Play and Creativity
in Psychotherapy

The Norton Series on Interpersonal Neurobiology
Louis Cozolino, PhD, Series Editor
Allan N. Schore, PhD, Series Editor, 2007–2014
Daniel J. Siegel, MD, Founding Editor

The field of mental health is in a tremendously exciting period of growth and conceptual reorganization. Independent findings from a variety of scientific endeavors are converging in an interdisciplinary view of the mind and mental well-being. An interpersonal neurobiology of human development enables us to understand that the structure and function of the mind and brain are shaped by experiences, especially those involving emotional relationships.

The Norton Series on Interpersonal Neurobiology provides cutting-edge, multidisciplinary views that further our understanding of the complex neurobiology of the human mind. By drawing on a wide range of traditionally independent fields of research—such as neurobiology, genetics, memory, attachment, complex systems, anthropology, and evolutionary psychology—these texts offer mental health professionals a review and synthesis of scientific findings often inaccessible to clinicians. The books advance our understanding of human experience by finding the unity of knowledge, or consilience, that emerges with the translation of findings from numerous domains of study into a common language and conceptual framework. The series integrates the best of modern science with the healing art of psychotherapy.

A Norton Professional Book

Play and Creativity in Psychotherapy

TERRY MARKS-TARLOW
MARION SOLOMON
DANIEL J. SIEGEL

W. W. Norton & Company
Independent Publishers Since 1923
New York • London

For information about permission to reproduce selections from this book, write to
Permissions, W. W. Norton & Company, Inc., 500 Fifth Avenue, New York, NY 10110

For information about special discounts for bulk purchases, please contact
W. W. Norton Special Sales at specialsales@wwnorton.com or 800-233-4830

Manufacturing by LSC Harrisonburg
Production manager: Christine Critelli

Library of Congress Cataloging-in-Publication Data

Names: Marks-Tarlow, Terry, 1955– editor. | Solomon, Marion Fried, editor. | Siegel, Daniel J., 1957– editor.
Title: Play and creativity in psychotherapy / [edited by] Terry Marks-Tarlow, Marion F. Solomon, Daniel J. Siegel.
Other titles: Norton series on interpersonal neurobiology.
Description: First edition. | New York : W.W Norton & Company, [2018] | Series: Norton series on
interpersonal neurobiology. | Includes bibliographical references and index.
Identifiers: LCCN 2017017768 | ISBN 9780393711714 (hardcover)
Subjects: | MESH: Play Therapy | Creativity
Classification: LCC RC489.R4 | NLM WM 450.5.P7 | DDC 616.89/1653—dc23 LC
record available at https://lccn.loc.gov/2017017768

W. W. Norton & Company, Inc., 500 Fifth Avenue, New York, N.Y. 10110
www.wwnorton.com
W. W. Norton & Company Ltd., 15 Carlisle Street, London W1D 3BS

1 2 3 4 5 6 7 8 9 0

In memory of Jaak Panksepp
Rat Tickler and Father of Affective Neuroscience

and

To our patients
Who continue to teach us the power of play and
the courage of creativity

Contents

Contributors   ix
Introduction   1

1. Deer, Chicken, Hunting Dogs, and the Future of Humankind   13
   Mihály Csíkszentmihályi
2. A Closer Look at Play   21
   Stuart Brown and Madelyn Eberle
3. Play and the Default Mode Network:
   Interpersonal Neurobiology, Self, and Creativity   39
   Aldrich Chan and Daniel J. Siegel
4. How Love Opens Creativity, Play, and the Arts through
   Early Right-Brain Development   64
   Allan Schore and Terry Marks-Tarlow
5. Play, Creativity, and Movement Vocabulary   92
   Pat Ogden
6. A Cross-Cultural and Cross-Disciplinary Perspective of Play   110
   Theresa Kestly
7. Creativity in the Training of Psychotherapists   128
   Louis Cozolino
8. Awakening Clinical Intuition: Creativity and Play   144
   Terry Marks-Tarlow
9. Trauma, Attachment, and Creativity   167
   Paula Thomson
10. Resonance, Synchrony, and Empathic Attunement:
    Musical Dimensions of Psychotherapy   191
    Victoria Stevens

11. Playing with Someone Who Loves You: Creating Safety
    and Joyful Parent-Child Connection with Theraplay   217
    Phyllis B. Booth, Dafna Lender, and Sandra Lindaman
12. PLAY and the Construction of Creativity, Cleverness,
    and Reversal of ADHD in our Social Brains   242
    Jaak Panksepp
13. Nesting Dolls: A Playful Way to Illustrate a Valuable
    Intervention in Couples Therapy   271
    Marion F. Solomon
14. Rage, Comedy, and Creativity in Theater   287
    Jonathan Lynn
15. Rage Underlying Humor in Psychotherapy   299
    Rita Lynn
16. Developing Resilience with the Improviser's Mindset:
    Getting People Out of Their Stuck Places   309
    Zoe Galvez and Betsy Crouch
17. Cultivating Curiosity, Creativity, Confidence, and Self-Awareness
    through Mindful Group Therapy for Children and Adolescents   338
    Bonnie Goldstein
18. The Power of Optimism   359
    Steve Gross

Index   376

Contributors

Terry Marks-Tarlow, PhD, is in private practice in Santa Monica, California and is a core faculty member of the Insight Center, Los Angeles, where she conducts workshops nationally and internationally. She is an artist, illustrator, yogini, dancer, librettist, and author of *Psyche's Veil, Clinical Intuition in Psychotherapy, Awakening Clinical Intuition* (recipient of the 2015 Gradiva Nomination for Best Book), and most recently, *Truly Mindful Coloring*. As a member of the executive board of the Los Angeles County Psychological Association, she is cofounder and curator of the yearly art exhibition, "Mirrors of the Mind: The Psychotherapist as Artist." Dr. Marks-Tarlow is also guest editor of the "Special Issue on Interpersonal Neurobiology" for the *American Journal of Play*.

Marion F. Solomon, PhD, is a lecturer at the David Geffen School of Medicine at UCLA. She is cofounder and director of clinical training at the Lifespan Learning Institute, a fellow of the American Group Psychotherapy Association, and a member of the American Academy of Psychoanalysis and Dynamic Psychiatry, the California Psychoanalytic Society, and the American Psychological Association. Dr. Solomon is the author of *Narcissism and Intimacy: Love and Marriage in an Age of Confusion* and *Lean on Me: The Power Of Positive Dependency in Intimate Relationships*, coauthor of *Love and War in Intimate Relationships*, and co-editor of *The Borderline Patient, Countertransference in Couples Therapy, Healing Trauma, The Healing Power of Emotion*, and *How People Change*.

Daniel J. Siegel, MD, is a clinical professor of psychiatry at the David Geffen School of Medicine at UCLA, and is the founding co-director of the Mindful Awareness Research Center. He is also the executive director of the Mindsight Institute, an educational center devoted to promoting insight, compassion, and empathy in individuals, families, institutions, and communities. Dr. Siegel's books include *Mind, Brainstorm, Mindsight, Pocket Guide to Interpersonal Neurobiology, The Developing Mind* (2nd ed.), *The Mindful Therapist, The Mindful Brain, Parenting from the Inside Out, The Whole-Brain Child, No-Drama Discipline*, and *The Yes Brain*.

Mihály Csíkszentmihályi, PhD, is a Hungarian psychologist. He is best known for the concept of "Flow," his theory on the notion of happiness or satisfaction, which he presented in his seminal work entitled *Flow: The Psychology of Optimal Experience.* He is the Distinguished Professor of Psychology and Management at Claremont Graduate University focusing on human strengths such as optimism, motivation, and responsibility. He's the director the Quality of Life Research Center there. He has written numerous books and papers about the search for joy and fulfillment.

Stuart Brown, MD, trained in internal medicine, psychiatry, and clinical research and found a common theme of major play deprivation while researching the lives of mass murderers and other violent, antisocial men. This led to an enduring curiosity and exploration of play behavior, 6,000 detailed play histories, and a few years exploring the evolution of play in animals and humans with National Geographic Society–sponsored field observations. These pursuits led to the establishment of the National Institute for Play. Dr. Brown now advocates for the recognition and fostering of healthy play through the human life cycle. With play science as a newly emergent discipline, he enjoys continued exploration of its nature and benefits.

Madelyn Eberle is a Research Associate at the National Institute for Play in Carmel Valley, California. With a background in evolutionary biology and neuroscience, she advocates for playful learning at all stages of human development. Additionally, as a teacher of biology in California public schools, she aims to integrate play and cooperation in her classroom in order to maximize the intrinsic motivation and self-efficacy of young learners. Through playful and collaboration-based techniques, she hopes to foster a sense of social camaraderie, mutual respect, and empathy in today's learning minds, and tomorrow's future leaders.

Aldrich Chan, PsyD, received his doctorate from Pepperdine University. Throughout his training he was placed at several major hospitals, including Children's Hospital Los Angeles, Cedars-Sinai Medical Center, and the Ryder Trauma Center at Jackson Memorial Hospital. He is currently a post-doctoral fellow specializing in neuropsychology at the University of Miami. His research focus is on the theoretical and practical utility of understanding the default mode network in relation to neurologic and mental disorders.

Allan Schore, PhD, is on the clinical faculty of the University of California at Los Angeles Medical School. He is author of *Affect Regulation and the Origin of the Self, Affect Regulation and Disorders of the Self, Affect Regulation and the Repair of the Self,* and *The Science of the Art of Psychotherapy.* He is the editor of the *Special Issue of the Infant Mental Health Journal,* "Contributions from the Decade of the Brain to Infant Mental Health," is on the editorial board of the journal *Neuropsychoanalysis,* and has written the foreword to the reissue of John Bowlby's volume *Attachment*. He has been in private psychotherapy practice for more than four decades and currently resides in Northridge, California.

Pat Ogden, PhD, is a pioneer in somatic psychology and the founder and education director of the Sensorimotor Psychotherapy Institute, an internationally recognized school specializing in somatic-cognitive approaches for the treatment of posttraumatic stress disorder and attachment disturbances. She is cofounder of the Hakomi Institute, past faculty of Naropa University (1985–2005), a clinician, consultant, and sought-after international lecturer. Dr. Ogden is the first author of two groundbreaking books in somatic psychology: *Trauma and the Body: A Sensorimotor Approach to Psychotherapy* and *Sensorimotor Psychotherapy: Interventions for Trauma and Attachment*, both published in the Interpersonal Neurobiology Series of W. W. Norton. Her current interests include developing training programs in sensorimotor psychotherapy for children, adolescents, and families with colleagues, Embedded Relational Mindfulness, culture and diversity, couple therapy, and working with challenging clients.

Theresa Kestly, PhD, is a clinical psychologist, educator, and consultant. She is author of *The Interpersonal Neurobiology of Play: Brain-Building Interventions for Well-Being*, part of the Norton Series on Interpersonal Neurobiology. In her private practice in Corrales, New Mexico, she specializes in play therapy and sand tray therapy with children, adults, families, and couples. Theresa has worked with Native Americans over a number of years as a teacher and consultant, and she is the founder and director of the Sand Tray Training Institute of New Mexico in Corrales, New Mexico.

Louis Cozolino, PhD, is a clinical psychologist, consultant, and professor of psychology at Pepperdine University. Before discovering the joys of neuroscience and evolutionary theory, he explored the ins and outs of Buddhism, Sanskrit, and martial arts. Lou lives in Los Angeles with his wife and son and spends his spare time keeping his house from falling down and tinkering with a tribe of old cars he has collected over the years.

Paula Thomson, PsyD, is professor in the Department of Kinesiology, California State University, Northridge (CSUN). She is a licensed clinical psychologist and works in private practice in California. She is co-director of the Performance Psychophysiology Laboratory at CSUN, adjunct faculty at Pacifica Graduate Institute, OperaWorks faculty, professor emeritus at York University's Departments of Theatre and Graduate Studies (Canada). She was a professional dancer and continues work as choreographer and movement coach in dance, theater, and opera. Past professional choreographic company work includes Canadian Opera Company, Canadian Stage Company, Stratford Shakespearean Festival, Northern Lights Dance Theatre, Ballet Jorgen, and UCLA On the Edge of Chaos. In 2013, she was named one of the top 20 female professors in California.

Victoria Stevens, PhD, is a licensed clinical psychologist, psychoanalyst, musician, researcher, educational consultant, and educator. She is on the founding faculty for the CAP Teaching Artist Program at California Institute of the Arts, and adjunct faculty in clinical psychology at Antioch University, Santa Barbara, and Pacifica Graduate Institute. Through the Stevens Creativity, Imagination and Leadership Training, she consults for several nonprofit organizations including A Sense of Home and the Imagination Workshop. She conducts professional development trainings in schools nationally and internationally, focusing on creativity, the arts, trauma, and emotional regulation. Her most recent article is "To Think Without Thinking: Combinatory Play and the Creative Process: Implications for Neuroaesthetics" in the *American Journal of Play*.

Phyllis Booth, MA, is clinical director emeritus of The Theraplay Institute in Chicago. She collaborated with Ann Jernberg in developing the Theraplay method for helping children and families with attachment, trauma, and relationship problems. She is the primary author of the third edition of *Theraplay: Helping Parents and Children Build Better Relationships Through Attachment-Based Play* (Jossey-Bass, 2010).

Dafna Lender, LCSW, is a licensed clinical social worker and a certified trainer and supervisor in both dyadic developmental psychotherapy and Theraplay. She is program director for The Theraplay Institute in Evanston, Illinois. Dafna's main area of interest is in children with serious psychological problems caused by histories of abuse, neglect, trauma, and/or multiple placements. Dafna's focus is children's development of a secure attachment with their caregivers while resolving issues in their traumatic history.

Sandra Lindaman, MSW, MA, LSLP, LCSW, LISW, is a certified Theraplay therapist, supervisor, and trainer, and the training advisor for The Theraplay Institute in Evanston, Illinois. Sandra has been with The Theraplay Institute since 1990. She coauthored three chapters in the 2010 Third Edition of *Theraplay: Helping Parents and Children Build Better Relationships Through Attachment-Based Play*. Sandra develops Theraplay curriculum and has trained and supervised professionals in Theraplay across the U.S. and internationally.

Jaak Panksepp, PhD, is professor and Baily Endowed Chair of Animal Well-Being Science at the College of Veterinary Medicine at Washington State University. His scientific contributions include more than 400 papers devoted to the study of basic emotional and motivational processes of the mammalian brain. His recent work has focused primarily on the subcortical brain mechanisms of sadness (separation distress) and joy (play and animal laughter), work informed by exploring the consequences of basic knowledge about emotional endophenotypes for better understanding of human mental health, with implications for the treatment of depression and ADHD. He is the author of the monograph *Affective Neuroscience* (Oxford, 1998), *Textbook of Biological Psychiatry* (Wiley, 2004), and *The Archaeology of Mind* (W. W. Norton, 2012).

Jonathan Lynn is best known for the phenomenally successful, multi-award-winning BBC series *Yes, Minister* and *Yes, Prime Minister*, co-written and created with Antony Jay. Jonathan Lynn wrote the bestselling books *The Complete Yes, Minister* and *The Complete Yes, Prime Minister*, which cumulatively sold more than a million copies in hardback and have been translated into numerous languages and are still in print nearly 30 years later; *Mayday* (Viking 1993, Penguin 1994, revised 2003); and his latest book *Comedy Rules* (Faber and Faber), which also received rave reviews. He has directed 10 feature films. Numerous awards include the BAFTA Writers Award, Writers Guild (twice), Broadcasting Press Guild (twice), NAACP Image Award, Environmental Media Award, Ace Award for Best Comedy Series on U.S. cable, The Diamond Jubilee Award from the British Political Studies Association for Best Political Satire, and a Special Award from the Campaign For Freedom of Information.

Rita Lynn, PsyD, originally was a microbiologist. At the Hospital for Sick Children in Toronto, she worked with Dr. P. E. Cronen in cytogenetics, chromosome studies, and electromicroscopy, work related to congenital abnormalities. She was research fellow of the Lister Institute, London. She switched from applied science to psychotherapy, and was a psychotherapist at The London Hospital from 1980 to 1986. She was a senior member of The Institute of Group Analysis, London, and conductor of Clinical Supervision Seminars. Rita worked as co-therapist with Dr. Robin Skynner, one of the founders of group analysis in Britain, a group approach developed out of Foulkes's treatment of war victims. She was a psychotherapist at St Bartholomew's Hospital, London from 1983 to 1985, and taught fourth-year medical students. Rita served as Leverhulme Teaching Fellow at the Medical College of St Bartholomew's from 1985 to 1989. She also taught and supervised at the Southern California Counseling Center, and lectured at the Reiss-Davis Child Study Center. Rita dislikes writing, but has reluctantly contributed chapters to various books.

Zoe Galvez, cofounder of ImprovHQ, is one of the most beloved coaches and consultants of improvisation in the San Francisco Bay Area and beyond. She has introduced thousands to the magic of improv and is a pioneer in bringing improvisational theater to the world of business. From physician leadership at Kaiser Permanente to team building at Google, her leading-edge programs create lasting impact. Sharing her craft has taken her on adventures to Australia, Canada, and France, but you can always find her on the main stage in San Francisco, where she performs as a company member at BATS Improv. Zoe is passionate about sharing the power of improv's universal principles to connect us to our playful nature and innate creativity. She is coauthor of *The Improviser's Mindset* (provisional title).

Betsy Crouch is cofounder of ImprovHQ, is an executive coach, consultant, speaker, artist, poet, and improviser. She holds a BS in Economics from the University of Michigan, and as an executive coach she has conducted more than 5,000 one-on-one coaching sessions. With ImprovHQ she leads interactive learning experiences, keynotes, and executive coaching programs in the San Francisco Bay Area and beyond. She helps leaders and organizations develop effective communication, exceptional collaboration, and engaged cultures through the principles of improvisation. Betsy's purpose is to help people identify what makes them come alive and thrive through play and creativity. Betsy is a coauthor of *The Improviser's Mindset* (provisional title).

Bonnie Goldstein, LCSW, EdM, PhD is the director of the Lifespan Center for Psychological Services, offering integrative treatment through the lens of sensorimotor psychotherapy, interpersonal neurobiology and attachment, and the dynamic interaction of group psychotherapy. She offers training opportunities for clinical interns, who facilitate a dozen weekly therapy groups for children and adolescents transitioning to the next stage of life. Dr. Goldstein is an adjunct faculty at USC School of Social Work and co-editor of the *Handbook of Infant, Child, and Adolescent Psychotherapy*, Vol. 1 & 2, and *Understanding, Diagnosing, and Treating AD/HD in Children and Adolescents, An Integrative Approach*. She has published numerous professional papers, and is program director at the Lifespan Learning Institute, a nonprofit agency bringing together mental health professionals for continuing education and training.

Steve Gross, MSW, is the founder and Chief Playmaker of the Life is Good Kids Foundation, a 501(c)(3) nonprofit that partners with leading childcare organizations to positively impact the quality of care delivered to the most vulnerable children. Steve is a pioneer in utilizing play and meaningful relationships to help kids overcome the devastating impact of early childhood trauma. Steve's talents have been called upon to respond to some of the greatest catastrophes of our time, including the devastation caused by Hurricane Katrina, earthquakes in Haiti and Japan, and the 2012 Newtown school shooting. At the heart of his work, Steve helps others discover the power of optimism so that they can build resilience and bring greater joy, connection, courage, and inspiration to their lives.

Play and Creativity
in Psychotherapy

Introduction

PSYCHOTHERAPY IS SERIOUS business. Our patients frequently face life-and-death issues on the opposite end of the spectrum from fun and games. Psychotherapists harbor a tremendous amount of responsibility when encountering deep unhappiness, trauma, and at times, unthinkable horrors within their patients. Given such a somber state of affairs, what does play and creativity have to do with psychotherapy? On the surface, one might think, "Very little!" Yet, as you dive into the chapters ahead, we hope you'll reach the opposite conclusion; for this book arose out of our conviction that play and creativity have everything to do with the deepest levels of healing, growth, and personal transformation within psychotherapy.

From an evolutionary perspective, play became highlighted in the mammalian brain in service of open growth and flexible adaptation to ever-changing environmental conditions. Through play, young children learn the roles, rules, and relationships of culture, while expanding their window of tolerance for a wide range of emotions—areas that overlap tremendously with the domain of psychotherapy. Through play, children push to their very edges of what is tolerable and understandable as they wrestle, spin, twirl, hurl, and leap into novel states of mind. Certainly, novel experiences are necessary for change within psychotherapy. Apart from other mammals, children's play is uniquely characterized by imagination—an important aspect of the psychotherapeutic process that has been historically overlooked and theoretically undervalued. When lost in the fun and pleasure of a moment in play, children explore novels forms of thought, speech, action, and social interaction. Meanwhile, novel response is the hallmark of full engagement and healthy adaptation within psychotherapy.

Both developmentally and within psychotherapy, play that engages creative imagination represents a safe way to experiment with people, objects,

1

concepts, and culture at the very edges of being and becoming. Carl Rogers (1954) was a pioneer of psychotherapy in the middle of the last century who recognized the need for open, flexible minds. In his pearl of an essay, "Toward a Theory of Creativity," Rogers asserts presciently,

> In a time when knowledge, constructive and destructive, is advancing by the most incredible leaps and bounds . . . , genuinely creative adaptation seems to represent the only possibility that man can keep abreast of the kaleidoscopic change in his world...Unless man can make new and original adaptations to his environment as rapidly as his science can change the environment, our culture will perish. Not only individual maladjustment and group tension, but international annihilation will be the price we pay for a lack of creativity. (p. 250)

Rogers defined the creative process (p. 251) as ". . . the emergence in action of a novel relational product, growing out of the uniqueness of the individual on the one hand, and the materials, events, people, or circumstances of his life on the other." By not restricting creativity to some particular content, Roger's definition includes ordinary activities like discovering new sauces in the kitchen, or finding a clever new technique to communicate in our offices or to students in the classroom. Scholars often distinguish between Creativity with a big "C" versus creativity with a little "c." The big "C" variety is reserved for geniuses and savants who make major discoveries in science or who usher in new forms in art. The little "c" variety involves the creativity of everyday life, which includes micro-acts of novelty, spontaneity, humor, and improvisation that help each moment to sparkle and each day to stand out from the last.

When patients enter psychotherapy for trauma, the therapeutic process frequently involves the reduction of negative symptoms, including crisis resolution. Psychotherapists privileged enough to extend treatment beyond the short-term often enter more positive realms of deep connection and personal growth, which is where new unfoldings of personality become possible. Perhaps the most important little "c" type of creativity involves the creation of one's self throughout the lifespan. Within psychotherapy, the task of self-creation and the co-construction of the self become emergent relational processes. A playful attitude in therapists promotes an atmosphere of safety, support, and nonjudgment for patients, which sets the foundation for novel response and creative shifts. Simultaneously, a playful attitude helps therapists to stay curious and engaged, which protects them from burnout and empathy fatigue.

In so many ways, play and creativity speak to the heart and soul of what all psychotherapists engage in—or perhaps should engage in doing!

In the Chapter 1, Mihály Csíkszentmihályi presents a panorama of nature's drive toward creativity. Through his "deer-flavored morality tale," Csíkszentmihályi muses about how the young fawn must break away from its mother to eventually stand on its own wobbly legs in order to face life's novel challenges. The author's poetic image emphasizes those tiny, ongoing moments of creativity, with a little "c," as they parallel the existential human condition. Each of us must likewise move beyond the carefree play of childhood to flexibly face life's novel challenges with creative solutions.

Whereas the fawn deals with its immediate surroundings only, we humans face more open possibilities. Not only must we define *who we are*, but we must also define *who we want to become*. This creative mandate extends to how we view ourselves as psychotherapists. Each clinical moment, in turn, becomes an opportunity to practice the art of psychotherapy creatively, with a little "c," as we attend to the uniqueness of *this* patient in *this* moment with full presence and novel responses. In this way, we come to our work with a beginner's mind, an openness to be with whatever arises, as it unfolds in therapy.

In Chapter 2, Stuart Brown and Madelyn Eberle take a closer look at the nature of play itself, whose hallmark features include that it is inherently rewarding, voluntary, spontaneous and un-self-conscious. Play may seem frivolous on the surface, yet it serves an essential purpose in all mammals. Within animals, plays helps to socialize and develop adult skills. Within young children, play fosters creativity through imagination, while developing empathy through perspective-taking. Within adults, play helps to quiet the mind and bring pleasure to the player.

Alongside the capacity for positive emotions, intrinsic motivation, and rejuvenation throughout the lifespan, Brown and Eberle underscore the dark, potentially disastrous side of play's absence. Children chronically deprived of unstructured play in service of more "purposeful" activities can become excessively conformist on the surface, while struggling to manage rage and even murderous impulses underneath. The author's takeaway message is that play remains critical throughout the lifespan for everyone, for fostering adaptive minds, resilient emotions, and flexible bodies.

In Chapter 3, Aldrich Chan and Dan Siegel dive into brain processes underlying play, creativity, mindfulness, and other forms of meditation. The authors describe three interconnected neural circuits. The default mode network (DMN) is of primary interest in this chapter. The DMN remains highly active, even during resting states, such that it consumes a high percentage of the brain's metabolic energy. The DMN comes into play whenever we ponder introspectively, project ourselves into the future, think about our relationships, or engage our moral compasses.

The DMN works hand in hand with the salience network (SN), which consists of neural circuitry that determines what we consider as most important for us to attend to on a moment-to-moment basis. The SN operates like a kind of switchboard, shifting back and forth between inner concerns of the DMN and outer concerns as regulated by the central executive network (CEN). Whereas the DMN involves conceptual issues arising during imaginative play, mind wandering, and creative endeavors, the CEN regulates external tasks and environmental changes, as cued by perceptual events related to the five senses. In this chapter, Chan and Siegel also indicate which neural structures underlie various kinds of meditation practices, including what shifts and grows with greater expertise, as well as clinical implications of this research.

In Chapter 4, Allan Schore and Terry Marks-Tarlow propose a two-person, relational model of how mutual love "leavens" both play and creativity. Within early development, maternal and mutual love serve as primary motivational forces to energetically jump start positive emotions, motivations, and behaviors. During the first two years of life, the capacity to love and play concretely as well as symbolically originate in the emotional and relational processing of the right brain.

When brains, bodies, and minds are optimally cared for from birth onward, children naturally open up to novel experiences and explore developmental edges through play and imaginative activities. The mutual exchange of love fuels a young child's desire to explore the environment, drink in novelty, and eventually fire up the imagination in service of creativity. As children grow and develop, this initial dose of love gets internalized and becomes transmuted into passionate engagements throughout life, including a love for life itself.

In Chapter 5, Pat Odgen addresses the somatic, or body, side of things. She suggests that to be creative, we must extend beyond our comfort zone in order to take risks and push past the confines of the familiar. Yet, as creatures of habit, we humans also love to sink into routine and thrive in the comfort of the familiar. In general, the more secure we feel in our bodies, minds, and relationships, the wider our window of affect tolerance, and the more inclined we will feel to stretch beyond our usual boundaries.

The author presents five basic movements which underlie more complex sequences: yielding, pushing, reaching, grasping, and pulling. We yield to let go—into each other, into gravity, and into the comfort of our beds. We yield to open up to playful promptings and creative products of the unconscious mind. We push upon solid foundations: the fetus pushes out of the womb; we push to differentiate self from other and to push away that which offends, disgusts, or violates our boundaries. We reach to go beyond ourselves, often out of desire to connect with people or objects in the environment. Reaching manifests openness, interest, and curiosity—all ways to say "yes" to novel experience. We grasp to take hold of what we desire, gaining the opportunity to explore it further with multiple senses. Finally, we pull objects and people we desire closer, beginning in infancy with the nipple. Pulling epitomizes the positive, intrinsic motivation necessary for play and creativity. Ogden asserts that an extensive movement vocabulary provides the somatic foundation to support flexibility and variety in our physical actions.

In Chapter 6, Theresa Kestly examines play across cultures and disciplines, beginning with what she learned upon moving to the small Navajo village of Rough Rock, Arizona, where fire dances provided her first taste of how thoroughly play can be integrated into the sacred as well as ordinary spaces of indigenous peoples. Kestly became inspired to pursue a degree in psychology and then return to her growing fascination with play through sand tray therapy.

Kestly adopts the framework of interpersonal neurobiology to describe her cultural discoveries. She understands the sand tray to offer a right-brain language of touch and imagery that is developmentally more foundational than words. Sand tray is among many forms of play that enables a safe environment in which to experiment with novelty, as well as broaden positive emotions and motivations, while expanding behavioral repertoires. Kestly's chapter demonstrates increasing cultural attunement through her innovation of round sand trays to replace traditional rectangular ones, both with Navajo and Korean people, who naturally tend to "think in the round."

In Chapter 7, Lou Cozolino presents a personal look at play and creativity in the training of psychotherapists. He begins by contrasting early, idealistic images of what academia should be with his own rude awakening as a teacher within a "trade school" classroom. By recognizing how his preformed images stifled his creativity, Cozolino seized upon the opportunity to create his own philosophy and approach to teaching psychotherapy graduate students. Just as the author had to revamp his own expectations, so too must new therapists do the same in their clinical training, essentially by "starting from scratch." The creative challenge for any psychotherapy teacher then becomes cultivating an atmosphere of safety and trust that allows students to take emotional risks and play with new ideas. Cozolino accomplishes this by using humor, telling stories, and encouraging students to face their own demons. To be an effective psychotherapist requires that trainees take the heroic journey inwards, in order to identify personal wounds, dark corners of the unconscious mind, and the accompanying vulnerabilities that inevitably come into play during clinical sessions.

Cozolino identifies his own set of learning principles by sharing personal stories that embody them. Readers learn the importance of embracing the unexpected; providing a caring, receptive audience; working with rather than trying to dispel personal demons; and recognizing how profoundly we are shaped by unconscious aspects of mind and body. By revealing his own demons and struggles, including the trials and tribulations of his clinical training, the author evinces a creative attitude, models risk-taking, employs humor, and adopts a playful style in an essay that serves as a powerful teaching tale to inspire other teachers.

In Chapter 8, Terry Marks-Tarlow underscores the importance of play and creativity in psychotherapists in the form of clinical intuition. Whereas preset techniques and manualized treatment may address generalized symptoms, only clinical intuition can attune to the particulars of *this* person, in *this* moment, with *this* personal history, and *this* particular therapist. Not only is each individual patient unique, but so is the interpersonal chemistry that arises within each dyad. Whereas cognitive therapies and prefabricated suggestions rely on verbal, explicit processes initiated in top-down fashion, clinical intuition draws upon perceptual and emotional processing as guided from the bottom-up by implicit processes.

To be fully present, authentic, and effective, therapists must continually tune into interpersonal novelty, to render psychotherapy an inherently creative enterprise. Only clinical intuition, and not clinical deliberation, is grounded enough within the full context and complexity of each moment to register this level of nuance. Clinical intuition supports an open stance that permits spontaneity and the emergence of safe surprises. Psychotherapists who model this level of internal grounding in turn inspire patients to do the same. When two people take the risk of being fully present and authentic with one another, this promotes a truly intersubjective, two-person clinical space. Even in the face of hardship or trauma, a playful attitude in therapists can cultivate safety, curiosity, and freedom for mutual exploration and growth.

In Chapter 9, Paula Thomson explores the relationship between unresolved attachment issues, trauma, and creativity. During ancient times, Plato suggested that when the muse visits a traumatized artist, this can unleash transient states of madness. Prior to Thomson's research, such ideas have had little empirical investigation. The author describes how optimal early family experiences promote creativity and creative achievement throughout the lifespan. Her studies found that dancers and actors tend to demonstrate greater attachment security compared to nonclinical samples. Yet, Thomson's lab also found a higher distribution of unresolved mourning in artists compared to the general population. In addition, artists with PTSD demonstrated both more anxiety during the creative process as well as higher levels of shame, anxiety, depression, and dissociation. Dissociation is a common internal response to pain and trauma that allows children to disconnect from intolerable experiences and intensity of feeling.

Happily, participation in the arts appeared to promote positive states of mind including flow in all artists. This was the case despite the presence of unresolved trauma, as well as more negative states, such as anxiety, depression, dissociation, and shame. While various artists, like dancers, singers, musicians, actors, and comedians, may share similar career conditions, they also have unique stressors and needs; these differences must be understood and taken into account in order for psychotherapeutic treatment to be effective.

In Chapter 10, Victoria Stevens examines musical dimensions of psychotherapy, likening the ineffable quality of deep, relational healing to the experience of playing music. Both go beyond words; both involve the *feel* of things; both depend intimately on the art of timing. Stevens begins by discussing nonspecific aspects of treatment, asserting that technique is less important than the quality of connection. To create a strong therapeutic alliance depends intimately on the ability to read nonverbal, body-based, affective communications from moment-to-moment, both in ourselves and in others. Relevant cues include facial expression, posture, gesture, movement, and vocal prosody.

With relational skills so highly rhythmic, all psychotherapists are musicians at heart, as we move unconsciously in sync with breathing and postural changes in others, and flexibly adjust to tiny sensory and affective shifts. When analyzing musical dimensions of interpersonal neurobiology, Stevens identifies three important features: resonance, synchrony, and attunement. Resonating with the emotions and states of others enables patients to deeply "feel felt," as Daniel Siegel would say. Synchronizing with body movements and mental rhythms conveys empathy and understanding, while attunement to the inner worlds of our patients is how we convey safety and trust. By attending to all of the elements of music—rhythm, tempo, volume, pitch, timbre, melody, and harmony—therapists can enhance their own musical sensitivity in order to better read and respond to the nonverbal communications of patients.

In Chapter 11, Phyllis Booth, Dafna Lender, and Sandra Lindaman introduce the technique of Theraplay® as an engaging, play-based, and relationship-focused intervention that is interactive, physical, and fun. Within this system of psychotherapy, parents are included in sessions with their children, so that they may become more sensitively attuned and emotionally available. The aim is to create warm, responsive engagement that builds trust, facilitates emotion and arousal regulation, amplifies interactive repair, and ultimately leads to secure attachment, in hopes of ensuring lifelong mental health within children.

The authors review the history of Theraplay as connected to John Bowlby's attachment theory. Four key dimensions of the system are identified—structure, engagement, nurture, and challenge—and amply illustrated with case examples. The Theraplay clinician models and then guides parents to attend to their child's cues, and to reflect on the meanings of their own and their child's experience. The system focuses naturally on the pre-verbal, brainstem, and limbic levels of development, where synchrony, rhythm, facial expression, vocal prosody, movement, and play are the primary modalities. The play-based action is multisensory, aimed to induce calming, nurturing touch, stimulating fun, and soothing care. Clinical histories, dialogue, and reflections bring the case material alive. Through play-filled experiences described here, children learn how to connect with others, to enjoy human company, to experience happiness, and to reconnect with the feeling that life is worth living.

In Chapter 12, Jaak Panksepp, founder of the field of affective neuroscience, identifies seven emotional-motivational-action circuits in the mammalian brain that are genetically driven, yet in need of stimulating social and physical environments for healthy development. Among these are the urge to PLAY—a natural mind-body-brain "tool" designed by Mother Nature to facilitate higher cortical brain development and social adaptation. In the United States, the diagnosis among children of attention deficit hyperactivity disorders (ADHD) has been increasing at an alarming rate, alongside the prescription of psychostimulants. The author suggests that one major reason for the increased incidence of ADHD may be the diminished availability of real social play among children.

While psychostimulants may "work" to help children inhibit impulsive urges and increase academic focus, their long-term effects on growing brains remain inadequately characterized. Research shows that psychostimulants reduce playfulness in young animals and humans alike. They also appear to increase vulnerability for depression, and for drug addiction and abuse later in life. Panksepp struggled to obtain funding for his research on play; he feared that natural solutions to the problem of ADHD may be unpopular among social policy makers under the influence of big pharmacological companies. Panksepp calls out for careful evaluation of whether intensive social play interventions can alleviate ADHD symptoms without any side effects in children. His other recommendations include regular physical play incorporated into early education, as well as the establishment of play "sanctuaries" for at-risk children, in order to facilitate frontal lobe maturation and the healthy develop-ment of pro-social minds.

In Chapter 13, Marion Solomon extends the importance of a playful atti-tude into couple's psychotherapy. She notes that many, if not most, clients enter psychotherapy finger-pointing—identifying their partner as the source of the problem, and asking for help to change the other as the solution. Solo-mon resists this perspective, instead maintaining that each person needs tre-mendous support, love, and recognition, exactly as he or she is, in order to change within him/herself. As a way to cut under long-held defenses and help her clients recognize the incredibly vulnerable, need-filled core hidden deep within each person, Solomon introduces two sets of matryoshkas, or Russian nesting dolls, all of which possess the same shape, as encased each inside the other.

By encouraging clients to take the dolls apart and hold the tiniest ones in their palms, Solomon helps her clients to reconnect with the earliest develop-mental phases in themselves and in each other—times when they felt needy, vulnerable, and susceptible to relational ruptures and traumas. By reminding couples that this tiny childlike part remains perpetually alive inside, the author hopes to engender empathy and greater understanding of one another. Solo-mon emphasizes that we are all social beings with social brains that sync up and fire as well as wire together. Because we are built to thrive in company, the author suggests we resist cultural messages that pathologize our social needs and inadvertently promote loneliness by pointing toward individualistic achievement rather than relationships as the source of greatest meaning and fulfillment in life.

In Chapter 14, Jonathan Lynn transports us onto the theater stage, where through his extensive experience as a director, he serves partly as friend, parental figure, and boundary maker—not unlike leading a psychotherapy group. To facilitate high levels of creativity, Lynn wants his actors to feel safe in order to play and take risks. The task of creating emotional safety is akin to handling transference and countertransference issues, especially in learning how to distinguish everyone else's projections from the director's concerns. Meanwhile, the director must retain control over the group process, lest his cast and crew suddenly feel unsafe such that play becomes impossible.

Lynn specializes in comedies. He notes that laughter is clearly therapeutic, and we easily conceive of comedies as warm and fuzzy. Yet Lynn sees the underbelly of comedy as high in aggression, often in the form of ridicule. The dark side of humor is evident in language used by comedians of "killing" the audience or "knocking them dead." With ingredients of comedy fundamental to the human condition, the audience functions like a tribe, asked to identify with circumstances portrayed, in order to laugh *at* the victim. Meanwhile, plays often take the moral high ground of warning about terrible things that can happen to whoever breaks society's rules or taboos. There are cultural trends in what is considered funny, which means that the line between good and bad taste is ever moving and rather thin. After working with hundreds of comedians and comedy writers, Lynn concludes most of them to be angry and depressed under the surface. Comedy can serve as a safe outlet to express underlying rage, but unfortunately is *not* a cure.

In Chapter 15, Rita Lynn, a psychoanalyst with decades of experience, extends the explorations of her husband. Lynn observes from her own clinical practice that patients deprived of play as children are more likely to use humor as a defense. These are often high achievers who struggle to experience joy, and who oscillate between comedy and darkness, while stating everything of significance only indirectly, as an aside. Lynn shares poignant case examples of patients who use humor as a cloak while relaying some aspect of personal history as a joke. With the patient as the butt of the joke, the therapist is invited into the laugh. Meanwhile, the horror of it all remains hidden in shame, under histories of accommodation, out of terrors of abandonment or fears of overwhelming the therapist with the rage and pain that lurk underneath.

Only by cutting underneath the humor and attending to what is missing from the narrative can therapists hope address underlying feelings and help to heal old wounds. Yet, in the very same chapter that Lynn explores multiple cases of humor used as a defense, she also cautions us against simplistically dismissing the utility of humor in psychotherapy. Lynn believes humor can be used as a skillful clinical intervention for accessing underlying rage or as a creative way to express a needed metaphor. In depressed or overly serious patients, sometimes to share a laugh becomes a signal of healing.

In Chapter 16, Zoe Galvez and Betsy Crouch address the therapeutic potential of theater improvisation as a clinical intervention for building resilience. Given that no one escapes loss or other devastating circumstances in life, the difference between success and failure comes down to maintaining a positive mindset. This chapter offers improvisational exercises as a clinical tool to build confidence, gain comfort with the unknown, and address self-conscious attitudes that inhibit creative expression.

The exercises apply as readily to individual, couples, or group work. The "intentional listening" exercise invites players to slow down, really hear, and respond precisely to each other's verbal communications. "Make your teammate look good" helps players shift from an inward focus and self-conscious worry to an outward focus of attending and supporting partners instead. "Resilient response" helps people work more comfortably with mistakes.

"Yes . . . and" challenges players to open up more fully to life by accepting whatever comes our way in contrast to the more common everyday "No . . . but" stance and response. "Voice your ideas" grants permission to believe in ourselves and risk sharing our ideas. By the end of this chapter, readers are left with an embodied feel for improvisation as a whole mind-body-brain vehicle to prompt change and spontaneity.

In Chapter 17, Bonnie Goldstein explores elements of play and creativity in the treatment of early attachment issues with children and adolescents. By working with younger patients, the author capitalizes on children's plasticity of mind, body, and brain, in order to intervene before their sense of self or patterns of behavior become too deeply ingrained. By utilizing a group therapy milieu, Goldstein helps youngsters explore triggers and experiences related to loss, social anxiety, oppositional behavior, and other relational traumas. As anger, fear, a sense of danger, and other defensive responses emerge naturalistically, novel responses become possible within a context of safety, support, curiosity, and respectful response. By promoting a safe environment, Goldstein helps group members take in social feedback, gain new insights, and expand social repertoires.

Goldstein employs a somatic focus, by harnessing mindfulness techniques with a sensorimotor approach. The author's creativity is evident in her clinical descriptions of thinking "on her feet," as well as "out of the box." When a new member, Danielle, sits in her car, frozen with social anxiety and unable to enter the building, the author meets her exactly where she is by conducting "roadside therapy." Outside the building, Goldstein shows the teen how to tune into her breath, calm down, and ground herself through focusing on minute-to-minute, body-based experience; eventually, Danielle becomes ready to join the group. Goldstein's playfulness is evident in a group "moment of meeting" between Danielle, an immigrant who struggles with shame, and Ian, a bully who regularly expresses intolerance of differences. In order for the teens to engage more safely, Goldstein employs two large medicine balls. Each is encouraged to communicate with the other while bouncing, swaying, and dynamically regulating the distance between them. In this way, through play, the author choreographs a shared experience of co-regulated arousal, enhanced mutual understanding, increased trust, and self-acceptance.

In Chapter 18, Steve Gross demonstrates resilience in action through his play with traumatized children. In the United States, relational traumas resulting from abuse, neglect, or household dysfunction present a leading health and mental health problem for children. Toxic stressors disrupt play while derailing healthy brain development. To address these problems. Gross and his team of Playmakers travel wherever there is need. Using humor and play,

Gross strives to "grow the good" back in children, with moments of fun and laughter becoming a salve against the pain of tragedy.

Rather than defining play as an activity, or something we do, Gross defines play in terms of *how* we do anything. He identifies four important domains addressed through play: 1) *Joyfulness* involves enduring positivity, or a deep, felt sense of appreciation and contentment regardless of circumstances; 2) *Social Connection* highlights humans as social beings whose quality of life is defined by community and relationship to others; 3) *Active Engagement* requires the capacity to "be here now," enthusiastically immersed in every activity; 4) *Internal Control* promotes agency and the sense of being worthwhile, competent, and special, which becomes possible only after basic safety needs are met. Gross's underlying mission is one of optimism, of choosing to see and focus on the good in one's self, the good in others, and the good in the world around us. In this complicated, often distressing world, we could all use a bit of this salve from time to time, especially in our role as caregivers.

References

Rogers, C. (1954). Toward a theory of creativity, *A Review of General Semantics, 11*(4), 249–260.

1

Deer, Chicken, Hunting Dogs, and the Future of Humankind

Mihály Csíkszentmihályi

IT IS THE time of the year when in our valley you see deer raising their heads from one clump of grass to the next, looking with bewildered eyes at the strange contraption on wheels passing them by on the blacktop road. It must be particularly disconcerting to the smallest yearling, who was nudged uphill by his mother as soon as he could stand on his own legs, around late April, leaving behind the lush riverbanks for the stark mountainsides above.

Now, just as the fawn had become accustomed to the broad vistas and hard surfaces of the ridges, all the grown deer, including his mother, heeded their instinct to get back down to the muddy, dark banks of the river. There were advantages to this move, to be sure: good fresh water is right nearby, saving the long daily trip it took to take a satisfying drink. Also, by the end of August the nights were starting to feel a bit shivery up in the hills, while at the bottom of the valley, undisturbed by winds, it is still pleasantly warm even at night.

Yet the fawn could not stop wondering why life had to be so hard. First, unsure on his hoofs, he had to the trek up to the mountains to be cooled by the winds; then, just when he had learned to enjoy his new habitat, he had to move back down and relearn how to survive in very different surroundings. One thing the fawn had learned by the end of his first year was that the loose, spontaneous gamboling with which he started life was no longer a good idea. He had learned that the world was full of dangers: there were rocks that could break his legs if he did not step carefully, there were snakes that it would be best avoiding, roaming wolves to steer clear of, two-legged beings that the older deer feared more than anything else. He learned not to exhaust himself needlessly, to conserve his energy for the moment he needed a burst of speed to avoid getting into trouble.

Because of all this new knowledge, the life along the river was now very different from the first time he had lived there. Occasionally he remembered short snatches of how it used to be when he could leap into the ferns growing next to the water, and then splash for a while in the shallows, under the vigilant watch of his mother nibbling the grass on the banks. But now as the Autumn days get shorter and shorter, the fawn realizes that the playful times he had initially assumed to be what life was about were in fact only a prelude to life, and that now he had to figure out how to survive in a world that was harsh, unpredictable, and dangerous.

Is this what the fawn is thinking? I ask myself as I drive slowly by the small herd nibbling the fresh corn planted by our neighbor with such toil on his acres along the river. Alas, we will never know. Of course, whatever the deer is thinking is very different from the way we think; nevertheless, its brain has evolved to process information and to make decisions in changing environments just as our brain has evolved; so, *mutatis mutandis* (a term the deer, ignorant of Latin, would never use), I would expect that his brain would be struggling to make sense of the "facts of life" along the lines our much more upmarket brain does.

FIGURE 1.1
Courtesy of Terry Marks-Tarlow

This deer-flavored morality tale, based on an encounter that happened just about an hour ago, might not be true of ungulates, but it is a pretty good description of human life. Most of us—at least if we had the good fortune to be born into a reasonably nurturing family—start life as an adventure where every month provides us with new skills—crawling, walking, running, jumping; touching and then manipulating objects; pointing at or grasping the things we want, then learning to ask for them, remembering to say "please" first.

With each new skill, a new horizon of possibilities opens up, beckoning for attention. A normal child gets to believe that the world is a wonderful space to explore, to master, and to enjoy. Soon, however, the caretakers begin to direct and to control the child's attention. Many of the most interesting things to do are discouraged, and more and more of the attention must be invested in things that to the child seem boring and useless. After leaving school, most jobs will also use the young person's attention so as to perform tasks that are boring and seem useless. It is a rare person who can describe his or her job the way the leading cancer biologist George Klein described how he felt when working in his lab: "I feel the happiness of a deer running through a meadow" (Csíkszentmihályi, 1996, p. 280).

In fact, so long as we consider persons as just bundles of energy for producing and reproducing the species—or as the human equivalent of what Sir Peter Medowar used to say of poultry: "a chicken is just an egg's way of making another egg"—the issue of what makes people happy is a trivial, inconsequential matter. But is that all that people are? Or more to the point: is that all that we want a person to be—a productive/reproductive appliance? Because, given our highly evolved scientific and technological capabilities for controlling not only the environment but also our genetic makeup, for better or for worse, the main question we are facing now is not *Who are we?* but rather *Who do we want to become?*

So, if we could change the future of human existence for the better, what should we be concerned about? One can think of a formidable to-do list in answer to that question, ranging from a reduced human population load to the development of clean and renewable energy sources; from climate control to arms control; from peace among men to interspecies collaboration, and so on. All of these are urgent, and important goals to struggle for. But being a psychologist, I would add to the wish list a concern for the improvement of human life experience. After all, as far as we know we only have one life to live; therefore it only makes sense to try making this one-way trip as worthwhile as possible.

Even this single goal, however, leads to different, often contradictory directions. There is no single recipe that would result in an improved experience for humanity as a whole. So let us try to choose one that, while seemingly a low priority, has the advantage of being inexpensive and relatively uncontroversial—while at the same time, being more important than it would seem.

The key to a better future I shall propose is through freeing human consciousness. During the millennia of human evolution our race has learned to use attention to develop an unprecedented control over its environment. Rivers have been dammed, forests burned, other animal species used for food or as transportation. But all of this power which, to paraphrase Max Weber, at first rested on men's shoulder like a light velvet mantle, has become with time an iron cage. The machines we use, the bureaucracy that rules our behavior, have slowly leached life of joyful spontaneity, of a sense of personal control. Creativity has become a prerogative of a few, while conformity pervades the days of the multitude.

Regaining control of consciousness means, first of all, to give people, from childhood on, opportunities to explore different ways of thinking and acting; then to help them develop those ways of thinking and acting that the growing person feels most drawn toward.

Throughout the lifespan, men and women should be helped to stay free of the "iron cage" that their background, their training, and their adult responsibilities so often tend to become. Karl Marx, usually an untrustworthy guide to a better future, was right in his *The German Ideology* (with Engels, 1846) to describe a good society as one in which a person could be a fisherman in the morning, a farmer in the afternoon, and a theater critic in the evening—without in the process turning into either a fisherman, a farmer, or a critic.

For the last several thousands of years, as the division of labor made it possible for individuals to develop specialized skills, humanity has become more and more professionalized. This, of course, has allowed us to become masters of the material world. But the downside has been that too many people have lost the knack of being masters of their own selves. More and more our psychic energy, i.e., attention, is attracted, shaped, and used by institutions—from churches to corporations, from the media to advertising—so as to advance their own financial gains or political power.

Perhaps the time has come to change our priorities, and instead of training *professionals*, we should think of training *amateurs*. Today the word *amateur* has come to be a dismissive putdown: "Oh, he is such an amateur," we say of someone who does not seem to be doing a job as well as a professional. But it helps to remember that *amateur* is a word that originally meant *lover*. The new meaning of the word stresses performance and efficiency; the old meaning was about the state of mind of the worker. One way to improve the human condition would be to realize that love might be a better guide to a good life than efficiency.

So the next step in making life more worth living, meaningful, and fulfilling would be to make it more lovable, more enjoyable. More enjoyable in the sense that the Greeks two thousand and some years ago called *eudemonia*, rather than *hedonia*. Hedonia is more or less what we now call pleasure. Eudemonia, on the other hand, referred to states in which the person acted out his or her potential, and thus was fully living.

A current description of eudemonia is what I have called the state of *flow* (Csíkszentmihályi, 1975, 1990). It is what athletes describe when they say that they are at "in the zone"; what artists describe when they are doing their best work, or surgeons when they are successfully completing a difficult operation.

But this state of flow is not something that only elite performers of difficult tasks experience. It is actually a very accessible, very diffuse state of consciousness described by early Chinese texts as being the condition that allowed the cook of the Duke of Wei to carve an ox while dancing, or by Dostoyevsky when he described the serfs harvesting wheat as if they were dancing, and having a great time of it. I noticed the same intense concentration, the same focus of attention in our dog Cedric, bred to hunt small game, whenever he discovered a squirrel in the vicinity. *Mutatis mutandis*, it is how a scientist acts when she catches the spur of an interesting fact bearing on her theories.

It is a fact that the great poet Dante Alighieri noted seven centuries ago: every creature—whether hunting dog, butcher, or scientist—enjoys doing what it can do best; because in so doing it reaffirms its being. But the precondition for enjoying what we do is the feeling that what we do is our choice, that we are doing it freely, and that we can stop doing it whenever we chose to stop. Even a trivial act, like peeling potatoes for dinner, can be an expression of our being if we chose to do it freely; but if we see it as an obligation forced on us by necessity, we experience peeling potatoes as drudgery.

Freeing consciousness means to choose doing what we do, and therefore enjoy life as an expression of who we are and of what we can become. Unfortunately, for many people this simple solution appears to be an impossibly difficult task. When confronted by the constricting conditions of their environment, they seek to free their consciousness by artificial means—for example, the chemical hallucinogens that alcohol and drugs provide. This turns out to be a classic example of escaping from the frying pan by jumping into the fire; the illusion of changing reality by chemical means, instead of freeing consciousness, makes it even more dependent on external controls.

There are, of course, other solutions that human beings have devised to find some freedom by means that express their being through self-generated action, rather than the smoke-and-mirrors illusions of hallucinogens. One of the most universal forms is the category of activities that comes under the heading of "play." More specifically, the form of play that Huizinga calls *paideia*—which is spontaneous, often creative and improvised—as opposed to *ludus*, which is play that is organized, rule-bound, and evaluated by officials. Improvisational theater, a pick-up jazz combo, a hot-dogging skier are examples of *paideia*; while a symphony orchestra or an NFL game are more likely to be examples of *ludus*. But both of these two kinds of play have this in common: they exist in order to allow participants to express their being by performing difficult actions—and offer to their audience examples of freely chosen, highly skilled ways of being.

Play is often discounted as something for children, because it does not deal with important survival processes, because it is useless. But this is a profound misunderstanding. Play is important *because* it is useless; because it allows us to act not because of necessity or convenience, but in order to freely express our being. The problem, however, starts again when play becomes a profession—with all the external rewards and responsibilities that this entails. Musicians playing for leading symphony orchestras, or athletes playing for multi-million contracts with elite teams, no longer feel that they play to express their being, but instead start feeling that their skill is being used by others for their own ends. When that happens, instead of allowing for the free flow of consciousness, even play becomes part of the iron cage.

In fact, it is not play that leads to the freeing of the mind, but *playfulness*. One can be playful when working, or fighting a war, or having a conversation—just as one can play music or a sport and not feel playful at all. If you keep worrying about how well you are doing while playing a Mozart sonata, or while you are playing chess, you are still in the iron cage. But if all your attention is focused on the music, or on the next move on the chessboard, then you are out of the cage, free to allocate your psychic energy as you see fit.

It is in this sense that creative individuals are playful. Creativity involves paying attention to things that don't exist as yet, but will as a result of you investing psychic energy in them. You can't be creative if your mind is completely taken up with reality as we know it. The mind must be free to play with ideas, shapes, sounds that were never before expressed. And that, of course, will appear to be child's play to those who never dare to step out of the reality they know. The Nobel Prize–winning astrophysicist Subrahmanyan Chandrasekhar had this to say:

There are two things about me that people generally don't know. I've never worked on anything which is glamorous in any way. That's point number one. Point number two: I have always worked in areas which, during the time I have worked on them, did not attract attention. (Csíkszentmihályi, 1996, p. 122)

The former president of the American Psychological Association (APA), Donald Campbell, explains what his advice is to young scientists:

Don't go into science if you are interested in money. Don't go into science if you will not enjoy it even if you do not become famous. Let fame be something that you accept graciously if you get it, but make sure that it is a career that you can enjoy. (*ibid.*, pp. 121–122.)

And the biologist Barry Commoner, who ran unsuccessfully in the 1980 U.S. Presidential elections as the Citizens' Party candidate, explained his approach to life:

I enjoy doing things that other people won't do. Because what are they? They are usually things that are difficult and important—and that people shy away from . . . very often that puts me so far in front, that people are upset about it, but that's OK. (*ibid.*, p. 117).

Creative individuals like Chandrasekhar, Campbell, and Commoner have been fortunate in that their dissatisfaction with reality as we know it resulted in extensions of knowledge that were recognized and appreciated by society. But the point I am trying to make here is that even if they had not succeeded, their playful approach to conventional knowledge would have still resulted in freeing their consciousness to explore limits, discover new perspective, and break into unknown territory.

Such people work within established disciplines, so that when they come across something new, they are recognized as pioneers in their fields. But one does not have to be an artist, or a scientist, to unmoor consciousness from an externally controlled, conventional reality. That's what consciousness is for: to be aware of reality, and then to interpret it, and give it meaning. In that sense, every person can be creative. It is what in the trade is known as creativity with a small "c"—to distinguish it from creativity with a capital "C" that is recognized by society and that changes the culture in which we live.

Small "c" creativity may not change anything, except the quality of life of the person who experiences it. But that in itself is a stupendous achievement: instead of a life determined by outside events, limited by convention; a life we endure as passive consumers, a small "c," playful consciousness allows us to be critical co-creators of our own experiences, and hence of our lives.

References

Csíkszentmihályi, M. (1975). *Beyond boredom and anxiety.* San Francisco: Jossey-Bass.

Csíkszentmihályi, M. (1990). *Flow: The psychology of optimal experience.* New York: Harper & Row.

Csíkszentmihályi, M. (1996). *Creativity: Flow and the Psychology of Discovery and Invention,* New York: Harper Perennial.

2

A Closer Look at Play

Stuart Brown and Madelyn Eberle

PLAY IS A state in which we flirt with reality, turning it to pleasurable ends this way and that, thereby expanding our potential for creativity. Characterized by imagination and risk-taking, this play state invites delight and surprise, quiets a chattering mind, and grants temporary relief from worry. During play, we entertain fantasies, break down preconceived notions, and become more socially and physically flexible. This enables us to navigate unfamiliar territory with greater finesse and ease. By playing, we foster empathy and relieve tension. A sense of safety, spontaneity, and curiosity prime the playful engine that resides in us all, and drives us to lighten up and join in on the fun.

To be considered "play," the experience must be apparently purposeless and done for its own sake. Play is voluntary, it frees the player from a sense of time pressure. It has improvisational potential, it is inherently pleasurable and we yearn for more when it's gone. While in a state of authentic exuberance, we delightfully engage with a playmate, play object, or playful thought. Each type of play evokes a state devoid of ego and therefore diminished self-consciousness. Each player contributes his or her own spin to play, exercising his or her own "play personality." Arriving in this "state" of play evokes intrinsic motivation, sustains engagement, and moves the player to the next level of mastery.

Background

Surprisingly, my analysis and advocacy for play began from a rather dark place. As a newly minted Assistant Professor of Psychiatry at Houston's Baylor

FIGURE 2.1
Play grants temporary refuge. (Courtesy of Madelyn Eberle)

FIGURE 2.2
Play promotes empathy. (Courtesy of Colin Brown)

FIGURE 2.3
Bear cubs playing in the water. (Public domain)

College of Medicine, I performed a retrospective assessment of Charles Whit-man. Whitman, a twenty-five-year-old UT student, an ex-Marine and former Eagle Scout, who had mounted the University Tower carrying an arsenal. Whitman soon became the man responsible for what was (at the time) the most devastating mass murder by one shooter in the United States. His vio-lent attack ended in his own death, almost two hours after his deadly accurate sniping had begun.

Texas Governor John Connally convened a diverse commission and drafted me to work to review three generations of his family history, plus as detailed as possible reconstruction of his overall life, taking note of any genetic and social factors that would predict a tendency toward violence. At the same time a team of pathologists meticulously evaluated his physiology and brain anatomy, searching for anything that might trigger violent behavior. As psychiatrists, we examined his upbringing from the prenatal period of his life all the way to his death on the Tower. We inevitably found evidence in his formative background, which would explain the impinging stresses during the final last months of his life.

Investigation revealed Whitman had an abusive family history—for exam-ple, his father fractured his mother's skull with a 2x4 when she was pregnant with him, and this pattern of abuse continued throughout Whitman's life.

The father's extreme measures of control, and continual oppression, and this oppression and his reactions to it were thought to have prodded Whitman's trajectory toward homicidal risk. His father had demonstrated obsessively grandiose expectations for his eldest son, which became the norm for Charles from birth onward. The Whitmans maintained an outward conventional charm and prosperity, however, that masked the domestic violence and dysfunction from all but close relatives.

I noticed, and the Commission concurred, that a curious absence of free play marked Whitman's life; social play and other natural play experiences that characterize and enhance socio-emotional development had been systematically denied to him throughout his early childhood and adolescence. During our chronological reconstruction of Whitman's life, Robert Stubblefield, a distinguished child psychiatrist and member of our team, noted that Whitman's father had severely suppressed playfulness. Additionally, interviews with his preschool teachers revealed how isolated and solitary he was, and that he was almost "too good" during these crucial years and thus fearful of making mistakes.

The father was heavily responsible in particular for what we came to recognize as Charles's play deprivation. From the earliest descriptions, any free time for him had to be "purposeful," which included hours of piano practice (beginning at age three), and at age 12 Charles became the youngest Eagle Scout in the US. To obtain the necessary merit badges, his father arranged for special consideration by scouting authorities, and encouraged him to con his way through, prematurely completing the exercises prior to reaching scouting age.

As a young adult, Whitman spent time in the US Marines, obtained a Naval scholarship to attend the University of Texas, married a small-town beauty, and prior to the August 1, 1966 tower tragedy, was majoring in architectural engineering. Although his life appeared to be happy and in many ways exceptional, his diaries revealed evidence of progressively increasing inner chaos. Academic overload was also noted by his professors. During the last months before the massacre, he was under significant stress, and had confided to a psychiatrist of his mounting inner rage. He had even expressed his desire to go up in the tower and "shoot people like pigs." Sadly, this violent rumination, along with other signs of severe depression and suicidal preoccupation, was not interdicted by follow-up professional help. The diaries he kept from this time exposed the conflict between his external, conformist lifestyle, with his deep inner torment.

The Tower Commission experts and I slowly reached a consensus that this ubiquitous "play deprivation" thwarted his ability to modify the violent impulses. Without free play growing up, Whitman had fewer outlets to manage aggression and disentangle himself from rage, or to create inner space to develop an authentic self-identity. By the time he reached adulthood, he had still never fully separated emotionally from his father's inflicted trauma. But even if he had been consciously aware of his father's acute impact, he kept these feelings buried. He conformed to a convincing mimicry of normalcy in order to cope with his father's cruelty and blend in with his peers. Outwardly, he was smart, good-looking, accomplished, and "securely masculine." Inwardly, he was filled with rage, resentment, and deep insecurity. On one occasion he beat his wife. His violent tendencies demonstrated earlier in his life became more formally recognized during Whitman's intermittent military service. Upon being recalled to active duty and losing his scholarship he threatened, bribed, and fought physically with fellow Marines—this combativeness and belligerence, revealed during posthumous review of his service records, surprised many who believed him to be a model citizen.

The Whitman tragedy led me to undertake a more formal evaluation of homicidal men in the Texas Correctional Facilities. This pilot study of young homicidal males concurred with an additional yearlong study of felony drunken drivers, which focused on fatally injured "Drivers who Die." Each research engagement was designed with deceased (drivers) and live (murderers) as well as many closely associated subjects, their families, and unique comparison populations. All underwent the same structured interviews. In the affected individuals, i.e., the fatally injured driver/felons and the incarcerated prisoners, we found remarkable psychological results. The interviews demonstrated that the highly violent, antisocial men were as a rule play deficient, and had been so growing up. We did not, however, find this with the comparison populations.

Ultimately, the studies conducted in the 1960s ignited the flame of my enduring interest in the nature and importance of play. The Whitman case was seen as a rare situation without precedence: he was a handsome, Southern man who served in the Marines, studied engineering in college, and had a happy marriage. This was not the archetype of a mass murderer in the 1960s nor now. So, where the anatomical, pathological, and outwardly conforming social evidence came short of explaining Whitman's horrifying actions, play and play deficiencies became a much more central question. At the time, play as an antidote to violence or its capacity to teach empathy was more or less absent from psychiatric medicine and public health.

The role of play in human social and emotional development clearly required a more considered examination. This led me to ask then and ever since, what *is* play, and why is it important to health and emotional harmony?

The Whitman case turned out to be the beginning of my understanding of play as a complex, emergent, evolutionarily designed "state" that aids in well-being, is integral to competency, but, more importantly, is essential to survival. As I transitioned from academia into a clinical role as Chief of Psychiatry at Mercy Hospital in San Diego, I felt a sense of urgency to integrate play fully into the Western attitude toward physical and mental health. I made the taking of "Play history" assessments routine in the course of many therapy sessions, and I encouraged residents and psychology post-doctoral interns to do the same. This led to the building of a large anecdotal repertoire on play from these clinical reviews. Gradually, I became convinced that play needed to be identified, further explored, honored, and nourished, instead of dismissed as a trivial, dispensable revelry.

Many years and six-thousand play histories later, I have come to better assay the contributions of healthy play and develop a clinical framework of serious "play deprivation" and its consequences throughout life. Lack of play results in delayed, but long-term, detrimental psychological, emotional, and physical health consequences. These reviews include cultural and gender differences, and range from the highly violent to Nobelists.

Play in Other Animals

Upon leaving clinical medicine full time in 1989, I have been fortunate to focus independent exploration and scholarship exclusively on play. For greater understanding of play in the context of violence, I contacted the primatologist Jane Goodall, who confirmed my conclusions through two homicidal chimpanzees within her Gombe Stream long-term studies. Goodall wrote me an eloquent letter indicating that Passion and Pom (her names for the homicidal chimpanzees) were extremely poorly mothered, did not play normally, and were not accepted into the extended chimpanzee family structures she had observed.

This led to an ongoing friendship with Jane, who suggested that if I really wanted to understand play behavior, I needed to see it across the spectrum of animal play behavior. At her suggestion, I obtained a grant from the National Geographic Society to study animal play behavior in the wild and review the scholarship of animal play worldwide. What fun! From 1990–1995, this sponsorship allowed me to discover a world of animal play and its connections to human play that certainly have shaped my understanding of play overall.

With the National Geographic, I spent summertime in Alaska with field biologist Bob Fagen observing brown bears during the salmon run on Admiralty Island from tree platforms. I later collaborated with ethologist

Marc Bekoff in Colorado, a play scholar with extensive field results in coyote and penguin populations In addition to the December, 1994 cover story for *National Geographic* magazine, we were able to film Marc and others for a *National Geographic Explorer*–TBS TV special release in 1995. Along the Geographic way, many other play scholars became my teachers. The Geographic was generous in allowing me to visit and interview play researchers worldwide. Without going through this entire list of play pioneers, Jaak Panksepp, Brian Sutton-Smith, Sergio Pellis, Steve Siviy, Jan Van 't Hooft, Irenaeus Eibl-Eibesfeldt, Gordon Burghardt, P. G Bateson, Fred Donaldson, and many others will always be play mentors for me. The array of scholars I had the pleasure of working with are responsible for launching play science as an emergent discipline in academia. The formation and my founding of the National Institute for Play, plus its Council of Advisors and mission, grew out of this background and these opportunities. It has been and continues to be a voyage of discovery.

This science is beginning to demonstrate that by allowing ourselves to play, we restore appreciation and gratitude, but we also restore exuberant engagement, sustained ambition and increased mastery. We handle irritations and stress with greater equanimity. Mutual benefit, respect, and vigor prevail during true play, and this vigor challenges nihilism and renews our joie de vivre. It bolsters our courage, strengthens our muscles, and steels us against despair. Thus, optimism is another benefit of play. By living and honoring a challenging and playful life, the player discovers that the hard stuff isn't so hard.

The Ineffability of Play

It's hard to describe play succinctly. We can certainly point out what is *not* play for us and could immediately tell you which activities we find boring or stressful. But to specify a playful state and say what play entails for each of us is harder to pin down. Play can be different for each person, within diverse cultures, yet its outcome can be surprisingly similar. To one child play consists of diving into the fallen autumn leaf pile. To another, it could be inviting stuffed animals to a tea party. For an imaginative player it could be writing a play for the livingroom stage. In a mother and child it could be a state of attunement, a harmony of emotion resulting from mutual tickling, cooing, and giggling. A play state entails and evokes a feeling of being wholly engaged, fulfilled, and delighted. These are states that we don't need to prepare for or reflect back upon. They are states where play functions as a catalyst for our authentic, creative, and blissful selves to shine through, whether we are aware of it or not.

Scholars who successfully hurdle the obstacle of fuzzy definitions might then encounter a cultural bias that assumes play equals frivolity and curtails

FIGURE 2.4
Stuart Brown in a tree house. (Courtesy of Colin Brown)

FIGURE 2.5
Stuart Brown Playing Tennis at age 79. (Courtesy of Colin Brown)

productivity. These obstacles make it difficult to understand one of the most basic and important human drives. However, in an age where technological novelty is fueled by creativity and where human intelligence and social competition are at an all-time high, the need for lifelong play is essential.

The Science

What is play at its most basic? Play is a *state of being*. My friend and affective neuroscientist Jaak Panksepp (1998; 2012), has outlined emotional systems that all mammals, some birds, and possibly a few reptiles share. He has shown that within our basal central nervous system, there are a series of predictable signals that indicate activity areas in specific regions of the brain (brainstem; limbic system; primitive cortex). His research comes down to this: we have seven basic emotional states that all living mammals possess, as deeply embedded neural circuitry within the subcortical brain: SEEKING, FEAR, RAGE, LUST, CARETAKING, GRIEF, and PLAY. Panksepp capitalizes these to note the universality of their special, fundamental, affective functions. In his research he and his former students observe, through optogenetics and EEG activity in real time, genetic activation and cortical synaptogenesis specific to PLAY.

In other words, Panksepp has coupled the brain scan evidence with the animal's play behavior at any given moment, and can demonstrate that PLAY, alongside each of these affective/motivational circuits, is unique and largely subcortical (i.e., mainly noncognitive). Panksepp offers a very complete picture of what actually happens inside the brain during these basic emotional states of being. He also unlocks some of the secrets of sustained, subcortical survival drives that underlie more "logical" thoughtful behavior.

While each of these systems does activate some cortical regions, many of them can still be experienced if the cortex— or, outermost region of the brain— is damaged. Thus, they are more like reflexes than cognitive functions, because they emanate from the subconscious and from brain regions farther below. The stimuli that trigger these states arise in the unique, individual circumstances during the course of play. All players communicate their readiness to play and their enthusiasm for play. Dogs wag their tails to initiate a mutually joyful romp, and humans, everywhere and in all cultures, display the smiling, open-eyed play face.

The PLAY affective system, aptly named by Panksepp, is more deeply rooted in the mammalian brain than many other higher-level processes. To thrive, however, play is a phenomenon that must be cultivated and harvested continuously, I believe, for the health and long-term survival of our species. Play is

FIGURE 2.6
Jasper and Frisbee. (Courtesy of Madelyn Eberle)

so deeply rooted in mammalian brain systems that it has been shown to be a fundamental drive, as are the drives for food, sleep and sex. For example, if you remove a rat's forebrain at birth but leave the rest of the brain and brain stem intact, it will not only survive, but also unexpectedly, will still play vigorously. This (albeit brute) technique will leave the rat's executive function debilitated no doubt, but ultimately: it will still eat, it will still sleep, and it will still play.

In my book, *Play: How it Shapes the Brain, Opens the Imagination, and Invigorates the Soul* (Brown, 2009), I outline how the impulse to play is internally generated and generally pre-cognitive. Consequently, just as sleep deprivation is known to lead to the kind of cortical imbalance contributing to impaired judgment, play deprivation has a similar effect. The differences arise in the periodicity of the impairment. Sleep deprivation can manifest itself in a matter of hours or days whereas play deprivation (as we sadly observed in the case of Charles Whitman) takes a longer time to make a serious impact. Nevertheless, suppression of this strong drive to play (seated in the survival centers of the brain) eventually inhibits healthy social development and can impair judgment and emotional balance.

So, now we have this picture: PLAY is a neurological circuit that is anatomically (and literally) beneath the cortex—with the cortex a relatively "new" addition on the evolutionary timescale. This way, it becomes apparent that play is a facet of not only mammals, but also our more ancient predecessors. It is *old* and has indeed evolved long before other [human-specific] cortical processes. In other words, the urge to play has grown over evolutionary time, integrated itself well into our large cortex, supplied us not only with adaptive strengths, but also has provided the key to innovative elegance. The urge to play is basic to survival and to living in a changing and demanding world.

The Play Paradox

If anything, play happens when we straddle the line separating what we find comforting and what we find provocative. That which is comfortable provides us with familiarity and boosts our confidence. That which is provocative keeps us coming back for more. In play, we navigate the gray area between what excites, arouses, or even frightens us, with what we recognize. Our playmates (or, "play muses") inspire us to consider new perspectives and challenge static beliefs. The state of play exists here, in between what we know, and what we don't. At the same time we desire both a sense of security and of thrill; play is a seamless union of both.

Play is thus a paradox in human evolution, precisely because it's so easy to dismiss it in order to prioritize other survival instincts. Simply, play distracts us from nutrient acquisition and potential predators. This seems to leave the player at a disadvantage over the long (evolutionary) haul. In this vein, it draws similar parallels to sleep. Both play and sleep tend to fall second to work or other structured activities we have built into our schedules to deliver food and shelter, warmth and security. In this way, it becomes tempting to deprioritize both play and sleep. Yet, without either, we succumb to exhaustion, implosion, or boredom as we suffer a deficit of energy and creativity. This suggests that play and sleep are basic human needs. The answer to the evolutionary conundrum is that play straddles arousal and comfort, enriching the player in the process.

Discord and Harmony

If play is a sultry tango with arousal and comfort, it's also a nimble dance between discord and harmony. In team sports, we play with the other team, but against them too. In drama and performance art, we put on a show *for* the audience. A lively debate among friends is characterized by opinions which resonate distinctly *among* the banter. But the truly playful moment exists when the audience and performer share a laugh, when the two teams pitted against each other are joined by their mutual appreciation for the game, or when our fervent words augment discussion, not discount the words of others. The type of discord we confront in play never reaches full-blown hostility or antagonism. And when we encounter an opinion we disagree with, a playful attitude allows us to navigate the situation with grace, fostering mutual respect. Through its discord, we find harmony. Harmony yields cooperation and peace. However unwittingly, certainly psychotherapists are familiar with this type of play during the back and forth dialog of therapy.

Some common misconceptions are that play is the opposite of work, or that we need to make a *conscious* shift in our psyche in order to experience a playful state. But it's risky to place a boundary on "time for enjoyment" and "time for work." This rigid separation we create undermines play's true essence—the state of *flow* (Csíkszentmihályi, 1996) that is spontaneously activated by our intrinsic motivators. It can happen anytime; we don't *necessarily* need to carve out a time for it or add it to our to-do list. If we do, we fall victim to extrinsic motivators for play. Play cannot be externally imposed upon us, or something that we have to force ourselves to do. On the contrary, it is a state that arises from our unique pleasure centers—it is only play to us if it comes from and leads to authentic joy in ourselves. Sure, it's silly and "purposeless" at times. But through its purposelessness we find purpose. We experience creative growth that carries over into the rest of our lives. By losing ourselves to play, we often find ourselves and our intrinsic motivations.

Intrinsic Motivation

We define intrinsic motivation as participating in an activity for its own sake, out of interest and for the pleasure and satisfaction from simply performing it. Intrinsic motivation does not necessitate an outside stimulus to foster its emergence, nor is it goal-oriented. Research in education shows that students with a more intrinsic motivational orientation will tend to outperform those who have been accustomed to extrinsic reward systems (Dweck, 1986; Malone, 1981; Rawsthorne & Elliot, 1999; Kohn, 1999). Education is not alone in these findings. Research in other fields has indicated similar results as it relates to job performance, innovation, self-management and more. Long-term behavioral change occurs when intrinsic motivators are engaged.

Stanford Psychologist Albert Bandura's social learning theory (1985), which emphasizes self-efficacy, highlights that external environmental reinforcement is not the only factor to influence learning and behavior. Bandura described intrinsic reinforcement as a form of internal reward, such as pride, satisfaction, or a sense of accomplishment. These internal states contribute to a belief in one's own competencies and capacities, i.e., *self-efficacy*. It is Bandura's research that has influenced David Kelley, Founder of IDEO, one of the world's most innovative design companies, and founder of Stanford University's famed school the Hasso Plattner Institute of Design. Bandura provided inspiration to David Kelley and his brother, Tom's, book, *Creative Confidence: Unleashing the Creative Potential within Us All* (2013). The Kelley brothers shatter the myth that only some people are creative. We each show our creativity in individual ways that express individual play personalities, and the Kelley brothers' curriculum patiently proves this.

Play Personalities

Out of these intrinsic motivators stems our intrinsic play personalities, which is the personality we exude during our most authentic and exuberant state. From my clinical play reviews, aided by known patterns of play present in all social mammals, I've discerned seemingly biologically organized "play personalities" that reside in all of us. These personalities, evident from infancy onward, demonstrate deep intrinsic motivation, including temperamental and cultural sculpting throughout one's lifetime. The human capacities obviously separate our play from that of non-human players, with imaginative, narrative, celebratory, ritual and other play experiences adding to the evolutionary foundation from which all play springs.

The artist, the joker, the collector, the narrator, the kinesthete might reside within us all, but it's fair to say that we each lean toward one specific play personality. In all social animals, including our species, self-organizing play patterns spontaneously emerge in infancy from subcortical areas through their play. Over time, those rudimentary play patterns become more sophisticated, refined, and blended to become play personalities. Environment, through epigenetics, activates, extends, and sustains the innate play drive. Yet it is the identification and actualization of individual intrinsic motivators through their corresponding play personalities that transforms precognitive motivators into a cognitive understanding of the human design to play, create, and innovate.

The play personality we each possess naturally enjoys various "play types" as well. Desire, pleasure, satisfaction all reveal themselves in the various types of play, and follow the formula below.

- Object Play involves the desire, pleasure, and satisfaction to tinker, construct, tear down, and use tools;

FIGURE 2.7
Caregiving play. (Courtesy of Madelyn Eberle)

- Social Play involves the desire, pleasure, and satisfaction to chat, flirt, tease, and joke around;
- Body Play involves the desire, pleasure, and satisfaction to dance, jump, run, touch, and tickle;
- Caregiving Play involves the desire, pleasure, and satisfaction to nurture pets or encourage a friend;
- Exploratory Play involves the desire, pleasure, and satisfaction to risk, assemble, and execute a plan, and to seek adventure.

Novelty

To me, the most fundamental aspect of both play and creativity is the pursuit of novelty, or the thirst for a sense of the new. When we find ourselves in a truly playful or creative state, it's exciting! And part of the reason it's exciting, is that it's new. For example, we might play the same game of SPUD in the backyard with our neighbors every afternoon, but that game can never be played the same way twice. The players, the moves, the fake-outs, the environment, the weather, and the state of mind we bring to the game are continually changing.

It may well seem that sports or active games with rules don't allow for creativity, and instead force us to conform to rules. But this needs some reconsideration. Within these rule-bound games, we employ our own nuance, our own finesse, and our own style. Soccer players try out different moves throughout the game and a butterfly effect determines the game's overall outcome. The game itself becomes an emergent system of the individual players and their unique style. No soccer game could ever repeat itself exactly the same way and this inevitability invites surprise and rejuvenation—two phenomena essential to a healthy mentality.

In this sense, we can observe creativity in even the most surprising places: at work, or amid exacting research, in clinical or legal practice, even at the higher levels of mathematics and invention. The ability to make the mundane beautiful, that is what is truly miraculous. Novelty is what unites play and creativity most deeply. To listen openly to anything that might guide the creative process and lead one further to unique results and synthesis.

Creativity extends to physical contests too. During rough-and-tumble play with other playmates, our dexterity, agility, innovation, spontaneous problem solving, and ability to compromise are all put to the test. And play fosters invention. As children play, they form languages with their playmates (or even just themselves) that are pre-verbal and preconscious. It's a state of intuition and instinct that needs to be encouraged, not neglected. Creativity is inexhaustible. To engage with open-ended freeform thought, indulge it, not stifle it. This too is the essence of play. To roll with the punches and yield to our playful urges. Both creativity and play are exploratory at their core—or when we yield to the exploratory process, playful creation begins.

The Daydream Effect

In play we begin to imagine, to fantasize, and to daydream. This dreaming might indeed be how we commit new information that we encounter to memory. We replay the most emotionally or intellectually significant events like a screenplay; sometimes, we warp this reality into an unruly daymare or, more optimistically, into a hopeful hero's journey. So, if dream is a state where we experiment with alternative or even nonsensical realities, then daydreaming is surely the playful equivalent that occurs while we're awake. Daydreaming is a safe haven for wonder and is the least structured function in human cognitive processing: there are no pointed mental rules to govern daydreaming. In daydreaming we might imagine different outcomes and possibilities for the very real scenarios we come across in our social, professional, or personal lives. When especially pleasing, we entertain idyllic reveries that play to our favor. Our mind is set free from time and space. The nagging voice that constantly reminds us of immediate responsibilities quiets and is replaced by an inner monologue that is more focused and heartening than before. When we daydream, we don't see what's really in front of us, but instead stare intently but distantly, while musing imaginary feats.

The most wonderful thing about the mind-wandering (or wondering) is this freedom. In wonder we explore outcomes that are both realistic and outlandish. When the waking mind is left free to roam to the farthest edges of imagination, it's easier to engage optimistic thinking and it's a harmless way to self-indulge. An obvious explanation for this is temporary comfort or relief from what worries us. And through this autonomous relief, we forgive ourselves a little bit. We might paint a slightly more virtuous version of ourselves than we usually picture. By forgiving ourselves we can be more forgiving of others. And thus an empathic cycle ensues.

When a playful child is left up to his or her own unfiltered, daydreaming devices, cooperation skyrockets, as does curiosity. Exploration of our physical environment gives way to exploration of ourselves—and vice versa. While at play, we never cease from exploration.

Play as an Emergent Process

Our play points in a direction. In addition to the characteristics or "properties" of authentic play, there are a series of emotional and physical states that each player experiences successively during play. Scott Eberle (2014) of the Strong National Museum of Play has outlined six stages that occur during play. These consist of:

Anticipation
Surprise
Pleasure
Understanding
Strength
Poise

It's important to note that each of these might be up- or down-regulated according to the type of play. For example, a hockey player may experience high levels of anticipation waiting for the puck to drop at face-off, while a dancer might be more poised than anticipatory waiting for her music to begin. But, the key notion here is that all of these elements are woven throughout each form of authentic play.

As an avid tennis player (even at 83!), I experience these play states of being every day. I situate myself on my side of the court, poised, and ready. Now seeps in the anticipation. I anticipate when and how my partner will serve. Usually he takes three bounces and a twitch of the left shoulder, but what if he doesn't this time? I expect his routine, but entertain the unexpected. He hits a diving top-spinning serve. Surprise erupts in me when it lands just shy of where I envision, but I am delighted to find I can hustle up to give a solid return. I build my age-ebbing strength and agility through this game, which has become a symbiotic dance that stems from, and also produces, joy. And as the match comes to an end, there's a mutual understanding that it's just a game. We've both lost and we've both won, and because of this we hanker for more. This, of course, is my play personality—a kinesthete. Likely, you can find in play how these elements reveal your basic personality profile.

A Recipe for Psychotherapists and a Role for Play

While many psychologists and social scientists have explored self-determination theories that include the roles of intrinsic and extrinsic motivation, many neglect to link the identification and development of intrinsic motivators with the survival drive to play. Perhaps this is because play was commonly denigrated as a "waste of time" and "unproductive" during the height of industrialized mass production. Meanwhile, focused attention on work was revered and nose-to-the-grindstone drive was considered what it took to get ahead. Or maybe its absence of recognition is because play has only been relatively recently demonstrated by neuroscientists as a fundamental survival drive. In any case, there is no question that there has been an historic bias against play on many levels.

Play science has been shown to complement therapy and especially drug therapy. Application of the proper play types can reduce and perhaps eliminate the need for drugs in the management of mild to moderate ADHD. Releasing excess hyperactivity through play could indeed achieve many of the same effects as the paradoxical calming of a psychostimulant. The same is thought to be true when dealing with such other afflictions as depression, autism spectrum disorders, obesity, vulnerability to addictions, and obsessive-compulsive disorders.

The evidence of mood elevation and exuberant engagement through intrinsically motivated play and the associated heightened immunity will soon be accompanied by more objective evidence of its contributions to preventive medicine.

The identification and activation of the play personality and subsequent design of an individualized health curriculum has huge self-motivating and self-sustaining preventive applications. Play is for a lifetime, and early fostering of spontaneous play in infancy continues throughout life. Its beneficence extends to effective compassionate care, even with dementia patients who have lost cognitive abilities, but retain their precognitive capacity to play. In fact, play which begins in anticipation and ends in poise suggests a model for both therapy and care.

We are built to play, and built through PLAY!

References

Bandura, A. (1985). *Social foundations of thought & action: A social cognitive theory.* Upper Saddle River, NJ: Prentice-Hall.

Brown, S. (2009). *Play: How it shapes the brain, opens the imagination, and invigorates the soul.* New York: Penguin.

Csíkszentmihályi, M. (1996). *Creativity: Flow and the psychology of discovery and invention.* New York: HarperCollins.

Dweck, C. (1986). Motivational processes affecting learning. *American Psychologist,* 41(10), 1040–1048.

Eberle, S. (2014). The elements of play: Toward a philosophy and a definition of play. *American Journal of Play, 6*(2), 214–233.

Kelley, T. & Kelley, D. (2013). *Creative confidence: Unleashing the creative potential within us all.* New York: Crown Business.

Kohn, A. (1999). *Punished by rewards: The trouble with gold stars, incentive plans, A's, praise, and other bribes.* Boston: Houghton Mifflin Harcourt.

Malone, T. (1981). Toward a theory of intrinsically motivating instruction. *Cognitive Science, 5*(4), 333–369.

Panksepp, J. (1998). *Affective neuroscience: The foundations of human and animal emotions.* New York: Oxford University Press.

Panksepp, J. (2012). *The Archaeology of the mind: Neuroevolutionary origins of human emotions.* New York: W. W. Norton & Company.

Rawsthorne, L. & Elliot, A. (1999). Achievement goals and intrinsic motivation: A meta-analytic review. *Personality and Social Psychology Review, 3*(4), 326–344.

3

Play and the Default Mode Network: Interpersonal Neurobiology, Self, and Creativity

Aldrich Chan and Daniel J. Siegel

Introduction

Play has been observed in all mammals. Our class of animals has many unique features, two of them being our dependence on caregivers for our survival in something called "attachment," and the other being our fundamental social nature. As a human species of this mammalian class, our attachment relationships are quite extended in time and our social networks quite complex over a range of systems of interaction. Our development and interactions are deeply shaped by both our genetic and cultural evolutionary history (how we've learned, as a group, to communicate and connect with one another through time). Because these ways of developing and being have grown to be so intricate, the need for experiences that enable us to explore how to behave in the world are profoundly important to our well-being—not just in childhood, but throughout the lifespan.

As with other mammals, we are reinforced in our neural circuitry to seek pleasure, and as humans we find significant joy in play. Indeed, play is an activity to which we are drawn and a process that is intimately interwoven into the fabric of our existence. Although it has sometimes been thought of as a purposeless activity, play has been determined by researchers to be crucial for human development and survival. From an evolutionary vantage point at the genetic and cultural levels, play is activity that enables individuals to engage creatively in novel situations, generating new, adaptive responses in potential future interactions or environments (Pellegrini, Dupuis, & Smith, 2007). Play has survival value for complex social creatures such as us.

Donald Winnicott (1989) emphasized the importance of play throughout the lifespan. He further described play as an experience where people act and feel genuine, free, filled with vitality, and fully absorbed in the moment. In this context, he viewed the process of play as integral to the discovery and maintenance of what he termed the *true self*. Living in such an authentic way may be something we discover only through the process of play, and may be important for a deep sense of well-being to emerge throughout our lives.

Human experience includes the ability to retrieve memories, evaluate present experiences, and construct imagined scenarios of the future—a form of "mental time travel" (see Endel Tulving, 2005). These capacities grow through time, providing humans with the opportunity to further the development of a self, while expanding their relationships with others and the world. Naturally, this increase in complexity is paralleled by the emergence of more complex forms of playing, from imaginary play with objects, to the composition of a romantic ballad, to the painting of a surreal landscape, to the writing of a chapter for a psychotherapy text.

Importantly, the ability to introspect provides us with a view into another aspect of the natural world: that is, the world as it is reflected in our minds. What is it, then, that allows humans to experience themselves as a subject of self-reflection? What makes it possible for a songwriter to engage the emotional experience of an audience? How does a poet evoke a deep sense of awakening? Or, at a more basic level, how does even an idea become expressed consciously and then into words? To explore these questions, we will focus in this chapter on some exciting contributions from the field of neuroscience.

The Default Mode Network

One of the contributing networks that social neuroscience has uncovered is the default mode network (DMN), a neural network popularized by Marcus Raichle and his research group (2001). Historically, research has focused primarily on neuroanatomical functioning in relation to specific tasks. However, the discovery of a *default mode* in brain functioning during its resting state has provided researchers with another lens into understanding human nature.

Although the DMN is known as a *task-negative network* (Jack, et al., 2013), for its tendency to become inhibited upon engagement with a task, recent findings have encountered several internally driven activities that activate the

DMN. Currently, the DMN has been correlated with autobiographical recall, prospection (Spreng, Mar, & Kim, 2009), self-referential processing (Lanius, Bluhm, & Frewen, 2011), social cognition (Mars, et al.. 2012), and moral sensitivity (Reniers, et al., 2012). Notably, there is a commonality underlying every function; namely, each serves self-related and social processes. Indeed, one way to remember it is as the OATS network, or a network dedicated to constructing energy and information patterns that deal with Others And The Self (See Siegel, 2017). In reference to the posteromedial cortices, structures housed within the DMN, Damasio (2010) eloquently stated that:

> It possibly reflects the background-foreground dance played by the self within the conscious mind. When we need to attend to external stimuli, our conscious mind brings the object under scrutiny into the foreground and lets the self retreat into the background. (p. 243)

Put simply, the same network involved with self-processes is also activated in social interactions. This correlation may advance contemporary understandings of the relationship between self-insight and social judgment (Alicke, Dunning, & Krueger, 2005), the importance of social relationships in the development of the self, and why our developmental experiences may influence the way we perceive others.

Given that DMN research is still in its infancy, discussion among researchers regarding its exact neuroanatomical correlates is still underway. Overall, areas that have been associated consistently with the DMN include the medial prefrontal cortex (mPFC), the precuneus, posterior cingulate cortex, bilateral inferior parietal and posterior temporal cortices around the temporoparietal junction (Mars, et al., 2012) and hippocampal formation (Buckner et. al., 2008).

Li, Mai, and Liu (2014) conducted a meta-analysis on the DMN, identifying three main subsystems: the ventral medial prefrontal cortex (vmPFC) in the medial temporal lobe (MTL) subsystem, critically involved with processing emotional features; the anterior mPFC and posterior cingulate cortex (PCC), responsible for the elaboration of the experiential feelings of self; and the dorsal mPFC and the temporoparietal junction (TPJ), central to theory of mind (mentalizing) and morality. The authors further highlighted two central nodes in the DMN, the PCC/precuneus and mPFC. The PCC/precuneus was found to be a central node involved with explicit emotional engagement (emotional word processing, face-perception), implicit emotional engagement (during self-directed attention or evaluation), and autobiographical memory. The mPFC was found to be critical in all of the reviewed studies, supporting simulation theory, which states that humans' social cognitive functions are contingent upon past experiences and their understanding of themselves, which serve as a platform for understanding others. They also indicated that mPFC activation increases with the complexity of tasks performed, with this complexity also manifesting in activations higher up in the frontal cortex. This pattern potentially reflects a bottom-up process by which nonconscious, effortless information processing emerges into effortful cognitive processing.

Table 1 summarizes relevant regions of the brain and associated functions.

Just as people do not live in isolation, neither do brain networks. More specifically, the DMN does not work in isolation; rather, it functions in relation to other neural networks: specifically, two closely related circuits are the salience network (SN) and central executive network (CEN). The SN is a neural network that determines the importance of internal and external stimuli (salience) as related to an individual's context, further orienting an individual to internal activity or the environment. It is composed of the ventrolateral

TABLE 1 Brain Areas Included in the Default Mode Network and Functions

Brain Regions	Functions
Medial prefrontal cortex (Mitchell, Banaji, & Macrae, 2005)	Information processing relevant to self and considering the minds of other people
Temporal lobes (Buccione, et al., 2008; Kapur, et al., 1992)	Role in memory for past events, affecting both autobiographical (i.e., episodic) and non-autobiographical (i.e., public events, general semantic knowledge) memory.
Temporoparietal Junction (Saxe, 2006)	Theory of mind, empathy
Parietal lobes (Beaumont, 2008)	Somatosensory perception, bodily perception, visual-spatial orientation, memory, symbolic synthesis, and cross-modal matching
Precuneus (Cavanna & Trible, 2006)	Mental imagery strategies related to the self, facilitation of successful episodic memory retrieval
Posterior Cingulate Cortex (Maddock, Garrett, & Buonocore, 2003)	Evaluative functions and mediation of interactions of emotional and memory-related processes
Hippocampal formation (Buckner, Andrews-Hanna, & Schacter 2008; Fair, et al., 2008)	Formation of new memories (both autobiographical and semantic), spatial coding, contextualization of memory

prefrontal cortex (vlPFC), anterior insula, anterior cingulate cortex (Sridharan, Levitin, & Menon, 2008), amygdala, and putamen (Patel, Spreng, Shin, & Girard, 2012). The distinct CEN is activated when the brain is engaged in a task, and its central nodes are the dorsolateral prefrontal cortex (dlPFC) and posterior parietal cortex (Sridharan, et al., 2008). The SN has been found to be responsible for transitioning between the DMN and the CEN (Goulden, et al., 2014). Anticevic and colleagues (2012) defined the DMN as a constellation of areas in the brain anti-correlated to frontoparietal regions such as the CEN, further labeling the DMN as a task-negative network (TNN) in contrast to a task-positive network (TPN), as the DMN deactivates when one is engaged in an external task. However, this notion has been found to be incorrect, as tasks involving self and social processes have also been found to activate the DMN (Mars, et al., 2012).

For the purposes of this chapter, the SN and CEN will only be discussed as they are related to the DMN. Figure 1 symbolically illustrates the relationship among these three neural networks.

How is the Default Mode Related to Play?

History has revealed that our main survival challenges in the past were related to hunting and foraging for food, placing us in danger of constant physical threats. Today, many of our battles are psychological in nature. Stress, anxiety, depression, and a whole host of mental disorders now afflict much of the world's population (World Health Organization, 2004). It has become increasingly difficult for us to remain present, spontaneous, and genuine in the face of such a chaotic world—our own intricate neural machinery can create disruptions to optimal functioning.

Sood and Jones (2013) distinguished between the perceptual (external reality perceived by five senses) and conceptual world (inner milieu built upon thoughts and emotions). The DMN helps us access the conceptual world, which consists of self-generated thoughts or contents of experience that arise from internal changes within an individual, rather than external changes cued by perceptual events (Smallwood & Schooler, 2015). Consciousness is the awareness of energy and information that is constantly flowing; sometimes we are aware of the flow, and at other times the flow unfolds without awareness. In this context, information processing can be divided broadly into two categories: focused and goal directed or undirected and spontaneous (Sood & Jones, 2013). In fact, it has been found that 46.9 percent of our time is spent engaged in spontaneous internal processes (Killingsworth & Gilbert, 2010). As will become clear, the way in which we regulate this flow determines our

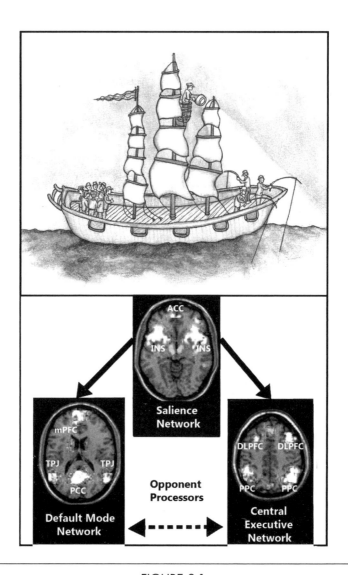

FIGURE 3.1

Symbolic relationship among DMN, SN, and CEN. (Courtesy of Terry
Marks-Tarlow) Top left: Group of sailors in a huddle represents the social
nature of the DMN. One individual is looking at where the ship has gone
(autobiographical recall) and another is looking at where the ship is going
(prospection). Top Center: The sailor on the mast represents the salience
network. He may only direct the light to one side at a time, directing the
focus of energy and information flow inwards or outwards. Top right: The
men fishing represent the CEN—as they are engaged in an external task.
Bottom: The three actual networks that are symbolized in the metaphorical
boat. ACC: anterior cingulate cortex, mPFC: medial prefrontal cortex, TPJ:
temporoparietal junction, INS: insula, dlPFC: dorsolateral prefrontal cortex,
PPC: posterior parietal cortex. Note: not all regions of DMN, SN, and
CEN are displayed in this diagram.

capacity to adopt an attitude receptive to play, as well as how we engage in the process of play.

So how does the DMN relate to play? The DMN is a network related to introspective processes as well as social engagement. As mentioned earlier, it is activated in the absence of an external demand or task. One activity that occurs when we leave our minds to idle without a goal is *mind-wandering*. The DMN has been associated with mind-wandering (Brewer, et al., 2011), or the tendency for our minds to *wander*, and this can occur with or without awareness. It is important to note however, that DMN activation is *not equivalent to* mind-wandering. In fact, Christoff, Gordon, Smallwood, Smith, and Schooler (2009) encountered neural recruitment in both DMN and CEN regions during mind-wandering. This finding was particularly prominent in "subjects that were unaware of their own mind wandering, suggesting that mind wandering is most pronounced when it lacks meta-awareness" (p. 8,719). Their findings suggest that mind-wandering may be a sort of intermezzo, facilitating a fluid transition from the internal world to the external.

Christoff, et al. (2009) found that regions of the DMN activated during mind-wandering include the ventral ACC, the precuneus, and the temporo-parietal junction, with two main executive regions, including the dorsal ACC and dlPFC. Outside the typical networks, they found activations in the temporopolar cortex, inferior and middle temporal gyri, anterior insula, and caudate nucleus. Interestingly, mind-wandering with meta-awareness has been associated with similar but weaker activation in both networks. In the words of Sood and Jones (2013), "The DMN has a dark side to it . . . specific DMN activity can produce mind wandering. Inability to suppress DMN activity can lead to attentional lapses and impairs task performance" (p. 138).

One principle of particular relevance that has received empirical validation is *perceptual decoupling*, which suggests that during periods of self-generated thought, attention is disengaged from perception. Other studies also suggest that emotional and episodic processes are involved with self-generation of mental content during mind-wandering. Moreover, there is evidence that executive control processes are important in the coordination of the mind-wandering state itself (Smallwood & Schooler, 2015).

From a positive perspective, Beaty, Benedek, Kaufmann, and Silvia (2015) found that both cognitive control and spontaneous thought were necessary for creativity. On a divergent thinking task, several core hubs were found to be activated in the default (PCC) and executive (dlPFC) circuitry. Increased coupling (bilateral insula) was found at the beginning and end of the task, suggesting a "focused internal attention and top-down control of spontaneous cognition during a creative idea production" (p. 1).

Thus, there are two sides to the utility of mind-wandering. Killingsworth and Gilbert (2010) suggested that the tendency for the mind to wander is a robust predictor of unhappiness; they concluded in their experiment that a wandering mind is not a happy one. Moreover, mind-wandering has also been documented to potentially interfere with learning (Sood & Jones, 2013). This is mind-wandering that happens without intention and interferes with the focus of attention on task-related cognition and behavior. On the other hand, Baird and colleagues (2012) found that mind-wandering during simple external tasks may facilitate creative problem solving. This can be an invited mind-wandering, distinct from the intrusive and un-invited mind-wandering associated with an unhappy mind. Similarly, Levinson, Smallwood, and David-son's (2012) study found that individuals with higher working memory capacity also reported more mind-wandering during simple tasks, without hindering performance.

Our internal mental life is a rich source of who we are. We learn and develop an identity based on our memories, use our imaginations to play out future scenarios, self-reflect to gain insight into our challenges, and activate our social cognition to engage in relationships. The default mode has been associated with all of these important self-defining processes. However, the DMN has also been associated with mind-wandering, which, as noted, is a controversial topic in current science in that uninvited it can be unhelpful while invited it can be helpful. What truly distinguishes mind-wandering as a negative from when it is positive?

In a review by Smallwood and Schooler (2015), they delineated the benefits and disadvantages of mind-wandering. The disadvantages include (a) comprehension impairment during reading and (b) reduced performance in complex tasks (especially tasks involving executive control). For example, the tendency to mind-wander is predictive of SAT performance (with increases in mind-wandering associated with poorer performance), and 49 percent of the variance in general aptitude.

In contrast, the benefits of mind-wandering include:

1. Improved capacity for delayed gratification via future planning in self-generated thought, which itself has been predictive of positive attributes such as greater intelligence;
2. Creativity or the capacity to generate novel creative thoughts, especially during simple tasks or in daily life;
3. Enhanced meaning: Engaging in mental time travel, particularly thinking about specific remembered or anticipated events, can enhance

self-reported meaning in life. Meaning in personal experience fosters well-being and enhances health outcomes.

4. Mental breaks: Mind-wandering (particularly future-oriented thoughts) has been found to reduce undesirable mood states associated with engaging in a boring task (Baird, et al., 2010; Ruby, Smallwood, Engen, & Singer, 2013); and

5. The simulation of negative content promotes preparedness for potential threats.

Another interesting concept proposed by Djiksterhuis, Strick, Bos, and Nordgren (2014) supports the DMN's association with creativity. They proposed that the DMN partially contributes to what they call *Type 3 processing* in addition to Type 1 (unconscious, fast, associative, automatic, and effortless) and Type 2 (conscious, slow, logical, rule based, goal-directed, and effortful) processing. They view it as "conscious intermezzi" (p. 360): a form of processing that is largely unconscious, very slow, abstract, exploratory, goal dependent, and largely effortless. They specified that two conscious intrusions bring Type 3 processing to light: (a) the awareness of an unconscious goal when progress becomes difficult; and (b) when an answer to a challenging question arises while doing something completely different, also known as a *eureka moment*. They view Type 3 processing as necessary in creative problem solving and making important decisions. They do, however, specify that working memory involvement is necessary, and as such the DMN is not solely responsible for all Type 3 processing.

These findings relate to a study by Schooler, Gable, Hopper, and Mrazek (2014), who examined situations surrounding the generation of creative ideas by professional writers and physicists. Every evening for 2 weeks, participants responded to a questionnaire that asked them to indicate if they had any creative ideas that day and, if so, to indicate the situation where the inspiration occurred plus estimated quality of the idea. Over 40 percent of the participants' creative ideas occurred when engaged in a non-work-related activity and/or thinking about something unrelated to the topic. Moreover, although creative ideas that occurred during mind-wandering were not rated overall as more creative, they were more likely to be characterized as involving an *aha!* experience and contributing to overcoming an impasse.

With this information in mind, how can we sculpt our own brains in such a way that can maximize the utility of mind-wandering while diminishing its disadvantages? How is the DMN involved? Is it possible to alter DMN functioning to improve overall well-being?

Mindfulness and Meditation

There has recently been a surge of literature supporting mindfulness meditation and other types of mental training as a way to focus attention on the present and develop an attitude of nonjudgment and acceptance (Brewer, et al., 2011). Interestingly, this attitude is reflective of play, in that playing occurs in the context of focused and relaxed attention while being in a state of acceptance and receptivity.

Mindfulness meditation has been found to improve attention and cognitive flexibility, decrease emotional reactivity, enhance executive processing, improve conflict monitoring and reactive control, and facilitate rational decision making (Sood & Jones, 2013). The use of brain scanning has allowed researchers to uncover the mechanisms underlying such improvement. Structurally, research has uncovered increased cortical thickness of right medial and superior frontal cortices and the insula of mindfulness meditators compared to controls (Lazar, et al., 2005). Other reports include increased cortical thickness and gray matter density (such as insula, somatosensory cortex, and parietal regions) (Lazar, et al., 2005) and the brainstem (Vestergaard-Poulsen, et al., 2009). These findings are consistent with evidence that mindfulness is accompanied by enhanced mood and well-being; improved attention, and cognitive performance; reduced stress, depressive symptoms, anger, and cortisol levels (Baer, 2003; Tang, et al., 2007; Jung, et al., 2010); and improved immune functioning (Davidson, et al., 2003). In fact, a variety of meditative practices have demonstrated benefits; Buddhist meditators engaged in a non-focal universal compassion meditation exhibited greater gamma synchrony between medial prefrontal and parietal areas during resting state compared to control subjects (Lutz, Greischar, Rawlings, Ricard, & Davidson, 2004). This finding has been interpreted to mean enhanced neural integration. Neural integration may be a fundamental neural correlate of conscious awareness of the present moment (Tononi, Edelman, & Sporns, 1998). Particularly relevant to this chapter, research has found detectable changes in default mode functioning between meditators and non-meditators, likely reflective of commonly reported experiences post-meditation (Brefczynski-Lewis, Lutz, Schaefer, Levinson, & Davidson, 2007; Brewer, et al., 2011; Farb, et al., 2010; Goldin, Ramel, & Gross, 2009; Hasenkamp, Wilson-Mendenhall, Duncan, & Barsalou, 2012; Jang, et al., 2011; Josipovic, Dinstein, Weber, & Heeger, 2011; Kilpatrick, et al., 2011; Pagnoni, Cekic, & Guo, 2008; Taylor, et al., 2013; Xu, et al., 2014).

Overall, meditation can be categorized into four types: focused attention (FA), open monitoring (OM), non-directed meditation, and non-dual awareness. FA involves selectively attending to a specific sensory or mental experience (breath, image, sound, thought, feeling), whereas OM is directly attending to whatever arises in the field of consciousness (Sood & Jones, 2013). In non-directed meditation, an individual places relaxed attention on a mantra while allowing spontaneous internal experiences to emerge (Xu, et al., 2014). Finally, in non-dual awareness, the process of meditation is equally given for experiences arising inside and outside the body (Josipovic, et al., 2012), with the intention of realizing that self and object are one process, and only separated by human abstraction.

One of the most vital systems in our biological constitution is the respiratory system. Breathing is essential to our survival, and an activity in which we must be engaged constantly. It is not hard to fathom why traditions that stress the importance of meditation place so much emphasis on this basic activity. Indeed, the use of diaphragmatic breathing has become the bedrock of several forms of meditation. One of the most common and widely known meditative practices is breath awareness, where an individual focuses on the breath, using inhalation and exhalation as a tether to the present.

Research on mindfulness meditation has yielded mixed results. Many studies seem to be confounded by the type of meditation, degrees of experience, demographic, study designs, and small sample sizes. In one study by Doll, Hölzel, Boucard, Wohlschläger, and Sorg (2015), just two weeks of daily breath awareness practice (20 minutes per day) with healthy participants led to increased internetwork intrinsic functional connectivity (inter-iFC). Increased mindfulness was associated with increased inter-iFC between the DMN and SN, as well as between the SN and left CEN. The authors concluded that this finding was suggestive of the adoption of a nonjudgmental attitude. In their review of other studies, they suggested that these relationships change through time; for example, they found that increased mindfulness was correlated with decreased connectivity between the anterior DMN and posterior DMN (mPFC/ACC with the PCC), which is congruent with the findings of some studies (Hasenkamp & Barsalou, 2012), but not with others. Some research has found increased connectivity (Jang, et al., 2011; Prakash, et al., 2013), whereas others have found no relation (Kilpatrick, et al., 2011; Taylor, et al., 2013). Doll, et al. hypothesized that these discrepancies may be related to demographics and study designs (i.e., methods that do not differentiate between aDMN and pDMN), but they also theorized that "more mindful individuals interpret the affective relevance of a given stimulus as less self-related" (p. 9).

Hasenkamp and Barsalou (2012) found that breath awareness meditation experience correlated with increased connectivity within attention networks, as well as between attentional regions and medial frontal regions. They suggested that this finding during non-meditative states (resting) reflects the generalization of these cognitive abilities into daily life.

In a randomized controlled trial, stressed out, job-seeking unemployed community adults were either randomized to a 3-day intensive residential mindfulness meditation program or a relaxation-training program. Pre- and post-intervention, 5-minute resting-state scans were employed along with a blood draw. A 4-month follow up blood draw ascertained the presence of interleukin-6 (IL-6), a marker of inflammatory disease. Creswell and colleagues (2016) found that mindfulness functionally coupled the DMN with the dlPFC, which was also associated with decreased IL-6. The dlPFC is a region that is part of the CEN, which Hasenkamp and Barsalou (2012) identified as related to focusing on present experience. Jang and colleagues (2011) similarly found this in non-meditative states of individuals who practice brain wave vibration meditation. They interpreted this neural recruitment as the adoption of increased attentional capacity.

This is a fascinating finding, as it suggests that self/social processing and cognition seem to have been somewhat conserved through evolution to function independently. These processes appear to predict different outcomes, and are usually associated with different neural networks. Jack and colleagues (2013) had two hypotheses on why this divergence may have occurred: The first was to increase effectiveness of predicting future behavior. There would be more room for error if the system used for predicting an inanimate object were used for predicting human behavior, and vice versa. Another possibility, for which the authors show preference, is the need to distinguish between conscious moral entities and non-conscious inanimate objects. It appears that mindfulness meditation allows one to integrate the adaptive aspects of cognitive reasoning into internal reflective processes, without the adverse effect of dehumanizing; however, with a notable adoption of a nonjudgmental and accepting disposition (see Farb, et al., 2007; Lueke & Gibson, 2014).

Brewer and colleagues (2011) scanned individuals who practiced three different types of meditation: concentration, loving-kindness, and choiceless awareness. In concentration meditation, the individual focuses on one object without interruption. Loving-kindness meditation is a meditative practice that aims to foster love and acceptance toward self and others. Finally, choiceless awareness opens up one's awareness, a form of open monitoring (OM), allowing whatever comes to one's attention to be the object of meditation.

Brewer, et al. (2011) discovered relatively decreased activation in the mPFC and PCC in the DMN of experienced meditators in all conditions. The decreases in these regions may reflect the development of an accepting and nonjudgmental attitude. They also found increased connectivity between PCC and task-positive regions (dACC and dlPFC), reflective of cognitive control and attention. Using the mPFC as a seed region, increased connectivity was found with the fusiform gyrus, inferior temporal and parahippocampal gyri, and left posterior insula in meditators relative to controls. They further noted that this was found in baseline connectivity as well. These regions are implicated in facial recognition, interoceptive awareness, and memory. Increased integration between the mPFC and these regions may very well facilitate a higher and more comprehensive level of internal and external awareness.

Differences were also noted in each meditation condition. In concentration meditation, less activation was found in the PCC and left angular gyrus as compared to controls. This finding supports the necessity to quiet down evaluative centers in the brain when meditating on a single object. Loving-kindness meditation correlated to less activation in the PCC, inferior parietal lobule, inferior temporal gyrus extending into the hippocampal formations, amygdala, and uncus. This finding also makes sense, given the attitudinal shift that loving-kindness meditation aims to produce. Finally, in choiceless awareness, less activation in the superior and medial temporal gyrus was observed in meditators as compared to controls. These regions have been implicated in auditory processing as well as social cognitive processes that mediate communication between the prefrontal cortex and amygdala (Adolphs, 2003; Bigler, et al., 2007).

Another question arises in response to the previous study; what other meditative practices have been studied, and how do they compare to other meditative practices in regards to brain functioning? Taylor and colleagues (2013) recruited 13 mindfulness meditators from Zen meditation centers with over 1,000 hours of training each. They were compared with 11 individuals without previous exposure to meditation and who trained in the practice for 1 week prior to the study. Overall, they found that experienced meditators had *weaker* functional connectivity involved in self-referential processing and emotional appraisal. In addition, experienced meditators had *increased* connectivity between DMN regions such as the dmPFC and right inferior parietal lobule. More detailed findings are summarized in Table 2.

Further research on Zen meditators was conducted by Pagnoni, et al. (2008), who recruited 12 Zen meditators with more than 3 years of daily practice each. They were asked to focus on their breath after processing and responding to stimuli. Compared with 12 control subjects who had no meditative experience, Zen practitioners displayed a reduced duration of neural responses linked to conceptual processing in regions of the DMN. The authors hypothesized that this finding suggests improved control over spontaneous semantic associations and internal regulatory capacity, a finding parallel to the results of a parallel study by Norman Farb and colleagues (2007).

TABLE 2 Differences in Brain Functioning between Beginning and
Experienced (>1,000 Hours) Meditators

Connectivity	Brain Region	Speculated Function
Decreased connectivity between vmPFC and:	dmPFC	Reduced emotional appraisal during self-referent processes; increased acceptance of thoughts, perceptions and feelings
	Right inferolateral Temporal cortex	Reduced retrieval or encoding of emotional self-referent memories
Decreased connectivity between dmPFC and:	Left IPL	Reduced analytical, self-referent processes
Stronger connectivity between right inferior parietal lobule and:	Precuneus/PCC	Reduced self-referential thoughts; greater global attention and moment-moment awareness
	dmPFC	Enhanced emotional resources and conscious awareness of present moment
	Left inferoparietal lobule	Greater emotional stability

Note: Adapted from "Impact of Meditation Training on the Default Mode Network During a Restful State," by V. A. Taylor, V. Daneault, J. Grant, G. Scavone, E. Breton, S. Roffe-Vidal, . . . M. Beauregard (2013). *Social Cognitive and Affective Neuroscience, 8*(1), 4–14. Copyright 2013 by the authors.

Western science has just begun to uncover the benefits of ancient meditative practices. One method that has received attention is a standardized and manualized 8-week intervention called *mindfulness-based stress reduction,* developed by Jon Kabat-Zinn (1990). Since its creation, numerous studies have emerged supporting its efficacy. One study by Kilpatrick and colleagues (2011) found that 8 weeks of mindfulness training sculpted DMN architecture to exhibit improved attentional focus, enhanced sensory processing, and improved reflective awareness of sensory experience. More specifically, they found increased functional connectivity within auditory and visual networks, as well as between auditory cortex and areas associated with attentional and self-referential processes. They concluded that these areas also demonstrate greater differentiation between regions of attention and unattended sensory cortex, as well as between attended and unattended sensory networks. This finding could possibly be indicative of improved processing efficiency.

Studies of the general impact of meditation become complicated, as they address different styles of practice, different methodological procedures, and different seed regions of the brain. The amount of time spent meditating, strategies used in meditation, sex, age, and other biological predispositions are variables that may further complicate findings. Extant literature seems to have focused mainly on two styles of meditation: FA (focused attention) and OM (open monitoring). FA meditation is understood as a form of voluntary endogenous or self-directed attention, mediated by the dorsal attention network (left lateralized). In contrast, OM style meditation relies primarily on involuntary exogenous attention/vigilance, which is mediated by the right-lateralized ventral attention network (Jha, Krompinger, & Baime, 2007; Raffone & Srinivasan, 2010). It is interesting to note that across meditation styles, similar activations and deactivations in brain activity have been encountered. As can be noted throughout several studies, the involvement of medial prefrontal cortical regions in structural and functional changes has been consistently associated with mindfulness meditation (Brefczynski, et al., 2007; Buckner, et al., 2008; Hölzel, et al., 2007; Lazar, et al., 2005). The involvement of self-processes, the adoption of a nonjudgmental attitude, and the practice of regulating information and energy may be activating similar areas in the brain. But are there any forms of meditation that differ significantly?

One form is non-directed meditation (NDM), during which individuals place a relaxed focus of attention on a mantra while noticing the stream of mental activity flowing in and out of consciousness. This form does not focus solely on an object as in FA, or merely allow spontaneous images to arise, as in OM. Rather, it includes elements of both processes. One NDM is a Norwegian technique called Acem. In one study by Xu and colleagues (2014), 14 Acem practitioners were examined. Notably, instead of a strengthening of attentional circuitry, this NDM practice was associated with increased overall DMN activity. They discovered that areas where thoughts and emotions were processed became highly activated. The authors suggested that this sort of meditation enables more room to process memories and emotions than during concentrated FA meditation. They also emphasized that this finding may also delineate a difference between circuitry related to relaxed attention and focused attention, with the former promoting DMN activation.

In a comparison study, Josipovic, et al. (2012) explored differences in functional connectivity among 24 experienced practitioners of Tibetan Buddhist Meditation practicing FA and NDA. They found an increased anti-correlation between extrinsic and intrinsic systems during FA meditation and weaker during NDA meditation in comparison to a control group (fixation, without meditation). FA and OM meditation led to stronger anti-correlations between intrinsic and extrinsic systems than were found among individuals who did not meditate. Anti-correlations mean as one system was bolstered, the other was diminished. Results support the theory that focusing on or monitoring external or internal experience actively increases the competition between extrinsic and intrinsic systems. In other words, they mutually inhibit each other. Consistent with Brewer (2011), they also found increased connectivity with areas involved with cognitive control and the PCC area in intrinsic systems—higher than among experienced meditators—both at rest and during meditation.

As a context-oriented approach, less anti-correlation was found between extrinsic and intrinsic systems in NDA approaches. NDA, being focused on the interrelations of elements of an experience, may thus be mediated by neural mechanisms that are different from the attentional systems mediating FA and OM, which are content-oriented, meaning that they are focused on the specifics of experience. Josipovic, et al. (2012) speculated that this sort of practice nurtures awareness of both external and internal experience, activating both systems at once, subsequently decreasing the competition between intrinsic and extrinsic systems. Thus, these practices may be reflected differently in the brain, as they are fundamentally distinct in their practice. Due to the levels of attentional engagement, FA and OM meditation styles have been regarded as effortful, thus leading to "constructed states," whereas NDA meditations are rooted in reflexive awareness and as such are regarded as "unconstructed" (Mipam & Hopkins, 2006). A range of meditation practices rest on a gradation of attitudinal and attentional flexibility, each with its own host of benefits. DMN research indicates that these methods of engaging our subjective world are reflected in our neural architecture.

Summary

The DMN supports introspective and social cognitive processes, helping people transform from merely sensory bound reactive organisms to individuals that can reflect on their cognition and actions and incorporate a complex array of socially relevant cognitive processes and behaviors. Despite this evolutionary advantage, the emergence of this network has also created a challenge: namely, the tendency for human minds to wander in unhealthy ways, preoccupying awareness with excessive worries about the self and others. This phenomenon is further complicated by research indicating that, in certain contexts, mind-wandering can facilitate the process of creativity, delayed gratification, meaning-making, regeneration (mental breaks), and preparation for potential threats. Fortunately, research has uncovered methods that can help reduce *maladaptive* mind-wandering: specifically, mindfulness and meditation-based practices in which mind-wandering is invited as part of the mental training. In this way, it may be that the intention behind mind-wandering may reveal its malevolent or benevolent impacts: Intentional "invited" mind-wandering is associated with positive outcomes such as creativity, whereas unintended "uninvited" mind-wandering is associated with negative outcomes such as impediments to problem solving and unhappiness.

Studies have yielded several benefits to meditation-based practices. Similar to the relationship between exercise and muscle groups, different forms of meditation may, at the very minimum, serve as mental exercises that increase levels of nonjudgment, acceptance, and cognition. A simple adage is "where attention goes, neural firing flows and neural connection grows." (Siegel, 2017). The common thread connecting all of these distinct methods is harboring a nonjudgmental attitude and an orientation to the present. With practice, such states can become traits of the individual, turning temporarily created associations of neural firing into structural changes in the connectivity among activated circuits. Neurobiologically, each of these studies involve the medial prefrontal cortex, a part of the DMN, and its relationship to other areas of interest to a particular practice. This finding brings to light the relationship between meditative practices and the self. Meditation can be understood as an activity that fosters awareness by nurturing connections between conscious self-states and other less conscious elements of the individual-environment interplay. This activity may then lead to higher levels of neural integration, promoting a more mindful existence. The results of meditation parallel conditions conducive to play, expanding our capacity to act from a more balanced and authentic perspective. In this vein, optimizing play states may improve overall functionality, a sense of wholeness, and well-being.

Clinical Implications

Similar to the shift in research paradigms from attention to externally based tasks to resting state activity, psychotherapy may benefit from attempting to understand how an individual's time is spent during moments of introspection. Practically, it is important to highlight that one of the core neural networks used for understanding relationships is also used for understanding the self (hence the OATS network). Thus, self-engaged states activated when "alone" are inherently relational, with relational cognition being influenced by disposition, history, and personal interpretation. This finding offers a neurobiological foundation for experiences such as transference, countertransference, projection, and reflexive attachment-based responses.

Studies of the default mode involve mind-wandering, which may be associated with the technique of free association with psychodynamically oriented psychotherapy. Consciously accessing this network through self-reflection, social cognition, prospection, and potentially free association, may indeed be beneficial, and it is possible to induce invited states of intentional mind-wandering. OM, NDA, and NDM types of meditation may be promising avenues to explore, as they may constitute a *royal road* to the quality of an individual's intrapersonal disposition as well as a window into how he/she relates to himself/herself. In addition, they may facilitate the processing of emotions and thoughts while increasing self-awareness. The most intuitive intervention would be to begin including meditation and mindfulness in psychotherapy. Psychoeducation and exposure to this way of engaging and relating to the self would be a great service to anyone's psychological and neurobiological quality of life.

Another possibility for gaining access to this sort of mind-activity involves a technique inspired by Killingsworth and Gilbert (2010). Similar to their approach, a therapist could ask patients to schedule their phones to alert them throughout the day, and, at the moment of being alerted, write down what they were doing, thinking, and feeling. Given that around half of our time is spent engaged in internal unintended mental processes, there is a high likelihood that an individual will be caught mind-wandering. This method would be beneficial in helping patients gain awareness of their own layers that form their mental flow.

Other creative ways of potentially tapping into this experience may be stream of consciousness writing, or the use of active imagination from analytical psychology. In fact, these interventions can be seen as forms of play that may engage the DMN, as they are guided by internal processes and introspection. In addition, these forms of imaginary play may shed light onto these processes, alongside an increasing awareness of internal dispositions.

Research on musicians, for example, who engage in improvisational jazz compared to those that perform from written, memorized classical pieces, reveal that the DMN and the anterior insula become highly activated with improv (Levitin, 2006; Limb and Braun, 2008; Müller, et al., 2013). This notion is that play may involve our bodily experience, enabling us to feel the fullness of our embodied minds, while also connecting to an open monitoring of awareness that involves intuition and reflections on our own emotional states. Improvisation in psychotherapy may facilitate the client/patient's engagement with the therapist, as is revealed in improvisational acting classes with fellow participants, in a form of "adult play" that activates the DMN.

These play states require what Steve Porges (2011) has described as the activation of the social engagement system that turns on with the state of trust. Without such open receptive engagement, we enter reactive states mediated by deeper, survival based brainstem and limbic reactions of fight, flight, freeze, and faint. Such reactivity under threat is the opposite of play. With the shift to an open state of engagement, we become receptive instead of reactive. In this way, playful states involve the social engagement system that reveals the interplay of the open self with the social world. New combinations of neural firing can emerge, new learning can be encoded, and new ways of being in the world of interacting with others can each contribute to the neuroplasticity needed for long-lasting change in psychotherapy.

From a systems perspective, when we define the mind as the "emergent self-organizing, embodied and relational process that regulates the flow of energy and information" (see Siegel 2012 and 2017), we come to the view that the linkage of differentiated parts of the system is the fundamental mechanism beneath optimal self-organization. That process can be simply called integration. Overall, we now know that neural integration is associated with states of health (Smith, et al., 2015) and compromised in mental dysfunction (Zhang & Raichle, 2010; Siegel, 2017). And interestingly, when we honor differences and promote linkages in relationships, this appears to cultivate the growth of integration in the brain. Across a range of studies, integration in the brain appears to be the fundamental mechanism beneath healthy self-regulation of affect, mood, attention, thought, behavior, morality, and relationships (Fair, et al., 2007; Siegel, 2012). Does playful engagement in psychotherapy similarly stimulate the growth of integration in the client? Does the chaos and rigidity of nonintegrated states diminish with playful engagement in therapy? Play could be a powerful mammalian way to differentiate new ways of being, new neural firing patterns, that enable engagement with new scenarios as practice in behavior and imagination. Also, play may involve the differentiated forms of attention, with focused, open, and a balance of the two forms becoming linked to each other in various aspects of the spontaneity and focus of play. Left and right hemispheres may be a part of this too, with the narrow focus of the left being differentiated and then linked to the open focus of the right (see McGilchrist, 2009). Linking these new firing combinations within the context of playful new narratives, enacting stories that tell the sequence of enacted events and reveal the mental states beneath those behaviors, may be how we as human beings—*Homo sapiens sapiens*, the ones who know we know—engage in the complex mammalian art of play.

Psychotherapy can be seen as the enacting and unfolding of co-constructive narrative with a therapeutic aim that promotes more integrative growth—in both client and therapist. As narratives can be both enacted and articulated, we can also see that both the nonverbal behavior as well as the linguistic sharing with therapy differentiate and link within the integrative process of playful narrative engagement. Since this requires the safety of trust, neuroplasticity in this state of activation of the social engagement system will be optimized.

Using different elements of attention—within FA, OM, and NDA—we stream an array of energy and information flow into consciousness both within therapist and client, and between the two. This is the shared intersubjective joining so essential in feeling felt within the therapeutic relationship. One study even shows that a simple empathic comment during a visit to a physician for a common cold will help the patient improve their immune function and get over their cold a day sooner (Rakel, et al., 2011). In many ways, then, playfulness within therapy reveals how person A and person B become a part of relationship AB within the playful immersion. This joining of two minds to create a relational mind may be part of the magic of therapy in which play becomes the nonjudgmental field Rumi described so long ago (Barks, 1995), a field where this is no wrong-doing or right-doing, a place where we can not only find each other, but where we can mutually liberate and create each other in this wild journey of life.

Questions for the Future

There is so much to learn about the interconnections among play, meditation, and psychotherapy. How the brain's circuitry participates in the dance of connection that is therapy needs to be explored with the possible reality that mind is much more than simply neural firing—mind is both fully embodied and fully relational. Play is a magnificent form of connection that reveals the importance of neural function and structure and the power of relational experience to transform the brain's structural connections. Future research focusing on maximizing the reduction of maladaptive mind-wandering habits while optimizing its benefits would be greatly beneficial for clinical purposes and may reveal how we can use the state of playful engagement to support an open mind's beneficial effects. Such openness is inherent in the relational trust of psychotherapy, and of play in its broadest applications for healing. The use of intentional mind-wandering, such as in NDA, NDM, and OM-based practices, would provide a good start for imagining which circuits may be involves in play and therapeutic transformation. Do all forms of meditation lead to easier access to play states? And does this lead to an increase in general well being? How about creativity beyond the play state? These and other intriguing potential outcomes of therapy and play may be exciting new discoveries in the future.

Another interesting variable to explore is the plastic nature, or inherent malleability, of the DMN. Experienced meditators exhibit resting states that are different than non-meditators do; does this new baseline serve as a platform where the usual detrimental effects of mind-wandering no longer hold true? How does play impact the DMN? More research is necessary to elucidate the relationship between shifts in attitude and mind-wandering tendencies and their potential therapeutic impacts.

In light of the benefits of play and mindfulness/meditative-based practices, the creation of a program based on empirical findings may be very useful. In this respect, creating a program that can be tailored to emphasize certain practices depending on an individual's disposition, vocation, challenges, etc., would potentially enhance psychotherapeutic efficacy. How meditative practice and play immersion may contribute to both relational integration and neural integration may lay the empirical foundation for how these practices may promote well-being in our lives.

References

Adolphs, R. (2003). Is the human amygdala specialized for processing social information? *Annals of the New York Academy of Sciences, 985*(1), 326–340.

Alicke, M. D., Dunning, D. A., & Krueger, J. (Eds.). (2005). *The self in social judgment.* New York: Psychology Press.

Anticevic, A., Cole, M. W., Murray, J. D., Corlett, P. R., Wang, X. J., & Krystal, J. H. (2012). The role of default network deactivation in cognition and disease. *Trends in Cognitive Sciences, 16*(12), 584–592.

Baer, R. A. (2003). Mindfulness training as a clinical intervention: A conceptual and empirical review. *Clinical Psychology: Science and Practice, 10*(2), 125–143.

Baird, B., Smallwood, J., Mrazek, M. D., Kam, J. W., Franklin, M. S., & Schooler, J. W. (2012). Inspired by distraction: Mind wandering facilitates creative incubation. *Psychological Science, 23*(10), 1117–1122.

Barks, C. & Moyne, J. (Trans.). (1995). *The essential Rumi.* New York: HarperCollins.

Beaty, R. E., Benedek, M., Kaufman, S. B., & Silvia, P. J. (2015). Default and executive network coupling supports creative idea production. *Scientific Reports, 5*, 1–14.

Beaumont, J. G. (2008). *Introduction to neuropsychology* (2nd ed.). New York: The Guilford Press.

Bigler, E. D., Mortensen, S., Neeley, E. S., Ozonoff, S., Krasny, L., Johnson, M., & Lainhart, J. E. (2007). Superior temporal gyrus, language function, and autism. *Developmental Neuropsychology, 31*(2), 217–238.

Brefczynski-Lewis, J. A., Lutz, A., Schaefer, H. S., Levinson, D. B., & Davidson, R. J. (2007). Neural correlates of attentional expertise in long-term meditation practitioners. *Proceedings of the National Academy of Sciences, 104*(27), 11483–11488.

Brewer, J. A., Worhunsky, P. D., Gray, J. R., Tang, Y. Y., Weber, J., & Kober, H. (2011). Meditation experience is associated with differences in default mode network activity and connectivity. *Proceedings of the National Academy of Sciences, 108*(50), 20254–20259.

Buccione, I., Fadda, L., Serra, L., Caltagirone, C., & Carlesimo, G. A. (2008). Retrograde episodic and semantic memory impairment correlates with side of temporal lobe damage. *Journal of the International Neuropsychological Society, 14*(06), 1083–1094.

Buckner, R. L., Andrews-Hanna, J. R., & Schacter, D. L. (2008). The brain's default network: Anatomy, function, and relevance to disease. *Annals of the New York Academy of Sciences, 1124*(1), 1–38.

Cavanna, A. E. & Trible, M. R. (2006). The precuneus: A review of its functional anatomy and behavioral correlates. *Brain, 129*, 564–583.

Christoff, K., Gordon, A. M., Smallwood, J., Smith, R., & Schooler, J. W. (2009). Experience sampling during fMRI reveals default network and executive system contributions to mind wandering. *Proceedings of the National Academy of Sciences, 106*(21), 8719–8724.

Creswell, J. D., Taren, A. A., Lindsay, E. K., Greco, C. M., Gianaros, P. J., Fairgrieve, A., Ferris, J. L. (2016). Alterations in resting-state functional connectivity link mindfulness meditation with reduced interleukin-6: A randomized controlled trial. *Biological Psychiatry 80*(1), 53–61.

Damasio, A. (2010). *Self comes to mind: Constructing the conscious brain.* New York: Vintage Books.

Davidson, R. J., Kabat-Zinn, J., Schumacher, J., Rosenkranz, M., Muller, D., Santorelli, S. F., Sheridan, J. F. (2003). Alterations in brain and immune function produced by mindfulness meditation. *Psychosomatic Medicine, 65*(4), 564–570.

Djiksterhuis, A., Strick M., Bos, M., & Nordgren, L. (2014). Prolonged thought: Proposing type 3 processing. In Sherman, J., Gawronski, B., & Trope, Y. (Eds.) *Dual-process theories of the social mind* (pp. 355–366). New York: The Guilford Press.

Doll, A., Hölzel, B. K., Boucard, C. C., Wohlschläger, A. M., & Sorg, C. (2015). Mindfulness is associated with intrinsic functional connectivity between default mode and salience networks. *Frontiers in Human Neuroscience, 9*(461), 1–11.

Fair, D. A., Cohen, A. L., Dosenbach, N. U., Church, J. A., Miezin, F. M., Barch, D. M., Raichle, M. E., Peterson, S. E. & Schlaggar, B. L. (2008). The maturing architecture of the brain's default network. *Proceedings of the National Academy of Sciences, 105*(10), 4028-4032.

Fair, D. A., Dosenbach, N. U. F., Church, J. A., Cohen, A. L., Brahmbhatt, S., Miezin, F. M., Barch, D. M., Raichle, M. E., Peterson, S. E., & Schlagger, B. L. (2007). Development of distinct control networks through segregation and integration. *Proceedings of the National Academy of Sciences, 104*(33), 13507–13512.

Farb, N. A. S., Segal, Z. V., Mayberg, H., Bean, J., McKeon, D., Fatima, Z., & Anderson, A. K. (2007). Attending to the present: Mindfulness meditation reveals distinct neural modes of self-reference. *Social Cognitive and Affective Neuroscience, 2*(4), 313–322.

Farb, N. A., Anderson, A. K., Mayberg, H., Bean, J., McKeon, D., & Segal, Z. V. (2010). Minding one's emotions: Mindfulness training alters the neural expression of sadness. *Emotion, 10*(1), 25–33.

Goldin, P. R., Ramel, W., & Gross, J. (2009). Mindfulness meditation training and self-referential processing in social anxiety disorder: Behavioral and neural effects. *Journal of Cognitive Psychotherapy, 23*(3), 242–257.

Goulden, N., Khusnulina, A., Davis, N. J., Bracewell, R. M., Bokde, A. L., McNulty, J. P., & Mullins, P. G. (2014). The salience network is responsible for switching between the default mode network and the central executive network: Replication from DCM. *NeuroImage, 99*, 180–190.

Hasenkamp, W. & Barsalou, L. W. (2012). Effects of meditation experience on functional connectivity of distributed brain networks. *Frontiers in Human Neuroscience, 6*(38).

Hasenkamp, W., Wilson-Mendenhall, C. D., Duncan, E., & Barsalou, L. W. (2012). Mind wandering and attention during focused meditation: A fine-grained temporal analysis of fluctuating cognitive states. *NeuroImage, 59*(1), 750–760.

Hölzel, B. K., Ott, U., Hempel, H., Hackl, A., Wolf, K., Stark, R., & Vaitl, D. (2007). Differential engagement of anterior cingulate and adjacent medial frontal cortex in adept meditators and non-meditators. *Neuroscience Letters, 421*(1), 16–21.

Jack, A. I., Dawson, A. J., Begany, K. L., Leckie, R. L., Barry, K. P., Ciccia, A. H., & Snyder, A. Z. (2013). fMRI reveals reciprocal inhibition between social and physical cognitive domains. *NeuroImage, 66*, 385–401.

Jang, J. H., Jung, W. H., Kang, D. H., Byun, M. S., Kwon, S. J., Choi, C. H., & Kwon, J. S. (2011). Increased default mode network connectivity associated with meditation. *Neuroscience Letters, 487*(3), 358–362.

Jha, A. P., Krompinger, J., & Baime, M. J. (2007). Mindfulness training modifies subsystems of attention. *Cognitive, Affective, & Behavioral Neuroscience, 7*(2), 109–119.

Josipovic, Z., Dinstein, I., Weber, J., & Heeger, D. J. (2011). Influence of meditation on anti-correlated networks in the brain. *Frontiers in Human Neuroscience, 5*.

Jung, Y. H., Kang, D. H., Jang, J. H., Park, H. Y., Byun, M. S., Kwon, S. J., . . . Kwon, J. S. (2010). The effects of mind-body training on stress reduction, positive affect, and plasma catecholamines. *Neuroscience Letters, 479*(2), 138–142.

Kabat-Zinn, J. (1990). *Full catastrophe living: Using the wisdom of your body and mind to face stress, pain, and illness.* New York: Dell.

Kapur, N., Ellison, D., Smith, M. P., McLellan, D. L., & Burrows, E. H. (1992). Focal retrograde amnesia following bilateral temporal lobe pathology: A neuropsychological and magnetic resonance study. *Brain, 115*(1), 73–85.

Killingsworth, M. A. & Gilbert, D. T. (2010). A wandering mind is an unhappy mind. *Science, 330*(6006), 932.

Kilpatrick, L. A., Suyenobu, B. Y., Smith, S. R., Bueller, J. A., Goodman, T., Creswell, J. D., Tillisch, K., Mayer, E. A., & Naliboff, B. D. (2011). Impact of mindfulness-based stress reduction training on intrinsic brain connectivity. *NeuroImage, 56*(1), 290–298.

Lanius, R., Bluhm, R., & Frewen, P. (2011). How understanding the neurobiology of complex post-traumatic stress disorder can inform clinical practice: A social cognitive and affective neuroscience approach. *Acta Psychiatrica Scandinavica, 124*(5), 331–348.

Lazar, S. W., Kerr, C. E., Wasserman, R. H., Gray, J. R., Greve, D. N., Treadway, M. T., & Rauch, S. L. (2005). Meditation experience is associated with increased cortical thickness. *NeuroReport, 16*(17), 1893–1897.

Levinson, D. B., Smallwood, J., & Davidson, R. J. (2012). The persistence of thought evidence for a role of working memory in the maintenance of task-unrelated thinking. *Psychological Science, 23*(4), 375–380.

Levitin, D. J. (2006). *This is your brain on music: The science of a human obsession.* New York: Dutton.

Limb, C. J., Braun, A. R. (2008) Neural substrates of spontaneous musical performance: An fMRI study of jazz improvisation. *PLoS ONE 3*(2): e1679.

Li, W., Mai, X., & Liu, C. (2014). The default mode network and social understanding of others: What do brain connectivity studies tell us? *Frontiers in Human Neuroscience, 8*(74).

Lueke, A. & Gibson, B. (2014). Mindfulness meditation reduces implicit age and race bias: The role of reduced automaticity of responding. *Social Psychological and Personality Science, 6*(3), 284–291.

Lutz, A., Greischar, L. L., Rawlings, N. B., Ricard, M., & Davidson, R. J. (2004). Long-term meditators self-induce high-amplitude gamma synchrony during mental practice. *Proceedings of the National Academy of Sciences of the United States of America, 101*(46), 16369–16373.

Maddock, R., Garrett, A., & Buonocore, M. (2003). Posterior cingulate cortex activation by emotional words: fMRI evidence from a valence decision task. *Human Brain Mapping, 18*(1), 30–41.

Mars, R., Neubert, F., Noonan, M., Sallet, J., Toni, I., & Rushworth, M. (2012). On the relationship between the "default mode network" and the "social brain." *Frontiers in Human Neuroscience, 6*(189).

McGilchrist, I. (2009). *The master and his emissary: The divided brain and the making of the Western world.* New Haven, CT: Yale University Press.

Mipam, G. & Hopkins, J. (2006). *Fundamental mind: The Nyingma view of the Great Completeness.* Ithaca, NY: Snow Lion.

Mitchell, J., Banaji, M., & Macrae, N. (2005). The link between social cognition and self-referential thought in the medial prefrontal cortex. *Journal of Cognitive Neuroscience, 17*(8), 1306–1315.

Müller, V., Sänger, J., Lindenberger, U. (2013) Intra- and inter-brain synchronization during musical improvisation on the guitar. *PLoS ONE 8*(9): e73852.

Pagnoni, G., Cekic, M., & Guo, Y. (2008). "Thinking about not-thinking:" Neural correlates of conceptual processing during Zen meditation. *PLoS One, 3*(9), e3083.

Patel, R., Spreng, N., Shin, L., & Girard, T. (2012). Neurocircuitry models of posttraumatic stress disorder and beyond: A meta-analysis of functional neuroimaging studies. *Neuroscience & Biobehavioral Reviews, 36,* 2130–2142.

Pellegrini, A. D., Dupuis, D., & Smith, P. K. (2007). Play in evolution and development. *Developmental Review, 27*(2), 261–276.

Porges, S. (2011). *The polyvagal theory: Neurophysiological foundations of emotion, attachment, communication, and self-regulation.* New York: W. W. Norton & Company.

Prakash, R. S., De Leon, A. A., Klatt, M., Malarkey, W., & Patterson, B. (2013). Mindfulness disposition and default-mode network connectivity in older adults. *Social Cognitive and Affective Neuroscience, 8*(1), 112–117.

Raffone, A. & Srinivasan, N. (2010). The exploration of meditation in the neuroscience of attention and consciousness. *Cognitive Processing, 11*(1), 1–7.

Raichle, M. E., MacLeod, A. M., Snyder, A. Z., Powers, W. J., Gusnard, D. A., & Shulman, G. L. (2001). A default mode of brain function. *Proceedings of the National Academy of Sciences of the United States of America, 98*(2), 676–682.

Rakel, D., Barrett, B., Zhang, Z., Hoeft, T., Chewning, B., Marchand, L., & Scheder, J. (2011). Perception of empathy in the therapeutic encounter: Effects on the common cold. *Patient Education and Counseling, 85*(3), 390–397.

Reniers, R. L., Corcoran, R., Völlm, B. A., Mashru, A., Howard, R., & Liddle, P. F. (2012). Moral decision-making, ToM, empathy and the default mode network. *Biological Psychology, 90*(3), 202–210.

Ruby, F. J., Smallwood, J., Engen, H., & Singer, T. (2013). How self-generated thought shapes mood—the relation between mind-wandering and mood depends on the socio-temporal content of thoughts. *PLoS One, 8*(10), e77554. doi:10.1371/journal.pone.0077554

Saxe, R. (2006). Why and how to study theory of mind with fMRI. *Brain Research, 1079*(1), 57–65.

Schooler, J. W., Gable, S., Hopper, E., & Mrazek, M. D. (2014, November). "When the muse strikes: Ideas of physicists and writers regularly occur during episodes of mind-wandering." Presented at the Psychonomic Society Annual Meeting, Toronto, Canada.

Siegel, D. (2012) *The developing mind: How relationships and the brain interact to shape who we are*, Second Edition, New York: The Guilford Press.

Siegel D. (2017) *Mind: A journey to the heart of being human*, New York: Mind Your Brain, Inc.

Smallwood, J. & Schooler, J. W. (2015). The science of mind wandering: Empirically navigating the stream of consciousness. *Annual Review of Psychology, 66*, 487–518.

Smith, S. M., Nichols, T. E., Vidaurre, D., Winkler, A. M., Behrens, T. E. J., Glasser, M. F., Ugurbil, K., Barch, D. M., Van Essen, D. C., & Miller, K. L. (2015). A positive-negative mode of population co-variation links brain connectivity, demographics, and behavior. *Nature Neuroscience, 18*(11), 1567–71.

Sood, A. & Jones, D. T. (2013). On mind wandering, attention, brain networks, and meditation. *EXPLORE: The Journal of Science and Healing, 9*(3), 136–141.

Spreng, R. N., Mar, R. A., & Kim, A. S. (2009). The common neural basis of autobiographical memory, prospection, navigation, theory of mind, and the default mode: A quantitative meta-analysis. *Journal of Cognitive Neuroscience, 21*(3), 489–510.

Sridharan, D., Levitin, D. J., & Menon, V. (2008). A critical role for the right fronto-insular cortex in switching between central-executive and default-mode networks. *Proceedings of the National Academy of Sciences, 105*(34), 12569–12574.

Tang, Y. Y., Ma, Y., Wang, J., Fan, Y., Feng, S., Lu, Q., . . . Posner, M. I. (2007). Short-term meditation training improves attention and self-regulation. *Proceedings of the National Academy of Sciences, 104*(43), 17152–17156.

Taylor, V. A., Daneault, V., Grant, J., Scavone, G., Breton, E., Roffe-Vidal, S., . . . & Beauregard, M. (2013). Impact of meditation training on the default mode network during a restful state. *Social Cognitive and Affective Neuroscience, 8*(1), 4–14.

Tononi, G., Edelman, G. M., & Sporns, O. (1998). Complexity and coherency: Integrating information in the brain. *Trends in Cognitive Sciences, 2*(12), 474–484.

Tulving, E. (2005). Episodic memory and autonoesis: Uniquely human? In Terrace, H. S. & Metcalfe, J. (Eds.), *The missing link in cognition: origins of self-reflective consciousness* (pp. 3–56). New York: Oxford University Press, Inc.

Vestergaard-Poulsen, P., van Beek, M., Skewes, J., Bjarkam, C. R., Stubberup, M., Bertelsen, J., & Roepstorff, A. (2009). Long-term meditation is associated with increased gray matter density in the brain stem. *NeuroReport, 20*(2), 170–174.

Winnicott, D. W. (1989). *Playing & reality*. London, UK: Routledge.

World Health Organization. (2004). Prevalence, severity, and unmet need for treatment of mental disorders in the World Health Organization World Mental Health Surveys. *The Journal of the American Medical Association, 291*(21), 2581–2590.

Xu, J., Vik, A., Groote, I. R., Lagopoulos, J., Holen, A., Ellingsen, Ø., Haberg, A. & Davanger, S. (2014). Nondirective meditation activates default mode network and areas associated with memory retrieval and emotional processing. *Frontiers in Human Neuroscience, 8*(86).

Zhang, T. & Raichle, M. E. (2010). Disease and the brain's dark energy. *Nature Reviews Neurology. 6*(1) 15–28.

4

How Love Opens Creativity, Play, and the Arts through Early Right-Brain Development

Allan Schore and Terry Marks-Tarlow

OUR VIEW OF human nature is intimately tied to our view of human love. Philosophers, poets, and psychologists have adopted one of two basic stances: either people are seen as inherently selfish and out for the good of themselves, or people are seen as inherently altruistic and out for the good of each other and society. Love has been slow to enter the psychological dialogue partly because Freud epitomized the former stance. In *Civilization and Its Discontents*, Freud hypothesized that the very origins of civilization arose from a collective need for checks and balances to counteract otherwise selfish motives. Only an authoritative, hierarchical structure of customs and laws could keep things fair for everyone.

The humanistic revolt of the 1960s not only rebelled against authoritarian and paternalistic aspects of Freud's model, but also against his very model of human nature, as did some of Freud's own disciples, including Donald Winnicott and Sándor Ferenczi who boldly asserted the essential importance of love in early development. The contemporary fields of modern attachment theory, regulation theory, and interpersonal neurobiology weigh in on this issue of human nature. The two opposing views of human nature represent the primary motives of each of the two hemispheres of the human brain. At a conscious level, the left side of the brain concerns itself primarily with power motives, while the right side of the brain is steeped in affiliation drives (Kuhl & Kazén, 2008; Hecht,

2014). Only one perspective can press forward into consciousness at a time; and as this occurs, the other perspective recedes into the background (McGilchrist, 2009). Schore's modern attachment theory (Schore & Schore, 2008; Schore, in press) and regulation theory (Schore, 1994; 2012) add an important developmental dimension to which set of motives is more primary in a particular social context. In a nutshell, from the start of life, infants thrive on mutual love, and the social, emotional, relational right brain is the cradle for a healthy brain. If a baby is adequately cherished, soothed, stimulated, and respected by receiving attuned response during the first two years of life, the right brain—the relational, emotional, social, somatically grounded side—becomes a healthy regulator for the more individualistic motives of the left brain.

In this chapter, we propose a two-person relational model of love, play, and creativity. We suggest that maternal and mutual love are primary motivational forces from the start of a baby's life. Love is capable of energetically jump starting all of the positive emotions and behaviors, including interest, excitement, joy, curiosity, exploration, and play in babies. The mutual exchange of love fuels a young child's desire to explore the environment, drink in novelty, and eventually to fire up imagination in service of creativity. As children grow and develop, this initial dose of love gets internalized into passionate engagements throughout life, including a love for life itself.

The early origins of the relational capacity to engage in mutual love as well as in creativity are both generated in the early developing right hemisphere. The most rapid development of the right brain over the first two years of life occurs over a period when the child is processing enormous amounts of social-emotional information, much of which is *novel* and increasingly complex. According to McGilchrist (2009) at all points of the life span "What is *new* must first be present in the right hemisphere, before it can come into focus for the left. . . . It begins in wonder, intuition, ambiguity, puzzlement, and uncertainty on the right . . ." (p.). Integrating interdisciplinary data Schore (2012) is now documenting that current neuroscientific models view creativity as the production of an idea that is both *novel* and useful in a particular social setting. Although the left hemisphere is specialized for coping with predictable representations and strategies, the right predominates for coping with and assimilating novel situations and ensures *the formation of a new program of interaction with a new environment. Indeed, the right brain possesses special capabilities for processing novel stimuli.* The experience-dependent growth of this hemisphere, which is promoted in right-brain-to-right-brain, intensely emotional, attachment communications embedded in mutual love transactions, thus allows the maturing infant to process novel intra- and interpersonal information, an essential functional aspect of creativity.

In the first part of the chapter, we examine historical precedents of love's investigation before turning to neurobiological and developmental origins of love as the guiding force for attunement, synchrony, and coordinated response. We argue that the paradigmatic expression of how the mother shapes the baby's brain *for the better* is expressed in an early bond of mutual love, and that this growth-promoting early emotional experience acts as a relational matrix for the emergence of the capacity to play as well of as the lifelong capacity for creative self-expression. We suggest that two kinds of maternal love—quiet and excited—help to expand affect tolerance in babies for high-intensity positive *and* negative emotions, preparing young children for the highs and lows of playful explorations that generate self-constituting creativity. We discuss recent neurobiological studies of mother-infant love and describe a developmental model of three stages of mutual love. We highlight the central role of the right brain in primary intersubjectivity and the onset of mutual love, interpersonal play, and creativity. We also offer support for Dissayanake's artification hypothesis, that art springs directly from the intimacy of the mother relating lovingly to her infant. The chapter ends by addressing some clinical implications of the importance of transferential-countertransferential mutual love within psychotherapy.

Love's Historical Investigation

Love is mostly thought to be the province of the arts, poets and writers, actors, dancers, and musicians; yet from the very beginnings of modern biology and psychology, science has also explored its origins and emotional expressions. Indeed, in his seminal work *The Expression of Emotions in Man and Animals* (1872), Charles Darwin proposed,

> The emotion of love, for instance that of a mother for her infant, is one of the strongest of which the mind is capable. . . . No doubt, as affection is a pleasurable sensation, it generally causes a gentle smile and some brightening of the eyes. A strong desire to touch the beloved is commonly felt . . . (pp. 224–225)

Specifically referring to the origins of perhaps this most essential expression of the human species, he speculated, "The movements of expressions in the face and body . . . serve as the first means of communication between the mother and her infant; she smiles approval, and thus encourages her child on the right path, or frowns disapproval" (p. 385).

At the end of the 19th century Sigmund Freud (1895) began his pioneering studies in psychoanalysis and initiated the field's long history of interest in the essential role of love in human function and dysfunction. Referring to his evolving position on the developmental origins of love, Schore (2003b p. 256) has suggested "Although for much of his career [Freud] seemed ambivalent about the role of maternal influences in earliest development, in his very last work he stated, in a definitive fashion, that the mother-infant relationship 'is unique, without parallel, established unalterably for a whole lifetime as the first and strongest love-object and the prototype of all later love relations' (Freud, 1940)."

Donald Winnicott, an important follower of Freud, studied the deepest origins of the capacity to love. He observed, "The early management of an infant is a matter *beyond conscious thought and deliberate intention*. It is something that becomes possible only through love," and that the mother "by expressing love in terms of physical management and in giving physical satisfaction enables the infant psyche to begin in the infant body" (1975, p. 183, authors' italics). Thus the early origins of love are expressed in the mother-infant experience of mutuality. Furthermore, Winnicott (1963) described two forms of love in the developing infant. "Quiet love" is seen in moments when the mother holds and handles (soothes, comforts, caresses) the infant.

FIGURE 4.1
Quiet love. (Courtesy of Sharon Austin)

"Quiet love" has been characterized as "a mutual dwelling of baby and mother where one and one make not two but one" (Ulanov, 2001, pp. 49–50).

On the other hand "excited love" occurs in moments of thrilling excitement and intense interest in interaction with the mother, and contains an energetic potential.

FIGURE 4.2
Excited love. (Courtesy of Ruth Anne Hammond)

In the middle of the last century another of Freud's followers, John Bowlby (1953), began his seminal writings on what would become attachment theory in *Child Care and the Growth of Love*. In that volume he asserted that a mother's love in infancy and childhood is as important for mental health as are vitamins and proteins for physical health. Following this explicit association of the origins of attachment and love, Ainsworth (1967) offered her classic *Infancy in Uganda: Infant Care and the Growth of Love*. In his later writings Bowlby (1969) concluded, "Many of the most intense emotions arise during the formation, the maintenance, the disruption, and the renewal of attachment relationships. The formation of a bond is described as falling in love, maintaining a bond as loving someone, and losing a partner as grieving over someone" (p. 130).

Also in mid-century another of Freud's disciples, Erich Fromm (1956), wrote the classic *The Art of Loving*, in which he described love as "the experience of union with another being," and "becoming one with another." In that volume Fromm described what he deemed to be the central problem in individual development: "What meaning—in both women as well as men—does our longing for a mother have? What constitutes the bond to the mother?" (p. 26–27). He stated that motherly love is an unconditional affirmation of the child's life and needs, and that it is expressed in two different aspects:

> [O]ne is the care and responsibility absolutely necessary for the preservation of the child's life and his growth. The other aspect goes further than mere preservation. . . . Motherly love, in this second step, makes the child feel: it is good to have been born; it instills in the child the *love for life* and not merely the wish to remain alive. . . . Mother's love for life is as infectious as her anxiety (pp. 46–47, authors' italics).

Note the overlap between maternal "care" and Winnicott's "quiet love," and between Fromm's maternal support of the child's love for life and Winnicott's "excited love" that contains an energetic potential. Winnicott and Fromm understood the significance of the mother's loving attitude for instilling emotional resilience plus a passionate stance in children that lasts a lifetime. Thus the major pioneers in the field conceptualized love as an "intense" emotion, indeed "one of the strongest of which the mind is capable," which when shared by another forms an "intense emotional union" that persists as an intrapsychic stance toward life itself.

Love, Attachment, and Emotional Regulation

The *Shorter Oxford English Dictionary* defines love as "a state or feeling," "*deep affection, strong emotional attachment.*" This raises the matter of the relationship of love to attachment, especially in light of the transformational impact of the shift of modern attachment theory from behavior and cognition to affect and an emotional bond between intimate individuals (Schore & Schore, 2008; Schore, in press). Love is defined as 1) a noun: a feeling of tenderness, passion, and warmth; and 2) a verb: to feel love for another person—actions including expressions of physical affection, tenderness, and acts of kindness. The first usage implies love as an intense intrapersonal emotion, the second as a strong interpersonal emotional communication. The contrast in these two definitions mirror the ongoing shift from a "one person" intrapsychic to a "two person" interpersonal perspective in psychology, including the most prominent theory in developmental psychology, attachment theory.

Although the humanities have a long history of exploring this deepest expression of the human heart and mind, the idea that the brain sciences can be used to explain the subtleties and depths of human love has been controversial. In the humanities, many feared that a reductionist science would simplify the complexities of love to a neural synapse or to a collection of neurochemicals. This idea is disputed by Schore's ongoing interdisciplinary work on emotion, a central component of love, which conceptualizes mind/body/brain well-being to emerge from early healthy relationship dynamics. To understand the attachment origins of the capacity to receive, feel, and express the emotion of love with another, the perspective of *interpersonal* neurobiology elucidates the biological *and* psychological development of the early bonds of *mutual* love. The mutual love between a mother and her infant is embedded in an optimal co-created, reciprocal, synchronized, bodily based, emotion transacting attachment relationship. In this manner the relational mechanism of mutual love, *"strong emotional attachment,"* is mediated by the mother's right brain interacting and resonating with the infant's right brain, amplifying intense positive arousal in both (Schore, 1994).

After nine months of gestation within the womb, a newborn human is quite helpless, requiring care from adults for years, a period that extends much longer than any other primate. It appears that "intense maternal care" or "intensive parenting" arose as early as 1.8 million years ago (Falk 2004; Flinn & Ward, 2005, Leakey, 1994; Rosenberg, 1992). The mother-infant interaction is an evolved adaptation, because all healthy infants are born ready to recognize, respond to, and coordinate their behavior with the signals and responses of primary caretakers.

Infants are much less responsive to adult-style discourse than to what Dissanayake (2017) calls "extra-ordinary" signals in the form of exaggerated facial expressions and vocal tone, to which babies respond with "beguiling wriggles, coos, and smiles." As Dissanayake notes, babies are not *taught* to engage with caretakers in this way, and if anything are more the teachers, who by their positive and negative reactions let caretakers know which movements, expressions, and sounds they prefer. Babies are not passive beings, but instead use their own positive and negative emotional experiences to actively elicit responses and shape the pace, intensity, and variety of signals that adults direct toward them.

All emotion is composed of two dimensions: valence (positive-negative, pleasant-unpleasant, approach-avoidance of discrete emotions), and arousal (intensity, energy, calm-excited). Furthermore, left hemispheric activity is associated with moderate levels of cortical arousal, while right hemispheric activity accompanies either high or low levels of cortical arousal. Shared right-brain states of reciprocated mutual love thus generate the most intense states of emotional arousal and positive affects in the human experience.

On the matter of a centrality of a mother's love, we would go far as to say that most if not all mothers have the conscious intention of loving their baby. Yet one of the major findings of science is that many of the essential processes involved in love operate at rapid time frames, unconsciously, at levels beneath awareness. For this reason, the relational psychobiological mechanisms that underlie mutual love can best be described by integrating observations and data from neurobiology and psychoanalysis, the science of unconscious processes.

Toward that end, rather than describing love as an ideal mental state we will suggest that love is embedded in a basic evolutionary mechanism located in the early developing emotion-processing right brain. A central purpose of this chapter is to highlight the structural and functional ontogenetic development of this evolutionary system, all of which takes place at nonverbal levels. In light of modern conceptions of nature-nurture interactions we now understand how a loving early beginning can optimally epigenetically shape the basic evolutionary processes that are expressed in human infancy.

In terms of regulation theory, the calming and soothing, dyadic context of Winnicott's "quiet love" represents a transition of strong negative affect from a high arousal sympathetic-dominant energy-expending psychobiological state to a low arousal parasympathetic-dominant energy-conserving psychobiological state expressed in comfort and relief from stress and distress. On the other hand Winnicott's "excited love" contains an energetic potential that represents a transition from a calm, alert state into a regulated high arousal, mutually accelerating, sympathetic-dominant energy-expending emotional state, expressed by expanding joy and excitement. In other words Winnicott's "quiet love" describes the down-regulation of intense negatively valenced emotional arousal into a positively valenced calm, intensely pleasant state, while "excited love" describes the up-regulation of emotional arousal from open engagement into an intensely positive, excited, and joyful state. Ultimately "quiet love" and "excited love" need to be integrated into the personality structure.

Three Stages of Mutual Love

A central thesis of this chapter is that during development the emergent capacity for mutual love evolves in three stages that correspond roughly to MacLean's (1985) three layers of the brain: reptilian, mammalian, and neocortical. For the first several months after birth, a mother's quiet love is dominant, exquisitely monitoring and attuning her to the physical and emotional needs of her baby. During this stage, both mother and baby are primarily engaged at the subcortical level of the amygdala, which mediates basic emotions and corresponds to Freud's deep unconscious, as well as MacLean's reptilian level of basic safety and trust.

Barrett, et al. (2012) report an fMRI study that demonstrates the importance of the mother's subcortical amygdala in response to the facial affective signals of her very young infant. Referring to the emotional parenting tasks specific to this early postpartum period they note that giving birth and becoming a mother is a "profound experience":

> Over the course of pregnancy and throughout the postpartum period, changes in levels of certain hormones likely influence the function of key brain regions to increase the likelihood that a mother is attracted to her baby, is attentive and sensitive to her baby's needs, learns from her experiences, and behaves appropriately . . . the early postpartum period is an inherently emotional and challenging time, associated with both positive and negative affect (p. 253).

The second stage of maternal-infant mutual love first appears at about two to three months, when the attachment system common to all social mammals comes online. Now mother and child are engaged with one another at the level of the anterior cingulate cortex, which mediates both engaged attachment and separation anxiety. In classic research Stern (1985) describes the transition from an early forming "emergent self" at birth into a "core self" at two to three months. He observes, "At the age of two to three months, infants begin to give the impression of being quite different persons. When engaged in social interaction, they appear to be more wholly integrated. It is if their actions, plans, affects, perceptions, and cognitions can now all be brought into play and focused, for a while, on an interpersonal situation" (p. 69).

As mother moves from quiet love in the earliest phase to excited love that is mutual, she naturally starts to play in intimate and affectionate ways that express reciprocal and intense engagement (Miall & Dissanayake, 2003). Daniel Stern (1971, 1974), Beatrice Beebe (1977, 1979), Colwyn Trevarthen (1979), and Ed Tronick (1978, 1979) have provided essential basic research on the extraordinary abilities of young infants to engage with their mothers in mutually improvised, spontaneously choreographed interactions. The mother-infant pair employ rhythmic head and body movements, hand gestures, and facial expressions plus vocal sounds to co-create and maintain exquisitely patterned temporal and communicative sequences. As Beebe (1986) demonstrated, even newborns show sensitivity to temporal sequence and pattern. Babies are ready to engage in behavioral turn-taking as early as eight weeks of age, when they expect social contingency, which consists of predictable back-and-forth interactivity. Infant research has established the importance of timing (Murray & Trevarthen, 1985; Nadel, et al., 1999).

Ellen Dissanayake (2017) suggests that the usual labels for the interaction, i.e., "baby talk," "infant-directed speech," or "motherese," fail to sufficiently emphasize two important features: its *dyadic* nature, where both partners influence each other, as well as its *multimodality*, where multiple senses are involved. Frame-by-frame microanalyses of videotaped mother-infant interactions that show the faces and upper torsos of both partners side by side, reveal that *facial expressions* and *head-and-body movements* are as significant in the interaction as vocalizations (Beebe, et al., 1985; Beebe & Lachmann, 2014; Murray & Trevarthen, 1985; Stern, 1971). During these interactions, Dissanayake emphasizes how much all three sensory modalities or "languages" of the engagement— body, facial, vocal—are processed as a whole in the infant's brain (Beebe & Lachmann, 2014; Stern, 1985). Schore (1994, 2003a, 2012, in press) provides a large body of evidence that gestural, facial, and auditory signals are processed in the infant's right brain.

The third stage of maternal-infant mutual love sets in between 10 and 12 months, as baby's neocortical, emotion-regulating area of the orbitofrontal cortex begins a critical period of growth. In 2008, Noriuchi and colleagues published "The Functional Neuroanatomy of Maternal Love: Mother's Response to Infant's Attachment Behaviors" in *Biological Psychiatry*. In this study, mothers of 16-month-old infants were shown two videos of infant attachment behavior. In the first situation, the infant was smiling while playing with his/her mother, and in the second video, the infant was asking for her while being separated from his/her mother. Note this use of both a play and separation context parallels infant studies in the psychological sciences for evaluating attachment as maternal up-regulation of positive states and down-regulation of negative states.

In the video of the play context, the smiling mother blew bubbles toward her infant, while in the video of separation context, the mother leaves the room and the infant is left alone, "unduly distressed," crying and calling for mother. They note, "While mothers may feel joyful by watching video clips of their own infant in the first situation, they may feel anxious and protective when shown video clips of their own infant in the second situation" (p. 415). They posit maternal love and "strong emotional attachment" would be invariant regardless of whether she was expressing affectionate behavior or vigilance and protectiveness" (p. 415).

The authors report that maternal love is associated with activation of the mother's right anterior cingulate and periaqueductal gray, areas "involved in maternal response to infant's pain of separation" (p. 421). They interpret this as indicating that the mother is paying attention to her infant, who is expressing strong attachment behaviors, and that she recognizes her infant's emotional and mental *states evoked by separation from herself.* They therefore conclude, "Positive emotions such as love and motherly feeling coexisted with negative ones such as anxious feeling and worry in the mother herself. In this complicated situation, the mother's emotional responses to her own infant might be appropriately regulated by monitoring her own emotional states and by inhibiting her excessive negative affects so as not to show negative expressions to her infant who is in distress" (pp. 422–423). Note the emphasis on the auto-regulation of negative states in a loving mother and also her ability to hold ambivalent feelings for the infant (see Schore, 1994; 2012).

In line with earlier cited studies, these researchers document that feelings representing maternal love were elicited by viewing the mother's own infant, regardless of the situation, and that activity in her orbitofrontal cortex was associated with this. Maternal love activates the mother's right orbitofrontal cortex, the highest level of the limbic system that regulates both positive and negative affect. The authors state that the orbitofrontal cortex plays an important role in the positive reward system (it receives ascending dopamine projections from the ventral tegmental area) and at the same time its activation reflects selection of appropriate strategies to reduce the negative distress of her infant. This finding fits nicely with Schore's ideas about the right orbitofrontal system acting as the control system of attachment that encodes strategies of positive and negative affect regulation in the mother's internal working model of her relationship with her infant. In summary, they conclude, "the amount of love with which a mother interacts with her infant is highly influential on the stability of the mother-infant relationship and the quality of the mother-infant attachment." (p. 415)

Brown and Dissanayake (2009) speculate that the functional properties of the orbitofrontal cortex provide important insight into the multimodal processing so central to the components of ritual behaviors, whether in mother-infant interactions or participation in group-wide rituals. In both contexts one finds entrainment, joint action, emergent coordination, planned coordination, chorusing, turn-taking, imitation, complementary joint action, motor resonance, action simulation, and mimesis (Phillips-Silver & Keller, 2012).

These studies indicate that loving affiliative behaviors and emotions, such as those created and reinforced by the operations of mother-infant interaction and participation in temporally coordinated and integrated multimodal (facial, vocal, gestural) behaviors, make lasting imprints in the orbitofrontal cortex and its connections into reward centers of the brain, such the ventral tegmental dopamine system and the periaqueductal gray involved in the emotional pain of separation (Carter, et al., 1999; Miller & Rodgers, 2001). In their groundbreaking study "The neural correlates of *maternal and romantic love*" Bartels and Zeki (2004) describe these enduring effects:

> The tender intimacy and selflessness of a mother's love for her infant occupies a unique and exalted position in human conduct . . . it provides one of the most *powerful motivations for human action*, and has been celebrated throughout the ages—in literature, art, and music—as one of the most beautiful and *inspiring* manifestations of human behavior. It has also been the subject of many psychological studies that have searched into *the long-lasting and pervasive influence of maternal love (or its absence) on the development and future mental constitution of a child* (p. 1155, authors' italics).

Primary Intersubjectivity

Onset of Mutual love, Creativity, and Interpersonal Play

Love is a strong motivating and growth-promoting force, both in caretakers and in their children, because love is intrinsically rewarding. Love fuels self-sacrifice and hard work because it is inherently emotionally powerful, and thereby meaningful. Like love, play and creativity also involve intrinsic motivation that is connected to inherently meaningful states of being and doing. Subjectively speaking, love, play and creativity are undertaken voluntarily, that is freely for the sake of their own pleasure, reward, and satisfaction. Mutual love between mother and child carves out a dopamine-rich, oxytocin-laden landscape of passion, joy, curiosity, intrinsic motivation and self-evident meaning that becomes preserved throughout life through other playful, passion-filled, and creative pursuits.

Indeed, Ellen Dissanayake observes that at two to three months, the initiation of a critical period of mutual love, there is a significant change of infant facial, voice, and gesture.

> What mothers convey to infants are not their verbalized observations and opinions about the baby's looks, actions, and digestion—the ostensible content of talk to babies—but rather positive affiliative messages about their intentions and feelings: You interest me, I like you, I am like you, I like to be with you, You please me, I want to please you, You delight me, I want to communicate with you, I want you to be like me (1991, p. 91).

This same time period represents the onset of right-brain-to-right-brain protoconversations within the dyad (Trevarthen, 1979). In these initial trans-

FIGURE 4.3
Exuberance at play. (Courtesy of Terry Marks-Tarlow)

FIGURE 4.4
Food play. (Courtesy of Terry Marks-Tarlow)

actions of "primary intersubjectivity" the baby, attracted to the mother's voice, facial expressions, and gestures, replies *spontaneously and playfully* with affection, while the mother replies *spontaneously and playfully* to the baby's nonverbal communications. A traffic of visual, auditory-prosodic and tactile signals induce instant emotional effects, namely dyadically amplified excitement and pleasure (*"excited love"*) builds within the dyad. These expressions of increasing accelerating positive emotional arousal represent products of "primary process communication" expressed in "both body movements (kinesics), posture, gesture, facial expression, voice inflection, and the sequence, rhythm, and pitch of the spoken words" (Dorpat, 2001, p. 451). The loving mother's and infant's right-brain-to-right-brain nonverbal communications expose the infant's rapidly developing right brain to high amounts of *spontaneous* inter- and and intrapersonal *novelty*, allowing for the multimodal *integration* of external and internal sensations (see earlier description of the appearance of Stern's core self at two to three months).

These same interpersonal neurobiological mechanisms contribute to the interpersonal origins of creativity. In the neuroscience literature, Chavez-Eakle, et al. (2007) conclude, "Creativity means *bringing into being;* it involves generation of *novelty* and transformation of the existent (p. 519) . . . creativity involves *spontaneity* and the production of unusual and original responses to the environment (p. 525)." Documenting right-lateralized activity in these processes they observe that *"inspiration,"* the first and deepest initiatory stage of creativity involves sensorial, affective, and cognitive integrations that take place rapidly at unconscious levels. In neuropsychological research Martindale (1984) demonstrated that creativity is associated with right hemispheric primary process cognition. In early psychoanalytic studies of creativity, Reik (1953, p. 9) suggested that creativity specifically activates unconscious primary process mentation, which involves "sounds, fleeting images, organic sensations, and emotional currents."

Mutual love, an interpersonal context of right-brain accelerating positive emotional arousal, thus is the source of right-brain intrapsychic creative inspiration, a function that occurs rapidly, "beyond conscious thought." The *Shorter Oxford Dictionary* defines "inspire" as "arouse in the mind, instill (a feeling or impulse)." Discussing Reik's proposal of "the origin of inspiration in childhood," Arnold (2007) describes the adaptive functions of "the creative unconscious." Creativity has long been associated with a feminine muse, which may be derived from an unconscious representation of mother's love, which Bartels and Zeki (2004) describe as "one of the most beautiful and *inspiring* manifestations of human behavior."

Indeed there is now agreement across disciplines that creativity is impor-

FIGURES 4.5–4.6
Left: Multisensory play. *Right:* The nutcracker's bride. (Courtesy of Terry Marks-Tarlow)

tant for social survival and individual wellbeing. Recall this adaptive function involves the production of an idea that is both *novel* and useful in a particular social setting, and that the right hemisphere predominates in coping with and assimilating novel situations and ensures the formation of a new program of interaction with a new environment, a description of the infant's social emotional development over the first two years. Attachment transactions directly influence the "early life programming of hemispheric lateralization" (Stevenson, et al., 2008, p. 852), and thus the creative loving mother's excited love and quiet love provide novel and more complex social and emotional stimuli that facilitate the growth and development of the infant's rapidly maturing right-brain emergent functions. In this manner the right-brain-to-right-brain intersubjective communications that begin to structuralize the core self at 2 to 3 months represent the primordial developmental crucible of mutual love, creativity, and play.

Along with being intrinsically motivating, love, creativity, and play also

FIGURE 4.7
Learning how to shop. (Courtesy of Terry Marks-Tarlow)

share emotion-regulating functions. Just as love permits the mother to endure hardship and willingly self-sacrifice in the face of adversity, as noted in the previous section, love also helps to stretch affect tolerance in young children, thereby permitting safety in novelty-seeking activities. Marks-Tarlow (2010, 2012) describes the emotion-regulating aspects of early play, designed by nature to implicitly carry babies to the brink of regulatory boundaries. Early games of peek-a-boo and later versions of hide-and-seek tap into the edges of abandonment fears. Throwing baby high up in the air becomes gleeful due to fears of falling and necessary trust of being caught instead of perishing. In all of these early games, the line between safety and danger, joy and distress is a thin one. Tickling so easily turns into painful distress if not conducted in an attuned fashion. To play on the edges of what is intolerable again and again helps young children to stretch those regulatory boundaries, such that later in life they can engage in passionate and creative pursuits that may be difficult, risky, and not always fun, yet nonetheless rewarding.

FIGURE 4.8
The open-mouthed joy of early risk-taking. (Courtesy of Terry Marks-Tarlow)

We suggest that excited mutual love in the form of play is the apex that drives the heights and breadth of the developing child's positive emotions, which in turn expand joy, broaden the attentional landscape (Frederickson, 2001), and enhance creativity (Estrada, Young, & Isen, 1994). Love signals the safety to be vulnerable and to take risks.

Love drives open perceptual doors through which children soak in novelty, revel in spontaneity, and tolerate frustration. Love inspires mutual play and creativity that continue throughout the lifespan, preserving open-hearted engagement with others and the world at large.

The Artification Hypothesis

Another central thesis of this chapter is that in young children, the neurobiology fostered by maternal love boosts a lifelong engagement with play and the arts, partly by fueling the physiology of passion, joy, curiosity, and full engagement, both with negative and positive emotions. In this section, we explore a direct link between mutual love, play, and the arts. One reason a mother's love has been so celebrated in literature, art, and music may be because a mother's love resides at the very origin of art making itself. This is the "artification" hypothesis put forth by Ellen Dissanayake (2017).

Dissanayake traces the evolution of the arts back to early mother-child relations within hominid culture. By artification, she refers to "the behavior, observed in virtually all human individuals and societies, of intentionally making parts of the natural and manmade environment (e.g., shelters, tools, utensils, weapons, clothing, bodies, surroundings) extraordinary or special by marking, shaping, and embellishing them beyond their ordinary natural or functional appearance." The same term can apply to behaviors within vocal, gestural, and verbal modalities that translate to what we call song, dance, poetic language, and performances of various types" (p. 148).

Due to unprecedented helplessness of human infants and their need for protracted maternal care after birth, Dissanayake suggests that multimodal intimate maternal practices that solidified the mother-child bond carried an evolutionary advantage and so became amplified. She (2017, 2009) describes how maternal behavior became ritualized, in a fashion first illuminated by ethologists for birds and other animals, such that vocalizations and body movements from ordinary contexts became altered to enhance communication. Often occurring in playful contexts, such behaviors were characteristically stereotyped or formalized, repeated, exaggerated, elaborated, as well as temporally manipulated in order to create suspense and surprise. Dissayanake also speculates that facial expressions and body movements that convey social affiliation and accord between adults became co-opted into extraordinary and noteworthy signals to attract attention, sustain interest, as well as to create and mold emotion. Indeed, Chong and her colleagues (2003) present a typology of exaggerated facial expressions universally employed by mothers, including a trio of facial expressions of love which is completely unique to maternal-child interactions.

Much like Winnicott, Dissanayake delineates an early, quiet kind of love, when a mother's vocalizations, movements, and facial expressions are primarily concerned with regulating the emotional state of her infant—soothing, showing endearment, or modulating distress. As infants' autonomic and central nervous system mature, excited love emerges at three months, and the infant now desires and seeks not just calmed, soothed states but also suspense, surprise, and fun. Over the first year, early exploration heightens into action games through play and songs like peek-a-boo or *This Little Piggy*. Repetition in a mother's vocal utterances, facial expressions, and body movements coordinates the two bodies, minds, and brains, serving to regulate the infant emotionally and unite the pair temporally. Dissanayake describes how repetition also enables manipulation of expectation during mother-infant interaction, which occurs by delaying what the baby anticipates. Sensitivity to regular repetition leads to prediction of what will come next, while manipulations in timing and beat induce pleasurable release of emotion (Kubovy, 1999). Consider how a mother playing "peek-a-boo" will delay the removal of her hands from her eyes in order to provoke amusement and laughter from her baby or similarly will wait to utter what the fifth piggy squeals—"wee, wee, wee, wee, wee—all the way home."

These games illustrate why early mother-infant interaction is often described, thought of, and experienced as a kind of play (Stern, 1977). It is spontaneous, improvised, and self-rewarding, with both partners actively showing how much they are enjoying themselves. Spontaneous play transforms a context into an enriched environment, one that facilitates processing of novel information and thereby improves learning capacity, including social-emotional learning (Schore, 1994). Play is common in all social animals (Burghardt, 2005; Panksepp, 1998). Humans and other animals tend to display special facial expressions and body postures to indicate their play-actions are not real-life behavior. In humans, this "as if" behavior morphs through play first into embodied metaphor and later into creative uses of the imagination. Marks-Tarlow (2012) details a two-stage neurobiological model by which free play of the imagination during childhood establishes a bodily, social, and emotional form of exploration that later permits intuitively grounded navigation of social space "from the inside out."

Dissanayake notes (2017) that ritualized maternal-child sequences that are patterned in time foster mutual temporal coordination, or interpersonal synchrony that includes a release of oxytocin ("the love hormone") and other endogenous opioids in both parent and child. Oxytocin is produced in the hypothalamus and serves as a key modulator of complex socioaffective responses such as affiliation, social approach, and attachment stress and anxiety (Bartz & Hollander, 2006; Meyer-Lindenberg, 2008). Release of these neuropeptides creates feelings of intimacy and trust plus relieves feelings of anxiety. Just as right-brain prosody, the musical dimension of maternal care, enhances emotional regulation and creates strong mother-infant bonding, so too in adults does music create strong social bonds, partly by synchronizing movements, emotions, and physiological responses. Dissanayake (2008) suggests a dual function of oxytocin: it both drives participation with others in coordinated music-making, as in the songs and dances of ritual practice, as well as relieves individual anxiety and emotional tensions in the process. Not only does group singing and individual music listening release oxytocin, but oxytocin also enhances interpersonal rhythmic synchronization broadly, thus contributing to its pro-social effects (Gebauer, et al., 2014).

Neurobiological studies of the right brain now confirm Dissanayake's artification and Schore's regulation hypotheses. A functional magnetic resonance imaging study of 1- to 3-day-old newborns reports that music evokes activation in the right auditory cortex (Perani, et al., 2010). In adults the right somatosensory cortex is involved in subjective reports of emotional experience induced by music, one of the most potent and universal stimuli for emotional mood induction (Johnsen, et al., 2009). More recently Swart (2016) offers interdisciplinary evidence to conclude, "as regards the emotional aspects involved, the right brain appears to contribute most to the emotional meaning of music as well as of speech" (p. 7). Referring to the developmental model of Schore and Schore (2014) she describes the communicative and relational aspects of "music's ability to process emotion—both in terms of intensifying as well as releasing emotion, and particularly in terms of its ability to bypass the conscious mind (Montello, 2002) and to "pierce the heart directly," to borrow the words of Oliver Sacks (2008)" (p. 14).

Further support for Dissanayake's proposal that maternal love is an essential origin of the arts is found in neurobiological research on artistic creativity.

FIGURE 4.9
Youth orchestra tuning up. (Courtesy of Terry Marks-Tarlow)

Julian Jaynes (1976) speculated that the "pre-literate" right mind is dominant '[d]uring periods when consciousness is significantly altered, such as during literary or musical creativity' (p. 223). More recently Wan, Cruts, and Jensen (2014) offer an EEG study of improvisation, an instantaneous creative behavior associated with different forms of art such as music and dance. They document the right frontal region plays a central role in a "let-go" mode of improvisational playing in a less technical, more emotional manner. Citing both Dissanayake's and Schore's developmental models Platt (2007) links poetry to the right hemisphere.

Indeed a large body of research demonstrates that the right prefrontal cortex is centrally involved in artistic creativity (e.g., Finkelstein, Vardi, & Hod, 1991; Bhattacharya & Petsche, 2005; Kowatari, et al., 2009; Drago, et al., 2009). Mihov, et al. (2010) report a meta-analytic review of lateralization studies that support right hemispheric superiority in creative thinking. Furthermore, research is now revealing the underlying neurobiological mechanisms of creativity. Mayseless and Shamay-Tsoory (2015) offer evidence to show that the early developing right frontal area mediates creativity, while the later developing left competes with or interferes with an original creative response. They suggest, "Altering the balance between the right and the left frontal lobes can be used to modulate creative production…reducing left frontal activity and enhancing right frontal activity reduces cognitive control, thus allowing for more creative idea production" (p. 173). Indeed, Kane (2004) suggests that the creative moment involves "a sudden and transient loss or decrease of normal interhemispheric communication, removing inhibitions placed upon the right hemisphere" (p. 52). These observations are relevant to both creativity in caregiving of infants as well as in the psychotherapeutic context.

The Emotion of Love in Psychotherapy

In sections above, we explored how maternal love expresses itself initially through facial expression, soothing, affective touch, and lullabies as quiet love. The excited form of mutual love subsequently builds to a crescendo through spontaneous play that includes coordinated exploration, novel pursuits, emergent interaction, turn-taking, and synchronized pleasure. In these ways, mutual love, play, and creativity are yoked together in multi-modal expression that dovetails with early interactive regulation and development of self and cascades into lifelong and collective creativity at a societal level.

According to Schore (2014) right brain processes are dominant in psychotherapy. There is now agreement that right brain creativity, a fundamental aspect of clinical expertise, is an essential contributor to treatment, both in establishing and maintaining the therapeutic alliance and re-establishing it after ruptures, especially in re-enactments of attachment trauma (see Schore, 2012). He observes that a spontaneous enactment can either blindly repeat a familiar pathological object relation or creatively provide a novel relational experience via the therapist's co-participation in interactive repair and the regulation of the patient's affective states. Regulated enactments also include moments of intimate intersubjective play. Indeed play has a long history in psychotherapy, championed by Winnicott (1971) who argued, "Psychotherapy is done in the overlap of the two play areas, that of the patient and that of the therapist...The reason why playing is essential is that it is in playing that the patient is being creative" (p. 54). Marks-Tarlow (2012; 2014) has also written extensively about the importance of play and creativity as a two-way street within psychotherapy. Contemporary neuroscience now emphasizes the adaptive value of creativity, which is also an outcome of a successful psychotherapeutic experience. Lindell (2011, p. 480) observes, "Flexibility of thought . . . when coupled with originality...allows a creative individual to respond efficiently and effectively to a constantly changing, and regularly challenging, environment." Directly relevant to psychotherapeutic mechanisms of change, Abraham (2013, p. 1) concludes, "The immense capacity of human beings to be creative can be gleaned from virtually all realms of our lives whenever we generate original ideas, develop novel solutions to problems, or express ourselves in a unique and individual manner."

On the other hand the right brain functions of love have had a long and controversial history in psychotherapy. In classical psychoanalysis, love was considered a natural aspect of the transference dynamic on the part of patients, yet was discouraged, if not forbidden within psychoanalysts by Freud, who tended to eroticize all forms of adult love. In an early essay on the matter of love within psychotherapy, Eric Fromm (1958) observed Freud's implicit mistrust of *all* emotions. Because Freud considered emotions to be irrational and inferior to thought and objective interpretation, affectively charged non-erotic love on the part of the psychoanalyst had no place in Freud's clinical methodology, nor in "the talking cure."

In the same essay, Fromm described how Freud's fallout with his early disciple, Sándor Ferenczi, arose precisely over the issue of love. Ferenczi was an early proponent of leveling the playing field between psychoanalyst and patient. Through a process he called "mutual analysis, Ferenczi established the centrality of mutual emotional experience generally, and love specifically. For Ferenczi the essential characteristics of parenthood were the essential characteristics of the psychotherapist. In a book about Ferenczi with the delicious title of *The Leaven of Love*, Izette DeForest (1954) expounded upon his position as follows:

> The offering of loving care cannot be given, either by parent or by psy-
> chotherapist, on demand or in answer to threat. It must be given freely and
> spontaneously as a genuinely felt emotional expression. And it must pro-
> vide an environment of trust and confidence and hope, so that the neurotic
> sufferer can gradually unburden himself of his conscious and unconscious
> anxieties; of his shame and guilt; of his hostility and plans of vengeance; of
> his rejected longing to love; of all his deeply hidden secrets...
>
> It must provide the environment (no matter how absurd it may objec-
> tively appear) which is essential to growth, to the unfolding of individual-
> ity. In other words, the therapist must give to the patient a replica of the
> birthright of love which has denied him, as an infant or a growing child, but
> which, if granted, would have assured him full stature as an individual in his
> own right" (pp. 16-17).

Love, one of the most powerful emotions, fits better into contemporary, relational psychoanalysis, a two-person psychology wherein intersubjectivity is both the goal and the medium for transformation. For example, Hirsch and Kessel (1988) review the influence of existential humanists on interpersonalist proponents of love, including Fromm, Searles, Wolstein and Ehrenberg. Shaw (2003) traces early proponents of love within the perspectives of Ferenczi, Suttie, Balint, Fairbairn, Loewald, and Kohut and concludes, "Our clinical theories call for and make use of the analyst's emotional responsiveness—in particular, the analyst's capacity to love authentically and use his love therapeutically (p. 257).

Within fields of interpersonal neurobiology, Schore's work highlights dys-regulated emotion at the heart of psychopathology, privileging the role of emotion over thought during corrective interactive regulation, while highlight-ing the role of implicit, embodied processes over explicit, verbal ones within psychotherapy. Marks-Tarlow (2012; 2014) also underscores the importance of implicit processes and emotionally informed perception to the centrality of clinical intuition during psychotherapy, which dovetails with maternal intu-ition. Only through intuition, can clinicians attune to the uniqueness of the individual, the moment, and the "chemistry" of the specific therapist-patient dyad. Furthermore, we suggest that deep and ongoing psychotherapy that goes beyond symptom removal and trauma resolution into full transformative growth is likewise modulated by both forms of Winnicott's quiet and excited love within the psychotherapist/patient dyad.

These experiences set the stage for emotional transferential-countertransferential exchanges between therapists and patients that mirror early life right-brain-to-right-brain exchanges necessary for secure attachment. Since "love is the leaven" of early development, we suggest that love is also the leaven for deep healing and post-traumatic growth during long-term, open-ended psychotherapy. Whether or not the strongly emotional experience of love is ever explicitly acknowledged, when therapists and patients internally and nonverbally express their love for one another, this serves to widen perceptual doors, expand tolerance of negative and positive emotions, permit more vulnerability to explore novelty and engage in playful interactions, and mutually amplify safety and trust on both sides of the therapeutic alliance.

We assert that the essential importance of this emotion, "one of the strongest of which the mind is capable" and the "most powerful motivation for human action" within psychotherapy lies in the fact that not only does mutual love provide an ideal holding environment for empathic resonance and deep, other-directed understanding, but also that love may be the ideal growth-facilitating environment for unleashing creative self-expression throughout life. We end this chapter with a metaphor for the power of love put forth by another psychoanalytic psychiatrist, Henry Krystal (1988) in his classic text on *Integration and Self Healing*,

> Just as white light contains all the colors of the spectrum, so love encompasses all the feelings reflecting our living process. When we get a chance to observe it, as in self-healing or in promoting the expansion of the conscious recognition of our selfness, we are especially prone to equate it with life forces, or the full enjoyment of our identity and unity. Love is the affective state that is favorable to the achievement of the most comprehensive self-representation (p. 78).

References

Abraham, A. (2013). The promises and perils of the neuroscience of creativity. *Frontiers in Human Neuroscience, 7*, doi: 10.3389/fnhum.2013.00246.

Ainsworth, M. D. S. (1967). *Infancy in Uganda: Infant care and the growth of love*. Baltimore: The Johns Hopkins University Press.

Arnold, K. (2007). The creative unconscious, the unknown self, and the haunting melody: Notes on Reik's theory of inspiration. *Psychoanalytic Review, 94*(3), 431–445.

Barrett, J., Wonch, K. E., Gonzalez, A., Ali, N., Steiner, M., Hall, G. B., & Fleming, A. S. (2012). Maternal affect and quality of parenting experiences are related to amygdala response to infant faces. *Social Neuroscience, 7*(3), 252–268.

Bartels, A. & Zeki, S. (2004). The neural correlates of maternal and romantic love. *NeuroImage, 21*(3), 1155–66.

Bartz, J. A. & Hollander, E. (2006). The neuroscience of affiliation: Forging links between basic and clinical research on neuropeptides and social behavior. *Hormones and Behavior, 50*(4), 518–528.

Beebe, B. (1986). Mother-infant mutual influence and precursors of self- and object-representations. In Masling, J. (Ed.). *Empirical Studies of Psychoanalytic Theories, vol. 2* (pp. 27-48). Hillsdale, NJ: Erlbaum.

Beebe, B. & Stern, D. (1977). Engagement-disengagement and early object experiences. In Freeman, N. & Grand, S. (Eds.). *Communicative structures and psychic structures: A psychoanalytic interpretation of communication* (pp. 35–55). New York: Plenum.

Beebe, B., Stern, D., & J. Jaffe. (1979). The kinesic rhythm of mother-infant interactions. In Siegman, A. W. & Feldstein, S. (Eds.). *Of speech and time: Temporal speech patterns in interpersonal contexts* (pp. 23–34). Hillsdale, NJ: Erlbaum.

Beebe, B., Jaffe, J., Feldstein, S., Mays, K., & Alson, D. (1985). Interpersonal timing: The application of an adult dialogue model to mother-infant vocal and kinesic interactions. In Field, T. (Ed.). *Social perception in infants* (pp. 217-47). New York: Ablex.

Beebe, B. & Lachmann, F. (2014). *The origins of attachment: Infant research and adult treatment.* New York: Routledge.

Bhattacharya, J. & Petsche, H. (2005). Drawing on mind's canvas: Differences in cortical integration patterns between artists and non-artists. *Human Brain Mapping, 26,* 1–14.

Bowlby J. (1953): *Child care and the growth of love.* London: Pelican.

Bowlby J. (1969). *Attachment and loss, Volume 1: Attachment.* New York: Basic Books.

Brown, S. & Dissanayake, E. (2009). The arts are more than aesthetics: Neuroaesthetics as narrow aesthetics. In Skov, M. & Vartanian, O. (Eds.) *Neuroaesthetics* (pp. 43–57). Amityville NY: Baywood.

Burghardt, G. M. (2005). *The genesis of animal play: Testing the limits.* Cambridge, MA: MIT Press.

Carter, S., Lederhandler, I., & Kirkpatrick, B. (Eds.) (1999). *The integrative neurobiology of affiliation.* Cambridge MA: MIT Press.

Chavez-Eakle, R. A., Graff-Guerrero, A., Garcia-Reyna, Vaugier, V., & Cruz-Fuentes, C. (2007). Cerebral blood flow associated with creative performance: A comparative study. *NeuroImage, 38*(3), 519–528.

Chong, S., Werker, J., Russell, J., & Carroll, J. (2003). Three facial expressions mothers direct to their infants. *Infant and Child Development, 12*(3), 211–232.

Darwin, C. (1859/1958). *The origin of species.* New York: Signet Classics.

Darwin, C.. (1872/1965). *The expression of the emotions in man and animals.* Chicago: University of Chicago Press, 1965. (Original work published 1872.)

Dissanayake, E. (2001). Becoming *Homo aestheticus:* sources of aesthetic imagination in mother-infant interactions. *SubStance, 94/95,* 85–103.

Dissanayake, E. (2008). If music is the food of love, what about survival and reproductive success? *Musicæ Scientiaæ,* Special Issue on Narrative in Interaction, 169–95.

Disanayake, E. (2009). The artification hypothesis and its relevance to cognitive science, evolutionary aesthetics, and neuroaesthetics. *Cognitive Semiotics, 5,* 148-173.

Dissanayake, E. (2017). Ethology and interpersonal neurobiology together with play provide insights into the evolutionary origin of the arts. *American Journal of Play,* 9(2), 143–168.

De Forest, I. (1954). The leaven of love: A development of the psychoanalytic theory and technique of Sándor Ferenczi. NY: Harper Brothers.

Dorpat, T. (2001). Primary process communication. *Psychoanalytic Inquiry, 3,* 448-463.

Drago, V., Foster, P. S., Okun, M. S., Haq, I., Sudhyadhom, F. M., & Heilman, K. M. (2009). Artistic creativity and DBS:A case report. *Journal of Neurological Sciences, 276*(1–2), 138–142.

Estrada, C. A., Young, M., & Isen, A. M. (1994). Positive affect influences creative problems solving and reported source of practice satisfaction in physicians. *Motivation and Emotion, 18*(4), 285–299.

Falk, D. (2004). Prelinguistic evolution in early hominins: Whence motherese? *Behavioral and Brain Sciences*, 27(4):491–541.

Finkelstein, Y., Vardi, J., & Hod, I. (1991). Impulsive artistic creativity as a presentation of transient cognitive alterations. *Behavioral Medicine*, 17, 91–94.

Flinn, M. V. & Ward, C. V. (2005). Ontogeny and evolution and the social child. In Ellis, B. J. & Bjorklund, D. F. (Eds.), *Origins of the social mind: Evolutionary psychology and child development* (pp. 19–44). London: The Guilford Press.

Frederickson, B. (2001). The role of positive emotions in positive psychology: The broaden-and-build theory of positive emotions. *American Psychologist*, 56(3), 218–226.

Freud, S., Riviere, J., & Strachey, J. (1963). *Civilization and its discontents*. London: Hogarth Press.

Freud, S. (1895). *Project for a scientific psychology. Standard Edition* I: 281–397.

Freud, S. (1940/1964). *An outline of psychoanalysis. Standard Edition*. London, UK: Hogarth Press.

Fromm, E. (1956). *The art of loving*. New York: Harper and Rowe.

Fromm, E. (1958). Love in psychotherapy. *Merrill-Palmer Quarterly (1954–1958)*, 4(3), 125–36.

Gebauer, L., Witek, M., Hansen, N. C., Thomas, J., Konvalinka, I., & Vuust, P. (2014). The influence of oxytocin on interpersonal rhythmic synchronization and social bonding. Poster session presented at *The Neurosciences and Music-V*, Dijon, Frankrig.

Hecht, D. (2014). Cerebral lateralization of pro- and anti-social tendencies. *Experimental Neurology*, 23(1), 1–27. http://dx.doi.org/10.5607/en.2014.23.1.1

Hirsch, I. & Kessel, P. (1988). Reflections on mature love and countertransference. *Free Associations*, 12, 60–83.

Jaynes, J. (1976/1999). *The origin of consciousness in the breakdown of the bicameral mind*. Boston: Houghton Mifflin Company.

Johnsen, E. L., Tranel, D., Lutgendorf, S., & Adolphs, R. (2009). A neuroanatomical dissociation for emotion induced by music. *International Journal of Psychophysiology*, 72(1), 24–33.

Kane, J. (2004). Poetry as right-hemispheric language. *Journal of Consciousness Studies*, 11(5-6), 21-59.

Kowatari, Y., Hee Lee, S., Yamamura, H., Nagamori, Y., Levy, P., Yamane, S., & Yamamoto, M. (2009). Neural networks involved in artistic creativity. *Human Brain Mapping*, 30(5), 1678–1690.

Krystal, H. (1988). *Integration and self healing: affect, trauma, alexithymia*. Hillsdale, NJ: The Analytic Press.

Kubovy, M. (1999). On the pleasures of the mind. In Kahneman, D., Kubovy, M., Kahneman, D., Diener, E., & Schwarz, N. (Eds.). *Well-being: The foundations of hedonic psychology* (pp. 134–154). New York: Russell Sage Foundation.

Kuhl, J. & Kazén, M. (2008). Motivation, affect, and hemispheric asymmetry: Power versus affiliation. *Journal of Personality and Social Psychology*, 95(2), 456–469.

Leakey, R. (1994). *The origin of humankind*. New York: Basic Books.

Lindell, A. K. (2011). Lateral thinkers are not so laterally minded: Hemispheric asymmetry, interaction, and creativity. *Laterality*, 16(4), 479–498.

MacLean, P. (1985). Brain evolution relating to family play, and the separation call. *Archives of General Psychiatry*, 42, 405–417.

Marks-Tarlow, T. (2010). Fractal self at play. *American Journal of Play*, 3(1), 31–62.

Marks-Tarlow, T. (2012). Clinical intuition in psychotherapy: The neurobiology of embodied response. New York: W. W. Norton & Company.

Marks-Tarlow, T. (2014). Awakening clinical intuition: An experiential workbook for psychotherapists. New York: W. W. Norton & Company.

Martindale, C., Hines, D., Mitchell, L., & Covello, E. (1984). EEG alpha asymmetry and creativity. *Personality and Individual Differences*, *5*, 77–86.

Mayseless, N. & Shamay-Tsoory, S. G. (2015). Enhancing verbal creativity: Modulating creativity by altering the balance between right and left inferior frontal gyrus with tDCS. *Neuroscience*, *291*, 167–176.

McGilchrist, I. (2009). *The master and his emissary: The divided brain and the making of the Western world*. New Haven, CT: Yale University Press.

Meyer-Lindenberg, A. (2008). Impact of prosocial neuropeptides on human brain function. *Progress in Brain Research*, *170*, 463–470.

Miall, D. & Dissanayake, E. (2003). The poetics of babytalk. *Human Nature 14*(4), 337–54.

Mihov, K., Denzler, M., & Forster, J. (2010). Hemispheric specialization and creative thinking: A meta-analytic review of lateralization of creativity. *Brain and Cognition*, *72*(3), 442–448.

Miller, W. & Rodgers, J. L. (2001). *The ontogeny of human bonding systems: Evolutionary origins, neural bases, and psychological manifestations*. Boston and Dordrecht, The Netherlands: Kluwer Academic Publishers.

Montello, L. (2002). *Essential musical intelligence. Using music as your path to healing, creativity, and radiant wholeness*. Wheaton, IL: Quest Books.

Murray, L. & Trevarthen, C. (1985). Emotional regulation of interactions between two-month-olds and their mothers. In T. Field and N. Fox (Eds.) *Social perception in infants* (pp. 177–97). Norwood, New Jersey: Ablex.

Nadel, J., Carchon, I. Kervella, C. Marcelli, D., & Réserbet-Plantey, D. (1999). Expectancies for social contingency in two-month-olds. *Developmental Science*, *2*, 164–173.

Noriuchi, M., Kikuchi, Y., & Senoo, A. (2008). The functional neuroanatomy of maternal love: Mothers' response to infant's attachment behaviors. *Biological Psychiatry*, *63*, 415–423.

Panksepp, J. (1998). *Affective neuroscience: The foundations of human and animal emotions*. Oxford: Oxford University Press.

Perani, D., Saccuman, M., Scifo, P., Spada, D., Andreolli, G., Rovelli, R., et al. (2010). Functional specializations for music processing in the human newborn brain. *Proceedings of the National Academy of Sciences of the United States of America*, *107*(10), 4758–4763.

Phillips-Silver, J. & Keller, P. E. (2012). Searching for roots of entrainment and joint action in early musical interactions. *Frontiers in Human Neuroscience*, *6*(26).

Platt, C. B. (2007). Presence, poetry and the collaborative right hemisphere. *Journal of Consciousness Studies*, *14*(3), 36–53.

Reik, T. (1953). *The haunting melody: Psychoanalytic experiences in life and music*. New York: Farrer, Straus and Young.

Rosenberg, K. (1992). The evolution of modern human childbirth. *Yearbook of Physical Anthropology*, *35*, 89–134.

Sacks, O. (2008). *Musicophilia: Tales of music and the brain*. Rev. ed. London, UK: Picador.

Shaw, D. (2003). On the therapeutic action of analytic love. *Contemporary psychoanalysis*, *39*(2), 251-258.

Schore, A. N. (1994). *Affect regulation and the origin of the self. The neurobiology of emotional development*. Mahwah, NJ: Erlbaum.

Schore, A. N. (2003a) *Affect dysregulation and disorders of the Self*. New York: W. W. Norton & Company

Schore, A. N. (2003b). *Affect regulation and the repair of the self*. New York: W. W. Norton & Company.

Schore, A. N. (2012). *The science of the art of psychotherapy*. New York: W. W. Norton & Company.

Schore, A. N. (2014). The right brain is dominant in psychotherapy. *Psychotherapy*, 51(3), 388–397.

Schore, A. N. (In Press). Modern attachment theory. In APA *Handbook of trauma psychology: Foundations in knowledge*, S. N. Gold (Ed.). Washington, DC: American Psychological Association.

Schore, J. R. & Schore, A. N. (2008). Modern attachment theory: The central role of affect regulation in development and treatment. *Clinical Social Work Journal*, 36, 9-20.

Schore, J. R. & Schore, A. N. (2014). Regulation theory and affect regulation psychotherapy: A clinical primer. *Smith College Studies in Social Work*, 84, 178–195.

Shaw, D. (2003). On the therapeutic action of analytic love. *Contemporary Psychoanalysis*, 39(2), 251–278.

Stern, D. (1971). A microanalysis of the mother-infant interaction. *Journal of the American Academy of Child Psychiatry*, 10, 501–07

Stern, D. (1974). Mother and infant at play: The dyadic interaction involving facial, vocal and gaze behaviors. In Lewis, M & Rosenblum, L. A. (Eds.). *The effect of the infant on its caregiver*, (pp. 187–213). Leonard A. Rosenblum. New York: John Wiley & Sons.

Stern, D. (1977). *The first relationship: Infant and mother*. Cambridge, MA: Harvard University Press.

Stern, D. (1985). *The interpersonal world of the infant: A view from psychoanalysis and developmental psychology*. New York: Basic Books.

Stevenson, C., Haliday, D., Marsden, C., & Mason, R. (2008). Early life programming of hemispheric lateralization and synchronization in the adult medial prefrontal cortex. *Neuroscience*, 155, 852-163.

Swart, I. (2016). New developments in neuroscience can benefit the learning and performance of music, *Muziki: Journal of Music Research in Africa*, 13, 113–136.

Trevarthen, C. (1979). Communication and cooperation in early infancy: A description of primary intersubjectivity. In Bullowa, M. (Ed.). *Before speech: The beginning of interpersonal communication* (pp. 321–47). Cambridge: Cambridge University Press.

Trevathan, W. (1987). *Human birth*. Hawthorn, NY: Aldine.

Tronick, E., Als, H., Adamson, L., Wise, S. (1978). The infant's response to entrapment between contradictory messages in face-to-face interaction. *Journal of the American Academy of Child Psychiatry*, 17(1):1–13.

Tronick, E., Als, H., & Adamson, L. (1979). The communicative structure of face-to-face interaction. In Bullowa, M. (Ed.). *Before speech: The beginning of interpersonal communication* (pp. 349–372). New York: Cambridge University Press.

Ulanov, A. B. (2001). *Finding space. Winnicott, God, and psychic reality*. Louisville, KY: Westminster John Knox Press.

Wan, X., Cruts, B., & Jensen, H.J. (2014). The causal inference of cortical neural networks during music improvisation. *PLoS ONE*, 9(12): e112776.

Winnicott, D. W. (1963). The development of the capacity for concern. *Bulletin of the Menninger Clinic*, 27(4), 167.

Winnicott, D. W. (1971). *Playing and reality*. New York: Routledge.

Winnicott, D. W. (1975). *The child, the family, and the outside world*. Harmondsworth, Middlesex, England: Penguin.

5

Play, Creativity, and Movement Vocabulary

Pat Ogden

Go and play. Run around. Build something. Break something. Climb a tree. Get dirty.
Get in some trouble. Have some fun.

—G. Brom, *The Child Thief*

TO BE CREATIVE is to experiment with new ideas, concepts, activities, and actions in ways that transcend rules and habitual modes of thinking, feeling, and moving. Existing norms must be inhibited in favor of taking the risks that will challenge learned ways of being. As Anna Freud said, "Creative minds have always been known to survive any kind of bad training." We must relinquish what we know as we go outside our comfort zone to teeter on the edge of our windows of tolerance (Siegel, 1999) where uncertainty reigns. However, human beings are clearly creatures of habit. The manner in which we think, feel, and act is based on early learning and established into routines over time. Habits, including those of movement, gesture and posture, afford us a sense of security and safety in that they are implicit "proven" adaptations to particular environmental conditions, designed to produce optimal outcomes: If a child's parents tout stoicism, her body and breath may constrict in an effort to conceal her vulnerable emotions, winning the acceptance of her attachment figures. Such habits, if unexamined, persist into the future regardless of whether or not they are adaptive to current conditions, squelching our vitality and inhibiting novelty. To be playful and creative is to challenge habitual responses in order to move, think, and feel in new, unfamiliar ways—to seek out and grapple with the risks that enliven us by their unpredictability and expand our windows of tolerance. This requires a spacious window of tolerance of tolerance to start with, and then expands the window further.

The borders of a window of tolerance lie at the extremes of hyper- and hypoarousal. If our windows are wide enough, we can tolerate and be present with the uncertainty and novelty inherent in play and creative endeavors without arousal reaching extremes of hyper- or hypoarousal. The width of each window of tolerance is directly related to how much stimulation is required to elicit a threshold of response. If we have a generally wide window, meaning our threshold of response to stimulation is relatively high, we welcome and even relish in the greater extremes of arousal. People with a generally narrow window, having a lower threshold of response, might experience the same extremes of arousal as unmanageable and dysregulating. The width of our windows naturally fluctuates throughout the day, but if we have a relatively

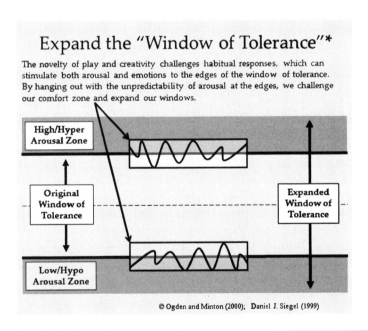

FIGURE 5.1
Window of tolerance chart. (Courtesy of Pat Ogden)

spacious window, we can process complex and stimulating information more effectively.

If we had caregivers who provided either comfort or stimulation as needed to prevent our arousal from remaining uncomfortably high or low for long periods of time, we are likely to more spacious windows. Such caregivers not only help their child recover from negative states of distress, fatigue, and discomfort, but also actively engage in play, producing ". . . an amplification, an intensification of positive emotion, a condition necessary for more complex self-organization" (Schore, 2003, p. 78). Through these salubrious early experiences with attachment figures and other persons of significance, we develop an internal confidence in our ability to regulate wide variances in arousal and respond flexibly to stimuli. This nourishes a safe base *inside ourselves* that can be relied upon throughout the lifespan as the ground from which we effortlessly seek out the novelty that expands our windows even more.

An extensive movement vocabulary supports flexibility and variety in our physical actions. In 1952, Roger Sperry stated, "The brain is an organ of and for movement. The brain is the organ that moves the muscles. It does many other things, but all of them are secondary to making our bodies move" (p. 298). In fact, only organisms that move from one location to another require a brain; and the brain depends on movement for its development (Ratey, 2002). The immediate action we make, whether reaching for a paintbrush, or shaking our heads "no" at the thought of an art class, is determined by what we expect to happen in the very next instant. Our brains continually compare the wealth of sensory stimulation from our immediate environment to memories of the past in order to make an action adaptive to present circumstance (Llinas, 2001). Movement habits reflect predictions about what is to come based on the repeated experiences of the past, the result of fitting sensory input into learned categories. Ratey (2002, p. 55) has pointed out that "We are constantly priming our perceptions, matching the world to what we expect to sense and thus making it what we perceive it to be." When actions become routine, they are relegated to procedural learned behaviors, and we no longer use top-down cognitive processes to regulate them, leaving our minds free to learn and tend to novel stimuli. Without the expectations that influence perceptual priming, each experience would be completely novel, and although we might engage in unique and creative ways with the environment, we could be quickly overwhelmed by the vast amount of information. So procedural habits are necessary, but they can constrain our movement vocabulary, truncate our impulse to play, and inhibit our creativity. This chapter will explore the interface between arousal tolerance, movement vocabulary, creativity, and play, and how to use movement to inspire the creative impulse that resides within us all.

The Role of Movement

Through movement the fetus, infant, child, and adult continually learn about themselves, others, and the world in an ongoing interactive dance. Each interaction, each movement adjustment, communicates one's location in space, the nature of human relationships, and one's place in the world. We develop movement memory, "achieved from a sophisticated feedback system that detects errors made as the movement is learned. The feedback system uses these errors as a basis from which to generate a new, more accurate [or adaptive] sequence of commands, eventually leading to a successful performance. We modify and learn through movement every second of our waking day whether we are active or inactive" (Ratey, 2002, p. 205). Movement memory develops over time, and is obvious in such tasks as tying shoelaces or playing a musical instrument, but often not so clear in subtle physical accommodations to environmental and interpersonal cues. For instance, if a child enthusiastically gesticulates and puffs up his chest while describing his latest fantasy, but is met with the mother's admonishment to stop making things up, a disapproving facial expression, and a pulling back of her body, the child's expanded chest deflates, his movements become restricted, and the excitement vanishes from his voice and eyes. If such interactions are repeated over time, this child's body will probably become chronically constrained. Mable Todd (1959) emphasized that function precedes structure: the same movement made over and over again will ultimately mold the body. It is likely that for this child, creativity, imagination, playfulness, and spontaneity will be truncated, because such a constrained physical organization will not support these qualities.

An embodied sense of self develops through the call and response of movement dialogue between the child and significant others. "Good enough," attachment figures advance the child's movement complexity so that "action sequences remain to some extent fluid and flexible throughout life; the nature of the consequences that are anticipated for a given action will change as the context of interaction changes and with development of the individual's powers" (Bucci, 2011, p. 6). Thus, as our brains compare current information with past data, there is the possibility of an "upgrading" (Llinas 2001, p. 38) of our movement, which expands our movement vocabulary further. However, schemas become more and more rigid in increasingly less functional environments, impeding new learning (Bucci, 2011) and constraining movement flexibility. Whether expansive or curtailed, the movement habits we form over time reflect and sustain implicit meanings and expectations, and thus can either encourage or inhibit creativity and play. The legacy of trauma and attachment failure, with their consequential neuropsychological deficits, constrains our bodies, inhibits the development of our movement vocabulary, and restricts a fluid response to novelty. Cannon (In Press) states that it may be that learning to live more in the "spirit of play" than in the "spirit of seriousness" is the end goal of all therapy.

Winnicott (1971) posited that psychotherapy patients could benefit from opportunities for "formless experience, and for creative impulses, motor and sensory, which are the stuff of playing" (p. 64). It is widely shown that movement improves creativity. Lakoff and Johnson (1999) assert that concrete embodied experience is at the root of cognition, and that concepts are embodied in sensorimotor systems. For example, gestures can provide a direct representation of spatial relationships and have been shown to both boost the ability to solve spatial problems and to improve the ease and facility of verbal expression (Goldin-Meadow & Beilock, 2010). Even a repetitious movement like walking enhances creativity. Opezzo and Schwartz (2014) found that going for a walk, especially outdoors, increased creative thinking by over 50 percent as measured by the ability to generate an analogy. They concluded that, "Walking opens up the free flow of ideas, and it is a simple and robust solution to the goals of increasing creativity . . ." (p 1142). Cognitive scientists often correlate fluidity of thought with creativity and play (Hofstadter, 1995). Slepian and Ambady (2012) hypothesized that "fluid, creative thinking is grounded in fluid movement." They explored the relationship between fluid movement and creative thought, through several studies that induced fluid and non-fluid body movement, finding that three domains were strengthened by fluid movement: creative generation, cognitive flexibility, and the ability to make remote connections. The authors noted that "Fluid movement enhanced creative but not analytic performance (only the former requires fluid thought) . . ." (p. 4).

Similarly, a variety of cross-cultural and cross-species studies show that spontaneous, fluid movements are characteristic of play and signal other members of the social environment to play as well. These include a relaxed, open body posture and a tilting of the head, often accompanied by a whimsical expression on the face (Bekoff & Allen, 1998; Caldwell, 2003; Donaldson, 1993). The physical movements of play are more random, fluid, and non-stereotyped. They change quickly and are spontaneously expressed in children and animals in a variety of leaps, rolls, and rotational movements (Goodall, 1995). In contrast, movements characteristic of non-playful or overly serious interactions tend to be constrained, stereotyped, rigid, agitated, or nervous (Beckoff & Byers, 1998; Brown, 1995).

It follows that psychotherapy that directly works to expand movement vocabulary and increase fluid movement might enhance our clients' capacity for play and creativity. Bainbridge-Cohen's five fundamental movements—yield, push, reach, grasp, and pull (Bainbridge-Cohen, 1993)—provide a useful map for exploring physical actions and expanding movement vocabulary. Each of these actions are defined below, and illustrated through case examples of clients who either overuse the action or have difficulty engaging it, both of which impede creativity and play.

Yield

To yield means to let go. We yield our weight to the force of gravity, letting go into the support of the ground; we yield to the care of another, or to the comfort of our beds as we fall asleep at night.

When securely attached infants experience a sense of safety in the arm of the mother, they are able to relax in her support and care. The capacity to actively relax in contact rather than passively becoming immobile is the hallmark of yielding (Aposhyan, 1999). Yield is a restful, alert state that encompasses qualities or receptivity, trust, surrender, and the taking in of nourishment. It pertains to being rather than doing. The body is at peace, the

FIGURE 5.2
Yield. (Courtesy of Terry Marks-Tarlow)

muscles let go, the breathing is deep, perhaps with an extended exhale. The dorsal vagal system, a primitive branch of the parasympathetic nervous system that promotes hypoarousal, is co-opted for quiet contact with the environment, with another, or with ourselves. When others induce or join us in these deeply pleasurable low-arousal states, the window of tolerance expands.

Being grounded—making a physical connection with the force of gravity, so that the energy of the body is drawn downward—is to yield. Grounding is the concrete sensation of connecting to the earth, as our body responds to the pull of gravity by settling downward, much as the water in a pitcher sinks to the bottom, the lowest level. Yielding necessitates trust and relinquishing control, we yield not only to gravity, but to another's administrations (as in relaxing into a hug or massage), or to an internal impulse, such as to curl up, or to an external stimulation like enjoying the sound of beautiful music. In such a receptive state, the mind can wander and the imagination can flourish. We become open to receiving new ideas, new ways of thinking, feeling, envisioning, and acting. Possibilities expand. The "ah-hah" moment often emerges from "yield," in which the mind drifts, the body relaxes, and both become deeply receptive to information that is unavailable in a "doing" state. The ability to yield is thus an essential quality of certain elements of creativity.

Associated with letting go, releasing, and letting down, yielding requires an even, relaxed muscle tone. However, if our muscles are lax and our bodies collapsed, yielding is compromised. Alternatively, if our muscles are tense and our bodies braced, yielding is also compromised. Some of us may fluctuate between these two conditions.

Lucy found it difficult to relax. Her body was stiff and her movements were awkward, telegraphing a nonverbal message of discomfort and stress. The tension throughout her body, and especially across her hunched shoulders, echoed her words that she could not let down her guard. She says she moves from one task to the next, her best friend calls her a workaholic, and her husband complains that she can't enjoy downtime. Lucy reported that as a child she was constantly worried about failing to meet her parents' expectations. She had been full of silent anxiety and did not perform well, to the dismay of her high achieving family that pushed her ahead faster than her developmental skills warranted. Lucy's energy was mobilized up and out, rather than settled down into a restful and rejuvenating yield. Having learned that she must please others or avoid making mistakes, she did not connect with herself sufficiently to develop her own internal base of support. Her fear of disappointing her parents or doing something "wrong" were impediments to her creativity and playfulness.

On the other hand, Jerry experienced the chronic shutdown/feigned death response, and he described himself as collapsed and "spaced out." Yielding is a form of inaction or immobilization without fear, but the "feigned death" response in trauma is immobilization with fear, as the dorsal vagal system is aroused to foster stillness in the hope of preventing attack (Porges, 2011). Jerry grew up in an abusive environment from which there was no escape. He said he felt stuck, collapsed, and shut down when he tried to relax. He had great difficulty falling asleep at night. Instead of a true yield, Jerry experienced immobilization with fear, which induces flaccid muscles, leaving him feeling collapsed, uncomfortably numb, and often unable to think clearly. Receptivity to novelty is lost, and the rejuvenation that can come from a true yield is compromised.

Both Lucy and Jerry needed to learn the action of yielding. In therapy, Lucy's explored "doing nothing" by allowing her body to rest into sofa and take slow breaths with a slightly longer exhale. Lucy first noticed impulses to move, uneasy emotions (nervousness, anxiety), and thoughts of "You're lazy. You're wasting time." She and her therapist worked through the pressure she felt from her parents that was there "as far back as I can remember" and that impeded her ability to yield. She placed her hands gently on her torso, using her own touch to soothe her anxiety and connect with the core of her body, sensing herself more deeply, and feeling compassion for the stress she had been under as a child. Gradually, Lucy began to feel and enjoy the sensations of her muscles relaxing, her breathing deepening as his energy settled, and she released the weight of her body to the force of gravity. Jerry learned to sense the support of the chair under him, and from there develop his ability to yield. This was very different from his usual collapsed body and shutdown state, which he described as "letting go into nothingness," because the yield was letting go into support. His ability to yield continued to develop as he worked with the pushing action.

Push

Yielding allows for the release of weight into a solid foundation of support beneath us, which provides the stability and leverage to push against, and thus is the foundation for pushing actions. Pushing occur in many ways. The fetus pushes with head and feet, lengthening the body, to be born, and later, the same pushing action enables an upright posture. Good posture requires a gentle push upward with the top of the head and downward into the pelvic floor in a seated position, or into the soles of the feet in a standing position.

The spine is the physical core of the body that provides support and stability to the entire physical structure and serves as an axis around which the limbs and head can move.

The first movements of an infant are initiated in the core of the body and radiate out to the periphery, then contract back inward to the core. These movements that strengthen the core (Aposhyan, 2004; Bainbridge-Cohen, 1993) and later, the vertical "push" when sitting and standing also develops the core. Kurtz and Prestera (1976, p. 33) note that the core of the body, the spine, has a psychological meaning as the "'place inside" to which we may "go for sustenance." Frank & LaBarre (2011) explains that as we push, ". . . the experience of weight condenses at the origin of the push, whether at head or tailbone, arms and hands, or legs and feet, as the act of pushing compresses tissues of the body" (p. 26). Our physical sensation is intensified with a pushing action, as we experience the density of our bodies:

"We push out in a variety of ways—with our arms, legs, spine eyes, energy and even breath. We push to create distance, separate, set a boundary, or defend ourselves."

The pushing action asserts our will, and is often associated with the word "no" that facilitates not only protection but also differentiation, self-identity,

FIGURE 5.3
Push. (Courtesy of Terry Marks-Tarlow)

and self-support. We learn who we are by saying "no" (pushing) to some stimuli, while being receptive (yielding) to others. Pushing is critical for differ-
entiating from others and developing our self-identity as autonomous. The
ability to push nourishes a locus of control inside ourselves, and a feeling of
command over our participation with our environment, which is essential in
playful interactions (Fisher, Murray, & Bundy, 1991; Levy, 1978).

Pushing is compromised either by pushing too much or too little. If our
spines remain chronically slumped (insufficient push head to feet), the core is
undeveloped, and the sense of one's boundaries and preferences is indistinct.
Without the strong sense of oneself that is enforced by an aligned posture, the
inner security necessary for the uncertainty of play and creativity is absent,
or at least jeopardized. We may feel dependent, inadequate, needy or passive.
Jerry's spine was perpetually slumped, turning his "yield" into a collapse, as
previously described. He also had trouble saying "no" to any requests that
came his way. On the other hand, a "military" stance, where the "push" is
exaggerated, induces feelings of inflexibility, being on guard and continually
on the defensive. An overstated push diminishes emotional intimacy because
it conveys a consistent message of "keep out" that went along with a gesture Jonah often made of putting his hands up, face out, in front of his body.
Jonah's stiff, rigid posture and the habitual gesture reflected a need to be in
control and keep stimuli at bay that he developed through his chaotic, but
demanding, childhood.

Both Jerry and Jonah needed to yield, then to develop a balanced, integrated "push." In therapy, Jerry first learned to yield by connecting with the
support of the ground under him, and then push off this base with the bottom
of his feet in a sequence of movements through the top of his head, strengthening his core and aligning his posture. Maintaining an upright posture, he
practiced a "no" gesture by pushing against a pillow held by his therapist, an
action that was weak and ineffective from a collapsed posture.

Jonah learned to yield by relaxing his tense body and releasing his weight
into the ground so that he could rest in the support beneath him. Then, he
could develop a relaxed and flexible push through his spine. He practiced
inhibiting his exaggerated tendency to push in favor of letting go into a yield,
and then pushing while sensing support.

Reach

Seeking proximity is the hallmark of attachment behavior. Bowlby (1969/1982)
observed that the attachment drive secures the nearness of attachment figures
through *approach behavior*, such as reaching, which, along with grasping and

pulling, is designed to bring one closer to the attachment figure. Whether or not a child reaches out is "based on that person's forecasts of how accessible and responsive his attachment figures are likely to be should he turn to them for support" (Bowlby, 1973, p. 203). Thus, reaching, like each of the five movements, is adapted and adjusted in accordance with the response of attachment figures.

However, to reach has implications beyond seeking nearness to attachment figures. Aposhyan (1998) writes, "Reaching is the way we extend out into space, toward others, toward objects. It is our ability to go beyond ourselves. Psychologically, reaching manifests curiosity, longing, desire, compassion" (p. 69). A reaching movement pertains to a desire to connect with another person or object in the environment. As we reach, we act on that desire, lengthening our limbs or spine to extend toward what we want.

When a reach is supported by the previous action, a push, the reach can be full and grounded. The reach could be thought of as symbolically saying "yes" to a person or object, but if we do not know what we want, we may need

FIGURE 5.4
Reach. (Courtesy of Terry Marks-Tarlow)

to first develop a push. Without the support of a push (evident in an aligned spine) the reach may have an empty, needy, or demanding quality that is not grounded or centered in the self. As previously stated, the "push" helps us differentiate ourselves and determine what we want to say "no" to. When that object or person is available for contact, literally within reach, then we can develop confidence in this action.

Depending on the previous two actions, and negative repercussions with past attempts to reach, we may be unable to reach out in a relaxed, tenacious, confident manner: with palms up, our arms fully extended in a way that conveys openness and assurance that our reaching will have a positive outcome. We may have a willingness to extend but reach out with a stiff arm, palm down, braced shoulders, or a rigid spine, already expecting an undesirable outcome. Or we may lack this willingness, and reach out weakly, shoulders rounded, holding the elbow close to the waist rather than fully extending the arm. This style of reaching inhibits creativity in different ways: one symbolizes a bracing against the unknown and the other symbolizes a "why bother" or giving up attitude. We may withdraw from relationships and from the world, shun physical contact, and have a hard time extending ourselves. Without the confidence to reach into the unknown, or the tolerance of the positive stress that accompanies uncertainty, our creativity and capacity to play is hampered.

Mike was a self-described loner. He said reaching out to others had never been a positive experience. He reported that his alcoholic father had abused him, and his mother did not protect him, so he learned at an early age that he was better off staying to himself. In his current life, Mike failed to initiate conversations, avoided eye contact, and often leaned back, looked away, and tightened his shoulders when someone approached him. In therapy, he found it unfamiliar and uncomfortable to reach out and did so awkwardly and stiffly. In therapy at the request of his wife, Mike couldn't even imagine participating in playful or creative activities with others.

On the other hand, Blanche reached out too intensely. Her husband Ron said he felt "crowded" because Blanche was so "demanding and needy." When their therapist asked Blanche to reach out to Ron, she leaned forward enthusiastically, with full extension of her arms and eager eye contact. She said she wanted to move closer to him; he pulled back, which she interpreted as rejection. As the therapist instructed Blanche to sit back in her chair and try reaching with a slightly bent elbow, Blanche said she didn't think Ron would "be there" unless she really "engaged." In fact, the opposite was true; Ron felt the impulse to reach back when Blanche's reach was less intense. Blanche slowly learned that as she learned to reach in a more spacious and relaxed manner, Ron was able to move toward her more fully.

Grasp

Once a reach is executed, the obvious progression of that action is to grasp or hold the object of the reaching, and, through the grasp, to discover the nature of the thing or person. Thus, grasping is the natural outcome of reaching, and these two actions are complementary. Frank (2011) clarifies: "Whereas reaching brings with it the risk of moving the edge of and beyond one's kinesphere, grasping can reestablish balance by holding on to what is grasped." A child needing reassurance reaches for and holds on to the mother, who responds in kind, reaching back and grasping the child, who regains a sense of security and equilibrium. Grasping is reaching fulfilled.

Once the reached-for object is within grasp, holding on to it affords exploration with senses not only of sight but also of touch. In a sense, to grasp is to hold on to the object of our desire and to gain understanding through discovery, as in the colloquialism "to have a solid grasp of something." To grasp something is to increase our understanding of it, to get to know its quality and significance through our senses. If the object is consistently out of reach—either physically or psychologically, as in too many restrictions levied by parents, confidence in this fulfillment and knowledge is truncated. We also cannot reap the benefits of grasping if control is exerted such that

FIGURE 5.5
Grasp. (Courtesy of Terry Marks-Tarlow)

the child only explores that which the parent chooses, rather than what the child chooses.

While reaching out can be a challenge for many clients, holding on can be equally challenging. Francine did not want to hold on to anything. She had not sustained a relationship longer than a year, kept most of her friendships superficial, and was not attached to her possessions. When her best friend told her he felt "disposable" Francine sought help for her "commitment problem." In therapy, Francine chose a pillow to symbolically represent her friend. She first placed the pillow in her lap, but rested her hands on top of the pillow although her therapist had instructed her to try holding on to it/him. Squirming as she struggled to grasp the pillow, Francine was clearly uncomfortable. She discovered she associated holding on to being needy: "better to let go than hold on" were her words. The granddaughter of Holocaust survivors, Francine has heard stories of loss her entire childhood from stoic parents who learned to survive, as had their parents, by keeping their grief and their needs at bay. Neediness was a despised trait in Francine's family, which manifested in her inability to commit.

For Marshall, reaching, grasping, and clinging were much more comfortable than pushing-away and letting-go action. His girlfriend told him that he was too clingy, and implied that his desperation drove her away. As a child, Marshall had been teased by the older children, so much so that he did not want to leave his mother. He was afraid to go on play dates, a fear his parents brushed off with "don't be silly—you'll have fun." He remembered clinging to his mother and pleading with her to not make him go outside to play with the neighborhood. In therapy, Marshall explored clinging (an easy, comfortable action for him) to a pillow. Slowly, he tried to let it go, releasing his grip, a simple action that he described as surprisingly scary. Grasping gave him a sense of security, but letting go thrust him back into implicit memories of his early years, just as holding on did for Francine.

Pull

Pulling involves both bringing an object or person closer to oneself, and/or bringing oneself closer to an object or person, and thus is also a proximity seeking action. Pulling makes one thing or person move toward another thing or person. The first actions of grasp and pull occur as the baby grasps the nipple with her mouth and pulls the milk by sucking, or as a tiny fist grasps on to the father's little finger and pulls it to the mouth. We can pull with the mouth, eyes, facial expression, as well as with the hands and arms. Pulling action symbolizes the satisfaction of getting what we want, of claiming it and owning it for ourselves. Pulling enables close proximity, which enables exploring sensory elements of the object or person—smell, taste, and possibly sound. Thus, it expands knowledge of the object or person through the senses.

Margaret was worried about finding a good job. As she spoke about her desire, her therapist asked her to make motions of reaching out and then bringing her arms toward her torso as if drawing something that she wanted in toward her chest. Her therapist asked her to repeat that motion mindfully, exploring it for meaning and memories. Margaret found words that went along with this pulling movement: "taking in" and "claiming what I want." She talked of being raised by a mother who did not demand much from life and, although bright, worked at a minimum wage job her entire life. Margaret remembered feeling ashamed as a child because she wanted more than what her mom had settled for. Margaret's learned beliefs and emotional reactions to opportunity conditioned her relationship with current opportunities, impairing her creativity and openness to new experiences. Practicing a pulling motion while imagining having the right to what she wanted for herself challenged these the belief that she didn't deserve good things, fueled her creativity, and expanded her confidence in getting a job she wanted.

FIGURE 5.6
Pull. (Courtesy of Terry Marks-Tarlow)

To pull something or someone toward us means to literally take what we believe to be our right. From this perspective, it has to do with positive entitlement. In pulling the object toward our person, we actualize the sense of having a right, or claim to that which is pulled. It speaks to an inherent sense of deserving to have that object or person. In the negative sense, it can pertain to claiming that which is not your right to claim. Tucker came to therapy because he had raped his partner when she was intoxicated and unable to give consent. His partner did not want to end the relationship but required that he do couple therapy. As he explored the pulling motion with a rope held by his partner, he pulled rather aggressively and said "She is my girlfriend. I have a right to her." Tucker was not only unable to discriminate about what is appropriate to pull toward him but he was also unable experience the nourishment (yield) from pulling something or someone toward him. Thus Tucker was never fully satisfied and persisted in asserting he has a right to pull and "take" what he wants.

Roddy found it easy to reach and grasp a pillow that represented something he wanted, held by his therapist. But as his therapist encouraged him to pull the pillow toward him, he said, "Why? It will just get taken away." Roddy had problems committing to what he wanted—he would begin going for what he wanted, such as learning to play the saxophone, but soon abandoned the activity. He grew up as an "army brat" who constantly changed locations. Gradually he learned not to go for what he wanted since he would lose it anyway. The simple act of pulling the pillow brought up his grief of all he had lost as well as elucidated his strategy of not claiming anything as his.

Note that a pulling action naturally leads to a yield. It is the completion of the action cycle of yield, push, reach, grasp, and pull. We spontaneously relax into the satisfaction of accomplishment and of receiving once we reach, grasp, and pull to ourselves that which we want, whether it is a job, a person, or an object. Janise was able to pull toward her what she wanted and achieved success after success in her life, but she did not experience the satisfaction of completion of that action—she could not yield into the rest of success because she went immediately to a "push"—on the next task in front of her.

Conclusion

It should be clear by now that these five basic movements spontaneously emerge in sequence (yield, push, reach, grasp, and pull) and each depends on the previous ones for its ultimate execution. The support afforded by yielding enables pushing; a full push is the foundation for reaching, the natural outcome of reaching is to grasp, which is organically followed by pulling the object grasped toward oneself. And, finally, pulling morphs into releasing the object that was pulled, giving way to yield. All the actions we make can be conceptualized as intricate combinations of these five fundamental movements.

Our movement is continually emerging in response to our ever-changing experience with others, the world, and ourselves, shifting moment to moment depending on who we are with, our circumstances, internal state, predictions, and many other variables. Our actions, at their best, are economical and efficient, with effort appropriate to the task at hand. The movement itself proceeds efficiently, beginning with its initiation, carried out through its execution, and ending with its completion, progressing easily into the next movement. Unnecessary tension or movements that contradict each other, like reaching out with the arms while pulling back with the upper body, are eliminated. When movement sequences are flexible and dynamic, we are better able to enthusiastically respond creatively to diverse activities of varying intensity.

However, as illustrated, we develop habits of executing each of the five movements, as well as habits moving through a combination or sequence of actions, that are useful for coping and filtering information but may limit our creativity and playfulness. Thus, movement habits need to be examined and changed when they have become default behaviors over other actions that would be more adaptive and innovative in current contexts. A resilient movement vocabulary enables us to welcome appropriate risks and respond to novelty in imaginative, life-enhancing ways. Our clients' response to novelty becomes ever more creative and playful when we can help them challenge their physical habits and develop expansive, innovative, flexible, and fluid movement vocabularies.

References

Aposhyan, S. (1999). *Natural intelligence: Body-mind integration and human development.* Baltimore: Lippincott Williams & Wilkins.

Aposhyan, S. (2004). *Body-mind psychotherapy: Principles, techniques, and practical applications.* New York: W. W. Norton & Company.

Bainbridge-Cohen, B. (1993). *Sensing, feeling, and action.* Northampton, MA: Contact Editions.

Beckoff, M. & Allen, C. (1998). Intentional communication and social play: How and why animals negotiate and agree to play. In Bekoff, M. & Byers, J. (Eds.). *Animal play: Evolutionary, comparative, and ecological perspectives* (pp. 97–114). New York: Cambridge University Press.

Beckoff, M. & Byers, J. (1998). *Animal play: Evolutionary, comparative, and ecological perspectives.* New York: Cambridge University Press.

Bowlby, J. (1973). *Attachment and loss. Vol. 2. Separation: Anxiety and anger.* New York: Basic Books.

Bowlby, J. (1982). *Attachment* (Vol. 1, 2nd ed.). New York: Basic Books. (Original work published 1969.)

Brown, S. (1995). Through the lens of play. *Revision, 17*(4), 4–14.

Bucci, W. (2011). The role of embodied communication in therapeutic change: A multiple code perspective. In Tschacher, W. & Bergomi, C. (Eds.). *The implications of embodiment: Cognition and communication* (pp. 209–228). Exeter, UK: Imprint Academic.

Caldwell, C. (2003). Adult group play therapy. In Schaefer, C. (Ed.). *Play therapy with adults* (pp. 301–316). Hoboken, NJ: John Wiley & Sons, Inc.

Cannon, B. (In Press). Authenticity, the spirit of play and the practice of psychotherapy. *Review of Existential Psychology and Psychiatry.*

Donaldson, F. (1993). *Playing by heart: The vision and practice of belonging.* Deerfield Beach, FL: Health Communications, Inc.

Fisher, A., Murray, E., & Bundy, A. (1991). *Sensory integration: Theory and practice.* Philadelphia, PA: F. A. Davis Company.

Frank, R. & La Barre, F. (2011). *The first year and the rest of your life: movement, development, and psychotherapeutic change.* New York: Routledge.

Goldin-Meadow, S. & Beilock, S. L. (2010). Action's influence on thought: The case of gesture. *Perspectives on Psychological Science, 5*(6), 664–674.

Goleman, D., Kaufman, P., & Ray, M. 1993. *The creative spirit.* New York: Penguin.

Goodall, J. (1995). Chimpanzees and others at play. *Revision, 17,* 14–20.

Hofstadter, D. R. (1995). *Fluid concepts and creative analogies: Computer models of the fundamental mechanisms of thought.* New York: Basic Books.

Kurtz, R. & Prestera, H. (1976). *The body reveals: An illustrated guide to the psychology of the body.* New York: Holt, Rinehart & Winston.

Lakoff, G. & Johnson, N. (1999). *Philosophy in the flesh: The embodied mind and its challenge to Western thought.* New York: Perseus Book Group.

Levy, J. (1978). *Play behavior.* New York: Wiley.

Llinas, R. (2001). *I of the vortex: From neurons to self.* Cambridge, MA: Massachusetts Institute of Technology Press.

Opezzo, M. & Schwartz, D. L. (2014). Give your ideas some legs: The positive effect of walking on creative thinking. *Journal of Experimental Psychology: Learning, Memory, and Cognition, 40*(4), 1142–1152.

Porges, S. W. (2011). *The polyvagal theory: Neurophysiological foundations of emotions, attachment, communication, and self-regulation.* New York: W. W. Norton & Company.

Ratey, J. (2002). *A User's Guide to the Brain: Perception, attention, and the four theaters of the brain.* New York: Vintage Books.

Schore, A. (2003). *Affect dysregulation and disorders of the self.* W. W. Norton & Company.

Siegel, D. J. (1999). *The developing mind: Toward a neurobiology of interpersonal experience.* New York: W. W. Norton & Company.

Slepian, M. L. & Ambady, N. (2012). Fluid movement and creativity. *Journal of Experimental Psychology, 141,* 425–629.

Sperry, R. W. (1952). Neurology and the mind-brain problem. *American Scientist, 40*(18), 291–312.

Winnicott, D. W. (1971). *Playing & reality.* London, UK: Tavistock Publications.

6

A Cross-Cultural and Cross-Disciplinary Perspective of Play

Theresa Kestly

WHEN I MOVED from Ohio to Arizona to the small Navajo village of Rough Rock at the end of a 15-mile unpaved and very rough road, I had no idea that I would be learning one of the more valuable lessons of my life. I went there in the mid-1970s to accept a position as a music teacher in a government-funded Navajo demonstration school. At that point I was not really thinking about the meaning of play or about issues in cross-cultural psychology, but now, looking back, I am deeply grateful for my experiences with the Navajo people and for the enduring relationships that I was fortunate to develop. This is the story of what I learned from the Navajos about play—not only that it is important, but also that it is integral to their sacred ceremonial life.

Becoming a *Biligana*

In Rough Rock there was one small trading post, and it meant that shopping at the supermarket was going to require a three-hour journey. I am reluctant to admit this, but I knew almost nothing about Native Americans. I did not know that some of them still spoke only their native language, Navajo. I had never even seen a photo of a hogan—a one-room home constructed of wooden logs and mud with no plumbing or electricity. I quickly learned that I was a *biligana*, meaning Anglo or white person, sometimes translated by Navajos as "one with whom I struggle." I also learned that I had come to live with the *Diné*, meaning

"The People" or "Children of the Holy People." Unknowingly, I had chosen to begin a rich and personally healing journey with the Navajo people.

Play at the Edge of the Fire

One of the things we biliganas liked to do to occupy our time on weekends was to find out where the ceremonies were being held and then challenge ourselves by trying to find the specific ceremonial sites, which seemed to us to be in the middle of nowhere. One of the first I attended was a fire dance. By the time we arrived at the ceremony, dusk had given way to a dark starry sky. The night air was crisp, and the warmth of the fire was welcoming as we approached the large gathering of Navajos who had come to witness the ceremony. As we drew closer the warmth intensified, and we realized that this was no ordinary bonfire. It was actually a huge, roaring, and very hot fire. We stood at the edge of the large circle of Navajos who had gathered, and I wondered how it was even possible for the dancers to be to be so close to the fire as I was feeling its intensity even at some distance.

The dancers were dressed in traditional leather skirts and moccasins, and their exposed skin was covered with gray clay. They had rattles in their hands, and they were moving around the sacred fire, singing and dancing perfectly to the beat of the drum. Never having seen anything like it, I felt deep awe. I began to relax, allowing myself to absorb the smells of the surrounding piñon trees and the night air, the sounds of the drums and dancers, and the soft talking of those around me. I soon fell into a bit of a trance as the dancers feet pounded steadily and rhythmically on the soft earth. It was comforting, and I gave way to the sense of being held in an ancient and sacred ritual that felt mysterious, yet familiar.

I was enjoying this trancelike state until I began to hear soft giggles here and there among the spectators. At first I couldn't figure out what they were laughing about, and then I saw the clowns. They were playing with the crowd. They pretended to be dancers, following along behind the circle of sacred dancers, except they kept falling out of step and out of line, drifting away from the fire so that they could pretend to be farting on the crowd of spectators. I was shocked by this display of crude behavior in public, but I was soon to learn that the clowns were called "sacred clowns," and it was their job to remind us not to take ourselves so seriously. There could be no sacredness without the clowns.

Balancing sacredness with play felt foreign to me, yet deeply intriguing and satisfying. Growing up in the mainstream of American culture, I had never encountered the idea that play could be a part of sacred life or even that play had any importance at all other than just being a fun way to relax and pass time.

I didn't fully appreciate this spirit of the playful clowns until years later when I participated in a Native American sweat lodge ceremony. The sweat lodge was built low to the ground, and it had been made especially for ceremonial purposes. To enter the structure we had to crawl on our hands and knees through a small opening that faced eastward. Inside we sat cross-legged on the ground in a circle around a bed of hot coals. Then came the songs, the prayers, and the passing of the sacred pipe in a repetitive fashion as water was poured on the hot coals at regular intervals to create steam. The medicine man's prayers were long as he prayed for everyone in the lodge, every relative and friend outside the lodge, all the leaders of the nation, and all the four-leggeds, the birds in the sky, and the fish in the sea. He prayed and prayed, and again as I had done at the fire dance ceremony, I found myself falling into a bit of a trance as he rhythmically and monotonously continued on and on. And then without varying his steady tone, the rhythm, or the inflection of his voice, he said, "And there are 25 shopping days left until Christmas." In that instant, as if shocked by electricity, I experienced the fusing of the sacred and the profane. I understood why the clowns and playfulness were an essential part of every sacred ceremony. That very ordinary act of sitting on the earth in a humble structure, listening to the sacred prayers in the presence of a playful medicine man, allowed me to experience the sacredness of the ordinary, and it happened in the context of a playful moment.

The Baby's First Laugh

In the Navajo culture, playfulness is highly valued. It is part of sacred life, and it is part of ordinary life, and sometimes they become one. The Navajos have preserved the value of play by including it in their traditional ceremonies. They even have a ceremony for a baby's first laugh. We are thrilled in Western cultures when our baby's first smile appears, but the Navajos have a ceremony as soon as they can after the baby's first laugh. The person who makes the baby laugh is responsible for organizing the celebration. So what makes a baby laugh? No doubt, it is play. Imagine what kind of silly play it would take to make a baby laugh, and imagine the pleasure of the baby learning about relational play. The Navajos believe that when a baby is born, it belongs in two worlds—that of the Holy People, and that of the Earth People. The baby's first laugh is a sign of joy that signals his or her desire to join the Earth family.

We lived in Rough Rock for 4 years, and by the time we were ready to move away from there, my daughter was 8 years old. She spoke Navajo well enough to play with her peers using their language. As a curious child, she participated in many of the Navajo traditions, including the butchering of the sheep for ceremonial purposes. The Navajo people welcomed her, and they treated her as one of their own. I had been told that the proper greeting when I met an older woman was, "*Yá'át'ééh Shimá,*" —"Hello, my mother." I am not certain about all the nuances of Navajo greetings, but this one felt true to me. I had a deep sense of family and belonging, and I knew that we were becoming acculturated. I had a sense that if we didn't leave soon, we probably never would.

My experiences with the Diné had made me very curious about cross-cultural issues, and so when we moved to Albuquerque, New Mexico, I enrolled in a cross-cultural psychology course just for fun. I wanted to make sense of my time with the Navajos. One thing led to another, and I was soon enrolled in a doctoral program at the University of New Mexico to pursue psychology.

During my doctoral program, I did an internship at a child guidance center, and in the process became very interested in play therapy and particularly the sand tray modality because it seemed to be so effective in grounding therapy in right hemisphere processes. I became so interested in the sand tray that I decided to offer some workshops to focus on the modality, and that is how I reconnected with the Navajo people and a number of other Native Americans. They began coming to the workshops I offered, and many of them told me that this modality was a good fit for them in their culture.

Playing in the Sand Tray

One of my workshop participants, Valencia Bizahaloni, asked me if I would be willing to do a one-day training for a group of women from Piñon, Arizona, a small community not too far from Rough Rock. They wanted to know more about using play with their children, and they were willing to come to my teaching studio in Corrales near Albuquerque where I lived. Prior to their arrival, I used a small round sand tray to create a scene with objects representing the four elements that are so important to the Native Americans—earth, air, fire, and water. I told them that I had learned from the Navajos at Rough Rock that when we had these elements, we had everything we needed to create a meaningful life. And then I invited them to play with the sand tray materials.

By then I had developed a deep trust in right-hemisphere processing, and I understood that lateral integration and metaphorical processes were essential if I wanted adults to experience the deep joy of play. At that time I did not

FIGURE 6.1
Earth, Air, Fire, Water. (Courtesy of Theresa Kestly)

yet know how to articulate these concepts, but intuitively they felt right. The articulation did not come until I began to study Allan Schore's concept of the primacy of the right hemisphere and Iain McGilchrist's work on the divided brain, but I trusted the power of the sand tray to enable patients to tell their life stories because I had witnessed it so many times in my clinical practice.

I invited the Navajo women from Piñon to tell their stories about their sand trays if they chose. Without exception they all spoke. They laughed. They used their gentle Navajo humor. Some of them cried, but I knew that each of them had touched something meaningful during their play. At the end of the day I asked them if they would each be willing to bring one image to the round sand tray in the center of the room with the four elements. Some of them spoke briefly when they placed their items in the tray. Others said nothing, and we just witnessed their pieces silently. When the community tray was complete, I asked if anyone knew a song that we could use as our closing. Of course they knew a lot of Navajo songs, and they were eager to sing. I felt very privileged to witness the bonding that occurred that day as the Navajo women played and told their stories. I had a lot to think about when the Navajo women left.

Margaret Lowenfeld and Nonverbal Thinking

Talking About Play in Korea

Margaret Lowenfeld (1993), the pediatrician and child analyst who originated the sand tray modality, was very clear about nonverbal thinking processes. Her motivation for creating this play modality came out of her experiences of working with traumatized children during and after World War I. Although she herself spoke seven languages, she was convinced that trauma could not be treated through the process of language alone. Lowenfeld talked about thinking in images. She was one of the first to question the prevailing notion of her time that infants could not think. She explained that of course infants could think. They just couldn't express their thoughts with words.

Based on my clinical observations of both children and adults playing in the sand, I was very convinced by Lowenfeld's idea of image thinking. I was so convinced that when I was asked to speak about the sand tray modality in Seoul, Korea in 2005, I decided to incorporate some hands-on play activities to illustrate these concepts. I knew that no matter how well I spoke about thinking without language, it would be impossible to convey the image thinking process in the absence of experience. There were about 120 mental health clinicians in the audience, and although many of them understood English, primarily they spoke Korean. My whole talk was to be translated, and the conference organizers had asked me to write out my presentation ahead of time. The translator was a lovely person who explained to me that she had already read my whole presentation so that she could do a better job of translating. I was drawing primarily from Dan Siegel's (1999) ideas about the storytelling brain and Antonio Damasio's (1999) "wordless storytelling" to talk about how neuroscience concepts could be really helpful in understanding how best to use the sand tray.

The translator and I had a few minutes to talk right before my presentation began. I don't remember her exact words, but she said something like this, "Your talk looks very interesting, but I think it is going to be difficult for this audience to grasp some of these academic concepts." I replied, "Well, I am planning to use some hands-on exercises that I think will help. I am going to ask them to play with some small objects to illustrate some of the concepts, and then we will talk together to help clarify." She said, "Oh, this audience is very shy. These people will never share publicly what they think." Now, this was not the first time I had used this experiential play strategy, but it was the first time I had spoken to Koreans, and so for one terrible moment, I thought she might be right. I was already being introduced, however, and there was no time to reorganize my plan.

I talked briefly about the sand tray in the context of neuroscience, and then we distributed my miniaturized version of the sand tray to each of the members of the audience—a Petri dish, 2 tablespoons of sand, and a small brown envelope full of the smallest figurines I could find. My instructions were simple: make a scene in your tiny tray—anything that pleases you. They played for about 10 minutes, and then I asked them to write for about five minutes to tell a story about their tray.

When they finished, I asked, "Is anyone willing to read your story?" Not only were they willing to read their stories, they were eager to share what it was like to participate in the play process. Over the next few days we used a variety of hands-on play experiences—including some group play— to ground the academic concepts in the right hemisphere. Of course, I was pretty relieved that the Koreans were willing to play and to talk. Actually, they were incredibly enthusiastic about their participation with each other and with me.

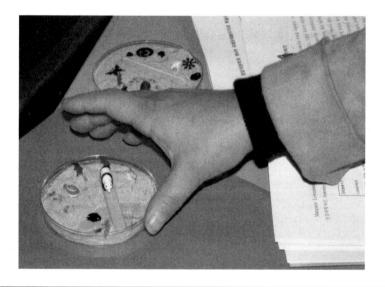

FIGURE 6.2
Play and storytelling in Korea. (Courtesy of Theresa Kestly)

Thinking in the Round

As you might imagine, the question of round sand trays came up since we had been playing in tiny round sand trays, and because I had shown them a photo of a larger round tray. Traditionally most sand trays are rectangular, and I think they might have been wondering whether or not the round tray was legit. So I talked with them about my work with Native Americans, and how they usually expressed preference for the round shape when they came to my workshops. I have both kinds of trays in my teaching studio, and I explained that I thought the round trays fit Native Americans better because they think "in the round" rather than in opposites, as Westerners tend to do. We Westerners often struggle in black and white terms: young or old, Democrat or Republican, good or bad. Although the rectangular shape of the tray seems to be well suited, in Carl Jung's terms, for transcending opposing energies— left-right, up-down, and even diagonally, one corner opposite the other, not all cultures think about the world in these terms. Many Navajos live in round hogans. There are no corners in their traditional dwelling places. Their philosophy about most anything begins with a circle. If you ask them what they believe about education, they will say, "It's like this." As they talk they draw a circle, and then they begin to explain.

I speculated with my Korean audience that some cultures think in the round, and others think in rectangular terms. I asked, "How do Koreans think, in the round or in a rectangular way?" They enthusiastically acknowledged that roundness was their choice. So let's talk about circles for a few moments. Are there really preferences in our different cultures for the way we humans prefer to use our divided brains? My short discussion with the Koreans about thinking in the round was mostly intuitive, based on my experiences of living with the Navajos and then teaching them about the sand tray and other ways of using play in their healing practices.

Recently, however, I was reading about linear versus circular processing in our divided brains in Iain McGilchrist's book, *The Master and His Emissary: The Divided Brain and the Making of the Western World* (McGilchrist, 2009). There is a section in his concluding chapter entitled, *IS THERE ROOM FOR HOPE?* He is asking if there is a way to achieve a better balance between the hemispheres of our brains in our Western cultures. He talks about the circle:

> . . . The shape that is suggested by the processing of the right hemisphere is that of the circle, and its movement is characteristically 'in the round', the phrase we use to describe something that is seen as a whole, and in

depth. Circular motion accommodates, as rectilinearity does not, the coming together of opposites. Cognition in the right hemisphere is not a process of something coming into being through adding piece to piece in a sequence, but of something that is out of focus coming into focus, as a whole. Everything is understood within its penumbra of significances, in its context—all that encircles it. There are strong affinities between the idea of wholeness and roundedness. The movement of the right hemisphere is not the unidirectional, instrumental gesture of grasp, but the musical, whole-bodied, socially generative, movement of dance, which is never in a straight line towards something, but always ultimately returns to its origins (p. 447).

The circle, then, or this movement of the right hemisphere, like music, returns us to our origins. This brings us to McGilchrist's idea of the right-left-right progression of hemispheric processing that is necessary for good story-telling. Stories begin nonverbally in our right hemispheres as we experience life in our bodies through our senses. To bring these "lived" encounters to the level of language, we journey into our left hemispheres where the experiences are "unpacked" to use McGilchrist's term. This unpacking involves processing our experiences in referential form with words that refer to our experiences. Our experiences are represented, or as McGilchrist says *"re-presented"* by the left hemisphere using language, sophisticated syntax, and bits and pieces of highly focused data. Through metaphorical language, we then return our "lived" experiences to the right hemisphere where once again they find their connectedness to the world of bodily experience.

The Navajo culture is one of metaphor and storytelling, and I believe that the reason the Navajo people like the roundness of the sand tray process is that it fits with their preference for right hemisphere metaphorical thinking and this right-left-right progression that McGilchrist describes.

The Piñon women asked for more—much more. After our one-day workshop, they asked me to come to their place for a five-day training in play therapy. Being with the Navajos for five days, this time with both men and women, was such a joy. No matter what materials we used or how we played, they used the metaphors of their culture to understand what I was trying to teach. We used puppets, sand trays, clay, games, arts and crafts, and costumes, and we made photo journal books about our experiences together. I taught and modeled as best I could how we attune with each other while we play. I even taught them Dan Siegel's hand model of the brain. I described briefly how the model worked—where the brain stem could be represented, and then the limbic system and the cortex. I told them that sometimes people even think about the arm as being like the spinal cord leading up to the brain stem.

I gave them face paints and asked them to paint the model on their hands so that they could visualize it. Immediately they began using their own cultural metaphors. Corn is one of the sacred plants in Navajo teachings, and it is often used symbolically and metaphorically to teach about personal growth and learning. One woman painted a corn stalk on her arm to represent the spinal cord. She clearly saw it as fundamental to the brain in the palm of her hand. I then asked them to pair off and use their hand models to teach each other about how the brain works. I wanted them to practice a little so that they could use this play activity with their children. My instructions were in English because I don't speak Navajo, but immediately they began teaching each other using their own Navajo language. I knew then that they had taken ownership of the model. They became especially animated when they explained the part about "flipping" your lid.

Playing with the Navajos is just so easy because they are so comfortable in metaphorical thinking and right-hemisphere processing. Luckily for me, they have continued to ask me to be involved in these play therapy intensives, and so in our most recent adventures we decided to try a different hands-on play activity, but one that also relies on metaphorical thinking processes. It is called Lego® Serious Play®, and we used an adaptation of it to help mental health clinicians and teachers develop skills in getting adolescents to communicate better.

So what is Lego Serious Play? I had to laugh when I first heard the word serious being used to modify the word play. As I read on, however, I learned that only adults used Lego Serious Play. The adults who use it are usually business people, but some are architects, government officials, and engineers, and I quickly realized that it would be almost impossible to get adults to buy into the idea of Lego play if they did not include the word *serious*. The process actually developed sometime around 1998 when the Lego Group was facing near bankruptcy, and so they decided to take seriously what they had been encouraging children to do all along—to use the bricks "to build their own dreams," thus envisioning their futures. The Lego Group needed to find answers to their financial problems, and they decided to try accessing their own imaginations with the Lego bricks to envision a more positive future for the company. The assumption was that the answer to their financial problems was already within them. They just had to find a way to access what they already knew. The process came to be known as "thinking with your fingers."

The Lego people often reference neurologist Frank Wilson (1998) who claims that the unique structure of the human hand and its evolution in cooperation with the brain is the reason that we humans became the most intelligent, advanced animal on the planet. There is no question in my mind about the close relationship between our hands and our brains. I can hardly talk without using my hands. In fact, Iain McGilchrist (2009) cites some interesting research by David McNeil about gestures slightly anticipating speech. He quotes McNeil (1992), "Gestures do not merely *reflect* thought, but help *constitute* thought . . . . Without them thought would be altered or incomplete" (p. 189, note 62, chapter 3).

Could that be? Is it possible that our hands are central to our thought processes? The Lego people seem to think so. They talk about "hand knowledge" to refer to what your hands know that is not yet conscious in your brain. Lego Serious Play involves a lot of free-form building, in contrast to building from a set of instructions. Generally, a trained facilitator poses a question about a particular problem, and then asks participants to build a model showing their understanding of the particular issue. Then the facilitator says, "If you don't know what to build, just start building. Trust your hands."

McGilchrist (2009) also seems to think that the hands are important for the thought process. He devotes several sections to it in his book. One is titled "Language and the Hand." He suggests that language may not have originated as a drive to communicate but as a means of manipulating the world. He is clear that language is not necessary for thought. He says that just because we are aware of how we sometimes think explicitly using words we "should not deceive" ourselves "into believing that language is necessary for thought" (p. 107). McGilchrist (2009) suggests that language is sometimes an impediment to thought. He says,

> Most forms of imagination, for example, or of innovation, intuitive problem solving, spiritual thinking or artistic creativity require us to transcend language, at least language in the accepted sense of a referential code. Most thinking, like most communication, goes on without language (p. 107).

Perhaps the Lego concept of "hand knowledge" and "thinking with your fingers" is not so far off. One thing is clear. It is hard to build anything with Legos without using both hands, and when we do that, we know we are activating both sides of the brain.

Once again, the Navajos enthusiastically entered into the model-building that is such an important part of Lego Serious Play. The Lego play came easily for them because it, like the sand tray, allows for the process of thinking without language, and it uses metaphor to collaborate with the brain's natural tendency to move in a circular fashion in the right-left-right progression that McGilchrist describes.

During the play intensives with the Navajo people, play opened up some of the most interesting and deeply moving conversations about cross-cultural issues. Within the context of safe relationships, play allows us to engage simultaneously with our social engagement systems *and* the positive arousal of our sympathetic nervous systems. Stephen Porges (2011) describes this phenomenon as the polyvagal definition of play—a blend of the social engagement system (neuroception of safety) *and* the sympathetic system (mobilization of the nervous system in the absence of danger). We know that we are "just playing," and in this zone it seems to me that we have special access to working on traumatic experiences at the edges of the window of tolerance. In this context, the window of tolerance means the degree of emotional intensity we can experience while still remaining connected to the person or persons who are with us. For example, children use a lot of pretend play in therapy, and when they use play themes to work unconsciously on a trauma incident, they will often check the play therapist's face to make sure that it is "just play." Because the striated muscles of our faces are entangled with the social engagement branch of the nervous system, we telegraph *safe* or *not safe* through often subtle changes in our faces. When others look toward us, their autonomic nervous systems are drawn toward whatever state we are in. Porges says that this face-to-face play allows us to assess the intention of the other in terms of danger or safety, and to learn the signals when the boundary is being crossed into danger.

Perhaps it is this face-to-face play with the Navajo people, and this neuroception of safety, that opened up some important conversations regarding cross-cultural issues. I have heard stories from them about how painful it is to try to adapt to Western medicine as they watch their traditional medicine practices disappear. They have expressed feelings of being lost between two worlds. Although they appreciate much of what Western medicine has brought them, it does not really fit with their worldview (the circular versus the linear—to use McGilchrist's words). They told me that there was a time when almost every extended family had its own medicine man or medicine woman living within their traditional family compound. They had immediate access if a problem arose. Now, if Navajo people want to visit a traditional medicine man, they must first find the money, or some kind of goods that can be used in exchange, and then set up an appointment to visit a medicine man who might live miles away, and then take a day off work to do so. Access is a real issue. I had to share with them that I thought we Westerners have lost our way, too. And then our discussion led to the question, "What will it take to find our way again?" Perhaps this is what McGilchrist is asking when he writes, *IS THERE ROOM FOR HOPE?*

In his concluding chapter, McGilchrist (2009) also writes a section entitled, "What we might learn from Oriental culture." As I was reading it, I realized that most of what he was saying would still ring true if I substituted the word "Navajo" where he was referring to Oriental cultures. Perhaps the culture we could learn from is closer than we think. Maybe, instead of us bringing our Western ideas to Native Americans, we should stop to see if we might benefit from allowing ourselves to understand the deep wisdom of being grounded in our right hemispheres where relational, intuitive, artistic, spiritual, and innovative ways of being flourish. McGilchrist believes that we may still be able to learn from the cultures of the world that have not yet been completely submerged by Western thought. He thinks that the pattern of psychological differences between non-Western people and Westerners lies in the different relationship between the two hemispheres.

He gives us a comprehensive view of why Westerners have become so left-centric. He believes that historical changes such as the Industrial Revolution have supported the materialistic view of the left hemisphere which has now become entrenched, and that the two main sources of non-materialistic values that could have countered this trend have all but disappeared from Western culture. McGilchrist suggests two things that could have helped: a coherent tradition, and contact with nature.

Both of these non-materialistic values are deeply embedded in Native American cultures. We see these values in the medicine wheel and in their ceremonial traditions. The medicine wheel appears to be a universal metaphor for Native Americans. There are many versions of it, and they use it at many different levels to talk about the balance that is necessary for life to flourish. I think we can begin to learn a lot from the Navajos even if we just consider what might happen if we had a more healthy attitude toward play in Western cultures. We would be doing ourselves a great favor if we did not submerge the Navajo culture in an attempt to make it more like Western cultures.

If we could combine what we know from affective neuroscience with what we can learn from the Navajos about allowing play to enhance our lives, it would be a wonderful step forward. Jaak Panksepp (1998; Panksepp & Biven, 2012) and colleagues have shown us through their laboratory work that PLAY [Panksepp used capitals when he wrote about the seven emotional systems (one of them being PLAY) to remind us that he was referring to one of the specific core circuits identified as being intrinsic to all mammals, not just humans.] is one of seven primary motivational systems that we inherit at birth. It has its own dedicated circuitry in the subcortical part of our brains. Panksepp calls PLAY one of our ancestral tools for living—a tool that can help children learn the relational rules of the road, and a tool that can make our adult lives so much richer. And yet, in Western cultures, we are building schools without playgrounds, and many schools have eliminated recess altogether. Play is all too often viewed as a child's waste of time.

For the Native Americans, play is a way to achieve the balance that they value so highly. Play is embedded in their medicine wheel, the circle that embraces their core teachings—all things in balance. I want to close this section with the words of Black Elk (Niehardt, 1932 p. 164), who speaks about "The Great Circle."

> You have noticed that everything an Indian does is in a circle, and that is because the Power of the World always works in circles, and everything tries to be round. In the old days when we were a strong and happy people, all our power came to us from the sacred hoop of the nation, and so long as the hoop was unbroken, the people flourished. The flowering tree was the living center of the hoop, and the circle of the four quarters nourished it. The east gave peace and light, the south gave warmth, the west gave rain, and the north with its cold and mighty wind gave strength and endurance.

FIGURE 6.3
Medicine Wheel, Albuquerque, New Mexico. (Courtesy of Theresa Kestly)

Crossing Cultures and Scientific Disciplines to Understand

How We Create Resilience through Play

Since the UCLA conference, *Play, Creativity, Mindfulness & Neuroscience in Psychotherapy* in March 2015, I have been thinking a lot more about play, not only across cultures, but also across scientific disciplines. Integrating some of the ideas from the conference presenters and from other neuroscientists who talk about play, I created a handout (Figure 1) for a journal article (Kestly, 2016) to illustrate how resilience is created in the nervous system through play.

The first column shows the three branches of the nervous system as Porges (2011) delineates them with the social engagement system (ventral vagal) placed in the middle to emphasize its position relative to the over- and under-arousal of the sympathetic and parasympathetic dorsal vagal systems. This social engagement branch is also sometimes called the *window of tolerance*, a term coined by Daniel Siegel (1999). We often use the words *fight/flight* for the sympathetic system and *collapse* for the parasympathetic dorsal vagal system. From the numbering we can see that the social engagement branch is our first preference if we are feeling safe. When we neuroceive safety, we are able to connect with each other through smiling, attentive listening, relaxed facial muscles, and good eye contact. If we don't feel safe, the sympathetic branch (number 2) comes online, and we become hypervigilant, with increased body sensations, emotional reactivity, intrusive images, disconnection from others, and cognitive impairment. Then if our attempts to fight or flee do not work, we automatically move to the third branch, where the parasympathetic brakes bring us to a collapsed state where we experience shutting down with decreased or even absent sensations, incapacitated cognitive processing, immobilization, feelings of emptiness or deadness, passivity, complete disconnection, and numbing of emotions. In the middle column, I listed these behaviors and symptoms associated with each branch.

The *Polyvagal Definition of Play* is that ". . . play shares with the defensive fight-or-flight behaviors a neurophysiological substrate that functionally increases metabolic output by increasing sympathetic excitation. Concurrent with the sympathetic excitation is a withdrawal of the myelinated vagal pathways that characterize the vagal brake. Just as the primitive mechanisms mediating immobilization in response to life threat can be co-opted to support loving and nutrient processes, so can mobilization mechanisms be involved to facilitate both defensive flight-or-fight behaviors and pleasurable 'play'" (Porges, 2011, p. 276). Column 3 integrates Porges's polyvagal definition of

PLAY IN THE NERVOUS SYSTEM
Hierarchy of Arousal Zones

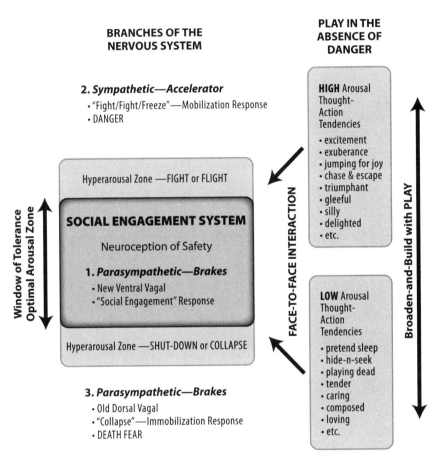

FIGURE 6.4

Creating Resilience through Play. Copyright © 2016 by the American Psychological Association. Reproduced with permission. The official citation that should be used in referencing this material is: Kestly, T. (2016), Presence and play: Why mindfulness matters. *International Journal of Play Therapy, 25*, 14–23.

play and the research of social scientist, Barbara Fredrickson (2009, 2013, 2015; Frederickson & Losada, 2005; Kok & Frederickson, 2010) to suggest that play in the absence of danger co-opts both the sympathetic (mobilization) and the parasympathetic dorsal vagal (immobilization) systems to broaden our capacity to manage the entire range of our autonomic nervous systems in the context of positive emotions that we experience during play.

Fredrickson's broaden-and-build theory asserts that the purpose of positive emotions is to build a repertoire of potential behaviors (thought-action tendencies) that is broad enough to be effective when we are challenged by negative life circumstances. Here in the handout we show the overlapping of the social engagement branch with the sympathetic (in the absence of danger), where we learn to manage positive high-arousal emotions such as excitement, exuberance, and delight. Generally we associate the sympathetic system (fight/flight) with danger leading to a restriction of cognitive processing and behavioral options as the autonomic nervous system seeks to protect itself, but in the case of play, face-to-face interactions allow the dyadic players to assess the intentionality of the other and feel the influence of the other's playful state so that they can use the high-arousal energy of the sympathetic branch of the nervous system (without fear) to build a repertoire of positive thought-action patterns involving high arousal, thus broadening behavioral options. Conversely, there is an overlap of the social engagement and the ventral vagal parasympathetic branch (in the absence of danger) where we learn to develop and manage positive low-arousal emotions such as tenderness, caring, and in children, pretending to sleep, or playing hide and seek, where immobilization is required.

Choosing Play Consciously

McGilchrist (2009) suggests that we could potentially learn from other cultures about finding a way to balance our right- and left-hemispheric thinking processes in Western cultures. Perhaps what we might learn from Native American cultures lies in the circle of their medicine wheel, the sacred hoop that teaches—*all things in balance*. Although in our Western cultures we don't seem to have any traditions that honor play the way the Navajos do in their sacred ceremonies, we Westerners may be developing the science that makes it difficult to refute the benefits that play offers. In the absence of a cultural tradition honoring play, we may need to choose it consciously, and maybe the abundant research that is now flowing from neuroscience will help us do just that. As Fredrickson (Kok & Fredrickson, 2010) has shown in her laboratory research, it is possible to cultivate positive emotions that directly affect our biological health. Who can afford to ignore an improved immune system, less inflammation, and better cardiac health? Fredrickson wrote a beautiful research report about this relationship with a title that included the words "Upward Spirals of the Heart . . . " pointing out the reciprocal nature of positive emotions and social connectedness in developing autonomic flexibility. Perhaps the ancient rituals of ceremony, community, and play are more scientific than we might think. To me, what McGilchrist suggests about cultures who have maintained balance in their hemispheric processing through their traditions and contact with nature may be the important lesson that our neuroscience is now illuminating.

References

Damasio, A. (1999). *The feeling of what happens: Body and emotion in the making of consciousness.* New York: Harcourt Brace & Company.

Fredrickson, B. (2009). *Positivity: Top-notch research reveals the upward spiral that will change your life.* New York: Three Rivers Press.

Fredrickson, B. (2013). *Love 2.0: Creating happiness and health in moments of connection.* New York: Penguin Group.

Fredrickson, B. (2015) Updated thinking on positivity ratios. *American Psychologist, 68*(9), 814–822.

Fredrickson, B. & Losada, M. (2005). Positive affect and the complex dynamics of human flourishing. *American Psychologist, 60*(7), 678-686.

Kestly, T. (2016), Presence and play: Why mindfulness matters. *International Journal of Play Therapy, 25,* 14–23.

Kok, B., & Fredrickson, B. (2010). Upward spirals of the heart: Autonomic flexibility, as indexed by vagal tone, reciprocally and prospectively predicts positive emotions and social connectedness. *Biological Psychology, 85*(3) 432–436.

Lowenfeld, M. (1993). *Understanding children's sandplay: The world technique.* Cambridge, UK: Margaret Lowenfeld Trust. (Original work published 1979.)

McGilchrist, I. (2009). *The master and his emissary: The divided brain and the making of the Western world.* New Haven, CT: Yale University Press.

McNeill, D. (1992). *Hand and mind: What gestures reveal about thought.* Chicago, IL: University of Chicago Press.

Niehardt, J. G. (1932). *Black Elk Speaks.* New York: William Morrow & Company.

Panksepp, J. (1998). *Affective neuroscience: The foundations of human and animal emotions.* New York: Oxford University Press.

Panksepp, J., & Biven, L. (2012). *The archaeology of mind: Neuroevolutionary origins of human emotions.* New York: W. W. Norton & Company.

Siegel, D. J. (1999). *The developing mind: How relationships and the brain interact to shape who we are.* New York: The Guilford Press.

Siegel, D. J. (2012). *The developing mind: How relationships and the brain interact to shape who we are* (2nd ed.). New York: The Guilford Press.

Todd, M. (1959). *The thinking body.* Princeton, NJ: Princeton Book Company.

Wilson, F. (1998). *The hand: How its use shapes the brain, language, and the human culture.* New York: Vintage Books.

7

Creativity in the
Training of Psychotherapists

Louis Cozolino

AS A STUDENT, I had an image of the teacher I someday hoped to become—a repository of knowledge and a wise elder, influencing generations of learners. I imagined a cozy campus and gothic architecture with ivy gumming up window hinges. I wanted to instill my love of libraries and books and the deep appreciation I had for the influence of history on contemporary life. I imagined sitting around heavy tables in musty conference rooms as I led classes though in-depth examinations of ideas and theories using well-honed Socratic methods.

These images, rooted in novels and the black-and-white movies of my childhood, were later reinforced by a decade at Harvard and UCLA. It may have also been a wish to find a safe and predictable place after growing up in a chaotic world. Despite my nostalgia for all things academic, these images gradually became outdated and stifling to creativity. Instead of heading back to the East Coast in search of the academic position I had always dreamed of, I ended up at a small teaching-oriented university in Los Angeles.

This world was very different from what I had imagined. I found myself in modern office buildings with browning plants and vending machines. Few students were interested in exploring theories or engaging in philosophical discussions; they were mostly interested in what questions would be on the exams. During my first year as a teacher, a student complained to the dean about me, claiming that I was using foreign words in my class and that no one had told her that there was a language requirement. (It turns out that I had used the word Gestalt in a sentence.) Most of my students were not aspiring academics; they had come to a trade school to learn how to do psychotherapy.

It had never occurred to me to think of psychotherapy as a trade. For me, trade school was a place where you go to learn carpentry or how to drive a tractor-trailer. I always thought of psychotherapy as an intellectual and emotional endeavor—a personal journey taken by a therapist and client—that utilizes ideas from philosophy, anthropology, evolutionary theory, and neurology. Despite feeling ill prepared and a bad institutional fit for a trade school, I also saw the potential value of this way of thinking. I already knew what my future would look like in academia, but I was curious about where this path would lead. Needless to say, teaching psychotherapy has been a wild ride, and I have learned a few things along the way.

Psychotherapy and the Classroom

Becoming a therapist requires learning a great deal of information about everything from diagnosis to medication, to law and ethics. For these subjects, the classroom works just fine. On the other hand, teaching the actual skills of psychotherapy doesn't work well in a classroom setting. It's not the room, chairs, or whiteboards, but the assumptions that students bring to a classroom: outward focus, remembering and regurgitating information, looking good, and competing for grades.

Psychotherapy training requires the opposite state of mind: inward focus, emotional awareness, wisdom, and an ability to listen to your heart. All of these abilities become inhibited when we are afraid that we might make a mistake or get a bad grade that will ruin our career. This is probably why in their early clinical sessions students are surprised to find that after years of classes, they still feel clueless. They're nervous and frightened, and they revert to filling out intake forms and checking off symptoms from the DSM. New therapists are surprised to find out that they are starting from scratch and that no one ever warned them. *We really should warn them.*

The creative challenge for a psychotherapy teacher is to cultivate a culture that subverts most of what students have been taught to expect in a classroom. We need to establish a classroom culture where putting your worst foot forward is rewarded and where personal vulnerability replaces looking good. An environment where awareness of your body and articulating your own emotions are valued above being able to repeat what the teacher says. Where social intelligence, analytic introspection, and uncovering unconscious conflicts is valued over grades.

What makes it even more of a challenge is that most students training to be psychotherapists haven't been in therapy themselves. Many don't believe that therapy would work for them. Many students don't even believe in the unconscious. Although they are months or weeks away from seeing their first clients, the only model many have of psychotherapy is from videotapes of Carl Rogers and old *Sopranos* episodes. Students are often surprised to learn that therapy is something that we do with another person, not something we do to them. Most students believe that they can sit back and think about the right thing to say and that their book learning will give them what they need to help people. In truth, that's just a small portion of what makes therapy successful. Both teaching and therapy require tenacity, sensitivity, toughness, transparency, and good improvisational skills.

The Heroic Journey

The path to becoming a psychotherapist is more akin to a heroic journey than matriculating through a degree program. Success as a therapist has nothing to do with a degree and everything to do with the courage it takes to come to know yourself and the desire to be the best therapist possible. While the surface journey consists of the trials and tribulations of surviving a graduate degree program, this inner journey puts students face-to-face with their demons and inner brokenness. We all have demons, and we are all broken in some way.

Often, it is our brokenness that unconsciously guides us to become therapists in the first place. Think of it as an impulse to heal combined with a lack of wisdom or courage to get the help we need. When our demons appear during the process, we become frightened, trying to hang on even more tightly to defenses like knowing the right answers and getting excellent grades. Because these demons separate us from our true selves, confronting them is essential if we are to reach our full potential as therapists and as people.

Fear makes us stupid, and our demons scare us to death, so we are not at our best when we come face-to-face with them. Sometimes our minds lead us to believe that our supervisors, teachers, and therapists are the demons, a clever trick our minds play to distract us. Paradoxically, the way we learn who we are is by peering into our own abyss and allowing our teachers to guide us through the process. If we are afraid of being vulnerable or of being labeled as emotionally unstable, we run the risk of solidifying our defenses.

Most of us assume that we need to be psychologically healthy and mentally well balanced to be psychotherapists. If this were in fact the case, we would have very few psychotherapists. The process of learning to be a psychotherapist and the process of self-healing are one and the same. However, if you believe that you need to hide your demons from others and even from yourself, your first meeting with them can not only be unsettling, but also threatening to the way that you perceive your entire career path. If we first face these demons while working with clients, it will hinder our ability to help our clients. Our reactions, if not contained, may even damage the therapeutic relationship.

Before we guide students to come face-to-face with their demons, we need to provide them with a way of understanding what's happening that doesn't lead them to retreat from the challenge. And once their demons are confronted, we need to be present and supportive in a way that boosts their emotional strength so that they can survive the challenge.

If psychotherapy training is a heroic journey, then teaching is more akin to being a wise and benevolent guide than a dispenser of information. This requires so much creativity and the ability to tune into the emotional climate of the moment that it feels more like performance art than lecturing. Telling stories becomes a big part of training because this is how humans have learned social-emotional lessons for a hundred thousand years. Humor is another excellent tool because, if used correctly, it helps us to accept difficult truths more readily. As guides, we support and challenge, cajole and comfort, and sometimes just sit quietly as our students ponder the significance of what has just happened. This suggests to me that training to be a psychotherapist is an interactive creative process between students and teachers.

As teachers and guides, we have quite a task. We have to simultaneously create a safe place that encourages curiosity and exploration while holding students to high standards, holding up a mirror that stimulates their fears, and riding the rapids of their emotional reactions with them. Over these many years, I've had students who thought that I am the worst teacher they've ever had and others who have thought that I was the best teacher. However, I happen to believe that both groups are right. It isn't just who I am and what I'm able to do; it's the proper connection and attunement with students at the right time in their development.

So the question for every teacher is how do we create this safe space? My teachers have been many, and I've engaged in inner dialogue with myself from an early age. Here, I share what I believe to be important through some stories that embody basic principles of learning.

Embracing the Unexpected

In 1965, my twelve-year-old self was in bad shape. My parents had gotten divorced; my mother was struggling with bills, a deep depression, and six of us living in a one-bedroom basement flat in the Bronx. This felt like hitting bottom. At first I sought solace in books to escape the painful realities of my life. I remember discovering science fiction and immediately connecting to these new worlds and alternative realities. It occurred to me one day that I felt so out of place in my life that I must have been placed on earth by an alien race as an experiment. I clearly recall looking up at the sky and saying "It's okay to come get me now; I think we've got enough data." Awkward, overweight, and having no idea of how to express my feelings, I discovered the ability to express myself through music.

On one particular Wednesday, I showed up for my usual drum lesson, but things were different at the school. There was a crowd gathered in the drum section, and an old timer was holding court, talking and playing riffs in turn. I was told that my regular teacher was ill and that I would be having lessons with the old guy that everyone seemed so interested in. While my usual teacher was punctual, precise, and dull, this guy seemed full of life and in no hurry to get the lesson started. My teacher made me play the music note by note and validated Buddha's belief that life is suffering. I was about to have a very different experience with Philly.

As I walked over, Philly said, "Okay. Who's my first victim, I mean student?" I timidly raised my hand, my other arm filled with drum books and sticks. He said "Okay, young man. Let's go!" and we walked downstairs to the lesson rooms.

As we descended the stairs to the lesson rooms, he asked me what kind of music I liked. I was surprised because my teacher had never asked me that question. I told Philly that I liked the Beatles and the Temptations. "Hmm!" He responded, "Why?" I must have said that they were fun to sing to or something like that. When we got to the lesson room, the first thing he said was, "Where are the drums?" I told him that we didn't do our lessons on real drums, but on squares of rubber glued to pieces of wood. "Bullshit . . ." he growled softly as he began searching the other rooms for drums. I heard him say, "Come here, boy" in a way that made me feel happy and excited. When I entered the room, Philly was setting up two sets of drums face-to-face.

"Take a seat," he said and pointed to the smaller of the two sets. "Now you're going to have a drum lesson." "Play," Philly told me. "What about the music?" I asked, holding up my lesson books. His words said, "We'll get to that later," but his eyes said, "Burn those damn things." "Play" he said, and I sat there staring at him. "What should I play?" I asked. He said, "Play what you feel." I had no idea what he meant, so I just started playing a basic rhythm. Philly watched for a while and began to play the same rhythm with me, varying the placement of the accent shots and playing lead to my rhythm. He then

FIGURE 7.1
Lou playing the drums. (Courtesy of Louis Cozolino)

stopped me and told me to play off of his rhythm, which I did for a while until I made a mistake and stopped. Here is where the lesson got really interesting.

"Never stop," he yelled over his playing. Never stop, what did he mean by that? I had been taught to stop when I make a mistake to make sure that I get it right. At the next break, I told him this, and my confusion about the "never stop." He said, "The Beatles and Temptations are very good for what they are, but they are designed to make you feel something; they don't ask you what you feel. Jazz is improvisation; you never stop because the secrets lie behind the so-called mistakes. What you call mistakes are opportunities to explore another part of your soul."

The second half of our lesson was about making mistakes and turning them into new rhythms. As we played together, I could see his mistakes and then him shifting to accommodate them. Gradually, I could see that when I made a mistake, Philly would shift to embellish some part of my mistake and help me find the value in where I had gone. I was slowly able to stop worrying about slip-ups and came to experience the mistakes as happy surprises that I could morph into the next phase of playing.

I didn't last long after my regular teacher returned to school the following week. Practicing rhythms and notes out of the book felt like wearing a straitjacket; it just wasn't for me anymore. I needed an environment where I could make mistakes and try new things while still feeling safe. When I began teaching many years later, I could hear Philly in my words when I encouraged students to reframe their mistakes as opportunities.

A few years later, a young guitarist named John McLaughlin was asked to sit in on a recording session with the legendary trumpeter Miles Davis. John arrived at the recording studio with no music and no preparation. Davis, who was taciturn, enigmatic, and often on heroin, gave the young man only one instruction in his deep, raspy, almost inaudible voice. "Play as if you have never held a guitar. Get to know the instrument for the first time—explore what it can do." The awe of the master must have been mixed with fear as the tech at Columbia Studios pointed the finger at John and said, "Go."

Instead of getting a ream of sheet music to play or specific directions to follow, Davis created an interpersonal space of attunement, collaboration, and sharing. He let the young man lead as he followed, picking up on his excitement, anxiety, exploration, and discovery. In turn joining him, then allowing

FIGURE 7.3
John McLaughlin. (Public domain)

himself to be joined as they flowed through the sounds and emotions of the music. If you're interested, the result of that afternoon and evening was an album called *In a Silent Way*. As a master guitarist in his old age, John still tells that story, a lot better than I do, and remembers the importance of that experience to his development.

The freedom to create, explore, and learn on our own terms is rarely granted, but this is when our best work is done. We can explore what we think we know, examine new perspectives, and incorporate new information into our worlds.

Loving and Learning

There is a clear connection between social connectedness and intelligence. This is because our minds emerge from the interaction between our brains and our relationships. Have you ever noticed that you feel smarter and more articulate with a receptive and positive listener? And how about the opposite situation, when your audience is hostile or disinterested, and you can almost feel your IQ melting away? An example of this type of experience happened to me while I was in college. A friend had asked me for a ride to a retreat center near our university. We arrived at a beautiful wooded setting and I excused myself to take a walk around the grounds.

After walking along a path for a few minutes, I came upon a lake with a viewing bench of which I quickly took possession. Not long after, a man strolled up to me, said hello, and sat down. His approach was so natural and relaxed that at first I assumed he had mistaken me for someone he knew. He introduced himself as Jon, told me that he was staying at the retreat center to work on a paper, and immediately began asking me questions. He asked about my studies and the ideas that I found most exciting. He engaged with me with such sincere interest and enthusiasm that he seemed to pull ideas out of my mind that I never knew I had. Within ten minutes, he knew more about me than anyone in my family and more than most of my friends. I felt emboldened by our connection and could feel that I was pushing the envelope of my thinking.

Time flew by as we bantered back and forth about everything from astronomy to philosophy. Eventually, we were interrupted by distant calls from my friend who was searching for me. Regretfully, I bid my new friend goodbye with promises of returning to renew our discussion. As my buddy and I drove back to campus, we discussed both of our experiences. When we pulled into the parking lot at school, I noticed a brochure about the retreat facility on my friend's lap and picked it up to have a look. As I unfolded it, I saw Jon's face on

FIGURE 7.4

Jonas Salk. (Public domain)

it with the caption Dr. Jonas Salk. Stunned, I sat there unable to say a word. Eventually, I told my friend that this was the man that I had been talking to for the last hour. My heart pounded as I began to think of all of the foolish things that I had just said to the genius who had cured polio decades earlier.

Had I known I was talking to Jonas Salk, I would have been overwhelmed with anxiety, self-doubt, and shame. If I were able to say anything at all, it would have probably been nonsensical or, even worse, I would have tried to sound smart, which would have made me sound both pretentious and stupid. Instead, my lack of self-consciousness combined with his sincere interest raised my game in a way that I will never forget. I now realize that the quality of his attention turbocharged the biochemistry of my brain. The synergy among a positive connection, enthusiasm, and a lack of social anxiety, provided an optimal neurobiological environment for creativity and learning.

Griffins and Fluffy Bunnies

Self-doubt, low self-esteem, and shame are common human struggles, and they are present in all learning environments. These challenges are amplified when students are convinced that they need to be devoid of personal struggles in order to work with clients. I experienced this need the first time that I was exposed to projective testing in an assessment class. There were fifty people in the class, mostly guys, around my age, who were pretty much like me. In preparation for the class I had read a chapter about the Rorschach but didn't have access to the cards. To get the discussion going, the professor put up a slide of the first Rorschach card and asked us to share what we saw.

The image fascinated me. I saw two griffins stretching their wings.
Ah, mythological creatures; look at me, such a vivid imagination.
I heard someone say they saw a jack-o'-lantern.
Oh yea, I see the jack-o'-lantern.
Next, I saw a woman in the middle wearing a transparent dress.
Okay, now it's getting good!
The next person saw dancers spinning really fast . . .
I guess, maybe mutant dancers.
Then, my griffins turned mean and started to pull on the woman's dress.
Oh Crap! Sadism, mother issues, repressed rage. . . . I started to worry about what I would say when my turn came.
"Rain clouds," said the next person . . .
Rain clouds! What makes them look like rain clouds, asked the professor? "They look fluffy to me" . . . I'm seeing a woman getting ripped apart, and you see fluffy rain clouds. What is wrong with me?

The longer I looked, the darker my images grew. Meanwhile, others were seeing ringing bells, flowers, mountain ranges, and fluffy bunnies. Fluffy Bunnies!!! It didn't occur to me that everyone might be struggling to look sane—or at least to not look like serial killers. What did occur to me, driven by my own shame, was that underneath it all I was a crazy person on the edge of insanity. I didn't think, "Hey, I should go to therapy and figure out what's going on in there." No! My impulse was to keep this broken part of me hidden from others in order to become a therapist.

And so I became introduced to a central theme of my early professional life: what do I do with my brokenness, insecurities, and fear of abandonment? How do I cope with my shame, how do I manage my vulnerabilities, and how do I tame my demons? The fact that I didn't consider getting help is telling. I believe that this desperate self-sufficiency is a kind of narcissism shared among helping professionals. We think we're different, and because of this, we fail to recognize the universality of our struggles. The upside is that our flaws allow us to connect and empathize with clients.

Supervision in Shambles

In 1980, I moved from Harvard to UCLA for my PhD. UCLA was dedicated to clinical training, and I had a wonderful array of supervisors in psychology, psychiatry, and neurology. During my first days at the clinic, as often happens, the universe sent me young depressed women to trigger my mother issues and press all of my pathological caretaking buttons. I tried to act like a therapist, but I was so unsettled by her sadness that I turned into a comedian. I did everything that I could to distract my client from her pain. It was me, not the client, who couldn't stand to be in the room with her pain.

At the end of the session, I dismissed the client and went into the observation room where three student colleagues and our supervisor were waiting to discuss the hour. I thought that I had done well because she came in crying and left laughing. However, I could tell by their expressions that they had a very different opinion.

My supervisor spoke first in the wonderful accent of his native Jamaica, "What da hell was dat, mon?" I had hoped for a little empathy, but the other students looked away with discomfort. "Um, therapy?" I offered. "No," he told me. "That was Richard Pryor mixed with George Carlin." "Tell me more," I asked. My curiosity opened the floodgates of expression in the room; my narcissism, pathological caretaking, and intellectualizing defenses became the focus of a two-hour discussion. I remember the experience vividly.

I was outed for things that I always knew but was never able to articulate. It was walking into my unthought known. I struggled to be open, stay in the room, and not dissociate. I had to make the decision to act strong or be real. Tears came to my eyes, and I let them flow. I was transported back to the Rorschach class, then to the trauma that surrounded me as a child, and then to the crushing fear caused by my mother's depression. I instinctually knew that this was a watershed moment and that the caring and respect I had for this professor and the other guys in the room made it possible. My professor and peers allowed me to look at my work honestly, which put me on course to becoming a better therapist. I realized that I had to reverse this process and begin healing. I had no idea it would go on for the rest of my career.

Holding it Together

As my career progressed, I transitioned from supervisee to supervisor and found myself in the role of providing guidance and support to students. In one class, I did a role-play with a male student in his mid-forties. We played therapist and client so I could demonstrate some therapeutic techniques. As we spoke, I found that it was difficult to follow the logic of what he was say-ing. His sentences were grammatically correct, but his overall communication lacked coherence. I couldn't follow him. After checking in with myself to look for any obvious signs of countertransference, I focused on my body to see if I was getting any communication from him at a somatic level. As I focused my consciousness into my chest and stomach, I started to feel constrained, almost suffocated. Breathing was difficult, and my body felt frozen in place. An image came to mind; I felt like an old wooden barrel, held together by metal hoops. While these hoops felt constricting, it seemed that without them I would fall to pieces.

While my "client" continued to talk, I focused my thinking on this image. During a pause, I asked his permission to share the image of the barrel. As he listened, he began to gently cry. When he was able to speak, he told me that his fiancée had been killed in a plane crash a month earlier. He said he had been walking around in a fog since the funeral, barely holding himself together. He was avoiding the reality of her death by scheduling every minute and socializing as much as possible. I came to realize that his words made no sense because their purpose was not to communicate, but to distract us both from his pain. He didn't want to think clearly about such a cruel and meaning-less world. I suspect that he needed me to put his feelings into words so that he could become aware of them. In fact, he later told me that our work together in class was the beginning of his grieving process.

I have been able to attune to clients on many occasions by remaining open to the feelings and images that come from my body. At first, I'm never sure if they have anything to do with the client or if they are just shadows in my own mind. I share these images with clients as products of my own imagination, and I leave it to them to accept, modify, or ignore them. Some clients just roll their eyes and move on while others immediately relate to what I may share. The important thing to remember about sharing our own associations is to not become attached to them and to be willing to immediately move on if they don't resonate with clients.

Heifetz and the Unconscious

Ten years later, I encountered a most interesting student. On the first day of the first class of the doctoral program, she was sitting in the front row with a skeptical look on her face. I tried to imagine why she was skeptical given the fact that she hadn't yet heard word one from me or anyone else. But there she sat with a resting facial expression that said to me "I don't believe you." It was as if I had told her that marshmallows could cure cancer. I focused on my notes and tried to avoid looking at her. It was probably all in my mind, I thought. A minute or two later, I began my introductory lecture for advanced abnormal psychology.

It didn't take long before she raised her hand to speak. In response to the DSM, she said, "I've heard it isn't valid"; in response to schizophrenia, "Thomas Szasz says it's a myth"; "psychotropic medication" a plot by Big Pharma, and so forth. Eventually, she began to notice the eye rolls from her peers and stood down for a while. She restrained herself until I used the U word, Unconscious—she lost control, "How can you believe in the unconscious? I thought you were a researcher." I could feel the impatience and anger heading up my throat toward my mouth, triggering words far more appropriate for the street than the classroom.

I composed myself enough to be able to point out: "It's interesting to hear that you disagree with nearly every premise of the field, yet here you are in a doctoral program." She didn't miss a beat: "I'm here to learn more about CBT, not about mythology and pseudoscience." "I'll do my best," I told her, swallowing a number of alternative responses. As the semester went on, she seemed to soften a bit, and occasionally found a few things interesting—especially if they sounded similar to something Tim Beck might say. I toyed with the idea of wearing a bow tie to see if that would help her connect with me.

At the end of the semester, I was glad to escape that skeptical resting face each week. I assumed I would never see her in another class again and that she was happy to see the end of me. Lo and behold the following year, there she was again. She had selected me over other professors who I assumed she found even more annoying. Because this was a seminar, we got a chance to get to know each other a bit during breaks and class discussions. I actually liked her; she was very bright, probably about 10 years older than I was at the time.

It turned out that she was from a wealthy family that did quite a lot of charitable work around Los Angeles; she was also very interested in classical music, a passion she and I shared. So our relationship deepened while she continued questioning my ideas and turning different shades of red at any mention of the unconscious. By the end of the semester, I assumed that this was the last class she would be taking with me, and I was happy to see our student-teacher relationship come to an end.

A couple of semesters later on the first day of a small seminar on assessment, there she was again. I was amazed to see her in this class because the focus was to integrate cognitive and personality testing into a coherent battery; there was no way to avoid the U word. "I'm really in for it now," I thought. I wondered how she's going to react to projective testing! Resting skeptical face reached a whole new level as I described Freud's projective hypothesis and his theory that the mind struggled to make sense out of nonsense.

During week three, I brought my testing case into class and pulled out the Thematic Apperception Test, better known as the TAT. I pulled out the first card, a picture of a young boy holding his head, staring at some sheet music, not playing a violin that was resting on the table in front of him. I read the instructions for the TAT to the class as they all looked at the picture. After a while I asked them, "What do you see? What happened? What is the boy feeling, and what will happen next?"

Before anyone else could respond, skeptical resting face practically flew out of her chair. Grabbing the picture, she said, "There's nothing projective about this. This boy's parents are forcing him to play the violin; he hates the violin, and he hates his parents. He refuses to practice, and as soon as he can, he's going to break the violin and never play it again. That's not in my mind; that's in his facial expression, and in the set up. That isn't projection, just what is obviously in the picture."

The students in the room sitting around the table looked at one another, with everyone's expression saying AWKWARD. I wasn't sure what to say at first, but I soon had an idea. I reached into my briefcase and pulled out the photograph on which this TAT drawing was based. Years earlier, I had learned that this young boy was actually Jascha Heifetz, a famous violinist. I had found the picture in a book years ago and kept it with my testing materials as a teaching tool.

I asked her, "Would you be interested to know who this is a picture of?" "It doesn't matter," she said. "It might," I said, and I slid the picture of young Jascha across the conference table. For the first time, she was speechless as she sat staring at the photograph. She said nothing for the rest of the class, but I could tell a lot was going on inside her mind, maybe even in her unconscious.

At the end of class, she told me what had been on her mind. She had met Heifetz as a young girl and idolized him. She tried to play the violin herself but could never get the hang of it. Practicing became a point of contention between her and her mother, and she ended up throwing the violin across the room, never to play again.

It became clear to her that what she saw in the TAT card couldn't possibly have had anything to do with Heifetz, and she said, as if in shock, that she could no longer deny the existence of her unconscious. The next week her resting skeptical face had become resting curious face. She had gone through the looking glass and became an active participant in the class. I ran into her a few years after she graduated, and she told me that she was in psychoana-

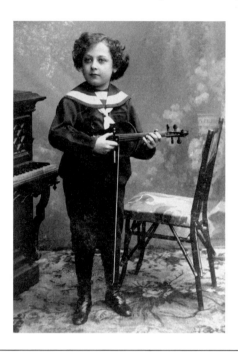

FIGURE 7.5
Jascha Heifetz. (Public domain)

lytic training at the Los Angeles Institute. Like a sinner gone to Jesus, she had become an avid explorer of her inner world and the inner world of others. Miracles do happen.

Shimmering

Students, teachers, in fact all of us, shimmer back and forth between being rational adults one moment and children the next; we are all desperate for love and attention. What I've tried to learn to do is to be sensitive to the shimmering of my students and clients, shimmering along with them. In other words, try my best to stay attuned enough to mirror their shifting consciousness and respond as a teacher, therapist, a father, or a wise uncle—whatever is called for in the moment. The trick for me has been to learn how to sense that shift as quickly as possible and to make the parallel shift within myself.

Creativity, wisdom, and emotional awareness are all needed to create a safe learning environment for trainees. They need to look inward, reflect, and understand their own inner demons. As supervisors, we do our best to guide them through this process, drawing on our own experiences for assistance. Because of my own intellectual defenses, I tend to get hyper-focused on the content of a conversation and miss (or avoid) the emotions that are also being expressed. Learning to listen to the second narrative, the life story of the storyteller vs. the content, has been one of my biggest challenges. This is something I've gotten better at over the years, but I still need a lot of work.

References and Selected Resources

Campbell, J. (2008). *The hero with a thousand faces* (3rd Ed.). New York: New World Library.

Collins, M. (1992). *Ordinary kids, extraordinary teachers.* Charlottesville, VA: Hamptons Roads Publishing.

Cozolino, L. (2004). *The making of a therapist.* New York: W. W. Norton & Company.

Cozolino, L. (2014). *Attachment-based teaching.* New York: W. W. Norton & Company.

Gruwell, E. (2008). *Teach with your heart: Lessons I learned from the Freedom Writers.* New York: Broadway Books.

Sacks, O. (2002). *Uncle Tungsten: Memories of a chemical boyhood.* New York: Vintage Books.

Salk, J. (1983). *Anatomy of reality: Merging of intuition and reason.* New York: Columbia University Press.

Szasz, T. (1974). *The myth of mental illness: Foundations of a theory of personal conduct.* New York: HarperCollins.

8

Awakening Clinical Intuition: Creativity and Play

Terry Marks-Tarlow

IN THEIR CLASSIC text, Kluckholm and Murray (1953) assert that each person is simultaneously "like all others," "like some others," and "like no others." We each resemble *all others* in how our mind/body/brains are wired and in facing the same laws of nature and basic existential conditions of life. We resemble *some others* by being inherently social creatures who participate in collective activities and social groups, as defined by culture, ethnicity, attachment style, sexual orientation, religious affiliation, etc. We resemble *no others* in how our many facets combine uniquely into precise developmental and family histories plus life trajectories.

When Kluckholm and Murray's formulation is applied to the enterprise of psychotherapy, being like all others leads researchers to conduct outcome studies in search of universal factors. Candidates include the quality of the therapeutic alliance (Geller & Greenberg, 2002; Messer, 2002) and memory reconsolidation, by which newly updated associations replace outdated, traumatic, or dysfunctional memories (Lane, et al., 2015). These pan-theoretical factors cross-cut all schools, orientations, and modalities of psychotherapy.

Within psychotherapy, our resemblance to some others highlights the issue of diversity. True empathy mandates psychotherapists to understand the social, cultural, and historical frames of reference of the people with whom we work. Meanwhile, symptom-focused approaches to treatments classify people into groups based on genetic factors and diagnostic categories. Whether people are grouped in terms of heritage, habits, or symptom clusters, no matter how sensitively this is done, psychotherapy necessarily proceeds according to gen-eralizations, broad formulations, and/or prefabricated treatment techniques.

It is Kluckholm and Murray's assertion that each individual resembles no other that invokes the realm of clinical intuition. In order for therapists to attend to the unique dynamics of *this* person, in *this* moment, given *this* attach-ment history, in *this* era, we must operate on the micro-scale of Daniel Stern's (2004) "now" moments. This is where the minute-to-minute expression of who we are determines the precise dynamics and interpersonal chemistry of the dyad. Only through clinical intuition can body-based perception tune into those tiny shifts in emotion, energy, posture, and information that fly back and forth across the room, often under the radar of conscious awareness. The purpose of this chapter is to explore the creativity and play of clinical intuition as it emerges in the realm of the unique.

Tuning in through Clinical Intuition

I define clinical intuition as the capacity to register and respond to inter-personal patterns in healing and growth-facilitating contexts (Marks-Tarlow, 2012a, 2014). Clinical intuition requires attuned response though which psy-chotherapists become anchored enough in their own bodies and perception to fully open their eyes, ears, hearts, and even souls without preconception. This is how we operate with full presence and authenticity, from the inside-out, grounded within our own sensibilities, emotional experiences, and unique perspective.

Whereas clinical theory offers abstractions that exist outside experiential realms, clinical intuition operates spontaneously, as a fresh response to a lived moment. No matter how many books we may read, workshops we may attend, or supervisions we may absorb, in the heat and heart of the clinical moment, we must put all of this aside. We render each moment both sacred and new partly by learning to bracket off past learning while laying future agendas aside. In this way, the science of clinical practice blends with the art of its timing through an unpredictable and present-centered dance of leading and following.

Implicit Knowing

Within talk therapy, attunement relates less to the content of speech, or *what* we say, and more to the processes of speech, or *how* we say it—tone and rhythm of voice (prosody), posture, body movements, facial expression, and eye gaze. These paralinguistic vocal, visual, facial, and postural cues are all part of the implicit relational knowing (Lyons-Ruth, 1998; Seligman, 2012), the primary form of learning and memory a baby uses for the first two years of life as guided primarily by right-brain processes (Schore, 2010, 2011).

Implicit knowledge involves emotional, relational, and body-based experiences that precede later-developing, explicit, cognitive, and verbal faculties. Implicit processes shape Bowlby's internal working models, helping us to form social expectations that determine relational openness or defensiveness and color the emotional tone of ongoing experience. I speculate that implicit learning and memory also account for the quality and landscape of repetitive dreams throughout life (Marks-Tarlow, 2012a, 2014b).

Whether psychotherapists work with children or adults, in order to pick up on these tiny, multimodal, implicit cues, *context* is everything. Both during early development and within psychotherapy, the full context is *always* too complex for any complete verbal description or future prediction. This is one reason why parental and clinical intuition take on such significance and how-to books pale by comparison. Only through nonverbal, intuitive channels can we register the full spectrum of interpersonal data, by drawing upon immediate sensory, emotional, and imaginal cues (Marks-Tarlow, 2012a, 2014a).

Because clinical intuition responds to nuance implicitly and subcortically, this is a fully embodied mode of perceiving, relating, and responding. In contrast to explicit levels of processing (e.g., thinking, analyzing, deciding), implicit responses are fast-acting and effortless; they operate automatically, in context, beneath the level of conscious awareness (Claxton, 1997). Implicit relational knowing draws more upon the right brain's deep connection to the stress and emotion-regulating aspects of the autonomic nervous system (Schore, 2010, 2011). The importance of implicit relational learning to psychotherapy also has been underscored by clinical theorists like Daniel Stern (1985, 2004), members of the Boston Change Process Study Group (2008), and infant researcher Beatrice Beebe (Beebe, et al., 2010, 2012). Beebe documents how tiny contingent moments of discordance or synchrony between caretakers and infants affect future attachment status.

Due to the primacy of this mode during psychotherapy, I assert that clinical intuition is what fills the gap between theory and practice (Marks-Tarlow, 2012a, 2014a and 2014b). Where theory is static, intuition is alive. Where theory exists outside of real time, intuition involves immersion within lived moments. When clinicians become immersed in this fashion, we often attain states of *flow* (Csíkszentmihályi, 1990, 1996) with our patients. When in a state of flow, therapists get caught up in the throes of implicit processes as intuitively guided. This is the realm of intersubjectivity, where self and other become physiologically and psychologically, if not spiritually, entwined (see

Marks-Tarlow, 2008a). Here, there may be emotional challenge, yet often little sense of effort.

As therapists and patients ride the waves of interrelatedness, it becomes easy to find smooth rhythms of exchange. Time flies by. Psychotherapy can take on an all-enveloping quality of wholeness. This sometimes feels like a dance where exquisitely coordinated movements are choreographed by no one and both people at once (see Figure 1). Or, verbal flows may feel like poetry in motion or a song of syncopated call and response. When psychotherapists are lucky enough to spend long periods intuitively immersed, despite intense, often negative emotional involvement, they can nonetheless leave work feeling energized and refreshed. Amid deep intuitive engagement, the relationship itself becomes vitalizing, pulling each person along, ideally nudging both into spontaneous, unexpected places.

Because of the effortless, non-conscious way that clinical intuition operates, it becomes all too easy to overlook its importance in graduate and postgraduate training programs. Yet, with the current emphasis on empirically validated

FIGURE 8.1
The Dance of Psychotherapy. (Courtesy of Terry Marks-Tarlow)

methods, if clinical intuition proves to be the most authentic and healing form of contact, I wish to boldly assert that it may be unethical *not* to pay attention to intuition as a vital dimension of clinical education. The issue is of crucial significance because clinical intuition appears necessary to fully tune into the uniqueness of each person and moment. The topic has hitherto received little formal attention because of the invisibility of its workings, its association with unscientific processes, as well as the difficulty of measuring its action.

Fortunately, all of these conditions are now shifting due to the burgeoning field of interpersonal neurobiology (e.g., Badenoch, 2008; Cozolino, 2002, 2006; Hill, 2015; Schore, 2003a and b; Siegel, 1999). This field deepens understanding of how relational exchanges tune the bodies, minds, brains, and spirits of individuals. Exciting advances in brain imaging increase capacity to measure two mind/body/brains in real time interaction with one another (Dumas, et al., 2011; Babiloni & Astolfi, 2012). Much like clinical theory has moved form a one-person to a two-person psychology, clinical neurology is currently enjoying a similar revolution in perspective (Schilbach, et al., 2013). We rapidly approach the day when the holistic workings of clinical intuition can be measured in real-life contexts.

Within the enterprise of psychotherapy, clinical intuition appears to be a necessary, though not sufficient, condition for change. Intuitively attuned response provides the safety to release defensive stances in service of emotional risk-taking and novel exploration. The change extends in both directions. As our patients heal and grow through connecting to and trusting their own intuitive foundations, we therapists grow and heal alongside them. The personal and interpersonal growth involved keeps us fresh over many years, arising as a natural byproduct of deep and meaning-filled connection with other human beings.

In Pursuit of Novelty

All factors considered, clinical intuition is the primary mode of response in psychotherapy for multiple reasons. Because clinical work deals with high levels of complexity, it is important to consider the full context. It is better for ideas to emerge from observations and direct experience, rather than to walk into the room with a preset theory or set of ideas, in search of supporting evidence. Despite operating with ambiguous information, conditions of uncertainty, and emotional urgency, we must detect what is most salient in hopes of stimulating and exploring novel territory. This is a creative act, and with respect to novelty, the right brain is foundational.

Because division of labor across the two sides of the brain is quite ancient, an evolutionary perspective is informative. Brain lateralization extends back more than 500 million years to early vertebrate development, long before the appearance of warm-blooded animals (MacNeilage, Rogers, & Vallortigara, 2009; see Figure 2). In reptiles and birds, the left side of the brain became specialized for tasks that are routine, such as eating a meal or building a nest. By contrast, the right side of the brain became specialized for tasks that involve novelty, such as detecting danger or seeking shelter.

With respect to clinical concerns, this distinction between hemispheres based on novel versus routine concerns broadens our context for understanding why intuition is so important during psychotherapy. In order to effect deep change, both therapists and patients must be open to what is new, which is inherently the domain of the right brain. Whereas the left brain can help people analyze problems, spell out choices, or make conscious predictions about what might come next, only the right side carries the creative capacity for something entirely novel, spontaneous, or unpredictable to emerge. Herein

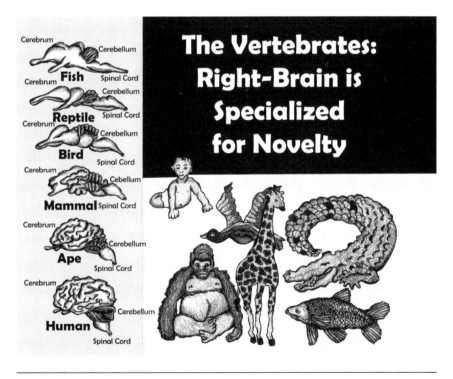

FIGURE 8.2
Right brain is specialized for novelty. (Courtesy of Terry Marks-Tarlow)

FIGURE 8.3
Safe surprises. (Courtesy of Terry Marks-Tarlow)

lies the importance of interpersonal creativity, including Philip Bromberg's (2003) concept of "safe surprises" (see Figure 3) by which the therapist/patient pair can break through old stale patterns to stumble upon something new.

Be Your Self

With his wry and characteristic humor, Oscar Wilde wryly suggests, "Be yourself: everyone else is already taken" (see Figure 4). Indeed, when we dedicate ourselves to discovering and expressing our true selves, we tap into our potential for unique self-expression. As mentioned, if we wish to be effective in helping others toward deep transformation, we must honor our own uniqueness as a precondition for honoring the uniqueness of patients. Herein lies the danger of charismatic teachers and manualized treatment approaches. When psychotherapists aspire to copy the style of someone they admire greatly, they run the risk of projecting a false self or of violating their own integrity—not in the sense of acting immorally, but more by failing to honor themselves fully,

FIGURE 8.4
Be yourself. (Courtesy of Terry Marks-Tarlow)

as an integral whole. Likewise, when therapists slavishly follow pre-scripted formulations such as appear in manuals, they run the risk of tuning out both self and other and rendering themselves robotic in the process.

Given that each practitioner's genetics, history, and developmental experience is highly individualized, it is no surprise that each clinician also sports his or her own highly individualized, intuitive repertoire. Whether emerging in the form of flashes, hunches, or gut feelings, radical uniqueness holds true both for ordinary levels of attuned response, as discussed so far, as well as for more extraordinary forms of knowing (Mayer, 2007). Here is a clinical tale of extraordinary knowing that appears in my book on clinical intuition (Marks-Tarlow, 2012a). A female psychoanalyst picked up a male patient in the waiting room. The man proceeded the therapist down a long hall toward the office and then turned the corner, out of sight. As he sat down in his usual chair, the patient let out a long sigh that sparked the therapist's sudden concern, "Uh-oh! I hope he doesn't need CPR." The therapist then rounded the corner, entered the office, and sat down in her usual chair. Immediately, the patient relayed a horrendous tale from the week before. He had been playing basketball with his best friend. Suddenly, the friend fell to the floor unconscious, needed CPR, but wound up dying shortly thereafter.

The psychoanalyst was astounded. In advance of the story, how did she pick up on such a central thread in the patient's narrative? While it may never be possible to know exactly how this happened, research from critical care nursing (Cioffi, 1997; Effkin, 2001; King & Appleton, 1997; Rew & Barron, 1987) reveals that clinical intuition is the most effective mode of response under conditions of emergency and high arousal.

It is my experience that most psychotherapists have at least one remarkable war story such as this one. Many of us keep these stories private, if not secret, for fear of judgment or disbelief. Nonetheless, the more seminal the moment, the higher the emotional intensity, and the greater our capacity to tune into invisible strings that continually interconnect the minds, brains, and bodies of people we love and care for. Dangerous, fearful circumstances appear to heighten receptivity, as communicated through body-to-body channels. In a carefully controlled study whose title begins, "Feeling the Future," social psychologist Daryl Bem (2011) claims to have proved something quite remarkable. With respect to survival-related cues, like sex and violence, our bodies implicitly may possess the precognitive capacity to tune into information that does not yet exist.

Extraordinary knowing aside, for one psychotherapist, an intuitive moment arrives as a flash of insight—an image or visual capacity to "see" an interpersonal pattern in a way that conveys new understanding or meaning. A clinical case described shortly involves a visual metaphor of this variety. For another practitioner, clinical intuition may take the form of a hunch, i.e., a cognitive sense of knowing that arrives fully fleshed-out, as if out of nowhere. As with the female psychoanalyst above, a sense of concern or certainty might surround information that is invisible to the naked eye or seemingly beyond the scope of one's reach.

At times, our intuitive repertoire appears not only to be unique, but also as downright idiosyncratic. One clinical psychologist I know is also a musician who reports hearing music as an ongoing, almost continuous backdrop during psychotherapy. Ominous music might signal a sense of emotional danger, while joyful tones appear to signal an intimate moment or recognition of progress achieved. No matter how individualized our intuitive repertoire might be, all clinicians share in common that intuition originates in the implicit, rather than explicit realm, as grounded in immediate, concrete sensory and emotional experiences as they inform higher symbolic capacities.

The Art of Psychotherapy

The art of psychotherapy has always stood in counterpoint to its science. Whereas the science remains behind the scenes in the form of theories, books, and formal lessons, the art shows up particularly in the timing of interventions. When to come forward with a remark and when to step back with respectful silence? Where do we place our attention and focus from among the myriad of possible aspects? Should we attend to the words a patient speaks? The way she slumps in the chair? Her breaks in eye contact? The flit of an association flooding our minds as we listen? The grumble in our stomachs when our bodies speak as loudly as our mouths? The art of psychotherapy is evident within all of these micro-second decisions about what is most salient and worthy of attention. To wade through a mountain of details is to sculpt a response. By whittling through the mounds of possibilities, we remain ever in search of truth, beauty, and even moral goodness in relational patterns.

Psychotherapy has been likened to musical or theater improvisation (e.g., Ringstrom, 2001), by others to a dance in the unconscious (e.g., Knafo, 2012), and still others to poetry in motion (e.g., Kurtz, 1989). Both art and psychotherapy revolve around making meaning. Dissanayake (2000) views art as an act of intimacy that begins in mother and child interactions. Over the course of human history art making comes from and creates emotional responses in the maker. Therapeutic art is a form of elaboration. Meaning is both found and made through physical means, hands on involvement, and cognitive operations. The function of the arts is to "make the ordinary special" as an effort to organize emotional, behavioral, and cognitive responses to experience (Carmic, 2007). One way we make the ordinary special in clinical work is by weaving a narrative that helps to mythologize the journeys of our patients.

Artistic process is a way of knowing through imagery and metaphor. Therapists actively create unique metaphors using empathy and mental models as we weave our narratives. Whether originating out of empathic attunement in the therapist or out of the safety to bring form to otherwise wordless realms, metaphors offer new possibilities for client and therapist to consider (Marks-Tarlow, 2008a, 2012a, 2014a; Sfregola, 2013).

As a case example of the power of metaphor, not just to illustrate, but also to heal, The Wild Woman depicted in Figure 5 arose spontaneously as a visual metaphor during a psychotherapy session (Marks-Tarlow, 2008a). The patient, previously given the pseudonym Charlotte, had a narcissistic mother and suffered from fibromyalgia. This left Charlotte feeling trapped—both in her own

FIGURE 8.5
The Wild Woman. (Courtesy of Terry Marks-Tarlow)

body and as well as in her mother's psyche. On the day when the Wild Woman emerged as a symbol, we were discussing the problem of Charlotte's stifled vitality and creativity, unable to find outer expression.

When the image of this fairy-like creature first arose, all the Wild Woman could do was to hold onto the bars of her cage, peer outside, and feel the despair of entrapment. This image, as later drawn by her therapist, illustrates nonverbally how stuck Charlotte felt by the appearance of things, at the front of the cage. The viewer can also see how the Wild Woman was riveted to looking outwards, as she longed for freedom.

In the months that ensued, Charlotte and I returned to this image over and over again. As we did so, the image itself began to morph. By working with its content and themes repeatedly, Charlotte could utilize the visual metaphor productively. Then one day, in a sudden and unexpected act of imagination, the Wild Woman found a way out of her imprisoned state of mind/body/spirit. Instead of remaining riveted to the bars at the front of the cage, the Wild Woman shifted her gaze, turned around, and walked instead toward the back of the cage. Here she discovered an open door, which held no lock and had always been open.

Simply by turning toward her back body, which in Yoga lore represents the unconscious, Charlotte could consider the cage from all angles. This more complex, higher dimensional view represented a path toward freedom. Through the transformative power of imagery, Charlotte discovered that the Wild Woman's imprisonment had been but illusion born of a limited perspective. As she and I continued to work with the image, the Wild Woman slowly emerged from her cage, timidly at first. But eventually, the Wild Woman opened her wings and took flight.

I was inspired to draw the image of the Wild Woman after this sequence had fully manifested. Charlotte loved the drawing, which now hangs in her house. In the decade or more since, I have found that many other people, especially women, feel intuitively drawn to the image, expressing how it moves them. One had recovered from brain cancer, another from sexual abuse, and a third from domestic violence. I am convinced that the entire clinical story vibrates and emanates from the image.

The case of Charlotte illustrates Daniel Stern's (1985) claim that the key challenge in psychotherapy is to find the central metaphor that captures the whole of things. This is the centerpiece of the work; from there the rest will flow. The case of Charlotte also illustrates a key ingredient of imagination as it manifests through metaphor: the very same image that initially illustrates the problem often later serves to illuminate the solution. This dynamic state of affairs attests to the healing power of spontaneous imagery.

Play therapists are well aware of the intrinsic, healing power of emergent symbols. Often, they feel little need to interpret or even translate the play process into words. Instead, their mission is to follow a child's lead in representing and working with stuck emotional places though the play of imagination.

A common goal of psychotherapy is a creative one: to assist a client to make new choices and changes which are adaptive and enriching. Both in the production of central metaphors and in how they infuse the body and direction in life, creative process is inherent in psychotherapy. It involves the play of innovation and adaptability on the part of the therapist and patient alike. It involves how the work becomes tailored to each unique dyad. The therapist uses metaphor and imagination like "a painter uses a palette, to create some-

thing that is both unique from, and similar to, all of his/her other paintings"
(Sfregola, 2013, p. 12).

The Importance of Imagination

Humans are genetically linked to the rest of nature to a surprising degree: we
share 18 percent of our genes with baker's yeast, 47 percent with a fruit fly,
and 90 percent with a chimpanzee (Zimmer, 2013). One by one, all scientific
attempts to divide *Homo sapiens* from our animal relatives have failed. Candidate distinctions include: tool use, language, grammar, symbolic thought,
problem-solving, self-awareness, and even an understanding of death. Fuzzy
boundaries separate humans from other animals in all respects. Nonetheless,
in a less formal way, the breadth and depth of the human imagination does
represent the pinnacle of evolutionary complexity. Through inner channels of
re-presentation, humans see deeply through the eyes of others, travel extensively back into the past, are able to anticipate long-term future consequences,
plus visit entirely imaginary places. A few theorists, including Arnold Modell
(2003) and this author (Marks-Tarlow, 2012a, 2014a) highlight the central role
that imagination plays during healing and trauma resolution within psychotherapy, a topic that has been largely underemphasized.

In a primitive way, imagination is wired into the body of even the most
elementary creature. Here it exists in the forms of intentionality and anticipation (Brentano, 1874/1995; Freeman, 1999), which hold even at the level of a
single cell operating well beneath the threshold of consciousness. Freeman's
lab studied the olfactory lobe of rabbits and found that previous exposure to a
particular smell changes how single cells respond to re-exposure to the same
stimulus, but only if the stimulus carries meaning to the animal. At its most
primitive level, organisms are forward-looking creatures who are moved by
anticipating the future.

From the perspective of neurobiology, we now know that the same brain
circuitry that underlies perception in the present moment also underlies imagination, including the capacity to project ourselves into the future (Addis,
Wong, & Schacter, 2007). At the global level of the whole person, the capacity
to envision a future that is different from the past is the essence of resilience
and a key ingredient that differentiates healthy from traumatic response to
challenging life events.

Although not the typical perspective, many psychological symptoms can
be interpreted as deficits in imagination (Marks-Tarlow, 2012a; 2014a). Depression represents an underactive imagination that is inhibited and unable to
conceive of an open future that is brighter than the bleak, closed sense of the

present. Anxiety represents an overactive imagination borne of a defensive and fixed gaze toward the future. Instead of relaxing into self-trust that surrounds inevitable uncertainties and ambiguities of life, people with anxiety disorders seize upon the imagination as an attempted protection against the unknown.

As psychotherapists, imaginative capacities that emerge from intuitive foundations form a critical part of our clinical repertoire (Marks-Tarlow, 2012a, 2014a; 2014b). Imagination is at the foundation of empathy, which according to Decety (Decety & Ickes, 2009) has two separate aspects: one inborn and affective, the other later developing and cognitive. The affective dimension of empathy involves emotional resonance. When we see a person in distress, it is natural to feel a bit of distress ourselves. This is why babies so easily cry when they hear another baby cry. The cognitive dimension of empathy involves perceiving the world through another person's eyes. This skill of mental rotation is an act of imagination that develops fully around age four or five. As therapists, it is the cognitive side of empathy that protects us from compassion fatigue and caregiver burnout. Through imagination, not only do we perceive where another person stands, but we also perceive where we stand in relation to the other, which includes all the differences between self and other.

As psychotherapists, along with empathy, we employ imagination as a vehicle for traveling beyond the present moment. For example, in response to a depressed patient's hopelessness, the therapist's capacity to imagine an open and different future for that person is an important service. By holding hope in the face of another's hopelessness, we allow patients to "lean into" our open perspectives until enough support, insight, and wisdom becomes internalized and supported. These are but two of many ways the psychotherapist's imagination serves to interactively regulate.

That the same brain circuitry underlies memory, ongoing experience, and imagination makes sense evolutionarily. The brain is designed to look forward. Ironically, the function of memory appears less to remember the past so much as to prepare us for the future (Klein, 2013). Effective psychotherapy takes imagination, which is the highest symbolic realm of a forward-looking arc that helps to organize our minds, bodies, and relationships. Every time a therapist plays creatively through the art of practice, he or she strengthens a muscle that is critical in many respects. A therapist's creativity is intrinsically healing, not just to ourselves, but also to our patients.

A Play Model of Healing and Growth

Creativity emerges developmentally and evolutionarily through play. As emphasized by Panksepp (see Chapter 12, this volume; 1998, 2012), PLAY is one of seven emotional/motivational circuits Panksepp identifies that is shared by all social mammals. Because play is essential to socialization, critical windows exist for the rough-and-tumble variety, prompting groups of youngsters to romp, roam, and wrestle together. Play assures the formation of peer bonds and social hierarchies. Play also affords opportunities to practice skills that are essential for adult life, like running, jumping, climbing, and fighting (Pellis & Pellis, 2010).

In humans, rupture and repair has been identified as the cornerstone for building trust (e.g., Safran, Muran, & Eubanks-Carter, 2011). Researchers (Bekoff, 2004; Bekoff & Pierce, 2009) have even identified a rupture and repair sequence during animal play, which they speculate indicates the evolutionary origins of morality. Rupture and repair enters into canine play as follows in the wild. A play bow (high rump, low head and forepaws) initiates an invitation to play. If an animal plays too hard by using excessive biting or other forms of aggression, all play will stop. The offender must then "apologize," by again adopting the play bow. Only then can play resume. If this sequence happens too often without proper curbs to the aggression, eventually the offender will be expelled from the pack. Because a lone canine is much more likely to die in the wild, play among animals is indeed serious business.

In human children, play is central to growth and general health, with its critical window extending well beyond early childhood, right into adulthood. Play is often considered the "work" of childhood, as babies and toddlers practice adult roles and rules, learn to take risks and to tolerate pain, and so expand the range of affect tolerance (Davies, 1997; Denzin, 2005; Garvey, 1977; Henricks, 2006; Nicolopoulou, 2005; Smilansky, 1990; Sutton-Smith, 1979, 1997). Unlike other mammals, fantasy, symbolic, and imaginative play adds to the human repertoire (Connolly & Doyle, 1984; Singer & Singer, 1990). Through the free play of imagination (see Figure 7), children explore social roles and rules from the inside-out. Through fantasy play, I have speculated that first children become oriented in social space, in such a way that equips them later to navigate their social worlds according to inner dictates and intuitive faculties versus outside pressures and external authorities (Marks-Tarlow, 2012a, 2012b).

It appears that play represents the cutting edge of cognitive, emotional, social, and behavioral growth in all animals. Within psychotherapy, a playful attitude, both on the part of therapist and patient, affords the positive spectrum of feelings (see Figure 8), as well as the motivation, energy, and curiosity to expand and grow, conditions that hold no matter how serious the explicit content. A trauma model of psychotherapy upholds rupture and repair as the

FIGURE 8.6
Free play. (Courtesy of Terry Marks-Tarlow)

cornerstone of relational work, by providing corrective emotional experiences, instilling trust and new expectations plus a sense of resiliency surrounding ties to others. Indeed, no therapist is perfect, and misattuned responses are inevitable. As I understand the process, trauma resolution and memory reconsolidation occur through rupture and repair, which brings the therapeutic dyad back to homeostatic balance. Then, from the solid foundation of mutual trust, it becomes possible to risk growth and experiment with novelty, and this occurs primarily through mutual play as intuitively guided.

The importance of play to psychotherapy has been emphasized by a few clinical theorists (e.g., Meares, 2005; Winnicott, 1971). Generally however, both play and imagination remain underemphasized factors. Perhaps life-and-death concerns cause clinical work to feel like serious business. But at implicit levels of social exchange, I suggest that play universally constitutes the deep structure of open-ended psychotherapy with hide-and-seek the prototypical game of psychotherapy (Marks-Tarlow, 2012a, 2012b, 2015). Patients hide from therapists, sometimes wittingly through lying or omissions, often unwittingly through shame and defenses against intimacy.

FIGURE 8.7
Glee! (Courtesy of Terry Marks-Tarlow)

Patients also hide from themselves, through self-deception, denial, and other internal defenses. Therapists hide from patients as well, and we all have blind spots and dissociative gaps that cause us to hide from ourselves. As a result, these implicit dynamics can get quite complicated and multilayered, with rules and games that morph along with shifting emotional stakes. The play of psychotherapy sets the timing for emotional revelation, while establishing rhythms of engagement and disengagement that operate quite independent of any explicit content.

Playful exchanges often take the form of humor. The dark side of humor has been long recognized (Kubie, 1971). Especially in the form of sarcasm, humor during psychotherapy holds great potential to belittle, shame, or serve as a defense against intimacy. Yet, its positive uses have also been well-documented (e.g., Marks-Tarlow, 2012a; Sands, 1984; Saper, 1988). Humor can serve as social glue, by signaling bids for contact and providing running commentary on the nature of the therapeutic bond. Humor is just one arena where each therapist playfully and often unwittingly inserts his or her idiosyncratic style of creativity.

Integrating Personal Idiosyncrasies

As a clinical psychologist, author, editor, librettist, curator, and artist (Marks-Tarlow, 2013; Marks-Tarlow & McCrory, 2014, 2015), one crucial way I tap into my own uniqueness is through illustrating clinical concepts (see all the Figures in this chapter). Throughout my early life I wrestled heavily with my own creativity. I loved to draw, yet didn't consider myself talented enough to tack on creativity as part of my identity, much less imagine myself to be an artist. Happily, after leaving art behind in my youth, I circled back round to it by necessity after becoming fascinated with nonlinear science, in particular chaos theory, complexity theory, and fractal geometry (Marks-Tarlow, 2008a, 2008b). I became transfixed with applying these visual areas of science and math to clinical concepts. Yet no images existed for what I needed, so I started producing them for myself.

The more I created my own drawings, the more I appreciated and even cherished my imagination. I realized the value of my art was not in some egoistic display of technical skill or burst of prodigious talent. Instead, I started to conceive of my drawings as a special form of communication—what Allan Schore might call "right-brain to right-brain" communication. During the UCLA conference giving rise to this book, Bessel van der Kolk challenged the scientific validity of this notion of right-brain to right-brain communication. While its empirical validation may remain controversial, I find that this concept invaluable at the level of metaphor.

In one way, my drawings seem to function like dreams, which also are right-lateralized (Scola, 2011). Alongside drawing images produced by patients, I have also drawn my own dreams. A significant one from childhood appears in Figure 10. I dreamt that the Statue of Liberty was a monster-like figure tramping from New York City across state lines toward my home in New Jersey in order to "get" me. I return to this dream again and again in order to milk new meaning. At times I have viewed the statue as a threatening, bivalent symbol of my mother, my freedom, as well as my own creativity.

Much the way dreams do, visual images lie close to primitive realms of the unconscious. They often correspond to early developmental periods as well as pre-verbal self-states. They are powerful partly because visual representations and other products of imagination bypass the explicit realm of words. Images are experience-near. They touch upon real perception rather than abstract thought. Partly for this reason, images travel straight to the heart, while creativity, intuition, and play supply invaluable coins to the emotional currency of the therapeutic alliance.

FIGURE 8.8
Liberty in hand. (Courtesy of Terry Marks-Tarlow)

References

Addis, D. & Wong, A., Schacter D. (2007). Remembering the past and imagining the future: Common and distinct neural substrates during event construction and elaboration. *Neuropsychologia, 45*(7), 1363–1377.

Babiloni, F. & Astolfi, L. (2012). Social neuroscience and hyperscanning techniques: Past, present and future. *Neuroscience & Biobehavioral Reviews, 44,* 76–93.

Badenoch, B. (2008). *Being a brain-wise therapist: A practical guide to interpersonal neurobiology.* New York: W. W. Norton & Company.

Beebe, B., Jaffe, J., Markese, S., Buck, K., Chen, H., Cohen, P., Bahrick, L., Andres, H., & Feldstein, S. (2010). The origins of 12-month attachment: A microanalysis of 4-month mother-infant interaction. *Attachment & Human Development, 12*(1–2), 3–141.

Beebe, B., Lachmann, F., Markese, S., & Bahrick, L. (2012). On the origins of disorganized attachment and internal working models: Paper I. A dyadic systems approach, *Psychoanalytic Dialogues, 22*(2), 253–272.

Bekoff, M. (2004). Wild justice and fair play: Cooperation, forgiveness, and morality in animals. *Biology and Philosophy, 19*(4), 489–520.

Bekoff, M. & Pierce, J. (2009). *Wild justice: The moral life of animals.* Chicago, Ill: University of Chicago Press.

Bem, D. (2011). Feeling the future: Experimental evidence for anomalous retroactive influences on cognition and affect. *Journal of Personality and Social Psychology, 100*(3), 407–425.

Boston Change Process Study Group (2008). Forms of relational meaning: Issues in the relations between the implicit and reflective-verbal domains. *Psychoanalytic Dialogues, 18,* 125–148.

Bowlby, J. (1969). *Attachment: Attachment and Loss* (Vol. 1). New York: Basic Books.

Bowlby, J. (1973). *Separation: Anxiety & Anger.* Attachment and Loss (vol. 2); (International psycho-analytical library no. 95). London: Hogarth Press.

Brentano, F. (1874/1995). *Psychology from an empirical standpoint.* Originally published in 1874; English edition edited by L. McAlister, London: Routledge and Kegan Paul 1973; reprinted with an introduction by Peter Simons, London: Routledge 1995.

Bromberg, P. M. (2003). Something wicked this way comes: Where psychoanalysis, cognitive science, and neuroscience overlap. In Bromberg, P. M. *Awakening the Dreamer: Clinical Journeys* (pp. 174–202).Mahwah, NJ: The Analytic Press.

Carmic, P. M. (2007). More than words: Bringing the arts into clinical psychology training. In Serlin, I. A , Sonke-Henderson, J., Brandman, R., & Graham-Pole, J. (Eds.). *Whole Person Healthcare* (Vol. 3.) *The arts and health* (pp. 259–282). San Francisco: Union Street Health Associates Press.

Cioffi, J. (1997). Heuristics, servants to intuition, in clinical decision-making. *Journal of Advanced Nursing, 26*(1), 203–208.

Claxton, G. (1997). *Hare brain, tortoise mind: How intelligence increases when you think less.* New York: Ecco Press.

Connolly, J. and Doyle, A. (1984). Relation of social fantasy play to social competence in preschoolers. *Developmental Psychology, 20*(5), 797–806.

Cozolino, L. (2002). *The neuroscience of psychotherapy: Building and rebuilding the human brain.* New York: W. W. Norton & Company.

Cozolino, L. (2006). *The neuroscience of human relationships: Attachment and the developing social brain.* New York: W. W. Norton & Company.

Csíkszentmihályi, M. (1990). *Flow: The psychology of optimal experience.* New York: Harper & Row.

Csíkszentmihályi, M. (1996). *Creativity: Flow and the psychology of discovery and invention.* New York: HarperCollins.

Davies, B. (1997). The construction of gendered identity through play. In Davies, B. & Corson, D. (Eds.). *Encyclopedia of language and education: Oral discourse and education* (Vol. 3) (pp. 116–124). Dordrecht, The Netherlands: Kluwer Academic Publishers.

De Botton, A. & Armstrong, J. (2013). *Art as therapy.* New York: Phaidon Press Limited.

Decety, J. & Ickes, W. (2009). *The social neuroscience of empathy.* Cambridge, MA: MIT Press

Denzin, N. (2005). Play, games and interaction: The contexts of childhood socialization. *Sociological Quarterly, 16*(4), 458–478.

Dissanayake, E. (2000), *Art and intimacy: How the arts began.* Seattle: University of Washington Press.

Dumas, G., Lachat, F., Martinerie, J., Nadel, J., & George, N. (2011). From social behaviour to brain synchronization: Review and perspectives in hyperscanning. *IRBM, 32,* 48–53.

Effkin, J. (2001). Informational basis for expert intuition. *Journal of Advanced Nursing, 34*(2), 246–255.

Elkind, D. (2007). *The power of play: How spontaneous, imaginative activities lead to happier, healthier children.* Cambridge, MA: Da Capo Press.

Fonagy, P., Gergely, G., Jurist, E., & Target, M. (2004). *Affect regulation, mentalization, and the development of the self.* London: Karnac Books.

Freeman, W. (1999). Consciousness, intentionality, and causality. *Journal of Consciousness Studies, 6,* 143–172.

Garvey, C. (1977). *Play.* Cambridge, MA: Harvard University Press.

Gazzaniga, M. (2005). Forty-five years of split-brain research and still going strong. *Nature Reviews Neuroscience 6,* 653–659.

Geller, S. & Greenberg, L. (2002). Therapeutic presence: Therapists' experience of presence in the psychotherapy encounter. *Person Centered and Experiential Psychotherapies, 1,* 71–86.

Henricks, T. (2006). *Play reconsidered: Sociological perspectives on human expression.* Chicago, IL: University of Illinois Press.

Hill, D. (2015). *Affect regulation theory: A clinical model.* New York, NY: W.W. Norton & Company.

Huizinga, J. (1949). *Homo ludens: a study of the play-element in culture* (F. F. C. Hull, Trans.). London: Routledge & Kegan Paul.

Knafo, D. (2012). *Dancing with the unconscious: The art of psychoanalysis and the psychoanalysis of art.* London, UK: Routledge.

King, L., & Appleton, J. V. (1997). Intuition: A critical review of the research and rhetoric. *Journal of Advanced Nursing, 26,* 194–202.

Klein, S. (2013). The temporal orientation of memory: It's time for a change of direction. *Journal of Applied Research in Memory and Cognition, 2,* 222–234.

Kluckholm, C. & Murray, H. (1953). *Personality in nature, culture, and society.* New York: Alfred A. Knopf.

Kubie, L. (1971). The destructive potential of humor in psychotherapy. *The American Journal of Psychiatry, 127,* 861–866.

Kurtz, S. (1989). *The art of unknowing: Dimensions of openness in analytic therapy.* Northvale, NJ: Jason Aronson.

Lane, R., Ryan, L., Nadel, L., & Greenberg, L. (2015). Memory reconsolidation, emotional arousal, and the process of change in psychotherapy: New insights from brain science. *Behavioral and Brain Sciences, 38,* e1–19.

Lewis, P. (1986). The somatic countertransference. Chicago: American Dance Therapy Association Conference.

Lyons-Ruth, K. (1998). Implicit relational knowing: Its role in development and psychoanalytic treatment. *Infant Mental Health Journal, 19*(3), 282–289.

MacNeilage, P., Rogers, L., & Vallortigara, G. (2009). Origins of the left and right brain. *Scientific American, 301*(1), 60–67.

Marks-Tarlow, T. (2008a). *Psyche's veil: Psychotherapy, fractals and complexity.* London, UK: Routledge.

Marks-Tarlow, T. (2008b). Alan Turing meets the Sphinx: Some new and old riddles, *Chaos and Complexity Letters, 3*(1), 83-95.

Marks-Tarlow, T. (2012a). *Clinical Intuition in psychotherapy: The neurobiology of embodied response.* New York: W. W. Norton & Company

Marks-Tarlow, T. (2012b). The play of psychotherapy. *American Journal of Play, 4*(3), 352–377.

Marks-Tarlow, T. (2013). *Mirrors of the mind: The psychotherapist as artist.* Los Angeles: Los Angeles County Psychological Association.

Marks-Tarlow, T. (2014a). *Awakening clinical intuition: An experiential workbook.* New York: W. W. Norton & Company.

Marks-Tarlow, T. (2014b). The interpersonal neurobiology of clinical intuition. *Smith College Studies in Social Work, 84,* 219-234.

Marks-Tarlow, T. (2015). Games therapists play: Hide and seek in the therapeutic dialogue. In Johnson, J., Eberle, S. Hendricks, T., & Kuschner, D. (Eds.). *Handbook of the Study of Play* (Vol. 2) (pp. 271-286). New York, NY: Rowman & Littlefield.

Marks-Tarlow, T. & McCrory, P. (2014). *Mirrors of the mind 2: The psychotherapist as artist.* Los Angeles: Los Angeles Psychological Association.

Marks-Tarlow, T. & McCrory, P. (2015). *Mirrors of the mind 3: The psychotherapist as artist.* Los Angeles: Los Angeles Psychological Association.

Mayer, E. (2007). *Extraordinary knowing: Science, skepticism, and the inexplicable powers of the human mind.* New York: Bantam.

Meares, R. (2005). *The metaphor of play: Origin and breakdown of personal being.* London: Routledge.

Messer, S. (2002). Let's face facts: Common factors are more potent than specific therapy ingredients. *American Psychologist, 9*(1), 21–25.

McGilchrist, I. (2009). *The master and his emissary: The divided brain and the making of the Western world.* Yale University Press.

Modell, A. (2003). *Imagination and the meaningful brain.* Cambridge, MA: MIT Press.

Nicolopoulou, A. (2005). Play and narrative in the process of development: Commonalities, differences, and interrelations, *Cognitive Development, 20,* 495–502.

Panksepp, J. (1998). *Affective neuroscience: The foundations of human and animal emotions.* New York: Oxford University Press.

Panksepp, J. (2012). *The archeology of mind: Neuroevolutionary origins of human emotions.* New York: W. W. Norton & Company.

Pellis, S. & Pellis., V. (2010). *The playful brain: Venturing to the limits of neuroscience.* Oxford, UK: Oneworld Publications.

Petrucelli, J. (Ed.) (2010). *Knowing, not-knowing and sort-of-knowing: Psychoanalysis and the experience of uncertainty.* London, UK: Routledge.

Rew, L., & Barron, E. (1987). Intuition: A neglected hallmark of nursing knowledge. *Advances in Nursing Science, 10*(1), 49–62.

Ringstrom, P. (2001). Cultivating the improvisational in psychoanalytic treatment. *Psychoanalytic Dialogues, 11*(5), 727–754.

Safran, J., Muran, J., & Eubanks-Carter, C. (2011). Repairing alliance ruptures. *Psychotherapy, 48*(1), 80–87.

Sands, S. (1984). The use of humor in psychotherapy, *Psychoanalytic Review, 71,* 441–480.

Saper, B. (1988). Humor in psychiatric healing, *Psychiatric Quarterly, 59*(4), 306–319.

Schore, A. N. (2003a). *Affect dysregulation and disorders of the self.* New York: W. W. Norton & Company.

Schore, A. N. (2003b). *Affect regulation and the repair of the self.* New York: W. W. Norton & Company.

Schore, A. N. (2010). The right-brain implicit self: A central mechanism of the psychotherapy change process. In (J. Petrucelli, Ed.) *Knowing, not-knowing and sort of knowing: Psychoanalysis and the experience of uncertainty* (pp. 177–202). London: Karnac.

Schore, A. N. (2011). The right brain implicit self lies at the core of psychoanalytic psychotherapy. *Psychoanalytic Dialogues, 21,* 75–100.

Schore, A. N. (2012). *The science of the art of psychotherapy.* New York: W. W. Norton & Company.

Schilbach, L., Timmermans, B., Reddy, V., Costall, A., Bente, G., Schlicht, T., & Vogeley, K. (2013). Toward a second-person neuroscience. *Behavioral and Brain Sciences, 36*(4), 393–414.

Scola, D. (2011). The hemispheric specialization of the human brain and its application to psychoanalytic priciples. *Jefferson Journal of Psychiatry, 2,* 2-11.

Seligman, S. (2012). The baby out of the bathwater: Microseconds, psychic structure, and psychotherapy. *Psychoanalytic Dialogues, 22,* 499–509.

Sfregola, E. (2013). Creativity in the process of psychotherapy and psychoanalysis. *San Diego Psychologist, 28*(4) 12–14.

Siegel, D. (1999). *The developing mind.* New York: The Guilford Press.

Smilansky, S. (1990). Sociodramatic play: Its relevance to behavior and achievement in school. In Klugman, E. & Smilansky, S. (Eds.). *Children's play and learning* (pp. 18–42). New York: Teachers College Press.

Singer, D. & Singer, J. (1990). *The house of make-believe: Children's play and the developing imagination.* Cambridge, MA: Harvard University Press.

Stern, D. (1985). *The interpersonal world of the infant.* New York: Basic Books.

Stern, D. (2004). *The present moment in psychotherapy and everyday life.* New York: W. W. Norton & Company.

Sutton-Smith, B. (1979) (Ed.). *Play and learning.* New York: Gardner Press.

Sutton-Smith, B. (1997). *The ambiguity of play.* Cambridge, MA: Harvard University Press.

Weaver, I., Cervoni N., Champagne, F., D'Alessio A., Sharma, S., Seckl, J., Dymov, S., Szyf, M., & Meaney, M. (2004). Epigenetic programming by maternal behavior. *Nature Neuroscience, 7,* 847–854.

Winnicott, D. W. (1971). *Playing & reality.* New York: Tavistock/Routledge.

Zimmer, C. (2013). Genes are us. And them. *National Geographic,* March 2017, *http://ngm.nationalgeographic.com/2013/07/125-explore/shared-genes.* Downloaded June 6, 2015.

9

Trauma, Attachment, and Creativity

Paula Thomson

"The man who arrives at the doors of artistic creation with none of the madness of the Muses would be convinced that technical ability alone was enough to make art . . . what that man creates by means of reason will pale before the art of inspired beings."
—Plato, C.388BC/1972, p. 32.

ACCORDING TO ANCIENT Greek mythology, one (or several) of the nine muses would visit and inspire a select group of artists by allowing them access to the universal memories preserved by their mother, Mnemosyne (Hamilton, 1969; Murray, 1994). Despite this gift of inspiration, the intensity of these memories often induced transient states of madness in the artists. In order to escape these painful memories, they were allowed to drink from the River Lethe to insure forgetfulness and end suffering. But, with the loss of memory, they became ghostlike shadows of themselves. They existed as if in a dream. When the artists could no longer bear this shadowy existence and decided to re-engage with the muses, all the pain from the past came flooding back. Even though the artists' hearts were full of sorrow and grief the muses also brought joy to them. While sharing their songs and dances, the artists were able to help ease the suffering of others who indirectly benefited from the visitation of the muses. As suggested by Plato, this was the process that ensured trans-formational creative works. Today, many artists continue to claim that the creative process resembles experiences with the muses; it is often a transfor-

FIGURE 9.1
"Communal Celebration of Music." (Photo by Chuck Valerio: Permission granted from California State University, Northridge; Guitar Player: Evan Rosenblatt)

mational experience that expands meaningful relationships between self and others (Nelson & Rawlings, 2009).

This ancient myth describes the transient states of creative madness; however, it also resembles a pattern that operates in individuals who relive unresolved traumatic memories. Traumatized individuals fluctuate between intense memories of past traumatic events and profound dreamlike depersonalized states. The description of being ghostlike shadows of themselves is now recognized in the *Diagnostic and Statistical Manual of Psychiatric Disorders, Fifth Edition* (DSM-5) as a dissociative symptom of posttraumatic stress disorder (PTSD) (APA, 2013). Like Mnemosyne, who is doomed to remember traumatic events until the world is brought into perfect order and harmony (Murray, 1994), individuals who remain in states of unresolved mourning must struggle with the disorganizing psychological and physiological effects of past memories until these memories are resolved and psychophysiological order is restored (Bailey, Moran, & Pederson, 2007; Stovall-McClough, & Cloitre, 2006).

Although Plato did not link trauma with creativity, when the muses visit traumatized artists, unresolved mourning may exacerbate their transient states of madness. The temporary joy while engaging in the arts may offer relief from suffering, but, like Mnemosyne, without the resolution of past trauma and loss, the disorganized psychophysiological states will intrude. Fluctuating between the shadowy realm of forgetting and vivid flashbacks of remembering is not only disorganizing but it may compromise the creative process. This chapter explores the relationship between trauma, attachment, and creativity, in particular the relationship in creative individuals. There are very few studies that have investigated attachment, trauma, and loss experiences in creative individuals (Kharkhurin, 2014) and this chapter addresses this deficit.

Creativity and the Educated Imagination

Creativity is defined as a syndrome or complex that involves novelty, process, and product (Sternberg, 2005). It can be witnessed in every stage of development and within every domain of creative expression, whether artistic or scientific (Runco, 2007). Creativity is also not exclusive to humans, as is evidenced by animal behavior such as mating dances, the ingenious problem solving solutions to obtain food, or the simple joy of play and exploration (Bailey, McDaniel, & Thomas, 2010; Kaufman & Kaufman, 2004). Although

FIGURE 9.2
"Tapping Joy." (Photo by Chuck Valerio: Permission granted by California State University, Northridge; Performers: Sara Adler and Angelica Abrahams)

creativity remains a distinct and independent function, it is also associated with intelligence, innovation, imagination, insight, and health (Runco, 2007). Ultimately, creative behavior indicates an increased capacity for resilience and adaptability (Bennett, 2009).

According to Northrup Frye (1963), regardless of dispositional creative ability, the imagination must be educated to nurture creativity. He claimed that an educated imagination involves the capacity to produce creative products and the ability to recognize and appreciate the created product. When creativity is distributed, collaboration with others, whether directly or indirectly, shapes new works that are inherently relational (Sawyer & DeZutter, 2009). The creative product must coexist between the creator and the witness, even if the witness is also the creator. Frye (1963) added that studying the imagination encourages tolerance for ambivalence and emotional intensity; "what produces the tolerance is the power of detachment in the imagination, where things are removed just out of reach of belief and action" (p. 32). Engaging in the imagination "stretches us vertically to the heights and depths of what the human psyche can conceive" (p. 42).

Imagination, especially when present in individuals with fantasy-prone traits, involves self-directed elaborations on imagined or real events (Bigelsen & Schupak, 2011; Dunn, Corn, & Morelock, 2004). Fantasy proneness provides an adaptive means of coping (Wilson & Barber, 1983; Waldo & Merritt, 2000), and can enhance creative capacity (Sànchez-Bernardos & Avia, 2004, 2006), athletic performance (Cumming & Hall, 2002; Shirazi, Dana, Jalili, & Behzadi, 2011; Taylor, Pham, Rivkin, & Armor, 1998), and facilitate intense absorption (Fuchs, Kumar, & Porter, 2007; Lack, Kumar, & Arevalo, 2003; Manmiller, Kumar, & Pekala, 2005). Imagination and fantasy proneness can also modulate depression, anxiety, posttraumatic stress (Rauschenberger & Lynn, 2002–2003), and shame (Schoenleber & Berenbaum, 2012). The role of imagination and fantasy, especially when it is educated, enhances psychological well-being. The educated imagination improves performance and augments coping strategies that promote adaptive resilience.

Trauma and the Traumatized Imagination

Unlike the educated imagination, a traumatized imagination is biased toward more negative imaginative activity, especially in dissociative individuals (Levin, Sirof, Simeon, & Guralnick, 2004). Becoming absorbed in alternative imaginative worlds is a common coping strategy to manage adverse childhood experiences such as sexual, physical, or emotional abuse (Rauschenberger & Lynn, 2002–2003). Because traumatic reminders can infiltrate cognitive processes, including the creative process, efforts to detach from these traumatic sensations and/or memories operate as distancing or avoidant strategies. When these coping strategies are operational in the creative process, either artists stop imaginative engagement (Myers, Fleming, Lancman, Perrine, & Lancman, 2013) or they get lost in elaborate fantasies that distance them from other relationships (Bigelsen & Schupak, 2011).

When fantasy proneness is persistent and intense, individuals are more vulnerable to increased distress. Because an excessive quantity of fantasizing interferes with actual relationships and daily endeavors, these individuals are at increased risk for intense shame-based experiences (Bigelsen & Schupak, 2011; Wilson & Barber, 1983). High fantasy proneness also exacerbates depression, anxiety, and posttraumatic stress (Lynn & Rhue, 1988; Sànchez-Bernardos & Avia, 2004; Waldo & Merritt, 2000). Research findings indicate that artists and performing artists not only manifest greater fantasy proneness, but they are also more dissociative (Chavez-Eakle, 2012; Thomson & Jaque, 2011b). When past trauma and loss remains unresolved artists endorse even greater fantasy and dissociative psychological processes (Thomson & Jaque, 2012a, 2012b).

Bessel van der Kolk (2014) claimed that traumatized individuals not only suffer mental disturbances but their bodies also manifest profound distress, such as chronic pain, fatigue, increased disease, and early mortality. He stated, "The body keeps the score." This reality is even more devastating for traumatized performing artists who rely on their bodies as creative instruments. No matter how many hours they train and how skilled they get, subtle, and sometimes not so subtle, traumatic symptoms may erupt unbidden. It is well known that performing artists may suffer stage fright that can be career ending (Langendorfer, Hodapp, Kreutz, & Bongard, 2006). They also are at increased risk for suffering toxic levels of internalized shame, especially because they must face public scrutiny (Budden, 2009; Dickerson, 2008; Dickerson, Gruenewald, & Kemeny, 2004; Gunnison, 1985; Thomson & Jaque, 2013). These career stressors are familiar in the performing arts (Barker, Soklaridis, Waters, Herr, & Cassiday, 2009); however, the complication of a traumatized imagination may exacerbate these stressors. Unresolved trauma affects the mind and the body; it affects the artist's imagination and their physical body. For example, artists with PTSD demonstrated more anxiety during the creative process (Thomson & Jaque, 2016a) and they had higher psychological states of shame, anxiety, depression, and dissociation (Thomson & Jaque, 2015a). They also had a higher frequency of family members with mental illness, more difficulty speaking about their trauma, more suicidal thoughts, and more childhood adversity and adult trauma. When compared to artists without

FIGURE 9.3
"Silent Guardian." (Photo by Lee Choo: Permission granted by California
State University, Northridge; Performers: Evan and Bethana Rosenblatt)

PTSD, artists with PTSD had greater fantasy proneness and they engaged in
more emotion-oriented coping when under stress (Thomson & Jaque, 2015a).
Emotion-oriented coping is the least adaptive compared to task-oriented
and avoidant-oriented coping strategies, primarily because it increases distress (Endler & Parker, 1990, 1994). This psychological profile may actually
increase psychological instability in artists with PTSD (Thomson & Jaque,
2015a). Consequently, artists with PTSD, a marker of unresolved trauma, may
have difficulty trusting their bodies and minds (their "creative instrument")
to perform with consistent reliability. Ultimately, no matter how much the
imagination has been educated, the traumatized imagination may compromise
creative performance and increase stress for artists with unresolved mourning.

Attachment, Unresolved Mourning, and Creativity

Attachment theory suggests that early experiences with primary caregivers
shape internal relational working models and establish organized strategies to
navigate stressful situations (Main, 2000). These working models are stored
at the implicit level of consciousness, and influence behaviors unconsciously
(Bowlby, 1988). When early attachment experiences are optimal, children are
able to explore their environment without excess anxiety because their care-

givers provide a safe haven that encourages confidence in self, others, and the world (Sroufe, Egeland, Carlson, & Collins, 2005). It has been speculated that optimal early family experiences, although complex, can promote creativity and creative achievement throughout the lifespan (Gute, Gute, Nakamura, & Csíkszentmihályi, 2008). However, sometimes attachment-related experiences, including experiencing traumatic events with primary caregivers and the loss of a significant loved one(s), are so dysregulating that exploration and a sense of safety are disrupted or lost (Hesse, Main, Abrams, & Rifkin, 2003). These states of mind and behavioral responses are inherently disorganizing and disorienting (Hesse & Main, 2000; Hesse & Main, 2006; Steele, 2003). Whether these early attachment experiences are secure or insecure, the patterns of coping tend to endure throughout life and influence attentional flexibility (Main, Hesse, & Kaplan, 2005) and emotional regulation (Creasey, 2002; Maier, Bernier, Pekrun, Zimmermann, Strasser, & Grossmann, 2005).

Assessing attachment states of mind can only be done through a semi-structured interview, the Adult Attachment Interview (AAI) (Main, Goldwyn, & Hesse, 2003). To date, self-report measurements do not capture these unconscious internal working models that operate outside of awareness (Jacobvitz, Curran, & Moller, 2002; Roisman, Holland, Fortuna, Fraley, Clausell, & Clarke, 2007). The AAI does not evaluate veridical truth (whether something happened or not), rather it assesses the state of mind of the speaker being interviewed. These states of mind are revealed in both the participant's capacity to collaboratively engage in the interview process and how they organize and narrate early attachment, traumatic, and loss experiences. These states of mind are strong predictors of parenting behaviors and the patterns of attachment transmitted to the offspring (Hesse & Main, 1999).

The detailed AAI scale coding analysis provides information about inferred childhood experiences with attachment figures such as the assessment of caregivers' loving, rejecting, involving/role reversing, pressure to achieve, neglecting, and unloving responses. The interview also reveals the participant's use of idealization, derogation, preoccupied anger, lack of memory, and passivity of mind. Each scale provides rich information about the speaker, and an overall classification can be derived to determine if the speaker's state of mind regarding attachment is secure or anxiously insecure. The participant can also be classified in one of three organized states of mind. If they are autonomous then it indicates that they are able to flexibly reflect on attachment experiences. They demonstrate an emotional balance coupled with a strong indication that they value attachment experiences. The two insecurely anxious classifications are dismissing (actively turning attention away from attachment-related experiences) or preoccupied (unable to disentangle from attachment-related thoughts). Both organized anxious states of mind are adaptive, but they are less resilient compared to the autonomous state of mind. When a participant is unresolved for past trauma or loss experiences, ruptures in the relational discourse manifest. These ruptures indicate that the participant's organized strategies collapse and become disorganized.

The AAI is the only measurement that can determine degree of resolution for all significant past traumatic and loss experiences. When assessing for unresolved trauma or loss, all microattentional lapses of monitoring are evaluated and all behavioral responses are incorporated into the assessment. For example, an unresolved speaker might shift from past to present tense, become absorbed by details of the event, have difficulty naming an event, or begin to speak in a eulogistic tone. Behaviors that indicate a lack of resolution include attempted suicide, avoidance strategies to escape memories, or high-risk self-injurious actions. There may be frequent lapses or one very brief but startling lapse in monitoring of reason and/or discourse. What makes them lapses is that they are not corrected or acknowledged (Main, Goldwyn, & Hesse, 2003). They indicate a dissociative fragmentation in a speaker's mind that might otherwise be coherent (Carlson, 1998; Ogawa, Sroufe, Weinfeld, Carlson, & Egeland, 1997).

Attachment security promotes active exploration, and exploration is a critical ingredient in the creative process. Studies from our laboratory suggest that artists demonstrate more secure autonomous states of mind when compared to nonclinical samples. A normal worldwide distribution of secure/autonomous individuals is approximately 55 percent (Bakermans-Kranenburg & van Ijzendoorn, 2009). Incredibly, in our study, 88 percent of the artists were classified as secure/autonomous (Thomson & Jaque, 2012a; 2012b). Because this study was not longitudinal it is difficult to determine whether a career in the arts enhances autonomous states of mind or whether these artists were more securely attached as infants. Attachment research suggests that security can be stable across significant portions of the lifespan and yet remain open to revision in light of experience (Waters, Merrick, Treboux, Crowell, & Albersheim, 2000).

Despite the high distribution of security in the artists, we also found a higher distribution of unresolved mourning compared to the general population. All but one artist had adverse trauma or loss experiences, 27.5 percent were classified with unresolved mourning, 36 percent met criteria for a dissociative disorder, and unresolved mourning was associated with pathological dissociative processing (Thomson & Jaque, 2012a). In a different study that examined actors compared to non-actors a similar pattern emerged (Thomson & Jaque, 2012b). The actor group also had significantly more individuals

FIGURE 9.4
"Exploring Connections." (Photo by Chuck Valerio: Permission granted by
California State University, Northridge; Performers: Dana Fukagawa and
Logan Schyvynck)

with secure autonomous states of mind but they also had more individuals
with unresolved mourning and elevated dissociation. These findings indicate
that they were unable to psychologically integrate past trauma and loss experiences. Compared to non-actors, they also had greater fantasy proneness,
which may have helped them manage the disorganized states of mind manifested in unresolved mourning.

Although not directly measured, the traumatized imagination may be manifested as unresolved states of mind identified in the AAI. To better understand
the unresolved mind, we conducted a third attachment study to investigate
the relationship between unresolved mourning, pathological dissociation, and
beliefs in the supernatural (i.e., paranormal experiences that include out-of-
body experiences, seeing and communicating with ghosts, telepathy). In this
study, the unresolved group had higher levels of dissociative processing and
endorsed more supernatural experiences (Thomson & Jaque, 2014). They
also had more inferred negative childhood experiences with parental figures.
Other studies demonstrated that individuals with unresolved mourning have
increased religious anxiety, greater belief in New Age supernatural/mysti-
cal spirituality (Granqvist, Hagekull, & Ivarsson, 2012), sudden conversions

FIGURE 9.5
"Lost and Found and Lost Again." (Photo by Lee Choo: Permission granted by California State University, Northridge; Performers: Elissa Brock, Cheyenne Spencer, Christian Vidaure)

(Granqvist & Kirkpatrick, 2004), increased experiences of personal contact with the dead (Granqvist, Ivarsson, Broberg, & Hagekull, 2007), and greater schizotypal personality disorder (Hancock & Tiliopoulos, 2010). Perhaps individuals who struggle with the disorganizing effects of unresolved mourning seek comfort from these anomalous experiences, or these anomalous experiences reflect their lack of internal psychological coherence.

The traumatized imagination may also reflect this pattern of supernatural beliefs, especially when considering that they are associated with individuals who are more creative (Gow, Lang, & Chant, 2004). These beliefs have been linked to more pathological dissociation (Klinger, Henning, & Janssen, 2009), fantasy proneness (Gow, et al., 2004; Irwin, 1990), and absorption (Gow, et al., 2004; Lynn & Rhue, 1988; Parra, 2006), and they are more frequent in childhood abuse survivors (Klinger, Henning, Janssen, 2009; Pekala, Angelini, & Kumar, 2001; Perkins & Allen, 2006). Although children tend to blur boundaries between reality and the paranormal (Irwin, 1990), abused children and children who experience violent loss of an attachment figure recount even more boundary blurring, supernatural belief systems, and a disrupted sense of self-continuity (Currier & Neimeyer, 2007; Lawrence, Edwards, Barraclough, Church, Hetherington, 1995). Supernatural belief systems may provide a sense of safety and control for these individuals (Lawrence, et al., 1995; Perkins & Allen, 2006); however, these coping strategies can also increase fragmentation and loss of a coherent sense of self (Sroufe, et al., 2005). In our study, pathological dissociation and supernatural beliefs were associated with unresolved mourning (Thomson & Jaque, 2014), a finding that may be related to the dysregulation experienced when the imagination is traumatized.

The studies from our laboratory indicated that artists had a higher distribution of unresolved mourning, but they also had a higher distribution of attachment security, autonomy, and attentional flexibility. The fact that the artists in our sample had "educated" imaginations may have allowed them to mindfully reflect on their past experiences. Perhaps their experience in the arts promoted self-reflection and awareness. It is noteworthy that all but one artist was exposed to a significant loss of a loved one and/or abuse by a caregiver. Even though 27.5 percent were unresolved, the greater majority of this group had an alternate classification of security. Although unproven, for these unresolved artists, their background of attachment security may have supported them during the education of their imaginations, or conversely, while being educated they acquired more autonomous states of mind.

Flow and Creativity

Creative individuals engage in the creative process because they enjoy and value it; it gives them meaning. Artists value intrinsic rather than achievement goals (Lacaille, Koestner, & Gaudreau, 2007). Aesthetic expression and enjoyment are particularly helpful to performing artists and these qualities enhance their intrinsic motivation. Further, harmonious passion, as opposed to obsessional passion, has been demonstrated as a performance augmenter. Harmonious passion supports increased mastery of goals, deliberate practice, and higher level performances; whereas, obsessional passion is associated with avoidance of goals and has a direct negative impact on performance (Bonneville-Roussy, Lavigne, & Vallerand, 2011). According to Mihályi Csíkszentmihályi (1990), these are essential ingredients necessary for flow experiences. Achieving optimal flow is considered a combination of personality traits and skill acquisition. Because all these variables are embedded in flow, it is considered a dispositional trait.

Flow is an excellent measure to determine artists' values and engagement in their particular artistic domain. Given the above findings regarding unresolved mourning and trauma, we wanted to understand the role flow played in these artists. The results were heartening. Flow was endorsed equally, regardless of adversity history, suggesting that artistic engagement can still be rewarding (Thomson & Jaque, 2016b). This result reinforces the theoretical foundation of

FIGURE 9.6

"Flamenco Passion." (Photo by Lee Choo: Permission granted by California State University, Northridge; Dancer: Jacqueline Eusanio)

positive psychology; by encouraging positive experiences such as flow, mental health is facilitated (Seligman, Steen, Park, & Peterson, 2005; Sheldon & King, 2001). Flow experiences are associated with reduced anxiety and pathological dissociation (Kirchner, Bloom, & Skutnick-Henley, 2008; Thomson & Jaque, 2011–2012; Thomson & Jaque, 2012c). As we age, the effects of high-quality flow in our daily lives facilitates high positive-affect arousal, decreases negative affect, and increases life satisfaction (Collins, Sarkisian, & Winner, 2009). Physiologically, flow is associated with decreased cardiac autonomic balance and regulation (Thomson & Jaque, 2011a). This finding is surprising since more autonomic regulation is usually related to better health and well-being (Berntson, Norman, Hawkley, & Cacioppi, 2008; Cacioppo, Tassinary, & Berntson, 2007; Porges, 2009). However, decreased autonomic regulation during flow experiences may suggest enhanced tolerance for physiological dynamic changes.

Neurobiologically, flow has been described as effortless attention. In a

FIGURE 9.7
"Quiet Beauty." (Photo by Chuck Valerio: Permission granted by California State University, Northridge; Performer: Tharini Shanmugarajah)

study by de Manzano (2010), flow was associated with lower thalamic gating thresholds, which means that there was an increase in thalamocortical information and decreased D2 receptor densities. Higher cortical activity was demonstrated in the frontoparietal regions, which might be related to high complexity during creative tasks. These response mechanisms during flow may explain the link between creativity and mental illness, and may shed light on the myth of the muses. Perhaps neuroscience is now illuminating what early philosophers such as Plato recognized.

Treatment Recommendations

Artists who enter treatment should be encouraged to participate in their preferred activities. Based on findings in our laboratory, traumatic events and childhood adversity experiences were similar among performing artists, athletes and healthy participants; however, athletes had less anxiety, shame and PTSD (Thomson & Jaque, 2015; Thomson & Jaque, 2016b). What is important to remember is that all were able to endorse high flow experiences, a variable that enhanced the quality of their lives (Thomson & Jaque, 2016b). Does engaging in art improve mood? Yes, participating in these activities does improve mood; it facilitates redirection from negative feelings and may serve as a cathartic function (De Petrillo & Winner, 2005). In a study on art-making, it was demonstrated that evoking positive emotions was more effective than venting, in short-term treatment (Dalenbroux, Goldstein, & Winner, 2008). This finding casts doubt on the assumption that artists improve their well being by expressing suffering. Rather the act of creative expression is related to flow experiences and it is the achievement of flow that enhances well being (Collins, et al., 2009; Csíkszentmihályi, 1990).

When looking at fantasy proneness, a variable that is regulating at moderate levels, performing artists had higher levels of fantasy. What is also important to note is that unresolved mourning and traumatic events predicted increased fantasy proneness. Perhaps engaging with the muses not only allows access to more memories of human suffering but more imaginative abilities to understand and express suffering. It suggests that the traumatized imagination may actually be serving to ease the suffering of individuals with PTSD and unresolved mourning. Increased mystical experiences and fantasy proneness are higher in performing artists, suggesting that the creative process may be helped by positive altered states of consciousness (Ayers, Beaton, & Hunt, 1999). Empirical studies have also demonstrated that these experiences are employed to ease symptoms of childhood sexual abuse (Perkins & Allen, 2006) and loss of perceived childhood control due to abuse (Watt, Watson, & Wilson, 2007).

Other complicating factors that must be considered when working with artists include financial limitations and lack of health insurance. Performing artists are incredibly vulnerable to physical injuries that are potentially career ending (Rickert, Barrett, & Ackermann, 2013, 2014a, 2014b), and their daily life is often unpredictable due to unexpected auditions, rehearsals, and performance opportunities. The psychological demands to maintain well-being are great, and if these artists are struggling to heal past traumatic wounds or attachment ruptures, their need for psychological healing is even greater. Adding to this list of difficulties, and based on clinical observation, many artists are sensitive to medication side effects and are often medication resistant. If medication is appropriate and they can tolerate it, then the lack of financial resources may compromise the maintenance of this treatment option.

Another complication is the fact that performing artists, in particular, actors, singers and dancers, have an enhanced ability to perceive internal

states in others. They have greater theory of mind capacity, while not necessarily having greater empathy (Goldstein & Winner, 2010–2011; Goldstein,
Wu, & Winner, 2009–2010; Nettle, 2006). Children begin this awareness that
others have different minds from theirs around the age of four years (Chaplin & Norton, 2014). Prior to four years of age they were eager to dance and
sing, but as they develop they gradually become self-conscious and hesitant.
Educationally and clinically, we need to enhance tolerance of public scrutiny.
This may explain why the performing artists in our sample had significantly
higher levels of internalized toxic shame (Thomson & Jaque, 2013). Given
this enhanced capacity, it is vital to support the emotional and psychological
needs of students during their creative training years. To become a skilled
professional performing artist, vast amounts of time and financial investment
are needed. It is essential to assist these artists so that they can move into
a professional career, whether it is performance or non-performance based
(Nagel, 2009).

Lastly, to gain the trust of these artists, it is necessary that clinicians have

FIGURE 9.8
"Interdependence." (Photo by Christopher Haggard: Permission granted
by California State University, Northridge; Performer: Lilia Kibarska and
Jacob "Kujo" Lyons)

some working understanding about the performance demands placed on them, and specifically, to understand the demands of each art domain. Dancers, singers, musicians, actors, comedians, etc. share similar career conditions, but they also have uniquely different stressors and needs (Hamilton & Robson, 2006). For example, studies have demonstrated that when actors are performing a given character, their self-perceived personality profile starts to become similar to the character during the rehearsal and performance period (Burgoyne, Poulin, & Rearden, 1999; Hannah, Domino, Hanson, & Hannah, 1994; Nemiro, 1997). They also have more emotional distress when assuming the role (Burgoyne, et al., 1999). Singers have anxiety associated with vocal health and a fear that they will not be able to perform (Kenny, Davis, & Oates, 2004; Sangren, 2009). Musicians struggle with career pressure, injury, and anxiety (Schneider & Chesky, 2011). These are only a few of the unique needs of each artistic domain and clinicians need to appreciate these differences.

Some of the common treatment focuses of performing artists include performance anxiety, depression, suicide, hypochondriacally based fears, low self-esteem, perfectionism and fear of failure, eating disorders, physical injury and loss of time performing, isolation from a performing arts community, travel and separation from family and home, career transitions, and substance abuse (Marchant-Haycox & Wilson, 1992; Wilhelm, Kovess, Rios-Seidel, & Finch, 2004). Added to this list are past traumatic events and childhood adversity. These factors are often hidden and are seldom queried (Laugharne, Lillee, & Janca, 2010). Since the adverse childhood experience scale (ACE) is strongly associated with the AAI classification for security and insecurity, it is recommended that it be included in all screening protocols (Murphy, Steele, Dube, Bate, Bonuck, Meissner, Goldman, Steele, 2014). Without treating trauma, including childhood adversity experiences, the other ailments may remain treatment-resistant.

Sadly, most clinical and medical attention has focused on treating anxiety, neuromuscular strains, or cardiovascular diseases in artists. Although these ailments are real clinical problems, unresolved traumatic experiences may be compromising health and performance.

Conclusion

Creativity is readily engaged regardless of the dysregulating effects of unresolved mourning and PTSD. The only difference between artists with PTSD compared to those without PTSD is that they engaged in the creative process with greater anxiety and concern about their vulnerability, while creating. Despite a higher distribution of artists with unresolved mourning, most were still able to maintain attentional flexibility and emotional regulation while narrating their past attachment experiences. Further, regardless of their unresolved or PTSD classification, the majority of artists were able to enjoy optimal flow experiences while engaging in their preferred artistic activity. However, these artists also struggled with higher levels of anxiety, depression, dissociation, and shame. They also had higher fantasy proneness and they employed greater emotion-oriented coping strategies under stress. Although these strategies may support creativity, they also can increase psychological distress.

Why the artists maintained creative functioning despite the disorganizing effects of PTSD and unresolved mourning may be attributed to their educated

FIGURE 9.9
"Exuberant Dedication." (Photo by Christopher Haggard: Permission granted by California State University, Northridge; Performers: Sunny Reichert)

imaginations. When the muses visited these artists, despite their traumatized imaginations, they may have gained resilience, as evidenced by their capacity to organize discourse and remain engaged in a collaborative relational field. Perhaps the communal nature of the arts helps buffer the dysregulating effects of creativity. Trauma and unresolved mourning are disorganizing. Even though these artists were equally able to enjoy the artistic process, the disorganizing effects remained present. Treatment needs to address anxiety, depression, and dissociative processes, along with the toxic levels of shame that may be exacerbated by emotion-oriented coping and fantasy proneness. Artists bravely welcome the dysregulating influence of the muses. We can help them by recognizing that they may also need regulating resources to ensure their ongoing engagement with the creative process.

ACKNOWLEDGMENTS

Dr. S. Victoria Jaque, Professor and Co-Director, Performance Psychophysiology Laboratory, California State University, Northridge, Department of Kinesiology, 18111 Nordhoff St., Northridge

Mr. Maurice Godin, Actor, Director, Lecturer, California State University, Northridge

References

American Psychiatric Association. (2013). *Diagnostic and Statistical Manual of Mental Disorders, Fifth Edition.* Washington, DC: American Psychiatric Publishing.

Ayers, L., Beaton, S., & Hunt, H. (1999). The significance of transpersonal experiences, emotional conflict, and cognitive abilities in creativity. *Empirical Studies in the Arts, 17*(1), 73–82.

Bakermans-Kranenburg, M. J. & van Ijzendoorn, M. H. (2009). The first 10,000 Adult Attachment Interviews: Distributions of adult attachment representations in clinical and non-clinical groups. *Attachment & Human Development, 11*(3), 223–263.

Bailey, A. M., McDaniel, W. F., & Thomas, R. K. (2010). Approaches to the study of higher cognitive functions related to creativity in nonhuman animals. *Methods, 42*(1), 2–11.

Bailey, H. N., Moran, G., & Pederson, D. R. (2007). Childhood maltreatment, complex trauma symptoms, and unresolved attachment in an at-risk sample of adolescent mothers. *Attachment & Human Development, 9*(2), 139–161.

Barker, K. K., Soklaridis, S., Waters, I., Herr, G., & Cassiday, J. D. (2009). Occupational strain and professional artists: A qualitative study of an underemployed group. *Arts & Health: An International Journal for Research, Policy and Practice, 1*(2), 136–150.

Bennett, D. (2009). Academy and the real world: Developing realistic notions of career in the performing arts. *Arts and Humanities in Higher Education, 8*(3), 309–327.

Berntson, G. G., Norman, G. J., Hawkley, L. C., & Cacioppi, J. T. (2008). Cardiac autonomic balance versus cardiac regulatory capacity. *Psychophysiology, 45*(4), 643–652.

Bigelsen, J. & Schupak, C. (2011). Compulsive fantasy: Proposed evidence of an underreported syndrome through a systematic study of 90 self-identified non-normative fantasizers. *Consciousness and Cognition, 20*(4), 1634–1648.

Bonneville-Roussy, A., Lavigne, G. L., & Vallerand, R. J. (2011). When passion leads to excellence: The case of musicians. *Psychology of Music, 39*(1), 123–138.

Bowlby, J. (1988). *A secure base: Parent-child attachment and healthy human development.* New York: Basic Books, Inc.

Budden, A. (2009). The role of shame in posttraumatic stress disorder: A proposal for a socio-emotional model for DSM-V. *Social Science & Medicine, 69*(7), 1032–1039.

Burgoyne, S., Poulin, K., & Rearden, A. (1999). The impact of acting on student actors: Boundary blurring, growth, and emotional distress. *Theatre Topics, 9*(2), 157–179.

Cacioppo, J. T., Tassinary, L. G., & Berntson, G. G. (2007). *Handbook of psychophysiology.* New York: Cambridge University Press.

Carlson, E. A. (1998). A prospective longitudinal study of attachment disorganization/disorientation. *Child Development, 69*(4), 1107–1128.

Chaplin, L. N. & Norton, M. I. (2014). Why we think we can't dance: Theory of mind and children's desire to perform. *Child Development, 86*(2), 651–658.

Chavez-Eakle, R. A. (2012). The multiple relations between creativity and personality. *Creativity Research Journal, 24*(1), 76–82.

Collins, A. L., Sarkisian, N., & Winner, E. (2009). Flow and happiness in later life: An investigation into the role of daily and weekly flow experiences. *Journal of Happiness Studies, 10*(6), 703–719.

Creasey, G. (2002). Psychological distress in college-aged women: Links with unresolved/preoccupied attachment status and the mediating role of negative mood regulation expectations. *Attachment & Human Development, 4*, 261–277.

Csíkszentmihályi, M. (1990). *Flow: The psychology of optimal experience.* New York: Harper & Row.

Cumming, J. & Hall, C. (2002). Athletes' use of imagery in the off-season. *The Sport Psychologist, 16*, 160–172.

Currier, J. M. & Neimeyer, R. A. (2007). Fragmented stories: The narrative integration of violent loss. In Rynearson, E. K. (Ed.). *Violent death: Resilience and intervention beyond crisis* (pp. 85–100). New York: Routledge.

Dalenbroux, A., Goldstein, T. R., & Winner, E. (2008). Short-term mood repair through art-making: Positive emotion is more effective than venting. *Motivation and Emotion, 32*(4), 288–295.

De Manzano, O. (2010). *Biological mechanisms in creativity and flow.* (Doctoral dissertation). Retrieved from Karolinska Institutet, Scandinavia.

De Petrillo, L. & Winner, E. (2005). Does art improve mood? A test of a key assumption underlying art therapy. *Art Therapy: Journal of the American Art Therapy Association, 22*(4), 205–212.

Dickerson, S. S. (2008). Emotional and physiological responses to social-evaluative threat. *Social and Personality Psychology Compass, 2*, 1362–1378.

Dickerson, S. S., Gruenewald, T. L., & Kemeny, M. E. (2004). When the social self is threatened: Shame, physiology, and health. *Journal of Personality, 72*(6), 1191–1216.

Dunn, L. W., Corn, A. L., & Morelock, M. J. (2004). The relationship between scores on the ICMIC and selected talent domains: An investigation with gifted adolescents. *Gifted Child Quarterly, 48*(2), 133–142.

Endler, N. S. & Parker, J. D. A. (1990). *Coping Inventory for Stressful Situations: Manual (2nd ed.).* Toronto: Multi-Health Systems.

Endler, N. S. & Parker, J. D. A. (1994). Assessment of multidimensional coping: Task, emotion, and avoidance strategies. *Psychological Assessment, 6*, 50–60.

Fuchs, G. L., Kumar., V. K., & Porter, J. (2007). Emotional creativity, alexithymia, and styles of creativity. *Creativity Research Journal, 19*, 233–245.

Frye, N. (1963). *The educated imagination and other writings on critical theory 1933–1963.* Toronto, Canada: Canadian Broadcasting Organization.

Goldstein, T. R. & Winner, E. (2010–2011). Engagement in role play, pretense and acting classes predict advanced theory of mind skill in middle childhood. *Imagination, Cognition and Personality, 30,* 249–258.

Goldstein, T. R., Wu, K., & Winner, E. (2009–2010). Actors are skilled in theory of mind but not empathy. *Imagination, Cognition and Personality, 29,* 115–134.

Gow, K., Lang, T., & Chant, D. (2004). Fantasy proneness, paranormal beliefs and personality features in out-of-body experiences. *Contemporary Hypnosis, 21*(3), 107–125.

Granqvist, P., Hagekull, B., & Ivarsson, T. (2012). Disorganized attachment promotes mystical experiences via a propensity for alterations in consciousness (absorption). *The International Journal for the Psychology of Religion, 22*(3), 180–197. doi: 10.1080/10508619.2012.670012

Granqvist, P., Ivarsson, T., Broberg, A. G., & Hagekull, B. (2007). Examining relations among attachment, religiosity, and New Age spirituality using the Adult Attachment Interview. *Developmental Psychology, 43*(3), 590–601.

Granqvist, P. & Kirkpatrick, L. A. (2004). Religious conversion and perceived childhood attachment: A meta-analysis. *The International Journal for the Psychology of Religion, 14*(4), 223–250.

Gunnison, H. (1985). Group work with athletes. *The Journal for Specialists in Group Work, 10*(4), 211–216.

Gute, G., Gute, D. S., Nakamura, J., & Csíkszentmihályi, M. (2008). The early lives of highly creative persons: The influence of the complex family. *Creativity Research Journal, 20*(4), 343-357.

Hamilton, E. (1969). *Mythology: Timeless tales of gods and heroes.* New York: New American Library.

Hamilton, L. H. & Robson, B. (2006). Performing arts consultation: Developing expertise in this domain. *Professional Psychology: Research and Practice, 37*(3), 254–259.

Hancock, L. & Tiliopoulos, N. (2010). Religious attachment dimensions and schizotypal personality traits. *Mental Health, Religion and Culture, 13*(3), 261–265.

Hannah, M. T., Domino, G., Hanson, R., & Hannah, W. (1994). Acting and personality change: The measurement of change in self-perceived personality characteristics during the actor's character development process. *Journal of Research in Personality, 28,* 277–286.

Hesse, E. & Main, M. (1999). Second-generation effects of unresolved trauma as observed in non-maltreating parents: Dissociated, frightening and threatening parental behavior. *Psychoanalytic Inquiry, 19,* 481–540.

Hesse, E. & Main, M. (2000). Disorganized infant, child and adult attachment: Collapse in behavioral and attentional strategies. *Journal of the American Psychoanalytic Association, 48,* 1097–1127.

Hesse, E. & Main, M. (2006). Frightened, threatening, and dissociative parental behavior in low-risk samples: Description, discussion, and interpretations. *Development and Psychopathology, 18*(2), 309–343.

Hesse, E., Main, M., Abrams, K., Y., & Rifkin, A. (2003). Unresolved states regarding loss or abuse can have "second-generation" effects: Disorganization, role inversion and frightening ideation in the offspring of traumatized, non-maltreating parents. In Solomon, M. F. & Siegel, D. J. (Eds.). *Healing trauma: Attachment, mind, body and brain* (pp. 57–106). New York: W. W. Norton & Company.

Irwin, H. J. (1990). Fantasy proneness and paranormal beliefs. *Psychological Reports, 66,* 655–658.

Jacobvitz, D., Curran, M., & Moller, N. (2002). Measurement of adult attachment:

The place of self-report and interview methodologies. *Attachment & Human Development, 4*(2), 207–215.

Kaufman, J. C. & Kaufman, A. B. (2004). Applying a creativity framework to animal cognition. *New Ideas in Psychology, 22*(2), 143–155.

Kenny, D. T., Davis, P., & Oates, J. (2004). Music performance anxiety and occupational stress among opera chorus artists and their relationship with state and trait anxiety and perfectionism. *Anxiety Disorders, 18,* 757–777.

Kharkhurin, A. (2014). Creativity 4in1: Four-criterion construct of creativity. *Creativity Research Journal, 26*(3), 338–352.

Kirchner, J. M., Bloom, A. J., & Skutnick-Henley, P. (2008). The relationship between performance anxiety and flow. *Medical Problems of Performing Artists, 23,* 59–65.

Klinger, E., Henning, V. R., & Janssen, J. M. (2009). Fantasy-proneness dimensionalized: Dissociative component is related to psychopathology, daydreaming as such is not. *Journal of Research in Personality, 43,* 506–510.

Lacaille, N., Koestner, R., & Gaudreau, P. (2007). On the value of intrinsic rather than traditional achievement goals for performing artists: A short-term prospective study. *International Journal of Music Education, 25*(3), 245–257.

Lack, S. A., Kumar, V. K., & Arevalo, S. (2003). Fantasy proneness, creativity capacity, and styles of creativity. *Perceptual and Motor Skills, 96,* 19–24.

Langendorfer, F., Hodapp, V., Kreutz, G., & Bongard, S. (2006). Personality and performance anxiety among professional orchestra musicians. *Journal of Individual Differences, 27*(3), 162–171.

Laugharne, J., Lillee, A., & Janca, A. (2010). Role of psychological trauma in the cause and treatment of anxiety and depressive disorders. *Current Opinion in Psychiatry, 23,* 25–29.

Lawrence, T., Edwards, C., Barraclough, N. Church, S., & Hetherington, F. (1995). Modelling childhood causes of paranormal belief and experience: Childhood trauma and childhood fantasy. *Personality and Individual Differences, 19*(2), 209–215.

Levin, R., Sirof, B., Simeon, D., & Guralnick, O. (2004) Role of fantasy proneness, imaginative involvement, and psychological absorption in depersonalization disorder. *Journal of Nervous and Mental Disease, 192*(1), 69–71.

Lynn, S. J. & Rhue, J. W. (1988). Fantasy proneness: Hypnosis, developmental antecedents, and psychopathology. *American Psychologist, 43*(1), 35–40.

Maier, M. A., Bernier, A., Pekrun, R., Zimmermann, P., Strasser, K., & Grossmann, K. E. (2005). Attachment state of mind and perceptual processing of emotional stimuli. *Attachment & Human Development, 7*(1), 67–81.

Main, M. (2000). The organized categories of infant, child and adult attachment: Flexible vs. inflexible attention under attachment-related stress. *Journal of the American Psychoanalytic Association, 48*(4), 1055–1096.

Main, M., Goldwyn, R., & Hesse, E. (2003). *Adult attachment scoring and classification systems.* Unpublished manuscript, University of California at Berkeley.

Main, M., Hesse, E., & Kaplan, N. (2005). Predictability of attachment behavior and representational processes at 1, 6, and 19 years of age: The Berkeley longitudinal study." In Grossman, K. E. , Grossman, K., & Waters, E. (Eds.). *Attachment from infancy to Adulthood: The major longitudinal studies* (pp. 245–304). New York: The Guilford Press.

Manmiller, J. L., Kumar, V. K., & Pekala, R. J. (2005). Hypnotizability, creative capacity, creativity styles, absorption, and phenomenological experience during hypnosis. *Creativity Research Journal, 17,* 9–24.

Marchant-Haycox, S. F. & Wilson, G. D. (1992). Personality and stress in performing artists. *Personality and Individual Differences, 13,* 1061–1068.

Murphy, A., Steele, M., Dube, S. R., Bate, J., Bonuck, K., Meissner, P., Goldman, H.,

& Steele, H. (2014). Adverse Childhood Experiences (ACEs) questionnaire and Adult Attachment Interview (AAI): Implications for parent-child relationships. *Child Abuse & Neglect*, 38(2), 224–233.

Murray, A. (1994). *Who's who in mythology: Classic guide to the ancient world.* London: Bracken Books.

Myers, L., Fleming, M., Lancman, M., Perrine, K., & Lancman, M. (2013). Stress coping strategies in patients with psychogenic non-epileptic seizures and how they relate to trauma symptoms, alexithymia, anger and mood. *Seizure*, 22(8), 634–639.

Nagel, J. J. (2009). How to destroy creativity in music students: The need for emotional and psychological support services in music schools. *Medical Problems of Performing Artists*, 24(1), 15–18.

Nelson, B. & Rawlings, D. (2009). How does it feel? The development of the Experience of Creativity Questionnaire. *Creativity Research Journal*, 21(1), 43–53. doi: 10.1080/10400410802633442

Nemiro, J. (1997). Interpretive artists: A qualitative exploration of the creative process of actors. *Creativity Research Journal*, 10, 229–239.

Nettle, D. (2006). Psychological profiles of professional actors. *Personality and Individual Differences*, 40, 375–383.

Ogawa, J. R., Sroufe, L. A., Weinfeld, N. S., Carlson, E. A., & Egeland, B. (1997). Development and the fragmented self: Longitudinal study of dissociative symptomatology in a nonclinical sample. *Development and Psychopathology*, 9(4), 855–879.

Parra, A. (2006). "Seeing and feeling ghosts": Absorption, fantasy proneness, and healthy schizotypy as predictors of crisis apparition experiences. *Journal of Parapsychology*, 70(2), 357–372.

Pekala, R. J., Angelini, F., & Kumar, V. K. (2001). The importance of fantasy-proneness in dissociation: A replication. *Contemporary Hypnosis*, 18(4), 204–214.

Perkins, S. L. & Allen, R. (2006). Childhood physical abuse and differential development of paranormal belief systems. *The Journal of Nervous and Mental Disease*, 194(5), 349–355.

Plato. (C. 388 BC/1972). Inspiration. In Rothenberg, A. & Hausman, C. R. (Eds.). *The creativity question* (p. 32). Duke University Press: Durham, NC.

Porges, S. W. (2009). The polyvagal theory: New insights into adaptive reactions of the autonomic nervous system. *Cleveland Clinic Journal of Medicine*, 76, S86–S90.

Rauschenberger, S. & Lynn, S. J. (2002–2003). Fantasy-proneness, negative affect, and psychopathology. *Imagination, Cognition and Personality*, 22, 239–255.

Rickert, D. L. L., Barrett, M. S., & Ackermann, B. J. (2013). Injury and the orchestral environment: Part I: The role of work organisation and psychosocial factors in injury risk. *Medical Problems of Performing Artists*, 28(4), 219–229.

Rickert, D. L. L., Barrett, M. S., & Ackermann, B. J. (2014a). Injury and the orchestral environment: Part II: Organizational culture, behavioral norms, and attitudes to injury. *Medical Problems of Performing Artists*, 29(2), 94–101.

Rickert, D. L. L., Barrett, M. S., & Ackermann, B. J. (2014b). Injury and the orchestral environment: Part III: The role of psychosocial factors in the experience of musicians undertaking rehabilitation. *Medical Problems of Performing Artists*, 29(3), 125–134.

Roisman, G. L., Holland, A., Fortuna, K., Fraley, R. C., Clausell, E., & Clarke, A. (2007). The Adult Attachment Interview and self-reports of attachment style: An empirical rapprochement. *Journal of Personality and Social Psychology*, 92(4), 678–697.

Runco, M. A. (2007). *Creativity: Theories and themes: Research, development, and practice.* San Diego: Academic Press

Sànchez-Bernardos, M. L., & Avia, M. D. (2004). Personality correlates of fantasy proneness among adolescents. *Personality and Individual Differences*, 37, 1969–1079.

Sànchez-Bernardos, M. L & Avia, M. D. (2006). The relationship between fantasy proneness and schizotypy in adolescents. *Journal of Nervous and Mental Disease, 194*(6), 411–414.

Sangren, M. (2009). Health anxiety instead of performance anxiety among opera singers. *Proceedings of the 7th Triennial Conference of European Society for the Cognitive Sciences of Music (ESCOM), Jyväskylä, Finland*, 468–474.

Sawyer, R. K. & DeZutter, S. (2009). Distributed creativity: How collective creations emerge from collaborations. *Psychology of Aesthetics, Creativity, and the Arts, 3*(2), 81–92.

Schneider, E. & Chesky, K. (2011). Social support and performance anxiety of college music students. *Medical Problems of Performing Artists, 26*(3), 157–163.

Schoenleber, M. & Berenbaum, H. (2012). Shame regulation in personality pathology. *Journal of Abnormal Psychology, 121*(2), 433–446.

Seligman, M. E. P., Steen, T. A., Park, N., & Peterson, C. (2005). Positive psychology progress: Empirical validation of interventions. *American Psychologist, 60*(5), 410–421.

Sheldon, K. M. & King, L. (2001). Why positive psychology is necessary. *American Psychologist, 56*(3), 216–217.

Shirazi, P. R., Dana, A., Jalili, F., & Behzadi, F. (2011). Comparison of mental imagination skill of male and female athletes of individual and team athletic fields. *Australian Journal of Basic and Applied Sciences, 5*(8), 316–319.

Sroufe, L. A., Egeland, B., Carlson, E., & Collins, W. A. (2005). *The development of the person: The Minnesota study of risk and adaptation from birth to adulthood.* New York: The Guilford Press.

Steele, H. (2003). Unrelenting catastrophic trauma within the family: When every secure base is abusive. *Attachment and Human Development, 5*(4), 353–366.

Sternberg, R. J. (2005). Creativity or creativities? *International Journal of Human-Computer Studies, 63*, 370–382.

Stovall-McClough, K. C. & Cloitre, M. (2006). Unresolved attachment, PTSD, and dissociation in childhood abuse histories. *Journal of Counseling and Clinical Psychology, 74*(2), 219–228.

Taylor, S. E., Pham, L. B., Rivkin, I. D., & Armor, D. A. (1998). Harnessing the imagination: Mental stimulation, self-regulation, and coping. *American Psychologist, 53*(4), 429–439.

Thomson, P. & Jaque, S. V. (2011a). Psychophysiological study: Ambulatory measure of the ANS in performing artists In Williamson, A., Edwards, D., & Bartel, L. (Eds.). *Proceedings of the International Symposium on Performance Science, Toronto, Canada, 24–27 August 2011* (pp. 149–154). Utrecht, The Netherlands: European Association Of Conservatoires (AEC).

Thomson, P. & Jaque, S. V. (2011b). Testimonial theatre-making: Establishing or dissociating the self. *Psychology of Aesthetics, Creativity, and the Arts, 5*(3), 229–236.

Thomson, P. & Jaque, S. V. (2012a). Dissociation and the Adult Attachment Interview in artists. *Attachment & Human Development, 14*(2), 145–160.

Thomson, P. & Jaque, S. V. (2012b). Holding a mirror up to nature: Psychological vulnerability in actors. *Psychology of Aesthetics, Creativity, and the Arts, 6*(4), 361–369.

Thomson, P. & Jaque, S. V. (2012c). Dancing with the muses: Dissociation and flow. *Journal of Trauma and Dissociation, 13*(4), 478–489.

Thomson, P. & Jaque, S. V. (2013). Exposing shame in dancers and athletes: Shame, trauma, and dissociation in a non-clinical population. *Journal of Trauma and Dissociation, 141*, 1–16.

Thomson, P. & Jaque, S. V. (2014). Unresolved mourning, supernatural supernatural beliefs and dissociation: A mediation analysis. *Attachment & Human Development, 16*(5), 499–514.

Thomson, P. & Jaque, S. V. (2015). Shame and fantasy in athletes and dancers. *Cognition, Imagination and Personality, 34*(3), 291–305.

Thomson, P. & Jaque, S. V. (2015a). Posttraumatic stress disorder and psychopathology in dancers. *Medical Problems in Performing Artists, 30*(3), 157–162.

Thomson, P. & Jaque, S. V. (2016a). Visiting the muses: Creativity, coping, and PTSD in talented dancers and athletes. *American Journal of Play, 8*(3), 363–378.

Thomson, P. & Jaque, S. V. (2016b). Exquisite moments: Achieving optimal flow in three different activity-based groups regardless of early childhood adversity. *American Journal of Play, 8*(3), 346–362.

van der Kolk, B. (2014). *The body keeps the score: Brain, mind, and body in the healing of trauma.* New York: Viking.

Waldo, T. G. & Merritt, R. D. (2000). Fantasy proneness, dissociation and DSM-IV Axis II symptomatology. *Journal of Abnormal Psychology, 109*(3), 555–558.

Waters, E., Merrick, S., Treboux, D., Crowell, J., & Albersheim, L. (2000). Attachment security in infancy and early adulthood: A twenty-year longitudinal study. *Child Development, 71*(3), 684–689.

Watt, C., Watson, S., & Wilson, L. (2007). Cognitive and psychological mediators of anxiety: Evidence from a study of paranormal belief and perceived childhood control. *Personality and Individual Differences, 42,* 335–343.

Wilhelm, K., Kovess, V., Rios-Seidel, C., & Finch, A. (2004). Work and mental health. *Social Psychiatry and Psychiatric Epidemiology, 39*(11), 866–873.

Wilson, S. C. & Barber, T. X. (1983). The fantasy-prone personality: Implications for understanding imagery, hypnosis, and parapsychological phenomena. In Sheikh, A. A. (Ed.), *Imagery: Current theory, research and application* (pp. 340–387). New York: John Wiley & Sons, Inc.

10

Resonance, Synchrony, and Empathic Attunement: Musical Dimensions of Psychotherapy

Victoria Stevens

"*To put it in a formula: [the analyst] must turn his own unconscious like a receptive organ toward the transmitting unconscious of the patient.*"
—Sigmund Freud, "Recommendations to Physicians Practising Psycho-Analysis" (1912)

"*People usually complain that music is so ambiguous, that it leaves them in doubt as to what they are supposed to think, whereas words can be understood by everyone. But to me it seems exactly the opposite.*"
—Felix Mendelssohn (1842)

"*Let us leave theories there and return to here's hear.*"
—James Joyce, *Finnegans Wake* (1939)

WHAT IS IT about the experience of psychotherapy that facilitates healing of suffering, strengthens vitality and sense of self, and increases clarity of purpose and meaning in life, while expanding consciousness in a patient? All of this happens, yet it is not clear exactly how or precisely why. When talking about their experience in therapy, patients often report noticing that they have a different way of being, perceiving, and feeling. They often express a deeply emotional sense of being seen, being heard, and feeling connected to another. Yet, they have difficulty putting into words what actually has happened. Is the difficulty verbalizing profound connection similar to the difficulty verbalizing how we are moved by music or other works of art? Our deepest, most transformative experiences with people, such as parents, teachers, friends, or therapists, seem to share an indefinable, ineffable quality characteristic of being in the presence of powerful works of art, nature, or spirituality.

In all cases, the experience lies beyond specific words, knowledge, techniques, or actions taken by the therapist or artist. The experience has more to do with *how* the words are said, and *how* the knowledge, skills, or techniques are used. The power of music does not lie in the written score nor in the notes themselves, no matter how perfectly executed. Similarly, a "correct" diagnosis or well-crafted interpretation does not by itself facilitate insight, connection, or new ways of being in psychotherapy.

In this chapter, first I will discuss the nonspecific elements of psychotherapy. Then I will show how music plays an important role in the creation of affective attunement between therapist and patient. The chapter ends with how therapists can develop their own musical sensitivity in order to better understand nonverbal communications of patients.

The Therapeutic Alliance

One way of conceptualizing the actual experience of the therapeutic alliance is that it is comprised of "moments of meeting," a term utilized by Karlen Lyons-Ruth, et al. (1998) and the Process of Change Study Group of Boston:

> What do we mean by a moment of meeting? A "moment of meeting" occurs when the dual goals of complementary fitted actions and intersubjective recognition are suddenly realized. Moments of meeting are jointly constructed, and require the provision of something unique from each partner. Sander (1995) has pointed out that the essential characteristic of these moments is that there is a specific recognition of the other's subjective reality. Each partner grasps and ratifies a similar version of "what is happening now, between us" (p. 286).
>
> [Footnote text: Sander (1995). Moments of meeting catalyze change in parent–infant interaction as well as in psychotherapy" (p. 286).]

The quality of the therapeutic alliance is entirely dependent upon the therapist regardless of theoretical modality. As Bruce Wampold (2015) states, "Putting aside the debate about whether some treatments are more effective than others, it is clear that if there are differences among treatments, the differences are quite small. Thus, we are left with the question: If the differences among treatments are nonexistent or are very small, are there other factors that do have an influence on the effects of psychotherapy? The answer is yes—the therapist who is providing the psychotherapy is critically important" (p. 3).

Wampold (2011) identifies skills that effective therapists possess, over and above basic education or training. These interpersonal skills include: verbal fluency, interpersonal perception, affective modulation and expressiveness, warmth and acceptance, empathy and focus on other, flexibility, awareness of verbal and nonverbal cues, willingness to be wrong, hypothesis testing, and the ability to make adjustments in manner or approach.

These skills contribute to the strength and authenticity of the therapeutic alliance. Each skill identified involves a kind of creative awareness, a way of being rather than doing on the part of the therapist. While necessary as skills, the question remains how these skills are utilized on a moment-to-moment basis so that a therapeutic alliance can be created and sustained.

I suggest the answer lies in the notion of the embodied mind, which highlights the importance of reading nonverbal communications from the patient as well as from the therapist in what is always a co-created interchange. All of these elements are part of the larger repertoire of clinical intuition. Emotions, body responses, and even unconscious states of mind are communicated nonverbally, through facial expressions, posture, gesture, movements, and vocal prosody—essentially the language of visual art, theater, dance, and music.

The musical quality to all communication is fundamental to how everyone expresses emotion, receives communications from others, and interprets meaning, with or without words. In this way, all psychotherapists are musical, as are our patients. We are continually singing to each other, while moving in sync during the ongoing dance we call psychotherapy. Meanwhile, the ability to flexibly adjust to sensory and affective shifts within a session is also highly rhythmic, ebbing, and flowing melodically with modulations of intensity, volume, pitch, sounds, and silences. Even though psychotherapists may not consider themselves "musical" or "creative," in fact they are involved in a highly musical and creative interaction every time they engage with a patient. In the intersubjective therapeutic matrix, facial expressions, breathing rate, gestures, posture, movements, and words are part of the narrative. The extra-linguistic, prosodic elements of verbal communication are intermingled within the patient and the therapist as well as between them, in a fluid interplay. Therefore, in this discussion, music can be seen as both a metaphor for the therapist and the therapeutic relationship, as well as a real element constantly in play.

The Music of Interpersonal Neurobiology

Our understanding of the mechanisms that lead to therapeutic change and transformation in patients of all ages has increased dramatically due to a confluence of studies that integrate interpersonal neurobiology with theories of early childhood development and attachment. This is particularly true with regard to our awareness of the exquisite, subcortical sensitivity that all people have to nonverbal communications at all levels. Developmentally, our affective and sensory experiences of love, safety, security, or the lack thereof were originally encoded during the first two years of life in these nonverbal forms. These conditions are fully consistent with how we process the elements of music. It is intriguing to note that many of the same words used most often to discuss early childhood attachment dynamics as well as the quality of therapeutic engagement are musical. These words, including "resonance," "synchrony," and "attunement," are briefly defined as follows:

Resonance: "The reinforcement or prolongation of sound by reflection from a surface or by synchronous vibration of a neighboring object;" "a quality that makes something personally meaningful or important to someone;" and "a quality of evoking response." (Merriam-Webster, 1983 p. 1004) From a psychological perspective, Dan Siegel (2007) states, "Educated as an attachment researcher, I know that resonance is the underlying mechanism beneath the attuned communication between parent and child in secure attachment" (p. 171).

Synchrony: "A simultaneous act, development or occurrence;" "the state of operating or developing according to the same time scale as something else" (Merriam-Webster, 1983 p. 1197). In child development, synchrony is understood as fluid patterns of interaction between a caregiver and infant, who respond to each other using coordinated rhythm and timing.

Attunement: "Being or bringing into harmony;" "to become aware or responsive" (Merriam-Webster, 1983 p. 114). Within psychotherapy, Richard Erskine (1993) describes attunement as "a kinesthetic and emotional sensing of the other—knowing the other's experience by metaphorically being in his or her skin. Effective attunement also requires that the therapist simultaneously remain aware of the boundary between client and therapist" (p. 186).

According to Siegel (2007), "Attunement can be seen at the heart of therapeutic change. In the moment, such resonant states feel good as we feel "felt" by another, no longer alone, but in connection. This is the heart of empathic relationships, as we sense a clear image of our mind in the mind of another. . . .

Attunement interpersonally and the nurturing of attunement internally are the central processes of psychotherapy" (p. 290–291).

As Schore (2003) proposes, "Empathic *resonance* results from dyadic *attunement*, and it induces a *synchronization* of patterns of activation in both hemispheres of the therapeutic dyad. *Misattunement* is triggered by a mismatch, and describes a context of stressful *desynchronization* between and destabilization within their right brains. Interactive *reattunement* induces a *resynchronization* of their right-brain states" (p. 51).

Each of these words echoes the others within them, while adding other musical dimensions, such as vibration, harmony, and rhythm. All are interconnecting strands that comprise the quality of connection that informs empathy. All promote the experience of Being and Existing in the eyes, mind, and heart of another. Here is a list of unique aspects of psychotherapy that facilitate transformative healing, and that can be considered both important processes as well as outcomes:

- Moments of intersection
- The creation of a space and states of mind enabling therapist and patient to safely play with a multiplicity meanings
- Deepening of affective states
- Freeing and mobilizing of body states
- Insight
- Transformative experiences
- Mutative and healing experiences through the new caregiving relationship

With these in mind, I next explore aspects of psychotherapeutic technique that can enhance these processes and goals. My aim is to help psychotherapists access various nonverbal modalities from moment-to-moment. I would also like to heighten their sense of the creative art of being with another person through musical awareness. Some relevant aspects of technique include: empathic attunement; multivalent attentional stance; emotional and energetic resonance; rhythmic synchrony; scanning; tracking shifts in body, affect, and prosody; imaginative play; creative flexibility and improvisation; translation, and interpretation.

Music

The basic elements of music are the same whether the music is instrumental or vocal, and whether it is classical, jazz, hip-hop, or any other genre, globally, or historically. These same elements are present in the musical interactions of everyday life. Music is considered to be the art of time. Music molds our perception of the flow of time, both in cyclical and linear forms. Music also represents the form of experience and emotion that holds its "meaning." Music represents the emotional quality of subjective, lived time, as made audible. Music sounds the way feelings feel, mirroring their ups and downs, motion and rest, emptiness and fulfillment, loss and change. The most fundamental aspects of music are patterns of vibrations, rhythms, waves, and energy, as shared with the physical forces of nature, including the quantum field.

Music is complex, mysterious, and ubiquitous. Known as a "universal language," music-making and listening have been shown to exist in all current and historically documented human societies. Call and response is one of the oldest forms of music, ritual, theater, and dance, harkening back to early interactions between caregivers and infants. In sum, music is the hallmark of all communication, including that which occurs in psychotherapy.

For every human being, music is present in all areas of human experience; from the musical matrix of the womb and the early emotional connections between infants and caregivers through songs, gestures, and rhythms, to the autobiographical memories in the elderly that are linked through emotional association to songs and music. Music is a unique and ever-present way of communicating, processing, and understanding emotional experience throughout our lives.

The basic elements of music are:

- *Rhythm* – patterns of sound and silence
- *Tempo* – patterns of time, faster or slower
- *Volume* – intensity of sound, louder or softer
- *Pitch* – higher or lower vibrational levels
- *Timbre* – tone, color, texture of sound
- *Melody* – pitch contours moving higher or lower
- *Harmony* – simultaneously produced notes that produce chords

These elements are present in every therapeutic encounter, both in the communications of the patient and the therapist, and are constantly shifting and changing whether with or without words. The fact that every session is a new experience in time and space evokes the musical analogy equating psychotherapy to jazz improvisation.

From the musical standpoint this would be described by the term "entrainment." Entrainment is the synchronization of two or more rhythmic systems into a single pulse. The body's physiological rhythms resonate with each other and the two voices or energetic vibrations move and change in response to

each other. The two voices are not fused into exact unison; nor do they mirror each other exactly. Ideally, they are always slightly off from each other.
They come together at key nodal points in time. Yet they also move in and
out of each other's rhythmic patterns, fluidly and responsively, continually
changing and morphing from one state to another. All of this happens on
an energetic level, occurring simultaneously with any verbal narrative being
spoken. Meanwhile, the words may or may not be synchronized or consonant
with the musical/emotional/physical dialogue.

Rhythmic synchronization and the effects of vibrations occur on all levels
of consciousness and throughout the natural world. The study of patterns of
vibrations has a long history in science from Da Vinci and Galileo through
today and is formally called "cymatics." Cymatics comes from the Greek word
for "waves" and is the study of sound and vibration made visible. Recent exper-
iments show how the vibrations from different sounds with varying musical
pitches and volume (intensity) affect particles and create unique patterns.

Here is what neuroscience and music expert Michael Thaut (2008) says:

FIGURE 10.1
Cymatics: Example of how the vibrations from different sounds create patterns in black sand. (Public domain)

Rhythm and time are among the most eminent concepts in understanding the nature of music as an organized and rule-based sensory language. The brain is neurologically superbly sensitive to processing the time elements of music in a rapid, precise, and meaningful manner. We may have reason to contemplate—if not the structured flow of time, made audible in music's temporal architecture of sound, rhythm, and polyphony—what it is that excited, moves, and gives order to our feelings, thoughts, and sense of movement when we engage in music (p. 59).

Psychotherapy, in addition to any cognitive elements, can be seen as a very high level of creative improvisational play between therapist and patient as they interact and communicate through the elements of music. During psychotherapy, we express emotions and other conscious or unconscious states through the body, words, and the musical dimension of the words and silences. With improvisation in music, as in psychotherapy, we play with the sounds and silences during call and response. Even as we play them, they transform into something new, and vanish.

Prosody

Prosody is a crucial vehicle for the communication of emotion through the music of language. The term prosody is used to describe the musical elements of vocal communication. While prosody has particular significance in early childhood, it also continues to play a part in conveying both emotional and semantic meaning within all linguistic and nonverbal communications throughout the lifespan. Prosody is present in lullabies, rituals, spoken languages, poetry, and songs throughout history and cross-culturally. Prosody is an important aspect of human expression central in the communication of emotion, meaning, and motivation through all of the modalities of music.

Prosody includes vocal rhythm, pitch, melody, tempo, and volume as part of the communication of emotional meaning, with or without words, and information about bodily, emotional, and cognitive states. Prosodic communication is characterized by variations in pitch, pitch and volume contours, and changes in tempo and emphasis that convey meaning irrespective of the words and grammatical construction (Mitchell, 2003).

Prosodic interactions play an important role in the following: the communication of emotional feelings and states; the facilitation of attunement and attachment; telling the difference between play and reality; the development of affect and self -regulation; and the development of affect synchrony between caregiver and infant.

It is mainly the right brain that processes the prosodic elements of language along with other important socioemotional information and body states which are central to the regulation of emotions (Schore, 2005). This right-brain regulatory capacity develops through the nonverbal, and playful interactions between the young child and an attuned caregiver. These interactions include gesture, rhythm, melody, tempo, facial expressions, and movements.

During infant development, I suggest (Stevens, 2008) that prosody reveals that the ontogenetic and phylogenetic importance of language has more to do with its musicality than our left hemispheric linguistic/semantic bias might lead us to believe. A large and continuously growing body of research provides evidence for this (e.g., Papousek, 1996; Trevarthan, 1999; Trehub, 2001). Given the general cultural emphasis on the semantic meanings of words, on linguistically based education, as well as on the content of the communication in psychotherapy, the importance of prosody as a vehicle for understanding has been vastly underestimated. Prosody is central to the developing brain, the nascent sense of self, as well as the processing of human relationships throughout the lifespan. We must help redress this imbalance by investigating how psychotherapists can learn more consciously to read the music of language, plus meanings conveyed by voiced emotions.

Empathic Attunement

Empathic attunement in therapists is a state of mind and being with the dual purpose of focusing in on the words and music of patients, as well as of simultaneously tuning into the words and music of our own responses. This is an intermediate state of consciousness, a kind of consciously active reverie, in which individuals open themselves up to sensory and emotional input from another, while simultaneously remaining aware of their own internal responses. These states allow for information stored in implicit memory to emerge consciously and intersubjectively. This information flow may include words, images, feelings, impulses, or prosodic inflections evoked from moment to moment.

The faculty that turns sensations, intuitions, and feelings into forms has been called "fantasy" and in more modern times "imagination." The sensory-musical imagination is a dominant activity of the mind, as it occupies a state of free-floating consciousness.

The creative function of imagination involves several skills:

- To discern relations between ideas, objects, feelings, or forms
- To see patterns within disparate elements

- To perceive both similarities and differences analogically
- To unite multi-modality linkages into new combinations

As Ogden (2001) states:

> The analyst's reverie involves a withdrawal from the logic, demands, and distractions of external reality that is analogous to the "darkness" of sleep (the insulation of the mind from the glare of consciousness)—a darkness in which dreaming, a continuous psychic event, becomes perceptible. As Freud (1912) put it, "I have to blind myself artificially in order to focus . . .on one dark spot" (p. 45). The analyst's reveries state is his waking sleep or sleeping wakefulness, a state in which he looks darkly at the productions of the unconscious (p. 6).

This state of mind has been called many things, including: "evenly suspended attention" (Freud, 1912); "primary maternal preoccupation" (Winnicott, 1956); "reverie" (Bion, 1967); "flow" (Csíkszentmihályi, 1996); and "mindfulness" (Siegel, 2007). It should be noted that these terms describe the therapeutic stance in some cases, as well as what occurs within the therapeutic interaction given the therapist's ability to hold that stance, in other cases.

Current interdisciplinary research emphasizes the importance of a therapist's ability to enter into and hold these states of mind/body. To do so facilitates tuning into patients' mind/body states, as well as understanding patient communications regarding the *feel* of their subjective experience. Much of this research comes from infant developmental neurobiology. Together with clinical observation and theory, this body of work focuses on the influence of caregivers on early affective, cognitive, and neurobiological development of the infant. Developmental findings affect how the clinician understands both the etiology and treatment of early forming psychopathology in patients of any age. This perspective becomes especially relevant in cases of attachment failures and instances of emotional misattunement.

The capacity for the therapist to receive communications from the patient's unconscious involves a right-hemisphere state of receptivity. This allows therapists to empathically attune to the affective and bodily states of patients. This also creates possibilities for resonances, or moments of synchrony, between the therapist and the patient, whether at unconscious, preconscious or conscious levels. Moments of attunement, resonance, and synchrony help therapists to empathically understand the patient's subjective experience and ways of constructing inner worlds. Moments of attunement, resonance, and synchrony also promote the patient's experience of being understood at a deep emotional and existential level.

Current research calls for a reexamination of the emphasis placed on verbal and historical thinking. We must also rethink the use of content interpretations within psychoanalytic technique in light of the importance of the nonverbal musical language of the right brain, plus other communications from the unconscious in all forms. This perspective carries important implications for the training and ongoing development of analysts and psychotherapists of all theoretical orientations. As Marks-Tarlow (2014) states, "In the heat of the clinical moment, it becomes unethical *not* to set aside empirically validated methods in order to sink fully into the depth of relational experience and complexity of information available only in the present moment" (p. xxvii, emphasis mine).

Improvisation

Improvisation is defined as "to make, invent, or arrange offhand" and "to fabricate out of what is conveniently at hand" (Merriam-Webster 1983, p. 606). The responsive give and take of improvisation is seen in the rhythmic affective attunement between infant and caregiver and continues in childhood pretend play, humor, creative invention and innovation, and in everyday interactions, whether verbally or nonverbally. Improvisation is spontaneous, creative interplay within a given context and structure. This holds for all forms of improvisation, including theater, dance, music, or psychotherapy. Improvisation can be seen in all forms of music, cross-culturally and historically, from the clapping sing-song games of children, to Mozart and Bach, and within all forms of jazz.

Jazz improvisation involves a musical context, harmonic, melodic, and rhythmic expectations, based on an overall structure. Simultaneously, improvisation involves the attunement of musicians to each other, as each listens to what the other produces. Improvisation also includes spontaneous creative responsiveness; each musician engages and plays off of what is offered in the moment by all of the others. From an analogic perspective, jazz improvisation comes the closest to the improvisational play of psychotherapy.

Improvisational play is directly related to structure and security, plus the ability to engage in free play. Improvisation of this sort is a sign of secure attachment, as well as of emotional health. Spontaneous improvisation serves as a means for connection, a method of empathic understanding, as well as an outcome of effective psychotherapy. As Winnicott (1971) says, "Psychotherapy takes place in the overlap of two areas of playing, that of the patient and that of the therapist. Psychotherapy has to do with two people playing together" (p. 38). He further states that the aim of psychological healing is "bringing the patient from a state of not being able to play into a state of being able to play. . . . It is in playing and only in playing that the individual child or adult is able to be creative and use the whole personality, and it is only in being creative that the individual discovers the self" (p. 54).

In psychotherapy, improvisational play necessitates staying grounded, and utilizing training, but not letting learned or preconceived theoretical models get in the way of being fully present to the human being who sits in front of us. An empathically attuned therapist who engages in creative improvisation is alert and connected to internal sensory responses as well as external cues from the patient. Improvisation requires the ability to flexibly and readily shift attention, based on intuition and observation in real time. This is the art of psychotherapy, which exists beyond technical competence. This art demands a mastery both of knowledge and technique. Yet by setting aside both knowledge and technique, clinical intuition and receptivity can come to the forefront of consciousness. When any skill reaches the level of creative mastery and becomes an art, it becomes hidden. We then arrive at a state of creative being that facilitates a co-created intersubjective space that feels vital and alive. At the same time, by definition, this space is messy, and demands a tolerance for ambiguity and an embracing of not knowing what comes next.

Tronick (2005) discusses the vital importance of messiness in the creative dyadic interchange between individuals in the following way:

> Connection is the regulation and co-creation of the age-possible meanings individuals make of the world and their place in it. The making of meanings is dyadic and continuous. . . . At best in the moment and with development they become increasingly coherent and complex. Perhaps more important, experience itself has to be seen as messily coherent. Even more vital is the need to recognize that no connection between individuals ever is perfect but out of all this imperfection unique meanings and connections emerge. Such is the wonder of the human condition—the emergence of the new out of messiness (p. 312).

Charles Limb, et al. (2008) have done fascinating research investigating what happens in the brains of musicians while they improvise. Limb's research has interesting implications for what states of mind are most conducive for therapists to remain present in an improvisational play space. He asked trained musicians to perform four different exercises while lying in an fMRI machine. First they played a C Major scale and then were asked to improvise on that scale. Then, he asked them to play an original blues melody that they had memorized with a pre-recorded jazz quartet playing with them, and finally, they were asked to freely improvise on their own, creating their own piece spontaneously with the same recorded background.

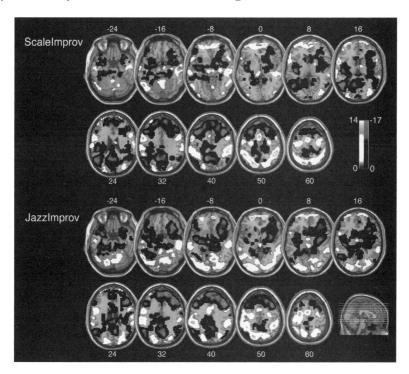

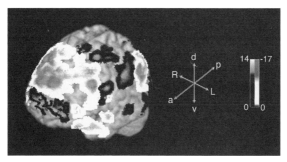

FIGURE 10.2

Three-dimensional surface projection of activations and deactivations associated with improvisation during jazz. (Courtesy Charles Limb)

In the analysis of the brain scans, similar patterns were found during both improvisations (on the scale and with the quartet). The brain turned off or shut down areas (the dorsal lateral prefrontal cortex and the lateral orbital frontal cortex) linked to self-monitoring one's performance, self-censoring, and self-inhibition. The brain also turned on an area (the medial prefrontal cortex) involved in organizing self-expression, and self-initiated thoughts and behaviors. In addition, the brain regions involved with all the senses lit up during improvisation, indicating a heightened state of awareness. Another fascinating aspect of the scans was their similarity to patterns seen during deep REM sleep, meditation, and hypnosis, pointing to possible connections between improvisation and dreaming. Limb also proposes that these patterns of activation and deactivation are likely to be key indicators of a brain engaged in creative thought.

Interestingly, Limb's findings correspond to how we understand the state of empathically attuned responsiveness in a therapist. It is critical for a therapist to have the ability to shut down the analytical self-monitoring system that has a more narrow cognitive focus and open up a responsive and self-expressive system that has a more diffused and sensory-emotional holistic focus. This creates a state of receptivity to a patient's shifting states of body, emotions, and mind, and is connected to both improvisation and creative thinking.

Recent research (Carson, et al., 2003) shows that individuals who are highly creative show reductions in what is called "latent inhibition," which refers to "the capacity of the brain to screen from current attentional focus stimuli previously experienced as irrelevant" (p. 499). These reductions in latent inhibition are associated with the personality trait of "openness" and associated with divergent thinking and trait creativity and with creative achievement. Such reductions have previously been associated with "susceptibility to or acute-phase schizophrenia" (p. 499). They conclude that "The highly creative individual may be privileged to access a greater inventory of unfiltered stimuli during early processing, thereby increasing the odds of original recombinant ideation" (p. 505). The ability to reduce latent inhibition would then be seen as crucial in the therapist's ability to both receive and be fully responsive to the sensory, emotional, and cognitive states and responses of a patient without being overwhelmed by them and to be able hold and feel them with the goal of understanding the patient and creatively transforming the nonverbal communications and experiences into meaningful interpretations.

Fine-Tuning the Therapeutic Ear

Fine-tuning the therapeutic ear to be a sensitive "receiver" or instrument begins with two basic preliminary stages. The first is that knowledge of all aspects of development, theoretical models, differential diagnoses, the history of the patient, the history of the analytic sessions, and the therapist's own history and personality development (including both transference and countertransference tendencies or vulnerabilities and defensive default modes) need to be so well known to the therapist that they are in "one's bones" as Winnicott (1971) put it.

Once that information is learned and practiced well enough, the therapist can consciously "forget" it in order to be fully present to the patient's communications at all levels. This involves what Bion (1967) called the "eschewing of memory and desire." Deliberate "forgetting" allows not only for the right-brain unconscious to "tune in" to the patient, but it also creates space for the therapist to imaginatively play with the sensations, feelings, actions and words in a way that enables them to understand the particular logic and meaning of the subjective experience of the patient. Once therapeutic "knowledge" and conscious memory and desire are released, the encounter with the patient moment by moment will evoke sensations, ideas, fantasies, memories, desires, impulses, daydreams, and associations that, if allowed to be stimulated and present, act as important signals that play in the therapist's preconscious.

This notion about the therapeutic stance implies an ability on the part of the therapist to tolerate frustration, disruption, and ambiguity, as well as the concomitant capacity to play with bodily sensations, feelings, images, sounds, and ideas without needing to prematurely "understand" what is going on. These abilities are the result of right-hemisphere self-regulatory capacities that allow the therapist to temporarily allow the preconscious/unconscious cues to be taken in, experienced, and processed.

Once the receiver is "tuned up," it becomes an instrument that can serve three main functions. The first is that it can receive communications from the patient in all forms. Secondly, it can allow itself to be "played upon" by the patient in the sense of being present to be used by the patient for multiple purposes, with transference a container to hold projections for all purposes, mirroring, thinking, a background object, and so forth.

Finally, it can play the music, poetry, drama and dance of what is happening moment by moment within the analyst's own body/mind while turning the many levels of internal and external stimuli into a series of coherent synthesized moments of understanding through interpretation. Wassily Kandinsky (1912), who was trained both as a musician and a painter, states something similar about the artist and the relationship between color in painting and music:

> Our hearing of colours is so precise. . . . Colour is a means of exerting a
> direct influence upon the soul. Colour is the keyboard. The eye is the ham-

mer. The soul is the piano with its many strings. The artist is the hand that purposely sets the soul vibrating by means of this or that key. Thus it is clear that the harmony of colours can only be based upon the principle of purposefully touching the human soul (p. 160).

The right brain is far superior to the left in terms of rapid scanning and the reception of nonverbal cues such as breathing, rhythm, facial expressions, posture, gesture, and movement, as well as the prosodic elements of verbal communication. As Mitchell, et al. (2003) state:

Temporal lobe regions in the right hemisphere are now known to be involved in the mediation of a range of linguistic functions, including the processing of metaphors, verbal self-monitoring and moral content. Since

FIGURE 10.3
Kandinsky, W. (1921) Segment Bleu. (Public domain)

prosody, whether emotional or linguistic, is a core component of language, right-lateralized activity in the current study adds to the growing sugges-tion that the right hemisphere plays a broader role in the mediation of lan-guage than was previously supposed (p. 1419).

The following are fundamental sensory-motor-emotional and musical cat-egories by which we make meaning out of experience metaphorically and that affectively inform nonverbal communication (Stevens, 2002):

Patterns of sound and silence	Rhythm/presence/absence/space/ Liveliness/deadness
Fast/slow	Tempo/time/movement
Warm/cool; light/dark; Smooth or soft/rough	Color/timbre/texture
Near/far	Space/distance/perspective
High/low	Pitch
Soft/loud	Volume
Part(s)/whole	Melody/harmony; theme/variations; Note/chord; form; narrative
Soothing/jarring	Consonance/dissonance; Synchrony/asynchrony; Resonance/disconnectedness Attunement/misattunement

All of these modes of communications have their own affective meaning depending upon where and how they emerge within the ongoing narrative of any given session. The essentially right-brain thinking needed to translate this emotional language involves the therapist observing, taking in, and hold-ing unexplained sensations, feelings, and ideas and letting them play until a pattern emerges. It is vertical in the sense that while the patient is providing the melody (horizontal) with the narrative and behavior of the session, the therapist is resonating vertically with a chordal structure throughout all levels of their being and providing both orchestration and accompaniment.

The Therapist's Body as an Instrument

The therapist's listening ear is not the only "receiver" of nonverbal communica-tions, in fact the therapist's instrument is their entire body. The attuned open therapeutic stance allows the therapist's body, affective, and predominantly right-brain states to constantly adjust themselves as they receive and resonate with the communications from the patient at all levels. This involves in a sense allowing itself to be "played upon" by the patient (being present and able to be used by the patient in multiple ways (transference, a holding function or container, mirroring, a background object, and so on).

The therapist resonates with the patient's internal state of arousal, modulates it, communicates it back prosodically in a more regulated form, and then (with rhythmically sensitive timing), verbally labels her states of mind/body/affect (Schore, 2003). Far from being a passive, trancelike state—the state of right-brain-dominant reverie and empathically attuned play is highly active and takes a great deal of discipline and attention on multiple levels simultaneously. It is a way of "thinking" and a technique that can be learned, practiced, and honed and one that is critical for both the art and the science of therapeutic work. This state is necessary not only for the ability to empathically attune to affective and bodily states of the patient, but also for the capacity for scanning and being able to discern patterns or themes in prosody, use of words and phrases, behavior, and metaphors.

FIGURE 10.4
The music of psychotherapy. (Courtesy of Terry Marks-Tarlow)

Unconscious Scanning—Ehrenswieg

Ehrenswieg in *The Hidden Order of Art* (1967) has an important piece to add to the discussion of the technique of the art of psychotherapy. He says that the creative individual is one whose ego is flexible enough to undergo the temporary dissolution of its surface, rational facilities, to reach deeper levels of unconscious sensing, which cannot be apprehended on a conscious level. Far from being mad, the artist must have sufficient ego strength (adaptability rather than rigidity) to allow a temporary dissolution of reality. Any act of creativity requires a temporary, cyclical paralysis of surface attention. A particular technique is needed to get hold of the visions filling the creative mind as a kind of absent-minded watchfulness. Ehrenswieg states that "Unconscious scanning makes use of undifferentiated modes of vision that to normal awareness would seem chaotic . . . the primary process is a precision instrument for creative scanning that is far superior to discursive reasoning and logic" (p. 5).

He also describes the function of unconscious scanning as that which enables the artist or therapist to discern a coherence from among a variety of simultaneous or sequential stimuli. This pattern-finding ability is crucial to the therapist's ability to hear themes and variations in the language and behavior of the patient. When allowed to play with consciously stored knowledge of the patient's personal history as well as the history of the therapeutic experience, all combine to form the groundwork for interpretation.

FIGURE 10.5
Kandinsky (1912) Improvisation. (Public domain)

His discussion of the stance of artists and musicians analogizes to the therapist:

> The musician like the painter has to train himself to scatter his attention over the entire musical structure so that he can grasp the polyphonic fabric hidden in the accompaniment . . . The trained musician allows his attention to oscillate freely between focused and unfocused (empty) states, now focusing precisely on the solid vertical sound of chords, now emptying his attention so that he can comprehend the loose, transparent web of polyphonic voices in its entirety (p. 25–27).

Interpretation: Reading the Language of the Unconscious

The stance and way of thinking that facilitates empathic attunement has been posited as an essential foundation for a vital and transformative interpretation, which is one that evolves out of the moment-to-moment intersubjective matrix of experience between therapist and patient. This kind of organic interpretation facilitates the process of linking feeling to thought and unconscious states of mind with conscious awareness. However, creatively attuned empathic resonance is a necessary, but not sufficient basis for creating those links through interpretation. Upon the foundation of this state of being are layered many other abilities that all together begin to describe the components of a vital interpretation.

These abilities include the therapist's ability to read all the levels and kinds of communications from the patient in the context of the narrative being communicated verbally and nonverbally. From the musical standpoint, this involves the therapist's ability to hear the themes and leitmotifs as they weave through the patient's language and history, as well as the subtext/accompaniment/orchestration underneath or surrounding the dominant themes or realistic content of a communication. These musical sensitivities then inform the therapist's ability to link all of the levels of communication with their understanding of the patient's history, the history of the analytic relationship, and the realistic details of the patient's life at the time of each session. The above abilities, when married to the empathic analytic stance, would lead to an intuitive sense of the "right timing" as well as content of an interpretation.

Themes and Variations

One of the ways of listening that enhances a therapist's ability to "hear" the unconscious narrative and the language of a particular patient is to listen for words and phrases that repeat or echo each other thematically both in a session and over time. This is a way of listening for the music and poetry of the unconscious regardless of the subject matter being talked about. It is assumed that *anything* the patient says or does when in a session has relevance to the transferential situation and is loaded with affective content. The unconscious has "selected" what is available to the conscious mind to say (like a dream) and the therapeutic questions regarding all communications are: Why this?; Why now?; Why this after (or next to) that?; Why here?; and Why with me? The answers lie in the words, themes, and events that rhyme and echo each other, which will only be heard if the therapist is listening on several levels simultaneously.

I take the phrase "events that rhyme" from Ogden (2001), who cites Italo Calvino's (1986) discussion about poetry where "he commented that the rhyming of words in poetry has an equivalent in prose narrative where there are 'events that rhyme.'" I would add that in the therapeutic setting there are conscious and unconscious feelings, thoughts, and other intrapsychic and intersubjective events, that rhyme—"that echo each other" (p. 111).

Words, phrases, metaphors, memory sequences, ways of characterizing people, as well as elements of prosody: tone, rhythm, timbre, harmony, dissonance, silences, and so forth all combine to create sequences of themes and variations within a session and over time, woven in increasingly complex and subtly changing patterns as the therapeutic process deepens.

Translation

The art of translation in the context of psychotherapy is like the skill of Orpheus as differentiated from an Aeolian harp. The Aeolian harp is an instrument that makes whatever music occurs when the wind has randomly stirred it. It is an instrument that is played upon by all of the stimuli that it receives by responding immediately. Orpheus takes in the stimuli from the world and from inside himself and organizes them into music within himself, which he then plays using himself and his instrument as vehicles for the music.

The art of interpretation in psychotherapy is to become Orpheus. All technique informs the music, and the music is the translated interpretation. Translation is a kind of transubstantiation. The patient communicates about life through verbal and nonverbal language, and the analyst/translator takes in that language and then moves from language back to life.

Just like an artist, paradoxically a therapist must be trained to creatively play. A sense for significant combinations must be developed, which is a highly

FIGURE 10.6
Kandinsky (1916) To the Unknown Voice. (Public domain)

sophisticated level of creativity and demands the sustaining of a highly trained diffuse awareness. The ability to translate also demands the capacity for play between states of mind and body, as well as self and other and to not get lost or to confuse oneself for the other. Ultimately it is our openness to the being of another and to perhaps frightening and overwhelming states of mind that allows us to transmute nonverbal and disorganized experience into an organized form and to name the unnamable or unnamed.

This act of translation is the facilitation of naming, thinking about, and giving meaning to experience, which then opens the way for transformation. The therapist's openness to the other is the act of allowing themselves to be utilized as a vehicle for a patient's experience of being alive, being real, and having a sense of self without losing one's own mind or sense of self. This is what I am calling "transparency to transformation" and I believe that it is a skill that can and needs to be developed as an essential tool for psychotherapeutic work. As Poincaré wrote in 1908:

> A first hypothesis presents itself: the subliminal self is in no way inferior to the conscious self; it is not purely automatic; it is capable of discernment; it has tact, delicacy; it knows how to choose, to divine. . . . It knows better how to divine than the conscious self, since it succeeds where that has failed" (in Hadamard, 1948, p. 23).

Conclusion

This brief investigation into the mechanisms that lead to therapeutic change and transformation in patients has focused on the importance for the therapist to develop the naturally existing exquisite sensitivity that all people have to nonverbal communications into a conscious and deliberate way of being, plus augmenting technique through the fine-tuning of a musical ear. Music as a form of communication is crucial, as is the art of time and the form of experience and emotion as it moves. Music reflects the emotional quality of subjectively lived experience made audible through the melodies, harmonies, rhythms, consonances and dissonances, sounds and silences of the voiced and unvoiced word. The ability to hear the music of another, from oneself and in the interaction between oneself and another, called for the honing of what T. S. Eliot (1933) called the "auditory imagination":

> What I call the 'auditory imagination' is the feeling for syllable and rhythm, penetrating far below the conscious level of thought and feeling, invigorating every word, sinking to the most primitive and forgotten, returning to the origin and bringing something back, seeking the beginning and the end. It works through meanings, certainly, or not without meanings in the ordinary sense, and fuses the old and obliterated and the trite, the current, and the new and surprising, the most ancient and the most civilized mentality (p. 111).

The question posed at the outset of this discussion was: What is it about the experience of psychotherapy that facilitates the healing of suffering, the strengthening of vitality and sense of self, increased clarity of purpose and meaning in life and expanded consciousness in a patient? Ultimately these questions may never be answered with words or understood by brain scans or any other quantitative, analytical measure. However, it is clear that we cannot underestimate the importance of repeated experiences of being seen and heard by another in terms of the effect these experiences have on the development of a sense of being-in-the-world. To be known by another provides a foundation for a person to develop a sense of existing in a personally meaningful world. The transformations that occur within the dynamically changing intersubjective space between human beings, facilitated by creatively attuned empathic resonance, occur at all levels: physiologically, emotionally, psychically, and perhaps most importantly—ontologically.

The interanimation of beings through moment-to-moment attunement opens up dimensions of a lived experience, where two separate individuals are united in synthetic moments of connection. The musical dimensions of the psychotherapeutic relationship: resonance, synchrony, and empathic attunement, become vehicles for the creative improvisational responsiveness of the therapist to the moment-to-moment experiences of patients and their interpretations of the world.

As of now, neither philosophy, psychology, nor neuroscience have been able to fully understand or explain the nature of the subjective experience or what is happening in those moments of connectedness, whether this occurs through music, a work of art, or an actual attuned human being. However, by engaging with the full spectrum of emotions, sounds, and images, we can begin to understand the qualitative range of experiences happening to different people when they feel seen and cared for by another, especially when wrenched by suffering.

As we expand our consciousness and increase the attentional focus and sensitivity of our sensory-musical awareness, we begin to fine-tune our ability to see and hear with the eyes and ears of the artist we all truly are. And then as we continue to engage in relationships with ourselves and others as explorers, wonderers, and keen observers, we can delight in increasingly deep moments of attunement, interconnections, synchronies, and epiphanies. Music, made up of vibrations, resonances, rhythms, patterns, melodies, harmonies, dissonances, colors, movements, gestures, shapes, and forms, is inside of us and all around us every moment, with or without words.

One of the many purposes of music, whether instrumental or vocal, formally presented or experienced as part of any interaction, is that it brings people together in a particular place and time to experience where we share the same sounds and ineffable series of moments together, yet do so with our own unique and deeply personal subjectivities, lives, and minds. Proust (1981) describes music as having the power to see with other eyes and says that it enables us to have something approaching "the communication of souls." And at the most profound level, this is what those healing, transformative "moments of meeting" in psychotherapy provide.

Perhaps in the end, if we open our ears to hear the songs being sung to us, music becomes a way through which time, space, and the exquisitely beautiful pain of being human are made clearly perceptible to the empathic heart.

References

Bion, W. R. (1967). Notes on memory and desire. *Psychoanalytic Forum*, 2, 271–280.

Carson, S., Higgens, D., & Peterson, J. (2003). Decreased latent inhibition is associated with increased creative achievement in high-functioning individuals. *Journal of Personality and Social Psychology*, 85(3),499–506.

Csíkszentmihályi, M. (1996). *Creativity: The psychology of discovery and invention.* New York: HarperCollins.

Ehrenswieg, A. (1967). *The hidden order of art.* Berkeley, CA: University of California Press.

Eliot, T. S. (1933). *The use of poetry and the use of criticism: Studies in the relation of criticism to poetry in England.* London, UK: Faber and Faber Limited.

Erskine, R. (1993). *Transactional Analysis Journal*, 23(4), 184–190.

Freud, S. (1912/1958). Recommendations to physicians practising psychoanalysis. *Standard Edition*, 12, 109–120. London: Hogarth Press.

Hadamard, J. (1945). *The mathematician's mind: The psychology of invention in the mathematical field.* Princeton, NJ: Princeton University Press.

Joyce, J. (1976). *Finnegans wake.* New York: Penguin Books.

Kandinsky, W. (1912). *Concerning the spiritual in art and painting in particular.* Munich: Verlag R. Piper & Co. In Lindsey, K. & Vergo, P. (Eds.). (1994). *Kandinsky: Complete writings on art.* (pp. 114–220). New York: Da Capo Press.

Limb, C. J., Braun, A. R, (2008). Neural substrates of spontaneous musical performance: An fMRI study of jazz improvisation. *PLoS ONE* 3(2): e1679.

Lyons-Ruth, K., et al. (1998). Implicit relational knowing: Its role in development and psychoanalytic treatment. Process of Change Study Group, Boston, Massachusetts. *Infant Mental Health Journal*, 19(3), 282–289.

Marks-Tarlow, T. (2014). *Awakening clinical intuition: An experiential workbook for psychotherapists.* New York: W. W. Norton & Company.

Mendelssohn, F. (1842). Letter to Marc-André Souchay, cited from *Briefe aus den Jahren 1830 bis 1847* (Leipzig: Hermann Mendelssohn, 1878) p. 221; translation from Felix Mendelssohn (Ed. Selden-Goth, G.) *Letters* (New York: Pantheon, 1945) pp. 313–314.

Mitchell, R., et al. (2003). The neural response to emotional prosody, as revealed by functional magnetic resonance imaging. *Neuropsycholgia*, 41, 1410–1421.

Ogden, T. (2001). *Conversations at the frontier of dreaming.* Lanham, MD: Jason Aronson.

Orange, D. (1995). *Emotional understanding: Studies in psychoanalytic epistemology.* New York: The Guilford Press.

Papousek, M. (1996). Intuitive parenting: A hidden source of musical stimulation in infancy. In Deliège, I. & Sloboda, J. (Eds.). *Musical Beginnings: Origins and Development of Musical Competence* (pp. 88–112). Oxford, UK: Oxford University Press.

Proust, M. (1981). *Remembrance of things past.* (Trans. Moncrieff, C. K. & Kilmartin, T.) New York: Random House.

Sander (1995). Identity and the experience of specificity in a process of recognition. *Psychoanalytic Dialogues, 5,* 579-593.

Schore, A. (2003). *Affect regulation and the repair of the self.* New York: W. W. Norton & Company.

Schore, A. (2005), Attachment, affect regulation, and the developing right brain: Linking developmental neuroscience to pediatrics. *Pediatrics in Review, 26:* 204-211.

Siegel, D. (2007). *The mindful brain.* New York: W. W. Norton & Company.

Stevens, V. (2002, May). *Metaphor and the poetics of the unconscious.* Paper presented for Psychoanalysis and the Humanities Lectures. Cambridge University, UK.

Stevens, V. (2008). The music of language: The importance of prosody and nonverbal communication in the dyadic interaction between infant and caregiver. In Izdebski, K. *Emotions and the human voice* (pp. 145–157). San Diego, CA: Plural Publishing.

Stolorow, R. & Atwood, G. (1992) *Contexts of being: The intersubjective foundations of psychological life.* Hillsdale, NJ: The Analytic Press.

Thaut, M. (2008). *Rhythm, music, and the brain: Scientific foundations and clinical applications.* New York: Routledge.

Trehub, S. E. (2001). Psychological predispositions in infancy. *Annals of New York Academy of Sciences, 930,* 3–16.

Trevarthen, C. (1999). Musicality and the intrinsic motive pulse: Evidence from human psychobiology and infant communication. *Musicae Scientiae, Special Issue* (1999–2000), 155–215.

Tronick, E. Z. (2005).Why is connection with others so critical? Dyadic meaning making, messiness and complexity governed selective processes which co-create and expand individuals' states of consciousness. In Nadel, J. & Muir, D. (Eds.). *Emotional development: Recent research advances* (pp. 293–316). Oxford, UK: Oxford University Press.

Wampold, B. (2011) Qualities and actions of effective therapists. *www.apa.org/education/ce/effective* therapists.

Wampold, B. (2015). How important are the common factors in psychotherapy? An update. *World Psychiatry. 14*(3), 270–277.

Webster's ninth new collegiate dictionary (1983). Springfield, MA: Merriam-Webster.

Winnicott, D. W. (1958). *Primary maternal preoccupation.* In Winnicott, D. W. (Ed.) *Through paediatrics to psycho-analysis: Collected Papers* (pp. 300–305). New York: Basic Books.

Winnicott, D. W. (1971). *Playing & Reality.* New York: Tavistock/Routledge.

11

Playing With Someone Who Loves You: Creating Safety and Joyful Parent-Child Connection with Theraplay

Phyllis B. Booth, Dafna Lender, and Sandra Lindaman

A father lies on the living room floor and smilingly invites his 3-year-old daughter to climb onto his knees. In a deep, resounding voice with a clear, engaging rhythm he chants:

One for the money—
Two for the show—
Three to get ready—
Pause while the excitement grows
AND FOUR TO GO!

He drops his knees open and she falls into his enfolding arms and a warm bear hug. "Again, again!" she shouts, and they continue till both are lying there in a contented glow of shared good feelings.

A mother and her 5-year-old daughter are making the beds together. The child runs ahead of her mother and crawls under the rumpled sheets, pulling the blankets over her head. Smiling, the mother starts to smooth the covers, saying, "Oh, there's a lump in the bed. What is it?" She rubs the girl's back warmly through the sheets and then searches underneath for the "lump." Feeling the girl's hair, she says, "It must be a mop!" The child pops out with a big grin and mother says, "Oh, It's My Girl!" After sharing a good, giggly hug, they settle down and make the bed.

Margaret, a Theraplay therapist, sits facing a child who is sitting in her adoptive mother's lap. With a warm, reassuring manner, Margaret takes the child's hands in hers and swings them side to side, chanting in a lilting voice, "La, La, La,—Hands" and Margaret and the little girl playfully touch hands together and look intently into each other's eyes. Having demonstrated the game, Margaret helps the child and her mother face each other so they can repeat the play. After the chanting, the mother calls out "Hands," then other body parts, "elbows . . . thumbs . . . foreheads." With each new turn they smile and laugh more. The mother's face is soft and open and the child's expression is focused and engaged. The child suggests "noses" and they touch noses and kiss.

WE HOPE THAT our title, "Playing with Someone Who Loves You," evokes happy memories from your own childhood and from your own experiences as a parent. Such experiences are the model for Theraplay®, our playful, interactive approach to helping parents and their children form more secure and joyful relationships. Our goal in this chapter is to introduce you to the broad range and richness of Theraplay.

The first two vignettes above are memories from my own childhood (PB). My playful, strong and steady parents created for me a sense of security and of well-being that has stayed with me throughout my life. The third vignette is a description of a typical Theraplay (registered service mark of The Theraplay Institute, Evanston, IL, USA, www.theraplay.org) interaction, which demonstrates its power to activate the relationship enhancing social engagement system (Porges, 2011). This four-year-old child, Angel, had been adopted at the age of 2.5 following extreme neglect in her birth family, which left her unsure of herself and wary of getting close to anyone. Margaret's plan for this particular session is to engage Angel in playful interaction that feels safe and comfortable. In the "La La" game, the simple, sing-song voice and the rhythm of the swinging arms, along with the delightful surprise of which body parts will come together, brings to life Angel's intrinsic capacity for curiosity and

FIGURE 11.1
Playful engagement with a young child. (The Theraplay Institute photo)

motivation to share experiences. Margaret's voice is melodic and her facial expression is inviting, soft and congruent with the mood and movements of the game. When it is her turn, the mother's voice is lilting and her face lights up with a similar warm and inviting expression. Under Margaret's sensitive guidance, Angel is able to feel safe and relaxed enough to enjoy moments of meeting and loving connection with her mother.

The Theraplay Model

Theraplay is an engaging, playful, relationship focused therapy that is interactive, physical and fun. It is modeled on the moment to moment interaction between "good enough" (Winnicott, 1965) parents and their children. These natural patterns of healthy interaction between parents and child lead to arousal regulation, secure attachment and lifelong mental health. Since the focus of treatment is the relationship itself, parents are included in sessions with their child and helped to become more sensitively attuned and emotionally available in order to create the kind of warm responsive engagement that leads to secure attachment. Bowlby (1988) supports our clinical application of attachment theory and the use of the healthy parent-child model when he says, "the pattern of interaction adopted by the mother of a secure infant provides an excellent model for the pattern of therapeutic intervention.. . . ." (p. 126).

Let us look more closely at what goes on in this interaction. In order to emphasize the amazing variety of things parents do with their young children, Ann Jernberg, the remarkable creator of Theraplay, gave the following description in her 1979 book, *Theraplay*:

Daily, the mother nuzzles her baby's neck, blows on his tummy, sings in his ear, . . . [plays] "peek-a-boo," and nibbles his toes. She picks him up, twirls him, rocks him, and bounces him. She holds him close and nurses him. She washes him, pats him dry, and rubs him with lotion. She whispers, coos, giggles, hums, chatters and makes nonsense sounds. She peeks at him . . . looks wide-eyed with surprise, and beams at him....defines his life space, . . . his relationships, his use of time. . . And finally, she remains one step ahead of him, thus encouraging him both to learn the art of mastery and to enjoy the challenge.

Her baby, in turn, coos at his mother, smiles at her, reaches for her, strokes her . . . imitates her and enjoys being mirrored by her; he gurgles with her, and, finally, he names her. Although her child may sometimes protest them, he responds to his mother's definitions, limits, and structures, and rises to her challenges. But above all he stares at her and gazes deeply into her eyes. (p. 4–5)

This great variety of responsive, engaging, nurturing, challenging, and playful interactions creates for the child a very positive view of herself, her parents and her world. The picture of herself that she sees reflected in the loving eyes of her parents will stand her in good stead throughout her life.

But what happens to children who are not so fortunate: whose parents are

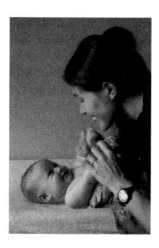

FIGURE 11.2
A mother defines her baby's life space through emotionally interactive playfulness

FIGURE 11.3
A father and child communicate through reciprocal eye gaze

preoccupied, neglectful or abusive? They do not feel good about themselves; they can't count on their parents; the world seems a bleak and frightening place. This had been Angel's experience and she and others like her are the children and their families that Theraplay is designed to help. In order to change this unhappy view, Theraplay provides direct, here and now experiences that help them feel safe and that create new neural connections and interactive expectations as well as new meanings in the relationship. In the same way that parent-infant interaction leads to maturation of emotional circuits, Theraplay "activates secure attachment processes, modulates fear and stress levels, and shapes an optimal biochemical arousal level that develops plasticity" (Mäkelä & Hart, 2011, p. 10).

The therapist's role is that of a sensitive, reliable guide who helps the parent and child experience the responsive, attuned and empathic interactions that are characteristic of healthy parents and children. In order to enhance parents' sensitivity and responsiveness in relation to their child, the therapist guides them to attend to their child's cues, and to reflect on the meanings of their own and their child's experience. As soon as they are ready, parents are encouraged to take over the leadership role.

Since our model is based on the interaction between very young children and their parents, Theraplay naturally focuses on the pre-verbal, brainstem, and limbic levels of development where synchrony, rhythm, facial expression, vocal prosody, movement, and play are the primary modalities. Theraplay stimulates and exercises the emotional brain. It is necessary for the autonomic and limbic systems to develop fully before higher level symbolic and mentalizing skills can be expected.

The action is multi-sensory, including lively proprioceptive experiences as well as calming, nurturing touch and soothing care. But above all it is playful. It has the character of the physically interactive play that parents intuitively do with their young children that meets early emotional needs and fosters a sense of connection and safety. Within these experiences children learn how to be with others, to enjoy human company, to experience happiness, and to feel that life is worth living.

How Theraplay Began

In 1967, Ann Jernberg, child psychologist, became clinical director of a program to provide psychological services to all the Head Start Programs in Chicago. She recruited a team, including me (PB), to go into the classrooms, identify children who needed help and refer them to existing treatment centers. During the first summer the number of children we found needing help far exceeded the help available at existing mental health clinics. Ann, a creative and enterprising woman, came up with a simple solution to the problem: We would recruit and train lively young people to go into the schools and play with the children who needed help. We asked them to engage each child assigned to them in the same way parents interact with their young children: sensitively, spontaneously, face to face, with no need for toys, simply inviting the child to join them in joyful, interactive play. In weekly supervisory sessions we helped these young mental health workers reflect on their own and the child's experience in order to be more attuned to each child's needs. Together we came up with new activities that we could use to engage and delight the

FIGURE 11.4
Sad and withdrawn children in Head Start programs benefitted from Theraplay provided by in-school mental health workers. (The Theraplay Institute photo)

FIGURE 11.5
Youth receiving Theraplay in Head Start improved rapidly in emotional
and social adjustment. (The Theraplay Institute photo)

children as well as to calm and comfort them. We saw the children 2 or 3 times
a week and averaged about 15 sessions per child.

And it worked: sad, withdrawn children became livelier and more outgo-
ing, angry, aggressive acting-out children calmed down and were able to
engage with others in a friendly, cooperative way. In order to demonstrate
the nature of our work as well as our success, we made two films about
four of the children: *Here I Am* and *There He Goes* (Jernberg, Hurst, Lyman,
1969, 1975).

When we revisited the children, three years later, they were all thriving.
The teacher of a boy who had been an angry, acting-out child in Head Start,
could not imagine that he had been so difficult. He was now lively, cooperative, and pleasant to have in the classroom. We found a formerly very withdrawn little girl skipping rope with friends in front of her house. When we
interviewed her parents, her father said, "I used not to notice her much. Now
she is my favorite child."

During the process of editing our first film, the film maker suggested the
name "Theraplay" to distinguish our hands-on, playful, relationship based
approach from other forms of play therapy.

In 1969–70, just as our program got under way, I (PB) spent a year studying at the Tavistock Clinic in London. Once a week I heard John Bowlby
describe his new theory about the role of attachment in healthy development, watched James and Joyce Robertson's films documenting the devastating
effects on young children of being separated from their parents, and attended
case conferences with Donald Winnicott. Looking back, I see that I was in at
the beginning of a groundswell of interest in the power of early attachment

relationships—what actually goes on between parents and their children—to create or disrupt long term social-emotional development.

When I returned to Chicago and to the Head Start program, I found myself making use of Bowlby's and Winnicott's ideas to explain our success with the children. I remember saying to Ann Jernberg, "We are providing them with the kind of 'holding environment' that Winnicott (1965) says is a crucial quality of a healthy relationship between a mother and her baby." Devoted mothers create an atmosphere of safety, focus exclusively on their child, respond empathically to his needs, and when he is ready, engage him in playful interaction. Bowlby's (1969) concept of the Internal Working Model also helped us explain our success. The lively faces and playful actions of the young mental health workers had reflected a much more positive view of each child as well as creating a new experience for the child of what he or she could expect from others. The dyadic experience of feeling safe, being sensitively responded to, validated and enjoyed, had created a new and more positive Internal Working Model.

In the 45 year history of Theraplay, our focus has always been on the model of healthy parent-child interaction, the present moment, social engagement, play and joy, touch and the body and arousal regulation. We are grateful to our fellow experts at this conference who have greatly enriched our understanding of the interpersonal processes that lead to healthy development. They have taught us about the importance of affect regulation (Schore, 1994), and interpersonal neurobiology (Siegel, 1999) and the emotional circuitry of the brain (Panksepp, 1998, 2012). Polyvagal theory (Porges, 2011) has given us much more insight into the elements of parent-child interaction and its effect on the developing brain of the child. A greater understanding of the mechanisms and impact of early trauma (Schore, 2003; van der Kolk, 1994; Perry, 2006) helps us fine-tune our approach to meet the individual needs of each child and parent.

Theraplay has now spread to sixty countries in various mental health and child and family service settings. Dyadic, family, and group Theraplay have been shown to be effective in improving emotional regulation, social-interaction, language development, and a number of other internalizing and externalizing problems. Theraplay has been rated as a promising procedure by the California Evidence Based Clearinghouse (2009). Published studies validating the effectiveness of Theraplay are listed at theraplay.org/research. The 3rd edition of the Theraplay text (Booth & Jernberg, 2010) is the current manual for best practice in Theraplay training, supervision and certification.

Theraplay Dimensions

In order to make use of the parenting model with its great variety of interactions, Ann Jernberg saw them as falling into four dimensions: Structure, Engagement, Nurture, and Challenge. The therapist initiates a sequence of activities chosen from these four dimensions to meet the needs of the parent and child for state regulating and attachment promoting experiences. Knowing the value and effect of a particular kind of interaction helps us choose activities that meet the needs of the dyad at any one moment: for example, creating safety, calming, energizing, or challenging a child to try something new.

Structure

The therapist is responsible for creating a good interactive experience for the parent and child. The reliable leader's actions create environmental regulation via organization, clear boundaries, and clear expectations, and relational regulation through pacing, choice of activity, and level of arousal. This guidance and regulation form the basis for predictability, safety and co-regulated interaction. As soon as possible, the parent becomes the leader of the activities and the therapist becomes a coach and helper. In group applications where parents are not present, such as classrooms or residential care, the therapist continues to interact directly with the children.

Engagement

The therapist initiates many engaging activities that create opportunities for attunement, synchrony and moments of meeting. Porges (2011) helps us understand the nature and importance of this activation of what he calls the Social Engagement System. The mammalian autonomic nervous system has features that serve social behavior. Areas of the brain that regulate the ventral-vagal pathways to the heart are integrated in the brainstem with the neural pathways that regulate the striated muscles of the face and head. The face-heart connection forms an integrated Social Engagement System that provides and senses signals of safety.

The Theraplay therapist uses her/his own Social Engagement System of in-the-moment contingent, warm, expressive facial expressions, prosodic voice and welcoming gesture and head movement to do the following:

- Engage the parent and child's Social Engagement System
- Promote a calm physiological state or neuroception of safety (Porges, 2011)
- Engage the parent and child in attachment enhancing experiences of attunement, synchrony, repair of mis-attunements, co-regulation, moments of meeting and intersubjectivity.

Nurture

The therapist sets up several gentle, caring and soothing activities per session including feeding the child. The therapist also looks for opportunities to express appreciation and concern and to take care of the parent and child throughout the session. These caring activities are down-regulating and stress reducing. A large body of animal and human research supports the value of touch in stimulating development of premature infants (Field, 1995), creating the capacity to relate to others (Harlow, 1958), reducing irritability and anti-social behavior (Suomi, 1995), reducing stress (Tronick, Ricks, & Cohn, 1982), and raising oxytocin levels with subsequent calming of adult and child (Mäkelä, 2005). Porges (2011) states, "both the giving and receiving of caregiving or love has the capacity to protect, heal and restore" (p. 295).

Challenge

The therapist supports the child's growth within the zone of proximal development (Vygotsky, 1978; Mäkelä & Hart, 2011) by partnering with the child in playful, physical activities that extend the levels of high and low arousal and encourage the child to try new things. Engaging successfully in these challenging activities creates a sense of mastery and helps the child feel more competent, confident, and courageous.

Play is an overarching element in all of our work. The therapist leads a series of simple face to face play activities, recruiting the parent's and child's PLAY (Panksepp, 1998) energies. The activities are frequently up-regulating but can be brought down in arousal as necessary. The focus is on joyful interaction, pleasure, success and cooperation. Panksepp (2012) describes how "the act of playing has remarkable effects on the cortex, programming it to be fully social" (p. 264). Porges describes play as a "hybrid state requiring features from both states of mobilization and social engagement" (2011, p. 278) with the power to down regulate fight/flight behaviors and "foster calm states that optimize learning and social behavior" (2015b, p. 3).

Case Examples Illustrating How Theraplay Works

We turn now to some vignettes that illustrate various aspects of Theraplay in practice. Photographs in Figures 6-10 were taken at The Theraplay Institute with nonclinical volunteers to illustrate the Theraplay process.

Creating Attunement and Repairing Mis-attunements

In the Theraplay vignette of Angel and her mother at the beginning of the chapter, we saw how a well guided but simple activity can provide opportunities for social engagement, synchrony, and moments of meeting that create a sense of safety and shared pleasure between a mother and her child. We now go back to the beginning of treatment to learn more about Angel's history and the pattern of interaction that had developed between her and her adoptive mother. These patterns were observed during our assessment using the Marschak Interaction Method (MIM) (Marschak, 1960; Booth, Christensen & Lindaman, 2011). The MIM is a structured, play-based assessment tool that we use to learn more about the relationship between parent and child and to help us plan treatment.

Background

Angel lived with her birth mother and grandmother until age 2 when she was found living in an abandoned building. She was dehydrated and sleeping on the floor in filth. There were bruises on Angel's body that indicated physical abuse. She was placed in two other foster homes before she was adopted at the age of 2.5 years by two experienced parents of 4 grown children. After a year and a half of struggle, they sought help. As she walked in to the clinic, Angel gazed up at the therapist with a penetrating look, which asked silently "Will you like me? Will you take me?" Her parents told us that perfect strangers consistently reacted to meeting Angel by saying "She is so cute, I want to take her home with me!" This reaction worried her parents, because at home Angel had a hard time connecting with them. She kept her distance and did not like to be touched or taken care of; however, her rejection was always masked by a smile and a giggle. When her parents tried to play with her or direct her in simple tasks like getting dressed in the morning, she flopped to the floor and refused to get up. Often she seems to hurt herself in the process, but when her parents tried to care for her injury, Angel pushed them away. Her mother, who spent the most time with Angel, felt rejected by her daughter and ineffective as a mother.

FIGURES 11.6–11.7
Left: Difficult behaviors often are signs of a child's distress. *Right:* Repair of misattunement brings relief and re-connection. (The Theraplay Institute photo)

Assessment: Marschak Interaction Assessment (MIM)

In the task, "Adult teaches the child something the child doesn't know," Lucille, Angel's adoptive mother, chose to teach Angel the colors on a stop light. Holding Angel's hands gently, she explained that the top light is red for stop, the middle is yellow for slow, and green is for go. Although Angel had above average cognitive skills, she hesitated when Lucille asked "What does red mean?" Angel looked up at Lucille as if trying to guess the right answer from her face, and said "Go?" Her mother corrected her and went over the colors again and then asked "What does red mean?" Angel giggled, leaned sideways and eventually flopped to the ground. Lucille sighed and tried again but her daughter was now lying on the ground giggling. She wouldn't answer, and she wouldn't get up. Lucille's face changed from a forced smile to a look of discouragement. She turned away from Angel and went on to the next task.

Session Example

As we saw in the first vignette, Angel and her mother experienced many pleasant, connected moments in Theraplay but it was not always as smooth. In a subsequent session, Margaret sets up a game where Angel moves back and forth between the therapist and Lucille, either slowly like a "slithering snake" or quickly like a "little mouse." Each time she reaches her mother, Angel gets a big hug. Angel seems to enjoy the play and goes fast or slow based on Margaret's directions. But then Margaret announces a change to the rules, saying "This time I'm going to switch to a different animal! Are you ready?" and takes a dramatic breath and pauses to increase the tension in the game. Then Margaret declares, "Hop like a bunny!" Instead of hopping, Angel walks hesitantly toward Lucille and then veers to the side, half running-half skipping and stops at the wall, where she flops to the ground. Angel looks at Margaret, her face trapped in a frozen smile, her eyes silently asking, "What's going to happen now?" Realizing that Angel is afraid that her reaction will bring disapproval or retaliation, Margaret pauses and her face changes from buoyant excitement to tenderness and empathy. She says, "Oh Angel, I don't think you liked it when you didn't know which animal was going to come next in our game. I think that scared you a little." Angel's frozen smile immediately disappears and her face looks apprehensive and serious. Margaret continues, "Oh that makes sense that you didn't like that, because I changed it and you weren't sure what to do." Margaret then beckons Angel to come back to the play area, saying, "Thank you for letting me know that. I'm not going to change the animal without telling you first."

Angel looks up at Margaret and then slowly approaches her. In a calm, gentle voice, Margaret says, "When I say go, you can go to hop, hop, hop like a bunny all the way across to your mother's side. OK?" Angel then hops across to her mother with ease. "Oh, that's better," Margaret says, "because you knew which one it was going to be so you could do it!" In order to help Lucille understand and reflect on Angel's experience and motivation, Margaret turns to her, saying, "I think Angel wasn't sure which animal it was going to be, so she got a little scared. That's why she ran to the side." Lucille nods in understanding. Then Margaret turns back to address Angel and says "Angel, are you ready to hop like a bunny one more time?" Angel nods her head. Margaret says, "Ready, set, go!" and Angel hops across to her mother and crawls quickly into her lap with a genuinely joyful laugh.

Reflections

Our efforts to understand what happened in the play sequence lead us to the following conclusions. As long as she fully understood the game and felt safe, Angel's movements were light hearted and she and her mother were in tune and having fun together. Margaret's unexpected raising of the interpersonal tension of the game (not telling Angel which animal was next) increased Angel's arousal beyond her level of tolerance. Angel must have worried, "Can I trust Margaret that nothing bad will happen when I don't know just what to do?" Instead of showing her fear overtly, Angel acted silly (high-pitched giggling) and resistant (veering off to the side and flopping to the floor with a frozen smile). Lucille read her behavior as uncooperative and her face showed her discouragement and dismay. Preoccupied with her own negative feelings, she retreated from the interaction, leaving Angel feeling rejected, abandoned and ashamed. Margaret, being alert to the possibility of such a rupture, immediately acknowledged her responsibility for what had happened. She then made sure that Angel understood the game so that she could happily hop to her mother's side. Then, she shared with Lucille her empathic understanding of what had happened. Margaret's attunement to the rupture in the relationship and her overture of repair provided an important step toward Angel's development of trust in adults.

Creating Opportunities for Connection and Shared Joy Using Playful and Nurturing Activities.

We turn now to look at another child and her adoptive mother to illustrate the power of nurture, play and shared joy to create a sense of safety and connection.

Background

Alissa is a 12 year old who was removed from her home at the age of 8 when she and her 5 year old brother were found home alone with no food in the house. She was separated from her brother and placed in three short-term foster homes before being adopted at age 10 by Fran, a single mother.

After struggling for over two years with behavior problems that she found frightening and disturbing, Fran sought treatment. She reported that Alissa refused to go to sleep at night and would get violent when Fran attempted to set limits or discipline her. Alissa would hit, kick and throw things when she didn't get her way, saying hurtful words, "I wish you would die!" "Why did you adopt me? Just so you could be mean to me?" She was openly defiant, saying, "NO, you can't make me," to simple requests such as being asked to turn off the TV. Alissa also had suicidal ideation and spoke of dying and becoming an angel or a fairy.

Fran's fear and discouragement were visible on her face as she talked about her adopted daughter. She described the early days when Alissa first came to her home. From the beginning, Alissa violently rejected Fran's touch or any comforting overture she made toward her. Alissa's rages paralyzed Fran and she felt so frightened of what Alissa might do next that she found herself doing all she could to avoid her. Alissa's constant rejection made Fran feel like a failure as a mother. With a look of defeat and despair, Fran told Ann, her therapist, that if she could, she would give Alissa back, "But where would I send her? There is nowhere to send her to."

Assessment: MIM

In order to get a picture of how a child responds to offers of nurture and care as well as of how comfortable the parent is in giving nurture, we use the task: "Adult and Child comb each other's hair." Alissa immediately grabbed one of the combs from the envelope so she could be the one to do the combing. She mechanically combed her mother's hair, taking no care to avoid snarls and painful yanks. She roughly pushed her mother's shoulder in order to direct her to turn her head sideways. She finished quickly and then announced "Done!" Fran responded in a frustrated tone, "What about me combing your hair?" As Fran took the comb and reached her arm out to begin combing, Alissa was silent for a moment, then grabbed the second comb and began combing her own hair, thereby blocking her mother's efforts. Fran exclaimed, "Hey! Can I do it?" and Alissa shook her head. Fran made another overture: "Can I put your hair in a ponytail?" and Alissa shook her head "No." Fran turned away in disappointment and as she reached to get the next task, she could not hide the hurt look on her face. This short interaction highlighted the pattern of isolation and rejection that they had settled into.

Session Example

Fast forward to Theraplay Session #9: Alissa and Fran are sitting on pillows on the floor with their backs supported by more pillows lined against the wall. The therapist, Ann, introduces a new game, which she plays first with Fran so that Fran can experience how it feels and also know what to do when it is her turn to play with her daughter. Ann puts lotion on her own hands and then taking Fran's forearms into her slippery hands, she lets her hands "slip" down Fran's arms as Fran pulls away from her. Ann exclaims in a progressively excited manner, "Oh no, I'm slipping away from you, I'm trying to hold on, OOOOooooh!" and then finally lets go of Fran's hands and rolls backwards in a dramatic fashion. Fran's smile gets progressively wider and her eyes sparkle with delight at the increasing tension of the dramatic "fall" about to happen. All the while, Alissa is watching her mother in joyful anticipation, bursting into happy laughter just as Ann falls backwards. After several more of these experiences, Ann arranges for Fran to face Alissa and offers her some lotion for her hands. Alissa eagerly offers her arms to her mother. Fran holds on and, looking smilingly into Alissa's eyes, slips her grip from Alissa's elbows down to her wrists as she chants, "Oh no, I'm trying to hold on!" As Fran falls backwards, Alissa erupts into explosive, rolling laughter that seems to have no end. In the moment it takes for Fran to get back up, Alissa stretches out her arms in anticipation, her eyes big and beckoning. Ann says excitedly, "Look Mom, Alissa's saying 'More Mom, more!'."

Following this moment of high excitement, Ann helps the two settle comfortably facing each other and holds a box of brightly colored feathers in front of them. "Fran, I want you to put a feather in Alissa's hair, and Alissa, I want you to put one in just the same place in your mother's hair." For the next few minutes they sit quietly, carefully placing feathers in each other's hair. When they are all done, Fran gives them a mirror and they gaze admiringly at their handiwork in a mirror: A pair of happy, smiling mother-daughter faces.

Reflections

How can we understand what just happened between Fran and her daughter? For those moments of the lotion and slip game, they shared a brand new dyadic state of consciousness created by and unique to them. Through their synchronized movements and shared laughter, they each gave meaning to the event. Suddenly, Alissa experienced in her whole being that it can be pleasurable *and* safe to be completely caught up in a moment of interaction and shared joy with another person. Once this had happened between them, there was no going back—a deeper sense of connection had been created that helped pave the road to a more secure attachment between Alissa and her mother.

Because of Alissa's chaotic life experiences and her mother's discouragement, we assume that their PLAY emotional circuits (Panksepp, 1998) were seldom activated prior to the Theraplay sessions. It is not uncommon when adopting a 10 year old child for parents and professionals to focus on developmental progress and forget about play and earlier forms of attachment building. We also know that Alissa often shifted into sympathetic arousal of fight and flight behaviors. The sensitive, guided play plus the social engagement of the Theraplay session regulated sympathetic arousal (Porges, 2011) and allowed her to experience the true goal of interpersonal play: social joy. Golding & Hughes (2012) point out that play can serve as a less intense form of affection for dyads who cannot tolerate direct, prolonged care. There were also some nurturing moments within the play as Fran put lotion on Alissa's arms before slipping away and tenderly decorated her daughter's hair with feathers. In both cases, Alissa's response was very different from her usual rejection of her mother's care.

It takes many moments like this in therapy for the child's relationship with her mother to become solid and secure. Alissa is now willing to accept her mother's nurturing touch. She comes in to bed in the evening to cuddle with her while watching TV. And she is no longer physically or verbally aggressive. She is still vulnerable to moments of fear and uncertainty and emotional upset, but now she seeks out her mother and welcomes her comforting presence until she feels better. Alissa spontaneously tells how much she appreciates her and loves her. Fran can feel that her daughter wants and needs her.

Although the therapist included other methods of treating trauma, Fran says she thinks the play was what made the biggest difference—it gave her the courage to reach out and connect with her child.

Providing Essential Co-regulation

Our next example highlights the Theraplay therapist's role in calming and co-regulating an agitated child.

Background

Sylvia was a bright, energetic, out-going and self-confident 5 year old girl. Her parents sought help because her high energy and need for attention were disruptive to the other students and teacher in her school classroom.

Theraplay Session

At her first session, Sylvia rushes into the Theraplay room and excitedly explores the materials that her therapist, Helen, has prepared for the session. She eagerly enters into each new activity and is quick to suggest new ways of doing it. When Helen challenges Sylvia to pick up 3 cotton balls with her toes, she grabs a big handful and insists on "thirteen!" Helen's calm but firm response "Three, this time," momentarily settles Sylvia. But when Helen gives Sylvia a ball to throw into the "basketball hoop" she has made with her arms, Sylvia throws it over her Helen's head. Sylvia's high level of excitement is palpable and Helen is hard pressed to find ways to calm her.

When it is time for a snack at the end of the session, Sylvia asks for "More, more, more!" before she can even finish the food in her mouth. Her voice reflects her increasing agitation. In order to help Sylvia experience the snack time as calm and relaxing, Helen matches the intensity of her response to Sylvia's high intensity, hoping to then modulate it. "Oh you just want, more, more, more!" Helen says emphatically while tapping her own leg for emphasis. Captivated for a moment, Sylvia laughs. In a softer voice, Helen says, "That's right, 'More, more, more.'" But the moment of calm is gone and Sylvia yells, "More, more, more!"

It is clear to Helen that Sylvia is in such a state of high arousal that it will take more than an ordinary calm response to help her settle into a more relaxed and regulated state. Perhaps moving more actively from matching to modulating would help. She says, "Say it louder. See if you can go (in a loud voice that matched Sylvia's earlier tone) 'more, more, more!'" Fully engaged with this game, Sylvia screams, "More, more, more!" Helen leans toward Sylvia and whispers, "More, more, more." Momentarily engaged, Sylvia leans toward Helen and matches her whisper, "More, more, more." Encouraged, Helen tries a lilting, sing-song version of "More, more, more, more." Sylvia's attempt to match Helen's "song" ends with a rising pitch, "More, more, more, more!" In order to practice the modulation between loud and soft, excited and calm, Helen suggests one more loud repetition, which brings a very high shriek from Sylvia as she reaches out toward Helen. Helen takes Sylvia's hands in hers to soothe her, saying gently. "Little voices can go really high. Let's see if we can both do the soft one." Still holding Sylvia's hands, she quietly says, "More, more, more." Sylvia mouths the words without a sound. Helen copies this and Sylvia repeats it again. For a moment the two feel calm and relaxed. Helen says, "We are so quiet." Following this, Sylvia accepts the rest of the snack—cookies and juice—in a quiet, content manner.

Reflections

The challenge for Sylvia's therapist was to find a way to meet her at her high energy and gradually modulate her excitement level to bring it within healthier bounds. The simple, comfortable play space which she provided created a level of environmental regulation. But this was not enough to help Sylvia settle in this first session. She also had to provide relational regulation through her efforts to get in synch with Sylvia's excitement, to modulate her arousal level and to engage her in playful interaction. Attention to these variables allows for co-regulation between therapist and client.

Working With Parents in Theraplay

A powerful aspect of the Theraplay model is the inclusion of parents in the treatment. Parents are helped to see, reflect on and respond to their child by participating in close, relaxed interactions of imitation, nonverbal dialogues,

FIGURE 11.8
Experiencing positive attention and nurture. (The Theraplay Institute photo)

FIGURE 11.9
A playful experience of co-regulation. (The Theraplay Institute photo)

FIGURE 11.10
Parents directly experience connection in the practice session. (The Theraplay Institute photo)

mirroring and attunement. As parents learn new skills and become more sensitive caregivers, their sense of self-esteem is strengthened. "By actually playing, nurturing, and attuning in Theraplay session new positive moments occur between parent and child that can promote changes in thoughts and feelings" (Mäkelä & Hart, 2011). After the assessment and before the parent-child treatment begins, or at various times when direct practice with the parent is felt to be useful, the therapist and parent may play together to prepare the parent for her role in the sessions and to address questions or reservations prior to bringing the parent and child together. Although parent role play has always been a possible part of the Theraplay process, the specific practice prior to commencing child treatment was developed by our Finnish Theraplay colleagues (Laakso, 2009) and further described in the Theraplay literature (Lender, 2012, Coleman, 2015).

Background

Tracey was the adoptive mother of Bree, an 8-year-old girl who experienced extensive abuse and neglect during the five years before she was adopted. Bree was often uncooperative at home and disruptive at school. In therapy, Bree's therapist, Allison, engaged Bree in interactive and nurturing games to give her experiences of relaxed fun and self-worth. Bree enjoyed the sessions very much and seemed to be benefiting from this type of positive regard. Tracey, however, was disappointed and dissatisfied with Allison's therapy method because she felt the games were a waste of time and that Allison was avoiding

Bree's "real" issues. Allison took time to explain the rationale underlying the approach but Tracey could not be convinced, saying, "When I was young, I would never have been able to get away with what Bree does!" Allison knew little about Tracey's own childhood, yet she sensed that Tracey's resistance was rooted in her own negative experiences in her youth. Knowing that the actual *experience* of the joy, connection and being cared for can effect a person on a deeper physiologic level than cognitive explanations, Allison suggested to Tracey that she come in without Bree for the next appointment so that Allison could have the opportunity to play the games herself. Surprisingly, Tracey said yes to the invitation.

Parent Session

In the next session, Tracey comes without Bree for her own Theraplay session. Allison prepares several fun and relaxing interactions for the two of them to do. They are both sitting cross-legged on the floor on comfortable pillows. They face each other and are close enough to make contact. Allison begins by touching Tracey's nose and chin and making funny "beeping" and "honking" noises. Tracey laughs in surprise. Then they build a "tower" with their hands, taking turns putting one hand over the others. As the hands go higher up in front of their faces, their eye contact is temporarily blocked. Allison lifts up her hand and quickly "peeks" at Tracey, saying delightedly "There you are!" Tracey's eyes light up with pleasure and she laughs again. Finally Allison asks Tracey to fill her cheeks with air and Allison "pops" Tracey's cheeks by gently pressing on them with her hands. Again Tracey lets out a rolling, hearty laugh.

After taking in the moment of shared joy, Allison pauses to explain that the games help create connection and a sense of togetherness, which is what her daughter missed out on when she was little. A look of reflection passes over Tracey's face as she says: "These are fun little games for kids, they'll like them, probably want to do all the time." This allows for a therapist-parent dialogue as follows:

ALLISON: What do you feel like when we are playing?
TRACEY: (Looking intently at Allison) Just connected, like it's you and me and the world, playing and having fun, real simple.
ALLISON: And you don't have to do anything to be noticed. That's why we do it, connecting with them without having to perform, like "get your school work done."

TRACEY: Yeah, that's really neat.

ALLISON: Did you ever get to be silly like this?

TRACEY: No I was always real serious. I didn't cause too many problems, didn't get in trouble at school. I almost felt . . . if I stay quiet. . . . There's so much drama going on, you don't want to cause any more drama in our house. Don't get in trouble. There was so much other chaos. My parents just thought I was okay. My step father said "I never worry about you." And now I'm thinking Wow!

ALLISON: The thing is, you didn't know what it was like to be noticed, feel comfortable with it, that it could be ok.

TRACEY: I still don't like people to do big stuff, make a big deal about me, I don't know what that's about.

ALLISON: Well, it's not safe; if you stay in the background it feels a whole lot more safe.

TRACEY: (Raises eyebrows, nods her head, assimilating this new insight) Oh!

At the end of the session, Allison sings a special version of *Twinkle, Twinkle Little Star* tailored just for Tracey: "What a special girl you are, soft brown hair and rosy cheeks, big brown eyes from which you peek, twinkle, twinkle little star, what a special girl you are." Tracey watches Allison intently through the entire song.

TRACEY: (looking very moved, and with her hand to her chest) Oh, I like all of that. That's so sweet. Wow, makes me want to cry, so sweet, wow.

ALLISON: (also visibly moved): You can cry.

TRACEY: You sure?

ALLISON: You can cry.

TRACEY: (With tears rolling down her cheeks) Wow, why does that affect me like that?

ALLISON: Probably because no one has ever sung to you like that, with no expectations. You can just be who you are and feel special, no performance, no approval, just be who you were meant to be

TRACEY: Yeah, (sniffling). Wow, that was sweet. (Looks directly at therapist), I enjoyed this! Thank you.

ALLISON: It's to experience what a child would feel; because you haven't had those experiences. It's especially for you, to find out how special this feels and a motivation for you to do it with your daughter.

TRACEY: Yes, wow, thank you so much!

Reflections

It is very common for parents not to recognize the value of interpersonal play and nurture as a primary focus of treatment. Parents are frequently focused on the behavioral problems and are worried about the negative outcomes that might result if their child's behavior does not improve. This skepticism is even more of an obstacle if the parent herself does not have the experiential foundation of being deeply embraced and delighted in by her own parents. In Tracey's case, no matter how hard Allison tried to explain the developmental theory behind Theraplay, Tracey simply could not relate to the experiences Allison was describing as essential for her daughter's healing. It was only through feeling the pleasure of the joint attention, connectedness and caring with Allison that Tracey was able to know on a limbic level what the goal was for her daughter. Furthermore, the experience of Theraplay enabled Tracey to reflect on how her own upbringing was linked to her current functioning. Reaching this type of insight into one's own history is directly linked to the development of a reflective capacity in the parent, which is a crucial indicator of secure attachment. This is the reason why we include Theraplay sessions for parents: to enhance both their personal as well as parental growth on all levels of their functioning.

Conclusion

Forty-five years ago Theraplay began with the simple idea of using interactive play to help troubled children in the Head Start Program. Following Bowlby's suggestion we patterned our play on that of loving parents with their young children. We found that creating this kind of experience can reverse the effects of early relational trauma and loss. Since our model is based on the interaction of very young children and their parents, we naturally focus on activities that stimulate deep levels of the autonomic and limbic systems in the emotional brain. Schore & Schore (2008, pp. 17–18) remind us of the importance of "early dyadic regulation, right hemisphere development and the formation of implicit procedural memory" in treating relational trauma. As they suggest, Theraplay focuses on pre-verbal, facial, vocal, and gestural communication and its importance in developing the limbic system right brain function and affect regulation. By bringing parents and child together in a relaxed and safe setting and helping them engage in loving, playful interaction, we are able to create the safety, intersubjectivity, synchrony, and co-regulation that lead to comfort and joy in their relationships.

References

Booth, P. B. & Jernberg, A. M. (2010). *Theraplay: Helping parents and children build better relationships through attachment-based play*. San Francisco: Jossey-Bass.

Booth, P., Christensen, G., & Lindaman, S. (2011). *Marschak Interaction Method (MIM) manual and cards (Revised)*. Evanston, IL: The Theraplay Institute, Inc.

Bowlby, J. (1969). *Attachment and loss: Vol 1. Attachment*. New York: Basic Books

Bowlby, J. (1988). *A secure base: parent-child attachment and healthy human development*. New York: Basic Books.

California Evidence-Based Clearinghouse for Child Welfare (December, 2009). cebc4cw.org/program/theraplay

Coleman, R. (2015). Parent training session in Theraplay: Adjusting for culture, boundaries, and gender differences between therapist and parents. *Newsletter of The Theraplay Institute*, 8–11.

Field, T. (1995). Infant massage therapy. In Field, T. (Ed.) *Touch in early development* (pp. 105–114). Mahwah, NJ: Erlbaum.

Golding, K. S. & Hughes, D. A. (2012). *Creating loving attachments*. London: Jessica Kingsley Publishers.

Harlow, H. F. (1958). The nature of love. *American Psychologist, 13*, 673–685.

Jernberg, A. M. (1979). *Theraplay: A new treatment using structured play for problem children and their families*. San Francisco: Jossey-Bass.

Jernberg, A. M., Hurst, T. & Lyman, C. (1969) *Here I Am* (Motion Picture). (Available from The Theraplay Institute, 1840 Oak Avenue, Suite 320, Evanston, IL 60201).

Jernberg, A. M., Hurst, T. & Lyman, C. (1975) *There He Goes* (Motion Picture). (Available from The Theraplay Institute, 1840 Oak Avenue, Suite 320, Evanston, IL 60201).

Laakso, M. (2009). Parent session in Theraplay: A way to consolidate therapeutic alliance and joint focus. In Munns, E. (Ed.). *Applications of family and group Theraplay* (pp. 183–196). Lanham, MD: Jason Aronson.

Lender, D. (2012, Summer). Working with parents before starting Theraplay with the child. *Newsletter of The Theraplay Institute*, 8–15.

Mäkelä, J. (2005). Kosketuksen merkitys lapsen kehityksessä (The importance of touch in the development of children). *Finnish Medical Journal, 60*, 1543–1549.

Mäkelä, J. & Hart, S. (2011). Theraplay: an intensive, engaging, interactive play that promotes psychological development." Unpublished English translation of chapter in Hart, S. (Ed.) *Neuroaffectiv psykoterapi med børn (Neuroaffective Psychotherapy for Children, pp. 1–28)*. Denmark: Hans Reitzels.

Marschak, M. (1960). A method for evaluating child-parent interactions under controlled condition. *The Journal of Genetic Psychology, 97*, 3–22.

Panksepp, J. (1998). *Affective neuroscience*. New York: Oxford University Press.

Panksepp, J. & Biven, L. (2012). *The archaeology of mind*. New York: W. W. Norton & Company.

Perry, B. D. (2006). The neurosequential model of therapeutics: Applying principles of neurodevelopment to clinical work with maltreated and traumatized children. In Webb, N. B. (Ed.). *Working with traumatized youth in child welfare* (pp. 27–52). New York: The Guilford Press.

Porges, S. W. (2011).*The polyvagal theory: Neurophysiological foundations of emotions, attachment, communication, and self-regulation*. New York: W. W. Norton & Company.

Porges, S. W. (2015a). Making the world safe for our children: down-regulating defense and up-regulating social engagement to "optimise" the human experience. *Children Australia, 40,* 114–123.

Porges, S. W. (2015b). Play as neural exercise: Insights from the Polyvagal Theory. In Pearce-McCall, D. (Ed.), *The power of play for mind brain health* (pp. 3–7). Available from *http://mindgains.org.*

Schore, A. N. (1994). *Affect regulation and origin of the self.* Mahwah, NJ: Lawrence Erlbaum Associates.

Schore, A. N. (2003). Early relational trauma, disorganized attachment, and the development of a predisposition to violence. In Siegel, D. & Solomon, M. (Eds.). *Healing trauma* (pp. 107–167). New York: W. W. Norton & Company.

Schore, A. N. & Schore, J. R. (2008). Modern attachment theory: the central role of affect regulation in development and treatment. *Clinical Social Work Journal, 36,* 9–20.

Siegel, D. (1999). *The developing mind.* New York: The Guilford Press.

Suomi, S. J. (1995). Interview. *The Journal of NIH Research, 7*(4), 74–76.

Tronick, E. Z., Ricks, M., & Cohn, J. F. (1982). Maternal and infant affective exchange: Patterns of adaptation. In Field, T. & Fogel, A. (Eds.). *Emotion and early interaction* (pp. 83–100). Hillsdale, NJ: Erlbaum.

van der Kolk, B. (1994). The body keeps the score. *Harvard Review of Psychiatry, 1*(5), 253–265.

Vygotsky, L. P. (1978). *Mind in society: The development of higher psychological processes.* Cambridge, MA: Harvard University Press.

Winnicott, D. W. (1965). *The maturational processes and the facilitating environment: Studies in the theory of emotional development.* London: Hogarth Press.

12

PLAY and the Construction of Creativity, Cleverness, and Reversal of ADHD in our Social Brains

Jaak Panksepp

[c]ertain actions, which we recognize as expressive of certain states of mind, are the direct result of the constitution of the nervous system, and have been from the first independent of the will, and, to a large extent, of habit.... Our present subject is very obscure, but, from its importance, must be discussed at some little length; and it always is advisable to perceive clearly our ignorance.

—Charles Darwin (1872)

THE CROSS-MAMMALIAN GENOME projects of the recent past have revealed that mammals (including humans) have only about ~22,000 genes in the cells of their bodies, including the neurons of our brains, despite earlier estimates—before modern technologies set us straight—that put expert estimates closer to ~100,000 genes. This brings us face-to-face with the reality that we are simply just another mammalian species. Many also believed, and still do, that *nurture* was more important than *nature* in the construction of the internal sophistication of our brains. Of course, both are essential.

A key issue is how to integrate them accurately and creatively, so neither

242

is marginalized. Neuroscience and genetics offer a new conclusion about the brain—lower brain functions are more genetically determined than higher brain functions where learning becomes ever more critical as encephalization increases. Thus, the critical importance of *nurture* is especially important for understanding the functions of our massive neocortical expansions—our "thinking cap," so to speak, that is essential for human cognitive creativity. In contrast, subcortical brain regions are functionally programmed much more by *nature*—since there are many more inborn solutions for living down there than in the initially "idea-empty" neocortex. In a sense, the subcortical affective powers of the mind facilitate creative programming of the upstairs brain. Thus, within the neocortex, developmental experiences, reflecting often the qualities of *nurture*, are of foremost importance, since life experiences program upper cognitive/neocortical brain regions to inhabit the world in thoughtful, individualistic, affective-, environmental-, and culture-dependent ways.

In short, modern genetics and neuroscience have not yet been able to decisively demonstrate that *any* cortical functions are genetically dictated, although there is abundant data that cortical programming arises from many *epigenetic* influences—i.e., how gene expression patterns within many brain regions are controlled by experiential factors (Keverne, 2014). Rigorous cross-species neuroscience work indicates that even the ability of our visual cortex to see is learned during early development (Sur & Rubinstein, 2005). Indeed, one can easily imagine that practically all of our cortical functions are refined initially through simple learning and ultimately by diverse cultural influences. Meanwhile, most of our in-built (i.e., unconditional, primary-process) "tools for living"—from our ability to dream to feeling our bodily states (e.g., HUNGER and THIRST) and the seven primal emotions to be introduced (the main focus of this essay)—are mediated by subcortical processes, which contain many, many more genetically dictated specializations than any newborn neocortex.

So what are the implications of all of this for understanding creativity? Here, I develop the idea that our inborn emotional systems, all of which are situated below our neocortical random access memory (RAM)-type brain systems (Panksepp, 1998a), are sufficient for the birth of young mammals, of all species, who already have abundant inborn affects—including *emotional* (within brain), *homeostatic* (body regulation), and *sensory* (pain, pleasure, and so on) affective varieties. We know this simply because, if one surgically eliminates all of the neocortex in higher brain regions of animals soon after birth (of course, such empirical work has been largely done in laboratory rats with much less work in other species), according to Kolb & Tees (1990) and Panksepp, et al. (1994), such animals grow up to be remarkably emotional creatures. The same is the case for humans born with massive neocortical deficits (Merker, 2007; Solms & Panksepp, 2012). Clearly, the unconditioned (i.e., instinctual) positively and negatively *valenced* (affective arousal-feeling) aspects of our emotional minds do not require abundant neocortex; just consider Shewmon, et al.'s (1999) work with hyranencephalic children, with many basic emotions intact, with practically no functional neocortex.

Humans born without neocortices (or animals that had their neocortices surgically removed soon after birth), are clearly affectively conscious, although they will never be cognitively "smart." Such animals exhibit very robust juvenile play, and can compete effectively (as determined by who *prevails* during rough-and-tumble juvenile play, as monitored with "pinning" measures—namely who ends up on top). Indeed, in a laboratory class of 16 students studying brain and behavior about a quarter century ago, the author prepared 2 animals for each student during the first week of class, one completely decorticated and the other simply having the sham surgery with neocortex left intact. After 14 weeks of study, the last laboratory practicum for each student was straightforward: Each was given 2 rats to observe for half an hour independently, one decorticated and the other not, with the assignment being to choose/decide which rat was decorticated. I thought it would be basically a matter of chance. To my amazement, 12 of 16 students chose the

FIGURE 12.1
Rough-and-tumble social play in rats. (Courtesy of Jaak Panksepp. Artwork by Lonnie Rosenberg)

decorticates to be the normal animals. In debriefing, the main reason for the incorrect selection was that students chose the animal that was more active, exploring vigorously (and hence interested), as being the normal one. Of course, in its supreme role in mediating cognitive skills, the neocortex often needs to inhibit and regulate emotionality, including what may be threatening in a new environment.

Clearly, it is unlikely that our genetic-hereditary stores provide enough information to construct a *fully* human higher social-emotional-cognitive mind that reflects anything close to our full potentials for creativity, as commonly inspired by our affective passions. In contrast, the genes provide many *subcortical* brain "skills for emotional-affective living," which probably help to inspire creativity in our cortices. Thus it is becoming ever clearer, for those paying attention to lessons from a cross-species *affective neuroscience*, that we do not scientifically understand the higher feelings of our brains and minds—from affective enthusiasms (especially via SEEKING) to creativity. The other basic emotions probably allow us to flow from RAGEful resentments to FEARful anxieties and shame, while PANIC can set the stage for deep sorrows and grief. Such flows help establish both creative and obsessive ideas in our upper minds, so to speak—and if so, we will not understand creativity, both positive and negative, until we understand the inborn (so-called "basic") emotional systems of our brains. Only animal research can provide us with clear neuroscientific evidence for the breadth and depth of the neuroevolutionary foundations (neuroanatomical, neurochemical, and neurodynamic) of our primal affective lives, which can both promote (usually the positive emotions) and hinder (via more negative ones) the capacity of our upper minds to be cognitively, often artistically and productively creative, as opposed to just narrowly obsessive.

Of course, each life trajectory will be different. Thus, developmentally, all of us neuropsychologically progress from *anoetic* (affective, without *knowing*) memories to *autonoetic* (knowing) states of mind, guided culturally as well as by individual experiences toward integrated affective-cognitive planning, based on remembrance of things past and imagined futures (Vandekerckhove & Panksepp, 2009, 2011). This has great implications for psychotherapy, where expert guidance is often needed for the turmoil of troublesome emotions to be guided toward positive affective shores, as through the powers of memory reconsolidation (e.g., see Lane, Ryan, Nadel, & Greenberg, 2015; Marks-Tarlow & Pankespp, 2015).

Thus, although our chromosomes contain enough genetic information to construct the sophisticated brains and *potential* minds that most of our babies possess at birth, they do not have enough information to construct mature, healthy, creative upper-minds. That must be achieved by living in rich affective environments and social worlds that program our neocortices (our "think-ing caps"), which have been evolutionarily constructed as initially "empty" neocortical random access memory (RAM)-type spaces) for programming our declarative-semantic and episodic-prospective memories into affectively and cognitively integrated strategies (Tulving, 2002). Many cognitive processes are consolidated-solidified by our fluctuating affective states in the midst of real-life affective experiences that arise from below (e.g., via subcortical *emotional*, *homeostatic*, and *sensory* valenced-value systems).

We are born (as are all other mammals) with various neocortical networks that can barely see and think at birth, which only gradually develop the full potential to think and plan and ultimately be creative (even cognitively clever). Only slowly, over the span of years, do we arise like phoenixes as the affec-tive flames of our subcortically organized passions guide our thinking and decision-making. It is very important for each human (and the psychological and psychiatric sciences) to come to term with the fact that our primal pas-sions and motivations come in various kinds of action-feeling neural networks, concentrated subneocortically, that we share with all the other mammals, and indeed, with many other vertebrates. In our neocortices, we become uniquely smart through interaction with cognitively rich and supportive environments. In short, our passions and motivations arise from the affective neural net-works of our ancient brain regions—to reiterate, from various survival-related, body-action-oriented, *emotional* networks, as well as *regulatory-homeostatic* and externally oriented *sensory-perceptual* systems that all motivate and control the construction of our memories. However, early vicissitudes can leave various emotional-cognitive wounds that can often be helped by therapists, espe-cially those who know how to treat affective "scars" by *reconsolidating* better memories through the power of positive emotions (see Lane, et al., 2015, with 28 commentaries). Still, it remains a scientific challenge to integrate human *cognitive neuroscience* and cross-species *affective neuroscience* approaches to under-standing the neural nature of emotional feelings (Panksepp, Lane, Solms, & Smith, 2016).

The *sensory-perceptual processes* of many neocortical brain regions allow us to experience the explicit structures of our worlds—to feel, touch, hear, and see. Meanwhile, the intrinsic *regulatory* and *emotional* systems, of much more ancient subcortical brain regions, code for our diverse bodily *homeostatic* needs-motivations that help assure our survival, from THIRST, HUNGER, and WARMTH to various *sensory* PAINs and PLEASUREs, as well as others that protect us from illness, through experiences such as DISGUST. Many other primary *emotional* processes allow us to mature into vibrant affective creative creatures that know how to behave with others and to find both physical and social environments where we can aspire to thrive. SEEKING, RAGE, FEAR, LUST, CARE, PANIC/SORROW, and PLAY are the major emotional/motivational circuits that Mother Nature built into the ancient subcortical regions of our mammalian brains, with the positive emotions (especially SEEKING, CARE, and PLAY) probably helping inspire productive creativity.

We capitalize the affective primes in order to highlight that they are empirically verified systems (Panksepp, 1998a), still incompletely understood (partly because so few are working on them, since it requires cross-species brain research). We know that various brain systems can evoke distinct emotional *behavioral* states that are also important for generating experienced *affect—positively and negatively valenced* states, because evocation of the above behavioral states with deep brain stimulation is uniformly rewarding or punishing in both animals (Panksepp, 1982, 1998) and humans (Panksepp, 1985). These are ancestral *emotional-affective, behavioral-integrated mind* systems from which our very special enthusiasms, survival urges, and rich (or impoverished) affectively constructed upper cognitive minds emerge through learning. In short, the ancient-evolved affective systems facilitate the construction of our upper minds—to learn essential life skills, to be both creative and clever, and with learning to communicate our survival and thriving needs and wishes to others.

The Creative Socialization of the Brain

Woe to a child who does not have emotionally responsive and resilient CARE providers. Woe to a child who has too much FEAR, RAGE, and PANIC, which can lead positive creativity to shrivel. Human socialization (and mental health) thrive when children have abundant opportunities for positive SEEKING and PLAY, especially in the context of devoted CARE, which can eventually (as symphonies of sex hormones mature at puberty) promote healthy LUST, when spiced with playfulness. When children's brains and minds are immersed in culturally rich, mind-supporting environments, children tend to thrive through many self-generated activities, commonly known as play, the primary-process, fundamental-evolved, subcortical-foundational version of this, shared with all mammals, at the very least; the PLAY label also reminds us that, most especially, it mediates the Prominent Ludic Activities of Youth, which are present in all young mammals, perhaps many other species, as well as healthy adults, who often have to share (or fight) for resources (Fig. 12.2).

The genes that control the growth of such brain systems are not yet known, but they provide rough-and-ready (*unconditional*, in psychological parlance) neural systems for survival—diverse affective and cognitive tools that allow

FIGURE 12.2
Even goats like to butt heads. (Public domain)

family and societal influences to create pro-social, functional minds, versus ones that will be in need of prolonged support (such as through psychotherapy) by diverse lifecoach wizards who understand and want to help heal broken human minds. Indeed, the practice of psychotherapy—the healing of emotionally damaged brains—is currently being increasingly enriched and facilitated by modern neuroscientific understanding of emotions, and a remarkable aspect of our dynamic memories, which can be re-molded toward positive perspectives in the context of supportive others (for extensive recent discussions and controversies see Lane, et al., 2015; Panksepp, et al., 2016).

To be sure, in order to use the gifts of Mother Nature well, we need to create learning environments that resonate well with the dramatic joyful play urges that our children naturally experience—namely environments where brain SEEKING and PLAY systems are among the main players in unfolding life activities. Here is how it works from a sensitive adult's perspective (vignette shared by personal communication by German psychiatrist Elisabeth Troje; see Panksepp 2008, p. 66):

Our big house in the Black Forest is surrounded by meadows and trees. In vacation time the family meets there. In my apartment are two grandchildren, who live in Antigua, West Indies and speak only English, Jasper, 10, and Imogen, 5 years old. There arrive two boys, grandchildren of my sister, 8 and 6 years, who live near London, speaking English and German. The four children stare at each other without a word. Then Jasper and Imogen begin to tease each other, using their feet, to knock each other, it looks dangerous, they hit the other's stomach and genital regions, but they do it softly, perhaps practised in Karate-like sports. They begin to laugh at each other without taking notice of their cousins, who stare at them, begin to move, to jump on the spot, begin to laugh, too. As soon as they move all in the same rhythm, Jasper turns to the door, running downstairs, behind him Imogen, behind them the two cousins follow immediately, they are running outside, and they disappear in the meadows and then between the trees, playing for hours, indulging in games of their own making.

Indeed, optimal psychotherapeutic environments help create opportunities for painful past memories to fade and be replaced by positive possibilities using that remarkable therapeutic tool known as memory reconsolidation, which has yielded tremendous excitement in psychotherapeutic communities around the world (for overview see Lane, et al., 2015), with abundant discussions (including our own commentary—Marks-Tarlow & Panksepp, 2015). Real PLAY, allowing deep SEEKING enthusiasms to be pursued with like-minded others, is an optimal environment for the development of mentally healthy citizens of the future. But appropriate open spaces are needed. Although many recognize such dilemmas for modern culture, surprisingly the importance of natural physical play (without toys) for our children was only recently documented (Scott, 2001; Scott & Panksepp, 2003; Panksepp & Scott, 2013).

At the point of discovering the importance of physical play for understanding ADHD, my colleagues and I had already been studying play for about three decades (Panksepp, et al., 1984), surprisingly without any government research support (of course we had asked). This sort of PLAY "work"—namely the Prominent Ludic Activities of Youth—was often considered frivolous. At the same time, a quarter of a century ago, the prescription of psychostimulants to reduce excessive childhood activities was on a meteoric, government-supported, rise. And all those psychostimulants dramatically reduce play (Beatty, et al., 1982), while increasing materialistic desires (Panksepp, et al., 2002).

Let me state it boldly: Without abundant PLAY and SEEKING, the mental health and positive creativity of our children will be compromised. Rather than enriching their early years in dynamic social environments where natural play is both permitted and promoted, increasing numbers of children, quite poignantly and most heavily in the USA, have been medicated with psychostimulants that certainly promote young and restless minds to sit more still, perhaps because such chemicals quiet the playfully distracting "ants in their pants." A few decades ago, Finland learned that lesson well, by decreeing that for every hour of elementary school instruction, there should be 15 minutes devoted to free play. Indeed, academic lessons become more "digestible" if those natural physical needs of their mind/body health and integration are satisfied. And we have known for a long time that the psychostimulants, still most widely prescribed in the USA, dramatically reduce playfulness—keeping many kids quietly "attentive," without much evidence that those addictive drugs clearly facilitate the kinds of pro-social humanistic learning that Mother Nature started promoting hundreds of millions of years ago. Abundant juvenile PLAY can even help reverse the consequences of upper executive-brain damage, as in the frontal cortices (Panksepp, et al., 2003).

I have gained undesired notoriety for advancing the premise that most of the diagnosed attention deficit hyperactivity disorders (ADHD) may often reflect cultural illnesses of our society, rather than a "real" neuropsychological disorder (Panksepp, 1998a; Panksepp & Scott, 2013). Our attempt to obtain a pittance of support from the National Institutes of Health (NIH) to deploy a "play sanctuary" intervention for ADHD in young children was soundly rejected three times in a row, although the failure to deploy such humanistic interventions may be a tragedy in the making (Panksepp, 1998b). Is our childhood mental health system in the pocket of Big Pharma, which is enriched by the widespread selling of potentially long-term disadvantageous and addictive mind medicines? Is there truly a dramatically growing brain disorder afflicting more and more of our children each year? Or perhaps childhood bodily enthusiasms are simply not sufficiently welcome in our educational system. In short, why are more than 10 million American children being chronically medicated with drugs, well known to be addictive, apparently at higher rates than in any other country in the world, while adults who consume cocaine, a neurochemical cousin of amphetamines, are persecuted and often jailed? The long-term psycho- and neurobiological effects of these drugs in animal models have long provided reasons for concern, including heightened incidence of depressive disorders when discontinued (Panksepp, 1998b, 2001, 2008).

Why are we not, at a national level, using the powers of social PLAY urges to promote childhood mental health more vigorously? Why don't we have a national "Day for Play" (perhaps facilitated by play-devoted Disney industries) to highlight this essential power in our lives, perhaps a key pillar of our sports-crazed society? Access to real PLAY, in the animal models we pioneered (Panksepp, 1981), dramatically elevated positive gene-expression pattern in the "thinking caps" (i.e., neocortices) of our juvenile rats (Moskal, et al., 2011)—some of the genes presumably enlivening and honing brain-gene expression patterns. In the future, PLAYful brain tools should be used to promote enthusiastic, self-motivated learning and positive social and ultimately healthy sexual emotional engagements. Our work for several score years (and tears, of non-fundable ideas).

When Tom Insel became director of the National Institute of Mental Health, I emailed a brief note of congratulations, at the end of which I asked whether he could foresee a day when our seminal work on rat-laughter (systematically evoked by tickling) might be funded. He responded graciously in a few hours, concluding "By the way Jaak, we have our own research priorities." Little could he anticipate that by studying the neurochemistries of rat laughter, we would develop a totally novel anti-depressant that, in preliminary trials, has been highly effective in reducing depression (Moskal, et al., 2011; Preskhorn, for overviews, see Panksepp, 2015, 2016).

Proper engagement of the PLAY system promotes healthy, pro-social brain maturation in the living present. To promote child mental health—"thrive by

FIGURE 12.3
Kids Can Play Anywhere. (Courtesy of Jan Goldstein)

five" policies, as in Washington State (thank you former Governor Christine Gregoir), or less focused "No Child Left Behind" policies in the rest of the country (and many other nations of the world)—we should also be creating optimal (play-enthusiasm-filled) learning environments. Such environments are characterized by natural, joyful, SEEKING, PLAYful activities with ample opportunities to enhance their evolutionarily appointed task of creating healthy, pro-social, creative-enthusiastic upper minds.

To reiterate, we inherit at least four genetically coded, *social*-emotional tools (shared by all mammalian brains), that can promote the construction of fully pro-social minds: 1) Throughout development, our childhood urge to PLAY should be seamlessly integrated with our 2) profound capacity to CARE for others, as well as to feel PANIC (separation-distress) when our social bonds are severed, and 3) to enthusiastically SEEK new knowledge and life perspectives (Panksepp, 1998b, 2005). Three of these inherited primal emotional action systems generate positive feelings (emotional affects) as they facilitate positive social feelings, social bonding, and ultimately feelings of empathy and devoted concern for others. In contrast, the psychological feeling of social-separation pain triggered by the PANIC system, highlights the profound need we have for supportive social others—from parents, extended families, and the pro-social policies of our communities and nation as well as the world at large. These fundamental powers of the mind, with some institutional devotion around the country, especially perhaps funding by rich play industries (should we not have a "National Disney Day of Play"?) could currently be much better used to promote joyful, positive enculturation of our children, and thereby also diminish the impact of the three negative primal emotions.

In the long term, lots of joyous physical PLAY probably helps build and strengthen the reflective, inhibitory resources that facilitate adult pro-social planning. At present, such inherited positive emotional forces of the brain are being used haphazardly. As we learn to use the fundamental brain pro-social tools for living more effectively, I anticipate we will have less willingness to use addiction-promoting, personality-changing psychostimulants that sensitize the brain (Nocjar & Panksepp, 2002) and partly compromise frontal-cortical, inhibitory functions that have not yet matured under the enthusiastic psychobiological guidance of the pro-social PLAY networks of our mammalian brains. Again, abundant PLAY promotes recovery from frontal-cortical damage (Panksepp, 2001, 2008; Panksepp, et al., 2003). Although psychostimulants can reduce the impulsivity of children diagnosed with ADHD, we clearly have better potential ways to deal with such developmental issues than are presently deployed in our school systems and culture. At a societal level, we need to institutionalize the power of PLAY, perhaps starting with

FIGURE 12.4
The Whole World is a Playground. (Courtesy of Jan Goldstein)

an annual "Day of Play" to help focus on and promote pro-social brain-mind maturation—including ability for cognitive reflection, imagination, empathy, and creativity as summarized below.

Our laboratory has now spent more than three decades of self-funded research studying the neural details of PLAY and the other most important affectively positive pro-social emotional tools-for-living, encoded in our genetic heritage, which help children mature into pro-social and productive members of society—the ancient subcortical SEEKING, PANIC, and PLAY systems (Panksepp, 1981, 1998b, 2001; Panksepp, et al., 1980, 1984)—all genetically provided, basic emotional tools for living: The dopamine-"fired" SEEKING system is a general-purpose system for all appetitive urges that can promote the enthusiasms and creativities of the LUST, CARE, and PLAY systems. Together, these allow for creativity in how we positively value others. Meanwhile, negative emotions, especially separation distress (i.e., PANIC states), promote crying in order to inform us of the disruption of social bonds. The pro-social feelings of PLAY help young children to value the creative company of others. CARE-givers, who invest in their welfare, become cherished companions. Without such attachments, children are less likely to optimally utilize the many opportunities that healthy educational environments provide.

PLAYfulness reflects that emotional system's urge to positively engage with others, routinely as well as creatively, allowing youngsters to learn about diverse social dynamics in affectively positive ways. This can lead children to CARE about others more while they SEEK to understand, and become affectively positive, productive actors in their social worlds. If unfulfilled, probably one of the societal consequences (and tragedies) is increased incidence of ADHD (Panksepp, 1998a). As we creatively learn to restore the full affective-cognitive powers of PLAY to preschoolers' lives, we may dramatically reverse the ADHD epidemic that continues to proliferate. In short, increased opportunities for "real PLAY" may promote the genetic and epigenetic construction of pro-social brains (Burgdorf, et al., 2011; Panksepp, 2001, 2008). This approach has already yielded novel medicines for the treatment of depression (Moskal, et al., 2011; Panksepp, 1980, 2015, 2016). An excellent guide for such neuroscientifically based, enthusiasm-promoting child rearing is Margot Sunderland's (2006) book on *The Science of Parenting* (now in the 3rd edition).

The Nature of ADHD and Minimal Brain Dysfunction

I will briefly overview some of our well-controlled experimental work on animal playfulness that may be relevant for understanding ADHD. Since we have so little access into the fine-grained organization of children's brains (with only low-level correlative knowledge offered by modern brain imaging), animal affective neuroscience models have been essential for tracking down the primary-process, emotional tools for living (Panksepp, 1998a, 2005). This helps us to relate developmental difficulties with basic brain issues (Barkley, 1997; Panksepp, 2001).

Obviously, impulse control problems reflect major difficulties during childhood, partly because of diminished frontal-cortical executive inhibition and regulation. As children develop creative ways to occupy themselves productively, these problems diminish. Much of this gets epigenetically and neurologically built into the brain, and ongoing positive social play is presumably a facilitator of such processes. Thus, emerging understanding of primary-process PLAY brain functions allows us to develop new pro-social ways to facilitate executive brain-mind maturation (Figure 12.5), leading to new perspectives on how to help children better regulate impulse control problems.

In sum, with the ADHD epidemic of the past quarter century, *most* of what gets diagnosed as ADHD may simply reflect natural variation of brain-mind maturation, often promoted by the social environments we have created, although genetic factors can obviously also contribute. What we firmly know neurally is that children diagnosed with ADHD are commonly a bit "shorter"

(~5 percent) in development of frontal lobe executive functions (Castellanos & Tannock, 2002). This has become a pharmacologically treatable social problem soon after children on low ends of the normal distributions enter school. They are not as able to follow instructions as readily as kids with more mature brain-mind regulatory functions. Although there are serious brain problems with a small minority of children, the majority diagnosed with ADHD probably have no clinically relevant brain disorder.

We should clearly be more creative and tolerant with such children. Perhaps many children with apparent impulse control problems simply have social compliance problems, because their compelling urges to play—powerful inbuilt tools for social living and creativity—are thwarted. Obviously, one first needs to consider psychobehavioral interventions that promote frontal brain region maturation (PLAY does that), before utilizing heavy-duty medications that can change the brain in less desirable ways. Obviously, provision of more play as a formal national policy, such as is deployed nationally in Finland,

FIGURE 12.5
The Open-Mouthed Joy of Discovery. (Courtesy of Jan Goldstein)

may work comparable wonders for positive classroom engagements among our own young children. Surely it is wiser for families and society to use positive psychobehavioral intervention with all children at the earliest and most plastic phases of brain-mind development to maximize optimal maturation of the mind.

But clearly, as we know from the USA experience, there are times when society will listen or not. Clearly ADHD has moved into the second category, and thus we have no national policies that systematically promote opportunities for play-facilitated socialization of our children's brains and minds. Obviously, the first line of defense should be implementation of creative pro-social natural play interventions, especially for the many young children who seem to be falling behind. If we had a national play initiative, we might dramatically diminish the perceived need to prescribe attention-promoting medications, whose long-term psychobiological and addictive consequences remain inadequately characterized. Wisdom dictates that all natural pro-social interventions should be properly evaluated before moving to powerful psychostimulants that are well known to have have long-term effects on brain plasticity in animal studies.

All the psychostimulants promote mental arousal and attention in everyone, but where is the solid human and cross-species *evidence* that they promote construction of pro-social brains and minds? Of course, psychostimulant drugs can reduce playfulness and thereby provide attention to focused scholarly activities without being ostracized by teachers and peers. But this needs to be weighed in the context of abundant, preclinical evidence that such drugs sensitize addictive tendencies and potentially reduce plasticity within socially desirable brain functions (e.g., Moll, et al., 2001; Robinson & Kolb, 2004). Surely, more abundant, well-supervised, PLAY-joy activities, where children do not marginalize or bully others could provide greater pro-social benefits for developing brains and minds. We were able to do a limited feasibility study in our public school system in Bowling Green, Ohio, and as already noted, the results looked promising (Scott & Panksepp, 2003; also see Panksepp & Scott, 2013).

ADHD, Psychostimulants, and Drug Abuse

It is well known that most psychostimulants long deployed as long-term treatments for ADHD (e.g., methylphenidate, amphetamines) have neurochemical effects comparable to cocaine. All these drugs can be highly addictive if access is unregulated. Indeed, there is data that children with ADHD treated with psychostimulants often have higher levels of drug abuse disorders later in life (see Biederman, et al., 1998; Wilens, 2004, for early work). This has also long been evident in animal models (Robinson & Berridge, 1993). Despite these findings, it has also been widely claimed that psychostimulant treatment of ADHD children has no such effects (Mannuzza, et al., 2003; Willens & Biederman, 2006), but such studies have often failed to include the amounts of psychostimulants prescribed by physicians in overall levels of drug intake (e.g., Biederman, et al., 1999). For instance, in the initial Biederman, et al. study, children placed on methylphenidate initially had substantially lower drug intake patterns than the unmedicated controls (0 percent and about 38 percent, respectively, with about 27 percent and 77 percent at four-year follow-up). It is hard to interpret subsequent intake patterns when baseline differences in drug consumption already exist. Might such differences also reflect the fact that kids getting medication are also receiving more psycho-social supervision? With children on the ADHD track, we clearly need more creative psychosocial research approaches to evaluate how positive-playful interventions work in the long run.

Neural Effects of Psychostimulants

In any event, it is important to have more formal evaluation of how psychostimulant-induced prophylaxis against behavior problem in ADHD-track kids may be modifying the brain-mind substrates that eventually lead to drug abuse. Many of the underlying emotional and motivational shifts remain poorly documented in children. For instance, do children chronically treated with such medications develop stronger drug cravings, as repeatedly shown in well-controlled animal studies? Do we have compelling scientific evidence that the brains of our psychostimulant-treated children do not exhibit higher cravings of such drugs later in life if opportunities arise? We do have that in animals, where it is clear such animals crave more rewards (Nocjar & Panksepp, 2002; Panksepp, et al., 2002). But that is exactly where the human data stream runs dry.

To my knowledge, changes in adolescent drug craving have never been as well measured in psychostimulant-treated ADHD children as they have in animals. Animal research has provided well-controlled data on the long-term consequences of psychostimulant exposure. Adult animals clearly become sensitized to periodic administration of all psychostimulants. Namely, their nervous systems become chronically hyper-responsive to various drugs of abuse. This increased responsivity is not only reflected in increased drug seeking (Berridge & Robinson, 1998), but also in elevated eagerness to pursue a diversity of hedonic rewards, from sweets to sexual opportunities (Nocjar & Panksepp, 2002). In the vernacular, this sensitization of the emotional-motivational system reflects a sustained elevation of normal desires, a psychological shift from "I want" (so to speak) to "I WANT IT, and I WANT IT NOW!"

It seems that psychostimulant sensitization of animal brains, especially their dopamine-energized SEEKING systems, makes them more urgently "materialistic"—with elevated eagerness for all rewards (Berridge & Robinson, 1998; Browning, et al., 2011). If there is anything we should wish to sensitize in the brains of ADHD children, it would be the urge for pro-social activities. But we don't know how to do that yet. In any event, it is long past time to formally (scientifically) evaluate whether psychostimulant-induced "sensitization" has transpired in the brains and minds of children medicated with psychostimulants for impulse control problems, namely ADHD. This could perhaps be easily done by contrasting the acute physiological effects of psychostimulants in children about to be placed on long-term psychostimulant medications, as compared to same-age children who have been chronically medicated in the past.

At present, the evidence remains inconclusive whether juvenile animals exhibit intensified (or diminished) addiction liability after long-term exposure to psychostimulants, with some evidence both pro and con (e.g., Andersen, et al., 2002; Brandon, et al., 2001). However, there is preliminary evidence that early exposure to such drugs does promote depressive tendencies later in life (Carlezon, et al., 2003; Mague, et al., 2005). One troublesome fact remains very clear: Psychostimulants are among the most powerful social play-reducing drugs in animal models (Beatty, et al., 1982). This should be formally evaluated in human children. Another piece of solace we do have is that younger animals do not develop psychostimulant sensitization as readily as older ones (Solanto, 2000), although adolescent rats certainly do sensitize (Laviola, et al., 1999; Panksepp, et al., 2002). In any event, psychostimulant exposure can promote long-lasting neurochemical and neuroanatomical shifts in the brain (Moll, et al., 2001; Robinson & Kolb, 2004). Most critically, there is no unambiguous evidence that such brain changes are desirable or beneficial.

In short, various compelling psychosocial issues remain to be considered: Might it be that many kids diagnosed with ADHD are simply receiving psychostimulants because they are normal kids who have intense, unsatisfied desires to play? Might it be that some of the perceived "benefits" of prescribed psychostimulants in rambunctious young children are due to these children simply *appearing* to *improve*, because such drugs reduce "disorderly behaviors" that actually reflect their intense urges to play? If so, that would constitute a national tragedy. Clearly there should be greater research investments evaluating and contrasting how abundant social play versus abundant psychostimulant prescriptions influence long-term brain organization of our youngsters, first estimated by the use of animal models. Certainly, we have to understand what chronic exposure to potentially addictive medications does to animals . . . and our children.

ADHD and the Pro-Social Effects of PLAY

Our work on the neurobiology of playfulness suggests that this important gift of nature is a primary-process tool for helping to construct social brains (Panksepp, 1998a, 1998b, 2001). Chronic psychostimulant use may abort the ability of PLAY to do this, as it fails to encourage kids to join the social structures in which they find themselves. Are the fluctuating play-stimulated gene expression patterns and neuropsychological benefits of childhood play diminished in children chronically treated with psychostimulants? As long as we don't scientifically know, we may be playing dice with the minds of our children.

Social play can activate growth factors such as BDNF in the brain (Gordon, et al., 2003). A recent, more comprehensive, brain gene expression analysis found that activity of approximately one third of the 1,200 brain genes we evaluated in frontal cortical regions are rapidly modified by play (Kroes, et al., 2006; Moskal, et al., 2011). It seems highly unlikely that psychostimulants will stimulate such a symphony of dynamically changing gene expression patterns. Since those changes probably reflect what Mother Nature built into our brains as adaptive tools for living, is it not reasonable to provisionally assume such dynamic brain changes evoked by play promote brain growth and mind maturation in pro-social directions?

Although psychobiological studies of the brain and mind benefits of social play remain in their infancy (i.e., surprisingly they have not been a national research priority), we have drawn out some potential implications for ADHD in our animal models of play. "Play therapy" in ADHD-phenotype rats significantly ameliorates impulse control problems later in life (Panksepp, et al., 2003; Panksepp, 2007, 2008). In contrast, treatment with methylphenidate, another psychostimulant that chronically diminishes social play in juvenile rats, promotes brain substrates for desire, as monitored by elevations in psychostimulant-induced, ultrasonic vocalizations (Browning, et al., 2011).

Since the urge to play in our children is an evolved psycho-neurological drive—an insistent emotional urge—might ADHD be, in part, such urges appearing in children in various social situations where rough-and-tumble activities may not be deemed socially acceptable? Indeed, opportunities for natural play have declined in our culture, as natural opportunities have diminished with the growth of enormous cities, car-filled roads, and regimented

FIGURE 12.6
When It's Time to Play Almost Anything Will Do. (Public domain)

education systems. In the final accounting, should such play-starved children be diagnosed with ADHD, and prescribed addictive psychostimulant medications to quell their natural ludic urges? Of course, some may consider such concerns presumptuous. After all: How, some might say, can research on *animals* illuminate the *human* condition? Obviously they have not been paying attention to the massive homologies at genetic, bodily, and brain levels that exist between humans and all other mammals.

For starters, we would predict that, 1) when data are empirically evaluated, we will discover that psychostimulants diminish the urges of *human* children to play, as it does in juvenile rats; 2) abundant physical play, each and every day throughout childhood, will diminish ADHD-type excessive acting-out urges, diminishing the rate at which children are placed on unjustified psychiatric "clinical tracks"; 3) more abundant play, when finally adequately evaluated, will be found to exert long-term pro-social benefits for children's brains and minds, while such effects will not be as evident in children treated with psychostimulants; 4) in contrast, administration of psychostimulants may sensitize young brains, thereby intensifying internally experienced materialistic urges, as well as eventually addictive mental desires, which, *if socio-environmental opportunities are available,* will be reflected in elevated use of diverse addictive drugs; and 5) if we ever obtain relevant genetic results in human children, the gene-expression profiles of children who have had abundant social play will be different (and more beneficial for life trajectories) than the effects of long-term psychostimulant medications. These are testable issues, yet no one is testing them. If such patterns of data were obtained, would that constitute a national tragedy? Perhaps. In any event, it seems likely that very different genetic and neurochemical "tunes" are "strummed" in diverse brain regions by psychostimulant medications as opposed to the social play experiences our children should naturally have (indeed what they naturally desire).

As data from animal models sustain our social concerns, profoundly different options exist in terms of the social policies we might support for childhood brain/mind development—1) those promoting abundant early physical play versus 2) those promoting abundant psychostimulant medications. Obviously this will be a very difficult issue to resolve. There are many resistances by different interest groups and government policy makers. Still, I suspect we would be wise to follow Plato's advice and encourage more free play—"those natural modes of amusement which children find out for themselves when they meet"—in *The Republic* (section IV). Plato insists that "our children from their earliest years must take part in all the more lawful forms of play, for if they are not surrounded with such an atmosphere they can never grow up to be well conducted and virtuous citizens." I anticipate that future research will provide definitive evidence for the conclusion that increasing daily rations of "real play"—namely the games that children themselves creatively design, along with those passed down culturally across generations—will help keep many children away from ADHD-psychiatric-medical tracks.

More Creative Play and Early Learning Social Policies

Many questions remain. Without any "national will" to get empirical answers to such critical culturally modulated brain-mind issues, the future of childhood in America may become haunting: Have we indeed restricted the playful birthrights of our children through various cultural and educational policies? Can a fully social brain emerge in mammals without abundant early social play? Let us again recall that in *The Laws* Plato extolled play's many social benefits, while encouraging free play in children.

> At the stage reached by the age of three, and after ages of four, five, six, play will be necessary. These are games which nature herself suggests at that age; children readily invent these for themselves when left in one another's company. All children of the specified ages, that of three to six, should first be collected at the local *sanctuary*—all the children of each village being thus assembled at the same place. Further, the *nurses* are to have an eye to the decorum or indecorum of their behavior (VII, 794, my italics).

Among many other social engineering ideas, one of his basic messages was that without abundant free social play, our children's future and the quality of the societies we create will be compromised. Without abundant early PLAY, we cannot become fully human. (See Chapter 2 in this volume by Stuart Brown and Madelyn Eberle.)

One of the wonders of play is that it takes children, all too creatively, to the edges of their emotional knowledge—what they can/should do with others, and what they can't/should not do. There will inevitably be conflicts among children, and some that may need to be promptly worked through toward satisfactory resolutions with the help of caring, creative adults (the social-educational assistants—Plato's *nurses*—at the periphery of new creatively constructed play *sanctuaries*, simultaneously both exciting and safe). Social difficulties are bound to arise during free play. Without gentle supervisors, such crises can lead to bullying. But with CARE-filled watchful eyes of young supervisors—who know how to gently educate at critical times—such moments can become wonderful opportunities for positive social learning (Panksepp & Scott, 2013). But this requires readily available caring people to help and assist.

Pursuant to the first well-controlled, ethological analysis of human social play (Scott & Panksepp, 2002), we evaluated this proposition in half-hour preschool play sessions for pre-kindergarten children (which took us great effort to implement—first getting all the principals in the school system to approve our pilot work with preschoolers, informing all relevant teachers as well as interested people in the local community (of Bowling Green, Ohio), and finally going through FBI background checks (to assure that none of our team had been a child molester). Our young undergraduate student supervisors (Plato's "nurses") were there simply to look on and intervene if naughty interactions happened . . . with a prompt return to the playing field being the reward, as long as a child explicitly indicated they would no longer participate in any hurtful behaviors. In other words, when pro-social expectations were gently but firmly conveyed and the reward was immediate continuation of play, young children understood well, and they rapidly internalized the social rule "do unto others" in order to continue having fun (Scott, 2001). We also concluded that PLAY enriches the many potentials for human creativity.

In summary, our past work developing animal models of ADHD demonstrated that long-term, daily "play therapy" reduces impulsive behaviors as juvenile rats mature (Panksepp, et al., 2003). Many questions remained to be addressed, largely because we never attracted the essential government funding for such work (not for lack of asking), leaving us to pursue preliminary work on our own dime/time. What we wanted to fully investigate was whether abundant early free social-play might be therapeutic for human children diagnosed with ADHD. Might abundant pro-social play help organize young minds in pro-social ways? Will there be lifelong negative consequences for pro-social neural maturation in children who have little chance to play normally (Brown, 1998), as happens in so many families today? Might the main accepted "evidence-based" treatment modality, namely psychostimulant medications, have permanent untoward effects on children's personalities? But the bottom line was that we were never able to attract funding for such a program of research.

Still, in order to promote optimal mental maturation in children who have excessive early impulse control problems we, as a nation, must give PLAY a chance! Hopefully researchers will eventually be able to evaluate such ideas formally in preschool children who seem to be on the ADHD track. So far we have only had the opportunity to do some feasibility pilot work indicating how one can get into a public school system and do a feasibility study with "normal" children (e.g., Scott, 2001). Indeed, I wish to note that we have never accepted the implication that ADHD-diagnosed children are not normal.

In any event, in our "Memorial Foundation for Lost Children", an organization previously established in Bowling Green, Ohio, for which I served as Director, we proceeded to guide parents through such interventions if they came to us with ADHD-diagnosed young children. We encouraged fathers willing to provide a daily diet of rough-and-tumble activities for their ADHD children each morning and evening to let us know how it worked. The reported benefits were substantial. Also, preliminary results by others indicate that access to play improves classroom behavior and academic performance (Pellegrini & Smith, 1998). Of course, many questions remain to be answered before we will have any solid evidence-based medicine in this area. As a population, ADHD children exhibit higher-than-normal risk for developing substance abuse disorders later in life. Despite debatable claims to the contrary, there is presently no replicated, credible evidence that early experiences with psychostimulants *diminish* urges to consume addictive drugs later in life. If anything, the data suggest the opposite, but well-controlled animal studies on such topics remain scarce because of national research policies, which from certain perspectives seem deplorable (learning more and more about less and less, where the basic nature of animal emotions and human values are too commonly ignored).

Is there any legitimate role for addictive drugs in childhood psychiatric medicine? Of course there is. We do know that psychostimulants can keep kids on task in classroom situations. As a result, highly impulsive children do not get marginalized, with potential lifelong negative consequences, as they might were they to be continued to be ostracized by teachers and playmates. Of course the benefits of highly debatable medical policies (treating young children with addictive medication) are being touted by those who have enormous investments in the use of such agents. As noted already, some experts claim, on the basis of scant data, that early exposure to psychostimulant medications may actually reduce future addictive drug urges. Those findings remain weak and without extensive replications. If such findings turn out to be replicable, we would still have the alternative that all that is being observed are desirable social compliance issues, as opposed to diminished underlying neuropsychological sensation-seeking urges (e.g., Nocjar & Panksepp, 2002). In any event, there are reasons to suspect that our culture will pay for the consequences of such policies—perhaps with the emergence of ever more materialistic, less pro-social societies.

Coda: Play Sanctuaries

Where are Plato's play *sanctuaries* for our times? Nature is no longer part of the lives of most of our children (Louv, 2006). Many youngsters are overprotected, regimented, and TV- and internet- egetated. Most young children, especially in single-child families, need more rough-and-tumble play partners (organized sports being a pale imitation of real PLAY). Many parents and educational systems don't explicitly recognize the profound value of physical social play for their children. Many believe that treating children like little adults helps to promote the emergence of wholesome social brains and minds. However, no compelling evidence exists that young minds can mature in healthy ways without daily opportunities for rough-and-ready emotional PLAY—affective tools that Mother Nature herself provided for our brains and minds, as fundamental forces to promote pro-social learning that facilitates positive social interactions throughout the life span.

Full social-brain and mind maturation appears to depend on regular and abundant early immersion of our youngsters in real social PLAY. To help assure that such treasures of the mind are seen as childhood necessities rather than luxuries, perhaps we should have a national conversation about societal responsibilities to build and create "play sanctuaries"—safe spaces where all children have optimal opportunities to integrate their PLAY urges with age-appropriate opportunities—namely socially enriched, emotionally fulfilling social (and eventually educational) practices. By using the creative powers of each child's SEEKING system (a powerful urge, with no fixed goals—that can range from despicable addiction to our highest artistic aspirations, so to speak), all children should have ample opportunities to become, creatively,

FIGURE 12.7
Tiger Cubs Playing. (Public domain)

fully "human" as well as lifelong learners. Culture needs to provide ample opportunities for abundant joyful social engagements, whereby pro-social living and superb learning and interacting become internalized habits. In short, I suspect that pro-social brain maturation cannot be optimized without abundant daily pro-social PLAY opportunities throughout the preschool (and perhaps all the remaining) years.

If animal data can be deemed a valid guide, as I believe it can, abundant play will facilitate more enriched maturation of the frontal cortical self-other cognitive-regulatory skills that become ever better integrated with children's other universal and often impulsive primary-process emotional urges. Perhaps abundant play (an evolved emotional motive of all our brains) requires more consistent cultural support—thereby providing optimal and most fertile evolutionary and cultural soil for promoting human creativity and thriving. The more our children are given opportunities for self-other indulgences of pro-social play, the sooner and more intensely they will develop invaluable mind functions—the precious, dynamically flexible, cognitive skills of maturing brains and minds.

With maturation, frontal lobe executive functions allow children, indeed all of us, to inhibit impulsive urges. That allows us to better "stop, look, listen, and feel." Such inhibitory skills promote enhanced capacities for adult self-reflection, imagination, empathy, and creative/play. The resulting frontal lobe working-memory abilities permit the kind of behavioral flexibility and foresight that constitute well-focused, goal-directed behavior. Such long-term developmental benefits of frontal lobe maturation can and should last a lifetime.

PLAY circuitry is surely a major tool for living, provided by our genetic heritage to promote full social flowering in our brains and minds, as nourished by the powerful daily sunshine of fun. This is the best antidepressant that we have—indeed we have developed a novel antidepressant, the neuropeptide GLYX-13—from studying the neurochemistries of PLAYful social JOY (Moskal, et al., 2011; Panksepp, 2015, 2016). The simple daily satisfaction of such primal social pleasures is bound to spontaneously reduce the incidence of impulse-control problems and disorders that might otherwise too often result in excessive RAGE/Anger and FEAR/Anxiety. Of course, the best of early infant social PLAY can only emerge in the safety of maternal CARE, which diminishes and allows better regulation of the PANIC (separation-distress) system, the basic emotional system that is the guardian of our emotional social-security, without which we cannot be fully human (Bowlby, 1969; Sunderland, 2006; and see Chapter 4 in this book by Schore & Marks-Tarlow).

There may be other, more mundane benefits. For instance, if short natural play interactions were indulged consistently, about half an hour before bedtime, in my experience, children's sleep problems diminish spontaneously. Another side benefit of early joyful living is the construction of pro-social brains that are resistant both to childhood and adult incidences of depressions. Joyful childhoods surely construct brain resources for joyful adulthoods (Burgdorf & Panksepp, 2006; Schore & Marks-Tarlow in this book). Lack of early play surely compromises both emotional and cognitive-mental health, as already outlined. Abundant play opens the doors to creativity plus deeper and more positive self-other feeling.

Although formal prospective data remain scarce, preliminary evidence indicates that children whose lives were impoverished by too little play all too often come to be too *well* (as in dark-hole) represented, as adults, in our prisons (Brown, 1998, and this volume). As Stuart Brown has noted, early play deficiencies are evident in violent men: Play-deficient creatures suffer from *"value laden adaptive map deficiency"* syndromes. Thus, children must be taught the requirements of intimacy and playfulness on an individual basis, for "a game deprived child may well become the socially dysfunctional adult who cannot handle the complexities inherent in the adult world" (p. 471, Gordon, 2015). From this vantage point, the remarkably consistent animal data that all psychostimulants reduce playful urges should be profoundly troubling. It apparently is not widely known that we are giving our ADHD-diagnosed children anti-play medications. In short, it is long past time for our postmodern, increasingly dangerous societies to provide abundant, well-supervised, free and open, pro-social, education-promoting play sanctuaries for our ever increasingly play-deprived children.

In closing, and with a more playful mood, when did jokes and puns begin to tickle us? I guess it must have been soon after the mushrooming of our cerebral cortices above and beyond those of the other anthropoid apes, soon after we learned how to speak, so let me share a couple of my favorites: "Did you hear about the Buddhist who refused Novocain during a root canal? His goal: transcend dental medication." This pun was downloaded from www.lkfshow. com/funfacts/puns.html. I thank Tom Verney for sharing the fruits of this fun website, as he shared this and other puns with many friends "with the hope that at least one of the puns would make them laugh. No pun in ten did." I also fear that I have shared a bit too much science, but remember: "When cannibals ate a missionary, they got a taste of religion."

References

Andersen, S. L., Arvanitogiannis, A., Pliakas, A. M., LeBlanc, C., & Carlezon, Jr., W. A. (2002). Altered responsiveness to cocaine in rats exposed to methylphenidate during development. *Nature Neuroscience, 5,* 13–14.

Barkley, R. A. (1997). *ADHD and the nature of self-control.* New York: The Guilford Press.

Beatty, W. W., Dodge, A. M., Dodge, L. J., Whike, K., & Panksepp, J. (1982). Psychomotor stimulants, social deprivation and play in juvenile rats. *Pharmacology Biochemistry & Behavior, 16,* 417 –422.

Berridge, K. C. & Robinson, T. E. (1998). What is the role of dopamine in reward: Hedonic impact, reward learning, or incentive salience? *Brain Research Reviews, 28,* 309–369.

Biederman, J., Wilens, T. E., Mick, E., Faraone, S. V., & Spencer, T. (1998). Does attention-deficit hyperactivity disorder impact the developmental course of drug and alcohol abuse and dependence? *Biological Psychiatry, 15*(44), 269–73.

Biederman, J., Wilens, T., Mick, E., Spencer, T., & Faraone, S. V. (1999). Pharmacotherapy of attention-deficit/hyperactivity disorder reduces risk for substance use disorder. *Pediatrics, 104,* e20, 1–5.

Bowlby, J. (1969) *Attachment and loss, Volume 1: Attachment.* New York: Basic Books

Brandon, C. L., Marinelli, M., Baker, L. K., & White, F. J. (2001). Enhanced reactivity and vulnerability to cocaine following methylphenidate treatment in adolescent rats. *Neuropharmacology, 25,* 651–661.

Brown, S. (1998). Play as an organizing principle: Clinical evidence and personal observations. In Bekoff, M. & Beyer, J.A. (Eds.). *Animal play: Evolutionary, comparative, and ecological perspectives* (pp. 242–251). Cambridge, UK: Cambridge University Press.

Browning, J. R., Browning, D. A., Maxwell, A. O., Dong, Y., Jansen, H. T., Panksepp, J., & Sorg, B. A. (2011). Positive affective vocalizations during cocaine and sucrose self-administration: A model for spontaneous drug desire in rats. *Neuropharmacology, 61,* 268–275.

Burgdorf, J. & Panksepp, J. (2006). The neurobiology of positive emotions. *Neuroscience & Biobehavioral Reviews, 30,* 173–187.

Carlezon, W. A. Jr., Mague, S. D., & Andersen, S. L. (2003). Enduring behavioral effects of early exposure to methylphenidate in rats. *Biological Psychiatry. 54,* 1330–1337.

Castellanos, F. X. & Tannock, R. (2002). Neuroscience of attention-deficit/hyperactivity disorder: The search for endophenotypes. *Nature Reviews Neuroscience, 3,* 617–628.

Gordon, G. (2015). Integrating conceptual divisions within and between the studies of play and wellbeing. In Johnson, J., Eberle, S. Hendricks, T., & Kuschner, D. (Eds.). *Handbook of the Study of Play* (Vol. 2)(pp. 467-476). New York, NY: Rowman & Littlefield.

Gordon, N. S., Burke, S., Akil, H., Watson, J., & Panksepp, J. (2003). Socially induced brain fertilization: Play promotes brain derived neurotrophic factor expression. *Neuroscience Letters, 341,* 17–20.

Keverne, E. B. (2014) Significance of epigenetics for understanding brain development, brain evolution and behavior. *Neuroscience, 264,* 207–217.

Kolb, B. & Tees, C. (Eds.) (1990). *The cerebral cortex of the rat.* Cambridge, MA: MIT Press.

Kroes, R. A., Panksepp, J., Burgdorf, J., Otto, N. J., & Moskal, J. R. (2006). Social dominance-submission gene expression patterns in rat neocortex. *Neuroscience, 137,* 37–49.

Lane, R. D., Ryan, L., Nadel, L., & Greenberg, L. (2015). Memory reconsolidation, emotional arousal, and the process of change in psychotherapy: New insights from brain science. *Behavioral and Brain Sciences, 38.*

Laviola, G., Adriani, W., Terranova, M. L., & Gerra, G. (1999). Psychobiological risk factors for vulnerability to psychostimulants in human adolescents and animal models. *Neuroscience & Biobehavioral Reviews, 23,* 993–1010.

Louv, R. (2006). *Last child in the woods: Saving our children from nature-deficit disorder.* Chapel Hill, NC: Algonquin Books.

Mague, S. D., Andersen, S. L., & Carlezon, W. A., Jr. (2005). Early developmental exposure to methylphenidate reduces cocaine-induced potentiation of brain stimulation reward in rats. *Biological Psychiatry, 57,* 120–125.

Mannuzza, S., Klein, R. G., & Moulton, J. L. (2003). Does stimulant treatment place children at risk for adult substance abuse? A controlled, prospective follow-up study. *Journal of Child and Adolescent Psychopharmacology, 13*(3), 273–282.

Marks-Tarlow, T. & Panksepp, J. (2015). Top-down versus bottom-up perspectives on clinically significant memory reconsolidation. *Behavioral and Brain Sciences, 38.*

Merker, B. (2007). Consciousness without a cerebral cortex: A challenge for neuroscience and medicine. *Behavioral and Brain Sciences, 30,* 63–134.

Moll, G. H., Hause, S., Rüther, E., et al., (2001). Early methylphenidate administration to young rats causes a persistent reduction in the density of striatal dopamine transporters. *Journal of Child and Adolescent Psychopharmacology, 11,* 15–24.

Moskal, J. R., Burgdorf, J., Kroes, R. A., Brudzynski, S. M., & Panksepp, J. (2011). A novel NMDA receptor glycine-site partial agonist, GLYX-13, has therapeutic potential for the treatment of autism. *Neuroscience & Biobehavioral Reviews, 35*(9), 1982–1988.

Nocjar, C. & Panksepp, J. (2002). Chronic intermittent amphetamine pretreatment enhances future appetitive behavior for drug- and natural-reward: Interaction with environmental variables. *Behavioural Brain Research, 128,* 189–203.

Panksepp, J. (1981). The ontogeny of play in rats. *Developmental Psychobiology, 72,* 261–264.

Panksepp, J. (1982). Toward a general psychobiological theory of emotions. *Behavioral and Brain Sciences, 5,* 407–467.

Panksepp, J., (1985) Mood changes. In Vinken, P. J., Bruyn, G. W., & Klawans, H.L.

(Eds.). *Handbook of Clinical Neurology* (Revised Series). Vol. 1. (45): *Clinical Neuropsychology* (pp. 271–285). Amsterdam: Elsevier Science Publishers.

Panksepp, J. (1998a). *Affective neuroscience: The foundations of human and animal emotions.* New York: Oxford University Press.

Panksepp, J. (1998b). Attention deficit hyperactivity disorders, psychostimulants and intolerance of childhood playfulness: A tragedy in the making? *Current Directions in Psychological Science, 7,* 91–98.

Panksepp, J. (2001). The long-term psychobiological consequences of infant emotions: Prescriptions for the twenty-first century. *Infant Mental Health Journal, 22,* 132–173.

Panksepp, J. (2005). Affective consciousness: Core emotional feelings in animals and humans. *Consciousness & Cognition, 14,* 30–80.

Panksepp, J., (2007). Can PLAY diminish ADHD and facilitate the construction of the social brain. *Journal of the Canadian Academy of Child and Adolescent Psychiatry, 10,* 57–66.

Panksepp, J., (2008). PLAY, ADHD, and the construction of the social brain: Should the first class each day be recess? *American Journal of Play, 1,* 55–79.

Panksepp J. (2015). Affective preclinical modeling of psychiatric disorders: Taking imbalanced primal emotional feelings of animals seriously in our search for novel antidepressants. *Dialogues in Clinical Neuroscience, 17,* 363–379.

Panksepp, J., (2016). The cross mammalian neurophenomenology of primal emotional affects: From animal feelings to human therapeutics. *Journal of Comparative Neurology, 524,* 1624–35.

Panksepp, J., Herman, B. H., Vilberg, T., Bishop, P., and DeEskinazi, F. G. (1980). Endogenous opioids and social behavior. *Neuroscience & Biobehavioral Reviews, 4,* 473–487.

Panksepp, J., Burgdorf, J., Gordon, N. & Turner, C. (2002). Treatment of ADHD with methylphenidate may sensitize brain substrates of desire. *Consciousness & Emotion, 3,* 7–19.

Panksepp, J., Burgdorf, J., Turner, C., & Gordon, N. (2002). Modeling ADHD-type arousal with unilateral frontal cortex damage in rats and beneficial effects of play therapy. *Brain & Cognition, 3,* 7–19.

Panksepp, J., Burgdorf, J., Gordon, N., & Turner, C. (2003). Modeling ADHD-type arousal with unilateral frontal cortex damage in rats and beneficial effects of play therapy. *Brain & Cognition. 52,* 97–105.

Panksepp, J., Herman, B. H., Vilberg, T., Bishop, P., & DeEskinazi, F. G. (1980). Endogenous opioids and social behavior. *Neuroscience & Biobehavioral Reviews, 4,* 473–487.

Panksepp, J., Normansell, L. A., Cox, J. F., & Siviy, S. (1994). Effects of neonatal decortication on the social play of juvenile rats. *Physiology & Behavior, 56,* 429–443.

Panksepp, J., Siviy, S., & Normansell, L. A. (1984). The psychobiology of play: Theoretical and methodological perspectives. *Neuroscience & Biobehavioral Reviews, 8,* 465–492.

Panksepp, J. & Scott, E. L. (2013). Reflections on rough and tumble play, social development, and attention-deficit hyperactivity disorders. In Meyer, A. L. & Gullotta, T. P. (Eds.), *Physical activity across the lifespan: Prevention and treatment for health and well-being* (pp. 23–38). Springer Science+Business Media LLC: New York.

Panksepp, J., Lane, R.D., Solms, M., & Smith, R. (in press). Reconciling cognitive and affective neuroscience perspectives on the brain basis of emotional experience. *Neuroscience & Biobehavioral Reviews.*

Pellegrini, A. D. & Smith, P. K. (1998). Physical activity play: The nature and function of a neglected aspect of play. *Child Development, 69,* 577–598.

Preskorn, S., Macaluso, M., Mehra, V., et al. (2015). Randomized proof of concept trial of GLYX-13, an N-Methyl-D-Aspartate receptor glycine site partial agonist, in major depressive disorder nonresponsive to a previous antidepressant agent. *Journal of Psychiatric Practice, 21,* 140–149.

Robinson, T. E. & Berridge, K. C. (1993). The neural basis of drug craving: An incentive-sensitization theory of addiction. *Brain Research Reviews, 18,* 247–291.

Robinson, T. E. & Kolb, B. (2004). Structural plasticity associated with exposure to drugs of abuse. *Neuropharmacology, 47* (Suppl. 1), 33–46.

Scott, E. (2001). Toward a play program to benefit children's attention in the classroom. Unpublished PhD dissertation, Bowling Green State University, Bowling Green, OH.

Scott, E. & Panksepp, J. (2003). Rough-and-tumble play in human children. *Aggressive Behavior, 29,* 539–551.

Shewmon, D. A., Holmes, G. L., & Byrne, P. A. (1999). Consciousness in congenitally decorticate children: Developmental vegetative state as self-fulfilling prophecy. *Developmental Medicine & Child Neurology, 41*(6), 364–74.

Solms, M. & Panksepp, J. (2012). The "id" knows more than the "ego" admits: Neuropsychoanalytic and primal consciousness perspectives on the interface between affective and cognitive neuroscience. *Brain Science, 2*(2), 147–175.

Solanto, M. V. (2000). Clinical psychopharmacology of AD/HD: Implications for animal models. *Neuroscience & Biobehavioral Reviews, 24*(1), 27–30.

Sunderland, M. (2006). *The science of parenting.* London: Doring Kindersley Limited.

Sur, M. & Rubinstein, J. L. (2005). Patterning and plasticity of the cerebral cortex. *Science,* 310) 805-810.

Tulving E. (2002). Episodic memory: From brain to mind. *Annual Review of Psychology, 53,* 1–25.

Vandekerckhove, M. & Panksepp, J. (2009). The flow of anoetic to noetic and autonoetic consciousness: A vision of unknowing (anoetic) and knowing (noetic) consciousness in the remembrance of things past and imagined futures. *Consciousness & Cognition, 18*(4), 1018–28.

Vandekerckhove, M. & Panksepp, J. (2011). A neurocognitive theory of higher mental emergence: From anoetic affective experiences to noetic knowledge and autonoetic awareness. *Neuroscience & Biobehavioral Reviews, 35*(9), 2017–2025.

Wilens, T. E. (2004). Impact of ADHD and its treatment on substance abuse in adults. *Journal of Clinical Psychiatry, 65,* Suppl. 3, 38–45.

Wilens, T. E. & Biederman, J. (2006). Alcohol, drugs, and attention-deficit/ hyperactivity disorder: A model for the study of addictions in youth. *Journal of Psychopharmacology, 20*(4), 580–588.

13

Nesting Dolls: A Playful Way to Illustrate a Valuable Intervention in Couples Therapy

Marion F. Solomon

Feeling Connected in an Age of Loneliness

We are hearing more and more about the feelings of loneliness and disconnection, even among people who are married or in committed relationships. There are some who believe that loving each other truly is enough to keep a strong loving connection and make a relationship work. But as described in my 2011 book with Stan Tatkin, *Love and War in Intimate Relationships*, unconscious needs of each mate that go back to early childhood, but remain unexpressed and not recognized by a partner, can destroy a relationship, with neither partner understanding how it happened. Some come to counseling sessions before they marry. Others seek help when relational problems begin.

Questions arise, such as, "Why are we having so much trouble communicating with each other?" Or, "What must we do to stop arguing, or to have a secure connection with each other?" This chapter introduces concepts that mental health professionals can creatively draw upon to help partners change the dynamics of the relationship. I have several methods of playfully using familiar objects to help bypass long-held protective defenses: throwing a ball back and forth while telling their stories; using one of the couch pillows to push against each other to see who is stronger; and taking apart a set of matry-oshka dolls (Russian nesting dolls).

The connective aspect of relationships feels deepest when we fall in love, but know each other least. The outer parts that we show each other are what we hope will convince someone we love to see us as worthy of their love. Kept hidden below is a tiny part that we don't even know ourselves. We are like nested Russian dolls that are built in the same pattern, one inside the other, but each shaped exactly in the same form. In this chapter I describe the use of these matryoshkas.

When a couple begins therapy, the goal is to keep the focus away from mutual blame and attack. Partners too often begin sessions with each want-ing to focus on, "What bad things have you done that you need to change?"

FIGURE 13.1
Dr. Solomon's Russian nesting dolls. (Courtesy of Marion Solomon)

FIGURE 13.2
Matryoshka dolls in a line on the fireplace mantle. (Courtesy of Marion Solomon)

The shift that I advocate is to enhance understanding of the need for secure attachment that we all have throughout the lifespan. Using the matryoshka nesting dolls, I can help partners recognize that we all have an "unthought known" (Bollas, 1989), a child part needing care and nurturing that is kept out of conscious awareness.

Some needs remain unstated, because the outer façade of competence and successful achievement is the one that many prefer to have their partner see. The child part remains deeply submerged, as it often feels shameful and immature. If this child part remains hidden away, the result may be that spontaneous play and creativity may also be kept submerged. Self-sufficiency and independence become the answer for some. They use their inherent resources, intelligence, talent, and hard work to succeed in life. It is this part of themselves that they show to a potential partner. People live together without sharing or even knowing the rest of themselves. I've worked with several couples who have filled their lives with buying homes, raising children, living a busy lifestyle; and as their children grew up and move away they discover that something was missing. Quite often they believe it is something missing in their partner. The answer, they may think, is ending the relationship and finding a new path to happiness.

The Importance of We, In a Culture of Me

Posted on a web page recently, I read, "It's not selfish to love yourself, take care of yourself, and to make your happiness a priority." Like a fish swimming in a lake who has no idea of water, there are things we don't think about because we are immersed in it. Moreover, the modern culture of autonomy does not promote enhancing intimate relationships. For years the message was popularized in social media as well as in the mental health professional literature. *How To Become Your Own Best Friend*, or *Living Alone and Loving It*, were well-received book titles that helped influence the "Culture of Me." This shift in expectations effectively resulted in an increased divorce rate of the generation between the Baby Boomers and today's Millennial generation. Therapists and patients agree that, "You have to love yourself before you can love another person." But every therapist can tell you about patients who do not love themselves, who have negative and punitive feelings toward themselves. When they enter a relationship, they try to get confirmation that they are seen by their mate as worthy, understood, accepted, and loved as they are. They even believe they are attuned and caring, and that their partner is failing to see how much they give. But it is only the receiver who knows what he or she is experiencing and whether the relationship feels nurturing. Too often they are told it is childish to want it. But there is a child living in each of us. Some received greater nurturing when they were young children. Others live with the feeling that they never had what they wanted, but can't explain what because they had what seemed like a good childhood.

Family therapists (e.g., Dicks, 1967/983) have long known that partners find one another at the same developmental level. So they each may be looking to the other for very similar things. Both soon become disappointed. In individual therapy, George reported that Margie blows up periodically for no reason that he can understand. "If this keeps happening, I'm going to have to get a divorce to get some peace," he says. Margie tells her therapist, "George never talks to me. His nose is always on television watching the sport event du jour. I may as well not be married." Both Margie and George feel their therapist understands, but that their partner is lacking the ability to relate with understanding. One is advised by a friend to see a great lawyer, another to see an experienced couples' therapist. I don't think there is a study of the odds for each couple.

I recently was on a panel of therapists at a parenting group meeting. I commented that I have often told couples in my office, "The secret of a successful relationship is paying attention to your partners' dreams, putting them into words in a non-shaming way, and supporting their dreams.

"And what do I get out of it," I was asked.

"A happy partner," I said.

"And what do I get out of that?" the questioner repeated.

Lieberman's (2013) research confirms the good feelings we get when we give to others. Therapists today have begun to look at the relationships of their patients through a more positive lens, as they find new ways to work with both partners conjointly.

Igniting Play

At the onset of many conjoint sessions, the tension is palpable. As we launch into our collaborative initial sessions, I point to the table with the matching

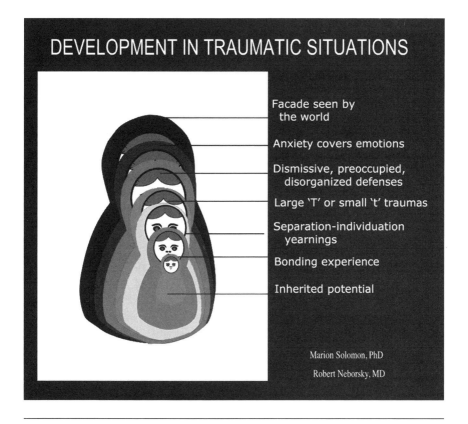

FIGURE 13.3
Courtesy of Marion Solomon and Robert Neborsky

sets of nesting dolls that are colorfully displayed. My office is filled with these matryoshka dolls, and I use them in a playful way to bring understanding, collaboration, and often laughter around a serious message. Our younger selves live deeply within our core. As adults, we may not be comfortable with this concept, or we may not understand the implicit parts of our history that affect our current experience of self and other. Shame and other feelings are mitigated through the use of the nesting dolls.

When one member of a couple talks of how they feel that we all need to take care of our own selves, I might playfully ask "How's that working for you?" "Not so well," one or both might respond. With curiosity and compassion, I respond, "Could it be that it is why you are coming to me for marital counseling, instead of coming alone to tell me what's wrong with your impossible partner?"

This is where the nesting dolls come to use. I will point to the fireplace mantle where I keep a set of matryoshka lined up, saying that we are all like these dolls. "We start out life as this one," pointing to the tiniest doll.

FIGURE 13.4
Layers of experience, each enfolded in the last. (Courtesy of Terry Marks-Tarlow)

I put two sets of matryoshkas on the table between us and hand one of the large dolls to each of them to hold. Then I ask them to take their doll apart, and hold the smallest one in the palm of their hand. As they hold the doll, I say, "That tiniest doll represents the part of each person that was once very young and vulnerable and totally dependent on someone else for life and safety. That part lives within us all, coming up at various times in our lives, often unbeknownst to us." I give them a fast lesson in attachment theory. The most important thing a baby gets is being held and nurtured securely. Asking each to let me hold the dolls that were in their hands, I help them caress the tiny doll. Some hold their doll with thumb and index finger. Some keep their hands far from their body.

I ask them to imagine themselves being held. Whatever they say at this point is right, even if they say they cannot imagine anything. This gives important information about how they experience the world. I point out that what we learn before words, during the first 18 months of life, got wired into the brain and likely still lives there. Throughout all the years of development, we grow new layers of experience, symbolized by the increasingly larger dolls. But the mold set in those earliest months and years of life influences whatever stages develop next. We don't lose what went before; we replicate it, while adding additional experiences.

Brain Development

As partners hold the tiniest dolls in the palm of their hands, I help them under-stand that this experience evokes feelings about a time in their lives when their brains were just beginning to develop. Whatever experience that little part had has become programed into the developing brain. Just as the matryoshka dolls are nested inside each other, our emotions and experiences from that time of life remain nested inside of us today. If needs at earlier times of life weren't met, an unconscious memory of those need remains. We may grow into larger and stronger versions of ourselves, but the tiny part that still lives within us longs for someone to love and care for us.

One or both partners often may oppose this, saying "Grow up;" "Don't be a dreamer;" or "I worked my whole life to not be dependent." Yet we have grown up, and have used all the resources available in order to become who we are. We succeeded in growing up by pushing away that tiny doll-like part, or by expressing feelings of shame or self-loathing when this part emerges. Sometimes people in therapy try to describe the missing part:

"I have a hole in my heart," said a captain of industry when he first entered therapy. "There is a darkness inside that sweeps over me at times," said the

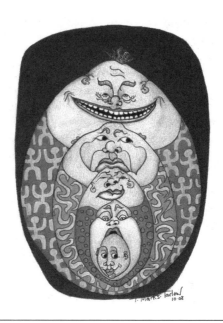

FIGURE 13.5
We never outgrow the earliest germs of self. (Courtesy of Terry
Marks-Tarlow)

successful principal of a high school. A comedy writer confessed, "Being
funny and making people laugh keeps my anger at bay and my feelings
in check."

Therapists often give a diagnosis to comments such as these. But to apply
a diagnostic label does not resolve the relational problem. I remind partners when I work with them that the old television comedies such as *The
Addams Family* and *The Munsters* offered seemingly odd individuals who were
happy together.

Nesting Dolls as a Surprise to the Unconscious

New insights often emerge in the room. Unconscious thoughts, feelings, and
memories are evoked as clients hold the nesting dolls. This offers a present
moment shift, opening up opportunities for mindful reflection of past experiences, good and bad.

Some couples grow quite reflective, as they recall snippets of experience. Holding the nesting dolls, taking apart the dolls, as they unearth

one within another, offers a tangible somatic experience. Emotions often arise, as they hold the tiniest dolls in their hands. Cognitions, perceptions, memories, thoughts, and feelings emerge through this playful yet powerful intervention.

I emphasize the importance of couples feeling safe and connected with one another as a fundamental element of satisfaction in lives which are filled with mutuality and otherness. This otherness is not simply with one another, but extends beyond the self and our individual relationships, as we look at the potential for a relationship in a world of others.

I ask for memories of experiences with others that were safe. Who in their lives, if anyone, could they go to for comfort? Who did they go to when they were hurting or afraid? Was there a teacher, a scout leader with whom they felt safe? Who was able to count on them?

Can they point to the doll that represented the best time for them? Can they remember a time of helping someone who needed support? My focus in these exercises is on feeling cared for and caring for others. It is through playful banter and introducing the nesting dolls as representative of the parts of people that were rarely or never allowed to see the light of day. Together we may achieve familiarity with their own, and their partner's hidden, needy core.

Through further discussion of these different parts and the earliest needs within us as represented through each of the dolls, people connect to the child states in the adult. Often tears come up by men as well as women. We discuss the dependent and needy aspects of self as not unusual and as commonly triggering pressure to get away from these childlike feelings by continuously succeeding. Some of the most accomplished people I know have intense needs to be nurtured, or to nurture another person that they love. Rather than offering messages such as "Grow up!" or "Behave like an adult!" I hand the largest doll to each of them saying, "When the child feels recognized and not shamed, the adult part does not have to spend enormous energy to deaden that needy, demanding baby inside."

Often I've been told that this is not a politically correct message in the culture of our 21st century mental health field. This is why I use psychoeducation to help the couple understand the impact of our modern culture.

Modern Culture

Modern culture has shifted from a focus on family and community to a focus on the self, with the importance of autonomy and separation complicating relationships. The emphasis on the nuclear family often discourages three generations living together, and "overly close" families are often described as enmeshed or needing differentiation and individuation (Bowen, 1978). People are often cautious and delay marriage until they feel more financially secure. Both partners may be paying off student loans, and both have to work in order to meet the rent, food, and other bills. Gender decisions are more flexible, and commitment varies. Despite this, even when surrounded by growing divorce statistics, people keep forming intimate bonds. They do not want that intolerable feeling of loneliness that is endemic in our society.

Consequently, we are becoming a nation of isolated individuals—lonely, longing, not integrated—all outgrowths of the Culture of Me. While adhering to the advice of popular gurus and the media, to "Do your own thing," become "self-actualized" (Maslow, 1943), or "Follow your bliss" (Campbell, et al., 1991), clients come to therapy thinking, "I've got the answer about how to be happy," yet also recognizing that something elusive is missing from their lives.

Fallout of the Me Generation

The widely quoted motto of Gestalt therapist, Fritz Perls (1972, p. i), strongly influenced the "Me" generation, and has remained a fixture of modern life.

I do my thing,
You do your thing,
I am not in this world to take care of you,
You are not in this world to take care of me,
I am I and you are you,
If by chance we meet, it's wonderful;
If not, it can't be helped.

The fallout of messages that centered on the self has had profound effects on social connections. We know that relationships take work. But for decades we have been hearing from social commentators, pop advisors, and a plethora of psychologists, that when we are having problems we in a relationship we may be codependent, or are in an emotionally abusive relationship. In essence we've been given the message, "Cut your losses; save yourself; go it alone." But this is a concept alien to the nature of the human social brain (Lieberman, 2013).

How Evolution Made us Natural Connectors

Evolution has created human beings who are strongly connected, brain-to-brain, cortex-to-cortex, core-to-core. We influence others and are influenced by the brains and minds of others. As much as we think we are autonomous individuals, research shows that there is no such thing as an autonomous individual. Just as an individual neuron cannot decide to be independent of other parts of the brain, human brains require other brains to survive and thrive (Lieberman, 2013; Siegel, 2007). We now know from a wide range of research on mirror neurons (e.g., Iocoboni, 2009) that the brain does not stop at the skull of one person, but sends and receives messages at the neuronal level. In fact, much of what we know about each other is known through awareness of somatic, sensorimotor (Ogden, Minton, & Pain, 2006), and neuronal attunement.

We send messages to each other, most often beyond the verbal, through nonverbal signs, expressions, movements, etc. Our ability to read body language and facial expressions varies in different people. Research has found that the brains of humans and other primates communicate with each other. In fact, as much as 95 percent of all communication between people are beneath our thoughts and words. Multilevel connections exist at the same time. Playful interactions foster a couple's mutual capacity to connect and attune to one another.

We know that these skills are first learned early in life, usually through

The part of me seen by the outside world. Wife, mother, therapist, author, a person who tries to show few flaws and looks strong no matter what the inner stresses.

The part that I share with the most intimate people in my life. The spirtual, emotional, sexual, private me that can be vulnerable, dependent, excited, or overjoyed, depending on the circumstances.

Aspects that are out of my conscious awareness. Others may see these in me more easily than I do, but I recognize them when made aware. Aspects that would cause me shame for you to know.

Unconscious, deeply imbedded emotions that may drive my behavior without my being aware of it. The part that comes out in behavior that is hard to understand, or in physical and emotional symptoms.

Innate, biological, temperamental aspects; a tendency to shyness, an analytic mind, high energy level, etc.

FIGURE 13.6A

Layers of the unconscious (a). (Courtesy of Marion Solomon; From *Lean On Me: The Power of Positive Dependency In Intimate Relationships.*)

interactions with parents and other people close to us. During infancy, our brains become wired to expect certain interactions, ranging from feeling loving and responsive, to feeling indifferent and hurtful toward those we are connected to. Subsequent relationships tend to recreate and repeat these relational feelings, including built-in beliefs that influence how we perceive others. Usually we manage to confirm our expectations, whether positive or negative. Our conscious minds develop narratives about how we experience others as well as how we feel about ourselves and others during encounters. But at levels below conscious awareness, another part of our mind, influenced by past experiences, is always reacting. Our ability to react with empathy and compassion is influenced by these subterranean beliefs.

Underneath it all, we want to be seen, understood, and accepted. As mentioned earlier, when we don't have these important experiences, we feel unsafe, concepts we've elucidated in *Love and War in Intimate Relationships* (Solomon &

The part of you showed to me when we first met, your success, charm, sense of humor and strength.

The part of you that I came to know as we began living together. Your values, beliefs, goals in life; what you were willing to do to achieve these goals.

The things about you that were different from the image you want to convey to the world. The habits, attitudes, vulnerabilities, imprints for relating to me and to others in your life.

Your unconscious. The things that I don't understand and never can change that affect your behavior and our lives together.

Innate, biological, tempermental aspects; artistic aptitude; intelligence; calm disposition.

FIGURE 13.6B

Layers of the unconscious (b). (Courtesy of Marion Solomon; From *Lean On Me: The Power of Positive Dependency In Intimate Relationships*.)

Taktin, 2011, p. 6). Among the myriad case examples are Richard and Christine, a couple who came for premarital counseling. They both had failed in relationships before and wanted to be sure this time. Each saw the other as perfect—the answer to a lifetime search for a secure love bond, someone on whom each could depend. We had two sessions, in which their love for each other was clear; I wished them a long and happy marriage. By the time they called for a "tune-up" two and a half years later, some problems had developed, and each was convinced the problem was the other. This is common in unhappy relationships, but changing the other would not fix the relationship. What was happening was the result of a recreation of the tiniest matryoshka doll within each—their past replaying in their current interactions. When the partners became intimately connected, they both began to re-experience their early learned attachment patterns. In fact, they were responding to wired-in expectations instilled in their neurons at a pre-verbal time in the lives of each.

The work of couple therapy as described earlier was to help both understand why they repeatedly behave in ways that seem to create problems. With the matryoshka dolls, I gently helped them develop an understanding of self-and-other through the lens of childhood experiences. Then it became possible to clarify with them how what happens in the here-and-now of their relationship was being caused by a recreation of the past in current moments. It was necessary to facilitate each member of the relationship so that they could self-regulate, fine-tuning their ability to be present and attuned to the deep core emotional pain of the other. For example, while using nesting dolls, my discourse with Richard and Christine was collaborative, my vocal tone was supportive, and the nature of my questions was both playful and nonthreatening. I provided psychoeducational interventions that were bite-sized and titrated, so that each member of the couple felt less threatened.

With the help of the nesting dolls, I was better able to help the pair understand the impact of their early childhood experiences upon their current relationship. Once they recognized and then calmed the angst and pain they each carried deeply in their cores, they were better able to understand one another, as well as experience the calming effect of being heard. This enabled both people to explore calmly, and to respond in healing ways toward one another. In this way, using the matryoshka dolls helps to open up the opportunity not only to heal the present, but also to lessen the pain of the past.

Conclusion

In our modern society there is a belief that a healthy person should not need other people in order to feel whole and content. Our cultural message is that

FIGURE 13.7
Russian nesting dolls all in a line. (Courtesy of Marion Solomon)

we should learn to love and nurture ourselves, while pathology is defined as the need to have others love and accept us, including telling us positive, enhancing things, so that we can feel connected and complete. But all of this is exactly what we *do* need! Modern messages abound, telling us this is at best an immature need, and at worst a disturbance that we must overcome.

We generally respond best to someone who is a cheerleader in our lives, who sees who we really are, including the needy childlike parts that we tend to keep hidden from the world. We want to be loved, admired, and adored, in spite of those parts that cause us to feel so inadequate. Since we are talking here about dark, hidden parts of us, a way that I have found to help partners engage in recollection of memories below a verbal level, is by stimulating dialogue surrounding various sizes of nesting Russian dolls.

Playfulness is a necessary component in our mental health profession. From the onset of a couple coming to therapy, I aim to elucidate the important shift they will both experience as they learn how to better merge their lives. Becoming a couple inevitably moves us from focusing on the individual toward focusing on one another. I suggest to everyone that there are many opportunities intimate partners have to facilitate hearing and feeling heard by one other, if they could only learn to listen beneath what is said, to locate the deep longings of each.

The Wonder of Me in a Culture of Me

There is much in our culture that tells us the need for others is a sign of immaturity, or even of pathological codependence or "love addiction." Contemporary society tends to measure individual success by personal achievements that have little to do with maintaining healthy social commitments. We place a premium on autonomy and independence, while identifying "needing" others with negative states. Yes, sometimes it is true that a strong craving for love and approval interferes with our functioning in relational life. But it is also true that the denial of the need for deep connection with others can be a real problem, resulting in loneliness plus a sense of emptiness and isolation.

In my writings and presentations I call this an epidemic of loneliness. The loss of social connections has reached epidemic proportions in our modern society. Individuals who join together to become a couple often do not understand what it takes to enter into and maintain relationships. People are easily confused by the myriad of social messages that say, "Take care of yourself first."

Through the playful and interactive modality of the matryoshka nesting dolls, clients can explore concepts of mutuality and relational interdependence in a safe and fun way. These dolls present an alternative to the complicated cultural messages described in this chapter. The use of nesting dolls as a clinical tool help clients begin to sort through confusing cultural messages, while simultaneously exploring the impact of early childhood experiences on who they are and what they might become in their current relationships.

Since I started working with couples more than 40 years ago, I have witnessed huge changes in male and female roles. Myriad possibilities now exist in how we choose mates, whether we choose marriage as the best way to achieve intimacy, the expectations we carry of one another, how changing roles affect partnerships, and what we can expect in the future. By referencing the nesting dolls in all varieties of relationships, couples' therapists can expand the possibilities for helping clients make significant shifts in how they love, work, and play together.

References

Bollas, C., (1987). *The shadow of the object: Psychoanalysis of the unthought known*. New York: Columbia University Press.

Bowen, M. (1978). *Family theory in clinical practice*. New York: Jason Aronson.

Campbell, J., Moyers, B. D., & Flowers, B. S. (1991). *The power of myth*. New York: Anchor Books.

Dicks, H. V. (1967/1983). *Marital tensions: Clinical studies toward a psychological theory of interaction*. London, UK: Routledge & Kegan Paul.

Lieberman, M. D. (2013). *Social: Why our brains are wired to connect*. New York: Crown Books.

Maslow, A. H. (1943). A theory of human motivation. *Psychological Review, 50*(4), 370–96.

Ogden, P., Minton, K., & Pain, C. (2006). *Trauma and the body: a sensorimotor approach to psychotherapy*. New York: W. W. Norton & Company.

Perls, F. (1972). *Gestalt therapy verbatim*. New York: Bantam.

Siegel, Daniel J. (2007). *The mindful brain: Reflection and attunement in the cultivation of well-being*. New York: W. W. Norton & Company.

Solomon, M. (1994). *Lean on me: The power of positive dependency in intimate relationships*. New York: Simon and Schuster.

Solomon, M. (In Preparation). *The wonder of we, in a culture of me*.

Solomon, M. and Tatkin, S. (2011). *Love and war in intimate relationships: Connection, disconnection, and mutual regulation in couple therapy*. New York: W. W. Norton & Company.

14

Rage, Comedy, and Creativity in Theater

Jonathan Lynn

I'M NOT A therapist. I'm not a neuroscientist. I'm not an academic. I have no background in research. I'm called "creative," and I haven't had a proper job since I sold records in a department store in 1966. Instead, I've spent my life as an actor, then a writer and director, and as a result I have some thoughts about the relationship between rage, comedy, and creativity (Lynn, 2011).

People often ask me, "What does a director do?" It's truly hard to explain, and it is much easier to say what I *don't* do.

- I don't demonstrate to professional actors how to act a scene. They would be insulted, and rightly so. An old English proverb states: You don't buy a dog and bark yourself.
- I don't write the script. (I do sometimes, actually, but not *qua* director; only if I'm also the writer, which is a different job).
- I don't design the sets or the costumes or the lighting.
- When I direct a film I am not the cinematographer, so I don't light it or operate the camera.
- I don't compose the music.
- I don't even get the coffee.

A director doesn't *do* anything, except choose the participants. (I select the actors, designers, composer, director of photography, and editor—the cast and crew, in short) and then coordinate the contributions of everybody involved with the production. My job is to get the best possible work out of each individual. I am asked a lot of questions. François Truffaut defined a director as "a man who answers questions." I must help those who are asking to find the answers for themselves.

The role I am describing must sound familiar to the psychotherapist. The director plays many roles akin to the therapist: friend; parental figure; boundary maker; comrade in arms; theorist about texts, academic and otherwise; and a subtle manipulator of events, emotions, and responses. Being a director is like being the leader of a therapeutic group. The object is different, of course—my job is merely to create a good entertainment. I am not trying to help any members of my group to improve their lives or to become better people. It's nice if they do, but it's not my business. But I do form a group, a huge group, not only of actors, but crew. The actors comprise a smaller group, a group within a group.

Playing and Risk-Taking

As director, I set the boundaries. I am the parental figure. My job is to enable the whole group to be a creative as they can be, which means that the actors have to be able to play. I must provide an emotional safety net, so that they feel free to take chances. Play is actually what it's all about. That's why what we create are called plays, or screenplays. That's why actors are called players. My wife Rita (whose chapter comes next) is a psychoanalyst. She says, "You can't leap a chasm in two steps." Just like patients in therapy, actors have to take emotional risks. Otherwise they give safe, mediocre performances. They can't play properly unless they feel free, and within safe boundaries, and with a parental figure whom they trust.

Directors, like therapists, have to deal with transference and countertransference, as well as with projection. Everyone comes to the director with their anxieties—the writer, the actors, the producers, the crew, the financiers, everyone! Everyone wants the director to share their anxieties, because then he/she may get permission to do what they want. I learned that I would never be a good enough director, no matter how good my taste, my eye, my organizational skills, or my dramatic or comedic ability, until I could deal with these issues of transference and projection. Sometimes I succeed; sometimes I fail.

The director has to learn to distinguish everyone else's projections from his own concerns. If not, he is no longer in control. And if the director is not in control, everyone else suddenly feels very unsafe—and playing becomes impossible. Everyone, consciously or unconsciously, is doing everything they can to make the director lose control over events, to push at the boundaries, to challenge authority; but they are all horrified if they succeed, and disorder or chaos results. Just like kids. Just like patients.

Comedy, Laughter, and the Nature of Audiences

A great deal of my life has been spent in comedy. All 10 of my movies are comedies, as are the TV series I've written and acted in. Laughter is therapeutic, we're told, for healing physical as well as mental illnesses. Beneficial biochemical changes apparently occur in the brain and body when we laugh (Cousins, 1979). According to Victor Borge: "Laughter is the shortest distance between two people." In my opinion, that's half true. It's true for the people who are doing the laughing!

We tend to associate laughter with warm, happy, relaxing experiences. But why?

Tony Jay, my friend and writing partner on my British TV series *Yes, Minister* and *Yes, Prime Minister* remarked that when we laugh "We bare our teeth and emit a barking sound." In every other species such behavior is immediately recognized as a warning, or as aggression. This is because all comedy is cruel. Will Rogers said "Everything is funny as long as it happens to somebody else." Many great comedies, and tragedies, revolve around being cruelly laughed at. Consider, for example, Malvolio's scenes in *Twelfth Night* on the one hand, a comedy, and the first two acts of *Rigoletto* on the other. That cruelty is why comedians regard audiences as a dangerous beast that has to be subdued and ultimately killed. So although we associate laughter with warm, happy experiences, it is the exact opposite if you're on the receiving end. It is when you are *laughed at* that you feel the aggression. Laughter is aggressive behavior. And it is a group activity. Laughing alone is often seen as a sign of madness. As Tony said, "What do you do if you're sitting on the bus or the train and you see someone laughing, out loud, all by themselves? You get out at the next stop."

As we all know, group behavior is different from individual behavior. Being in a large group changes people. Crowd psychology is different from individual psychology. To be in a crowd usually reduces the crowd's inhibitions and frequently makes people react with less empathy and more cruelty. We see this tribal or group behavior in football crowds, gangs, armies, politically inspired mobs . . . and audiences. This tribal behavior is one the reason why professionals have to try out comedy in front of an audience. So now we ask: What is an audience?

An audience is a collection of individuals. But it is more than that: An audience is a thing unto itself—a specific type of crowd. Each particular crowd needs to be made into a single and cooperative unit. That is why most people start a speech with a couple of jokes. By doing so they are organizing a bunch of 100, 500, or 1,000 separate individuals into one group, one audience.

Because laughter, from an evolutionary standpoint, is a tribal activity, there is safety in numbers. The effect is heightened if we all react together. For this reason, comedy goes better in a full house than in an empty one. It is always funnier to see a funny movie in a full theater than at home, alone, on video. Laughter is contagious!

Dark and Invisible Sides of Humor

Everybody who does comedy for a living is concerned about audience aggression. Consider the language comedians use. When their act goes well and gets big laughs they say, "I killed them. I knocked 'em dead. I slayed them!" When they get no laughs, they say, "I died." This accurately represents how they feel. The language tells us that comedians feel that they are in a life-and-death struggle with their audience. For a comedian, comedy means "kill or be killed." The comedian and the comedy are in a fight to the death with the audience. A draw is not a satisfactory outcome for either side. You have to "knock 'em dead!"

Once you have organized the audience into a coherent unit, instead of a group of random individuals, the audience needs to forget itself. That is why we watch plays and films sitting in the dark. This helps us to lose our individual identities and instead we assume a sort of collective identity. Why is this important? It's because theater originally had an anthropological purpose: to depict dangerous situations that threaten the safety or existence of the tribe.

If a play ends tragically, the audience is being asked to empathize with the victim. If a play ends comedically the tribe is being asked to laugh *at* the victim. Either way, the play says, these are the terrible things that will happen to you and to society if you break our rules and taboos.

If you are Oedipus and you commit incest, even unintentionally, you will suffer and die. Why is this lesson necessary? Because incest threatens the future of the species. In his essay, *Civilization and Its Discontents* (1929), Freud speculated about the necessity of getting across this message. If, in the kind of farces about marriage that used to be popular, the hero commits adultery, he will be exposed and ridiculed. Why? Because public shaming is an effective way for society to discourage adultery. Drama, therefore, is a training program for life.

Theater and the Search for Truth, Companionship, and Moral Leadership

Today the purpose of drama is mainly for entertainment. But even today, whether on the screen or the stage, dramas show people what not to do. Plays show people breaking the rules and suffering the consequences. So when we laugh we are, in fact, owning up. Laughter is recognition that what we as a tribe see enacted on the stage is true. That is why we bark with recognition, as the dogs do when we come home.

Tom Stoppard said: "Laughter is the sound of comprehension." That is true. I have always called it the sound of recognition, and that is why comedy can be so rewarding. When the audience laughs at something I have said or written it means that they understand my point of view. Joan Rivers once said: "I succeeded by saying what everyone else was thinking." If we don't recognize some truth about ourselves, even if truth is heightened or exaggerated for comic effect, we don't find the comedy funny. We say it's silly or stupid. But if we laugh, we are admitting "I've said that, I've done that. I've thought that" or, more likely, "I wish I'd said that or done that."

However, although you must control them, the audience can be your friend, not your enemy. The audience is like a dog, because not only does it bark and bare its teeth, it can be easily trained to love you. The audience wants leadership and enjoys being part of the pack. The audience gains confidence when the performers are confident; it wants the performers to be in control. The audience likes a safe pair of hands.

On the other hand, the audience reacts badly to poor leadership, lack of control, or failure to set boundaries. It starts to exhibit cruelty toward the players or comedian. Have you ever noticed how angry critics and audiences get if they go to see a comedy and it isn't funny? Why is that? They don't get angry if they go to a drama and it doesn't make them cry.

Members of the audience have made a commitment. They could be watching TV, playing video games, chess, or whatever they would do if they stayed home. They have not gone to a pub, a restaurant, a football game, or any other form of entertainment. They have come to see you, your show. And, usually, they have paid to see it. That is a serious investment of time and money. Like Alfred P. Doolittle in *Pygmalion* and *My Fair Lady*, the audience is wanting to like you; it's willing to like you; it's waiting to like you. On the other hand, it needs you to be confident, in charge, and to know what you are doing. Then it will relax and be happy.

None of the above applies, by the way, to people who have been given free seats. Free seats are called "paper." If the theater is full of people who have not paid, the house is said to be "papered." This will be a tough crowd. They are like patients who don't pay. They have made no commitment. They may think, or know, that they are doing you a favor by being there. They know that demand to see the show is inadequate, or they wouldn't have been given the comps. They have low expectations. Many, like the critics, or like court-mandated patients, are there not because they want to be but because they have to be. This kind of audience will never react as well as a house full of paying customers, but even they can be won round.

The ingredients of comedy are fundamental to the human condition. They are elemental. If you are looking for ideas, start with the Ten Commandments: Thou shalt not kill; Thou shalt not commit adultery; Thou shalt not covet thy neighbor's wife. Great stuff! Any Catholic readers need to look no further than the Seven Deadly Sins, the basis for all comedy. I keep a copy of them on my desk. Greed, envy, sloth, wrath, pride, lust—what else do you need?

There are other sins, not in that celebrated list, which are also intrinsically funny. Cowardice, for instance. Miserliness and cowardice were Woody Allen's stock in trade as a stand-up, and Jack Benny's too. Then there's hypocrisy, and treachery, which I think are subsections of greed, lust, or pride.

Laughter and Cultural Trends

Laughter is also subject to fashion. For instance, there are fashions in sexist jokes. In the sixties, many jokes were made by male comedians—that means virtually all comedians back then—about large boobs, knockers, tits, hooters, and other euphemisms. Today it is considered bad taste to make a joke about big breasts, or any other kind of breast. This has been one of the great successes of the women's movement.

Curiously, those jokes have now been replaced by jokes about small penises. These jokes *are* acceptable, and indeed appear to be almost mandatory for male comedians to demonstrate how enlightened they are. These jokes can, of course, be made by both men and women.

And this raises the whole question of taste. Does comedy have to be in good taste? The answer is that it's impossible! There is no such thing as good taste in comedy. All comedy, dependent as it is upon people's misfortunes, disasters, and embarrassments, is in bad taste. But if there is no such thing as good taste in comedy, there can be no such thing as bad taste either. Something is funny, or it's not funny. When comedy is funny, it tells a truth that might otherwise not be told. "Bad taste" is simply a way of describing when a joke has crossed the line into "not funny."

Why is comedy fundamentally about anger? Why are all comedians and comedy people angry and/or depressed? Because they are. It's a fact. Robin Williams's recent suicide raised that question again in many people's minds. Let me try to explain the psychology of the professional funny person.

I believe that comedians and comedy writers are universally angry, although they may not realize it. They may be in denial. They may repress their anger, or they may release its full destructive power. They may not show it if they're getting older, have had therapy, or have simply mellowed with age or success. But they are or were angry. I have met hundreds, worked closely with many, and lived with myself. In my experience it's invariable. Why is this so?

It is pretty well agreed among psychologists and psychotherapists of all stripes that everybody has, deep down, some primitive murderous rage from their childhood, a repressed desire to kill parents or siblings. (I'm not talking about tantrums here.) But rage is not acceptable in our society and is seldom expressed by a child because we are all required to be "good." As we mature, rage has to find other outlets. If it is expressed it in a safe place, like a therapist's office, a good marriage or a script, the guilt or shame about it may diminish, and so will the sadness, depression, and need for anger management. Comedy is one possible outlet for rage, a way to say or do things that "shouldn't" be said or done.

Many people to whom rage is forbidden and who are powerless to express it for personal or cultural reasons, or both, turn it against themselves. Shame is the result. This shame, in turn, causes profound sadness. In a psychological nutshell, this is why some people who are aggressive, prone to depression, melancholy, and despair become comedians. They are trying to express their rage in a way that doesn't make them feel guilty. Thus anger can be healthier than sadness. But it runs the big risk of upsetting people. This is why it is usually transmuted into comedy. It's safer that way.

For most people who do it professionally, comedy is an outlet for anger, but not, unfortunately, a cure. They are frequently unaware of the rage that is displaced into mother-in-law jokes, spouse jokes ("Take my wife. Please."), and jokes against all institutions of society. Comedy is on the attack! Satire is focused anger. It attacks the institutions of society. Comedy makes fun of marriage, sex, the in-laws, the family, the education system, the courts, the police, the military, the church, academia, the prison system, politicians, and everyone in public life. Art is criticism of life, and comedy is criticism of life by ridicule.

Get down from there! You're embarrassing me.

FIGURE 14.1
Hanged, by Oliver Gaspirtz. (Courtesy of Oliver Gaspirtz)

On the Attack, While in Search of Approval

Here is the paradox: comedians and writers of comedy enjoy being cruel but they also want to be liked. They want praise and approval. And, in purely practical terms, it's no good being the funniest person in the world if there is no audience to entertain. If a tree falls in a forest and there's no one there to see it, did it really fall? Here is comedian Henny Youngman's version of this famous philosophical conundrum: "If a husband is alone in a forest, is he still wrong?" That's an angry joke is ever there was one.

Here are some more of his one-liners:

"Why do men die before their wives? They want to."

"Why does divorce cost so much? It's worth it."

The late Robin Williams, seemingly the least depressed and sweetest comedian (but divorced three times!) quipped, "You know the difference between a tornado and divorce in the South? Nothing! Someone's losing a trailer, number one."

And, "Politicians are a lot like diapers. They should be changed frequently—and for the same reasons."

And, "See, the problem is that God gives men a brain and a penis, and only enough blood to run one at a time."

The angry, depressed man who made all these very funny jokes killed himself.

Women also make angry jokes. Joan Rivers said, "My best birth control now is just to leave the lights on."

She also said, "My vagina is like Newark, New Jersey. Men know it's there, but they don't want to visit."

And, "I hate housework. You make the beds, you do the dishes, and six months later, you have to start all over again."

Los Angeles's Hillcrest Country Club was founded in 1920 by a group of Jews who worked in films but were not allowed to join the LA Country Club. (They still wouldn't be allowed to join, by the way.) It is the club about which Groucho Marx famously remarked "I refuse to join any club that would have me as a member," although he did join, presumably because it was the only one he could join. It is said that Groucho was offered membership at one of the other golf clubs in LA as long as he didn't use the swimming pool, and he replied "My daughter's only half Jewish, can she wade in up to her knees?" (Another angry joke!)

But comedy writers know, either instinctively or consciously, that they have to keep their rage and their despair under wraps. It must come out in their work as funny, not angry. An angry *character* can be very funny, but an angry show, with few exceptions, is not. It is merely uncomfortable. We all know that, if we are in the audience at a bad play, it is embarrassing. I sometimes find that I have to look away from the stage, rather than watch people humiliating themselves. This is because I am in the same room as the actors who are embarrassing me, and probably embarrassing themselves. It may be a big room with a thousand seats in it, but it's still a room and I am still in it with them. I am a part of that aggressive beast, the audience, and I'd rather not be. Interestingly, this doesn't seem to apply to film. I can see a bad movie without suffering any embarrassment. This is because it's been made already, it's in the past, and the actors are not in the same room with me. Unless, that is, I am at a premiere; premieres have the potential to be really embarrassing occasions.

How are tragedy and farce/broad comedy related? They are two sides of the same coin.

Drama and comedy lie somewhere along the continuum between tragedy and farce, which are the two extremes of theater. Tragedy is drama at its purest. Farce is comedy at its purest. Some people use the word "farce" pejoratively because they don't understand what farce really is. Farce is not a synonym for silliness, stupidity, or chaos. A well-written farce is a brilliantly organized exercise in duplicity, lust, or some other human failing, full of insight into the human condition, and coldly analytical where a tragedy would be designed to elicit sympathy.

There are many great farces on film. Hollywood refers to them as broad comedies. Examples include *Some Like It Hot*, *His Girl Friday*, *Tootsie*, *What's Up, Doc?*, *Bridesmaids*, *The Hangover*, *Old School*. Tragedy is a drama of inevitable self-destruction induced by the flaws in the protagonist's own character, and farce is driven by the same inexorable, cruel logic, uncluttered by sentiment. A good farce is not about silly people doing silly things. It has to be about something important, to the characters and to the society in which it takes place. A farce is about deadly serious characters doing desperate things that are horribly embarrassing, but doing them because they have no choice.

I directed a farce at the National Theatre in London. Written by Georges Feydeau, John Mortimer translated it as *A Little Hotel on the Side*. In the play, a man is in a bedroom with somebody else's wife. They hear the husband coming up the stairs, and the lover takes off his trousers, and hides in the fireplace with his face up the chimney. This is *only* funny if this is the only logical thing to do in the context, and if he has no other choice. Otherwise it's merely silly.

In both tragedy and farce the protagonist starts a chain of events that inevitably will lead to his, or her, own destruction. Gradually these events spin out of control, leading eventually to madness. A situation is not funny unless there is a hideous dilemma for at least one of the characters. The defining difference between tragedy and farce is that in tragedy the protagonist dies, while in farce the *status quo ante* is restored. Thus comedy reassures the audience that its values are still intact and survival is possible, once punishment and humiliation have been inflicted.

Years ago, I was directing Eugene O'Neill's *Anna Christie* at the Royal Shakespeare Company, and my friend Ron Eyre was directing *Othello* in the other theater. He had an actor playing Othello who tended to overact. His show opened before mine. I saw him sitting alone in the green room one night, after *Othello* had had three previews. He was having a quiet, solitary, large whiskey. "How's it going, Ron?" I asked. "Not bad" he said. "We've got nearly all the laughs out."

FIGURE 14.2

A doctor and footman hurling pudding at each other in an attempt to make the obese patient laugh in order to cure his quinsey. Engraving by R. Newton, 1797. (Public domain).

In comedy you work to get the laughs in. In tragedy, you work to get them *out*. It's a choice, but it's the same process: You either make comedic choices or dramatic choices. The important thing to understand is that the events of the play or film are potentially tragic for the characters, whether it's a tragedy or a comedy. Leading actors in comedy should never reveal that they know they are funny.

Comedy has become more difficult since the advent of the permissive society in the 1960s. How do you do a romantic comedy, for instance, when practically nothing is forbidden anymore? If there's nothing to hide, there's nothing to laugh at. This is the major reason why film comedies are getting more and more gross. Romantic comedy is about what happens when two people who are—or might be—in love are kept apart by parental or other disapproval.

This is usually caused by class, economic, cultural, or ethnic differences. But you don't have a romantic comedy when two people want sex without love. In that case the romantic comedy becomes farce, the comic antithesis of *Romeo and Juliet*.

The next chapter, written by my wife Dr. Rita Lynn, considers the role of humor in psychotherapy. The next time you or your patients crack a joke during session, check out what may be going on deep under the surface. How much rage is there and why is it being hidden?

References

Lynn, J. (2011). *Comedy rules*. London, UK: Faber & Faber.

Cousins, N. (1979). *Anatomy of an illness as perceived by the patient: Reflections on healing and regeneration*. New York: W. W. Norton & Company.

Freud, S. (1929/1962). *Civilization and its discontents*. Ed. and Trans. by James Strachey. New York: W. W. Norton & Company.

15

Rage Underlying
Humor in Psychotherapy

*Rita Lynn**

I AM A psychoanalyst with many decades of experience seeing patients in London, both in National Health Service (NHS) hospitals, clinics, and private practice. I find that sometimes humor and creativity are used as a replacement or a defense by people who were play-deprived in childhood. Humor is an important aspect of creativity. In fact, in his classic book, *The Act of Creation*, Arthur Koestler (1964) identified humor as one of creativity's three pillars, alongside art and science. Since it is a lifesaver, creativity often produces extraordinary high achievers, brilliant people who appear almost superhuman in their accomplishment but who are grossly deficient in their capacity for joy. They often hide their unhappiness under massive achievement. Clinically, it is sometimes hard to bring this unhappiness and pain into the room. This is the kind of patient who unpredictably slips between comedy and darkness, saying everything of real importance as an aside.

My husband, Jonathan Lynn, in the previous chapter, made some points that I wish to follow up with clinical examples. First I describe two patients whose bodies told me what their brains could not: that humor was serving as a cloak. These patients provoked me into taking what I call the non-problems seriously. The question I always ask myself is: What is missing? What is missing from the narrative, which appears lighthearted and straight-

* The author wishes to acknowledge Terry Marks-Tarlow for transcribing and contributing to this chapter.

FIGURE 15.1
Humor as indirect communication: A doctor trying to sell youthfulness
potions to an elderly patient. (Public domain)

forward? So the question is, how do these patients use humor or comedy in therapy?

All psychotherapists have had the following experience at least once in their practices. A patient starts telling you some history, incidents from childhood, or some present occurrence. And they tell it as a joke, laughing themselves, making themselves the butt of the joke, inviting you to laugh with them. Often, these jokes contain immense cruelty and pain—physical and emotional. But the horror of it all remains hidden. And the therapist, sitting in an alert listening, is filled with a deep sense of sadness and pain in the countertransference.

Let me give you an example. A late middle-aged woman with a severe skin complaint, which could never be diagnosed, was recounting an incident from her childhood. She was never allowed into her parents' bedroom if the door was shut. She had fallen off her bike and broken her arm, which was swollen,

FIGURE 15.2
An April Fool's Joke in Denmark. (Public domain)

terribly painful, with the bone clearly protruding. She went to the door of her parents' bedroom, yet still was not allowed in, even though she said she was in great pain. Laughing, she told me, "I had to stay outside the door in pain all night." A great joke. This patient was trying to entertain me with her pain, in case I couldn't bear it. She was very surprised to see tears in my eyes, and shocked when I said that clearly there were tears and pain in the room, and they weren't actually mine. Mine were empathic and hers were missing. A lot of this patient's physical symptoms were relieved by this kind of empathic naming and mirroring of her abuse.

Bob Rodman, a well-known Californian analyst, once wrote that when you cannot cry, other organs weep (1977). What can't be expressed emotionally will be expressed in the physical body. So these kinds of patients try to entertain you with their pain in case you can't bear it, and because they can't bear the memory. Our job is to hear it, hold it, and give it back in small spoonfuls. By experiencing this sort of relational safety, their adult selves can have the compassion for their inner child who has suffered, so that they can understand and express the sadness and rage at the treatment of themselves as children, and to recognize the consequences in their present lives. In the case of this patient, the physical symptoms that she presented were entirely relieved as she was able to sympathize with her abused child rather than use her as a joke.

The Smiling Patient

When I worked at The Royal London Hospital (before 1990, The London Hospital, where the Elephant Man lived), I was sent some extremely ill patients with Crohn's disease and ulcerative colitis. It was a last resort, since the next step for them would be a colostomy. Eventually I collected about 10 of these patients, and so began to see a connection which was common to all of them. It was difficult to see at first, because these patients were almost all very affable people. Very pleasant, and in the case I will describe, smiling constantly. This young woman, in her late 20s, with severe Crohn's, had a hospital file 6 inches thick. And her story was difficult to put together. She was an adored only child of a possessive mother and a distant father. Her mother dressed her like a doll as a little girl and sat her on the bed where she had to stay clean and smiling. No anger of any kind was allowed. The parents did not live as a married couple, and she slept with her mum, also like a doll. In her preteen years, she started presenting with Crohn-like symptoms, abdominal pain, and dysentery, and started going to doctors. Drugs did not seem to help, and she continued to have to smile for her mother and be very good.

What brought her to us in the hospital was that when she was in college she smoked some pot, which resulted in lowering her inhibitions, and she became psychotically violent. When I saw her she was back to smiling and being good, and presenting all of her troubles with patience and an underlying sadness. I put her in a therapy group, and over the first year, we saw some signs of change, because the other people in the group challenged some of her goodness. The symptoms that she brought started to go up her body, from the colon to the diaphragm (she had trouble breathing), to her throat, which she experienced as having something stuck.

One night, driving home from group, she made a sudden stop at a red light and was hit from behind by another driver. He was very angry and came up to her window, shouting at her, and put his hands on top of her half-open window. At first, she was frightened and smiled in a placating manner. Then suddenly, his putting his hands on the window released something in her, and she wound up the window, trapping his hands. Once he could no longer get at her, she screamed back at him; she screamed and screamed like a terrible tantrum. The rage of years had finally come up her body and out. She processed this event in the group, carefully and with great understanding, and her Crohn's symptoms gradually receded.

In all 10 patients I saw with these diseases, there seemed to be a lot of suppressed rage and a great prohibition to expressing it. I wrote about this with Professor Sam Cohen in a paper I presented at The Royal London

Hospital called, "A Disease of Rage." In recent years I have met an extremely successful and talented young woman who also suffered from Crohn's, and had enormous trouble controlling it. She fell into the same patterns as I saw in the original patients. She did everything for everyone, always putting herself and her needs last, and having worse and worse attacks of Crohn's. It wasn't until she was with a doctor who was also a therapist that she began to come to grips with the underlying trigger events that brought on these attacks. Now, I'm not suggesting that these diseases are only of rage. They have other components, genetic predispositions being one, and diet being another. And obviously drugs are used to help. But in this young woman, the combination of her diet and therapy have produced remarkable relief. She was even able to have a second baby without exacerbating her Crohn's. But I also noticed that she is taking much more notice of her own feelings. She is also finding ways of expressing her anger that do not place it directly in her colon.

The Use of Humor to Treat Creative People

Patients are not the only ones to use humor in psychotherapy; psychotherapists frequently do as well (e.g., Marks-Tarlow, 2012, 2014). And humor isn't always a defense against full expression. Sometimes it becomes a well-crafted intervention. Obviously this is not by telling patients jokes, but by occasionally using language, which can express metaphor in a comic way.

Robin Skynner (who trained me) referred to this technique as paradoxical injunction. This can only be used by people who are adept at conveying humor while speaking very seriously, and should be used very carefully. And in America, perhaps the technique should not be used at all, since it involves the understanding and use of irony, which is not a popular concept in this country. Robin, Dr. Skynner, who did this very well, used Paradoxical Injunction to access the rage, which was not available any other way (see Behr, 2010). It is my experience that most creative people carry a lot of rage.

In Short-Term Dynamic Psychotherapy (STDP), which Dr. Habib Davanloo (1996) devised, he uses challenge and pressure as a technique. This produces very similar results to paradoxical injunction. Davanloo challenges the patient's defenses, and then pressures them when they increase the defense, eventually producing rage. But Robin Skynner used paradoxical statements or injunctions, for example, when a patient went on and on about their depression. Skynner quite seriously, but with a twinkle, would say "You know, I don't think you are depressed enough. Do you think you could really go for it?" The patient would usually be very startled, then very angry. And the

"Your choice, but remember:
You're damned if you do, damned if you don't..."

FIGURE 15.3
Humor as metaphor. (Courtesy of Terry Marks-Tarlow)

---

anger was in the room, which was the purpose of the whole exercise. He was very good at it, and I know, because he did it to me, when I was in my training analysis. I had finally reached some realization of my own depression, which I found very hard to access and very painful to describe. I was finally describing it, and at a very low point emotionally, when he made this paradoxical statement—that obviously I was not depressed enough. I became enraged at him, something he had been trying to get at with me. I had always seen him as my good father, and therefore had not been able to get in touch with some of my rage with my own father. I was avoiding this by making Robin the good father.

Robin believed that if you were training to be an analyst, you had to look in all your own dark corners and experience the difficulties, before you could treat patients with dark corners. Now this sort of enactment really worked on me, but I do not suggest this for the majority of patients. We are always looking for what is missing from the picture, and primitive murderous rage is hard to access and to hold in the room. I was often very entertaining, to hide mine, and Robin recognized this.

In searching for what is missing, psychotherapists are always looking for the discrepancy between the content and the affect. Another example: A patient who is probably the most creative of all my patients used his rage to create wondrous work, but the same rage trapped him in isolation in his intimate private life. He was, and is, a scientific genius, who used every moment of his working life to expand his brain, but cut off all access to emotions. It wasn't until his teenage daughter said that she would leave home if he didn't get help that he came to see me. He was a man in his early 40s, who had met his soulmate at university when very young. They had married and had two children. And then his wife contracted the very rare cancer in which he was the world's specialist. He could not save her. He swallowed his pain and rage and became even more expert in his field. But my patient's time was spent on only that and his children, and he had no relationships with anyone else. And, according to him, he had no feelings.

When this brilliant scientist came to see me, he spent the first few months distracting me in a rather assertive way to prove that he had done more, read more, and achieved more than me. All true. When he kept bringing examples of his brilliance, I finally had to say, "Look you will always be cleverer than me, academically and intellectually. But the area of your mind that you defend with your brilliance, i.e., your pain and rage and how to feel and express them, you know nothing about. This land of feeling, and recognizing it, is foreign to you. We are going to play in this area."

Eventually he accepted this, and the group I put him in began to help him with this deficit. At this point in my clinical narrative, I must digress for a moment. A number of years ago, our seven-year-old son Teddy was in the back of my car with his best friend Şam. We were driving past my office and he said to Sam, "There's my mum's school." Sam said, "Your mum goes to school? She's so old." Teddy said, "Well it's not really school, it's called group." "What's Group?" said Sam. Teddy replied, "It a sort of nursery school for adults where they learn to talk and play." My patient's professional creativity did not diminish, but he began to recognize emotions, even negative ones, first in others, and then in himself. He looked up in the lab one day and saw his coworker who had been there for some time, and saw that she had feelings for him. They married a year later. His daughters were pleased.

Stalking What is Absent

I look for what is missing from what the patient presents. From the one who was the stand-up comic, i.e., "Everything is a joke, especially my pain," to the one who cannot find anything to smile or laugh about. This latter patient, a very creative writer and poet, was intensely serious about everything, and he looked it. His eyes were wide and staring; he looked frightened and frightening. He was referred to me when his third marriage was breaking down, and he was extremely unhappy.

It gradually emerged that this man had never been happy, and actually felt that being happy would handicap his creativity. This creativity had saved him from controlling, cold parents who did not like him. In fact, he felt very unliked generally. When this patient got on a bus to come to my office, he felt that people moved away from him and avoided him. I understood why they would, as his penetrating stare was quite unsettling.

Jenni Diski (2015), an English writer and worker with deprived children, described the look on her face as "having taken in all the unfairness of injustice, rolled it up into small balls with spikey edges and shot them through her eyes killing dead the wrongdoer and the wrongdoer's representative" (p. 11). My patient's look was like this. He painted a bleak picture of his life as an outsider, even in his own family. He felt he had no rights, but felt he had to accept the decisions his wife and others made for him. His preferences were never noticed and, if indicated, were ignored. He didn't feel he had a place at home, and became increasingly depressed there—not a chair or corner was his. This echoed his childhood experiences, as this man came from a very formal, rigid, immensely rich family and was never considered or consulted about anything, while ostensibly having everything.

I began by asking how he saw himself. It turned out that he didn't see himself because there was no self to see. He had constructed a writer's persona, and said of himself, "What I was doing was being more involved with being a writer than with living. You swallow a notion of who the writer is, which is something quite different from who you are." A little later he wrote: "I think I didn't know, for instance, how to write with emotion, or I didn't know any sort of aesthetic that was life-enhancing. Basically, all sorts of things were missing from me."

So in the beginning we tried to get his feet under him and get him what I call some "edges." I use this kind of metaphor as, being a poet, he understood imagery as a shortcut to complex concepts. In order to have rights you have to be able to fight for them. In order to fight you have to be able to stand up. He wrote later, "I had no sense of edges. Barriers instead of boundaries." He grasped this concept rapidly, and then I used myself to mirror his effect on others—like his stare, which was able to move people away from him, and which no one had ever mentioned.

In the first months of this patient's treatment he did not smile or laugh once. As he gradually stopped pushing people away and started to soften his gaze he found that he could be, and was, liked. He said, "I even get along better with my mother. I think she notices I'm much happier. I didn't tell her about the therapy at all, she just recognized the change. It's nice to think you have a stretch of years ahead in which to give yourself a happiness you've not had."

His treatment was not a long one—a year—and about half way through he asked me if he could write about his therapy. He had been asked to contribute a chapter to a book which explored the patient's experiences of therapy. A lot has been written about the therapist's experience of psychotherapy but little about the patient's, and the two experiences may be very different. I said yes, thinking nothing would come of it. But to my surprise, just before we terminated therapy, he brought me the book. I was surprised and a little taken aback. I had never considered how I would feel being written about. I was nervous reading the book and could not find a chapter that seemed to describe me; all the chapters were written anonymously.

It is very unusual for psychotherapists to get reviewed. Sometime we get a little feedback after a patient has left but never a full chapter reviewing our work. When I finally identified the chapter, I realized why it took me a moment to recognize myself: It's fascinating how differently others see us, and very funny I think. After a rather unflattering description of my appearance, I read on and I found that although his description of me bore no resemblance to me—in my opinion!—his description of our therapy fit mine exactly. This was the most gratifying review one would ever want.

Even now, as I re-read the description all these years later, I was moved by this patient's conclusion after finding his missing self, "Probably humor is the only thing you've got which will allow you to handle everything. You have your strength, you have order and you have your brains. You have this marvelous palette and everything coming at you at once, and you've just got to handle it."

Although humor results in people trying to manage their primitive murderous rage, another way of expressing these feelings safely is though play. My patient never played as a child. I think in his year with me he felt free to explore areas foreign to him, just as children do when they play, which brings to mind Winnicott's famous declaration.

Psychotherapy takes place in the overlap of two areas of playing, that of the patient and that of the therapist. Psychotherapy has to do with two people playing together. The corollary of this is that where playing is not possible then the work done by the therapist is directed towards bringing the patient from a state of not being able to play into a state of being able to play. (1971, p. 44)

My patient was able to try on different parts of himself and experience different emotions without lethal results. His creativity was not diminished but enhanced. I got a new book of poems from him this Christmas.

References

Behr, H. (2010). Malcolm Pines, et al.: The art of teaching group analysis. *Group Analysis*, *43*(3), 241–252.

Davanloo, H. D. (1996). Unlocking the unconscious. In Groves, J. (Ed.), *Essential papers on short-term dynamic therapy* (pp. 300–334). New York: New York University.

Diski, J. (2015). Why didn't you just do what you were told? *London Review of Books*, *37*(5), 9–12.

Koestler, A. (1964). *The act of creation*. New York: Penguin Books.

Marks-Tarlow, T. (2012). *Clinical intuition in psychotherapy: The neurobiology of embodied response*. New York: W. W. Norton & Company.

Marks-Tarlow, T (2014). Awakening clinical intuition: An experiential workbook for psychotherapists. New York: W. W. Norton & Company.

Rodman, T. (1977). *Not dying*. New York: Random House.

Winnicott, D. W. (1971). *Playing & reality*. New York: Tavistock/Routledge.

16

Developing Resilience with the Improviser's Mindset: Getting People Out of Their Stuck Places

Zoe Galvez and Betsy Crouch

What I learned in improv crept into my life and still enriches it. In 2005, my son died in a car accident when he was only 20. To say that I was devastated is to put it lightly. For some reason, open and vulnerable and out of my mind, really, I signed up for improv with Ms. Galvez. We were encouraged to make one another look good, and when we did, it was reciprocated. We created scenes and stories together as if we had one mind with many bodies. We watched and laughed and cried. We were trying even if it wasn't perfect. Once a week, I came out of my tormented self and lived for two marvelous hours. There was something about the coalescing of the group that made me feel invited back into the family of man. I loved how we said 'yes . . . and' to everything, and if we didn't we would have to start over. No 'yes, but's.' No 'no's.' It made me realize how often in life I had heard the latter rather than the former. And it made even the death of my beloved son more palatable, because just like the Zen of improv 'This is what life is.' Improv is community. It is fun. It is spiritual. It saved my life.

—Lisa, student

IMPROVISATIONAL THEATER, OR improv, is much more than a comedy show. Improvisers are trained to adopt a mindset that allows them to face uncertainty and fear with a sense of gratitude and playfulness. Everyone experiences loss, loneliness, scarcity, and even devastation in life. Success is determined by how you respond to life's challenges. The improviser's mindset provides a new way to face times of uncertainty. We've created principles to harness the improviser's mindset by synthesizing the most effective philosophies of improv theater and expanding them beyond the stage. Our practice and framework are informed by decades of experience in improv, business, theater, performance, dancing, coaching, and teaching. We have observed, universally, an improvement in resilience, optimism, vitality, and adaptability when individuals commit to holistically practicing these powerful principles. We are intentional about creating a strong value system and a safe environment conducive to personal development and transformation. Over the course of this chapter we will dive into each principle, share exercises, and explore the psychological benefits of practicing improv.

What is Improv?

When you think of improv, you might picture a stand-up comedian at a microphone or the popular TV show *Whose Line Is It Anyway?* Improv is often humorous, yet it can also be poignant and dramatic. There are many different expressions of improvisational theater. The most basic component is actors creating characters and stories without a script. These stories can be short scenes or full plays. Imagine a group of improv actors creating an entire play from scratch, on stage in front of a paying audience, with just this opening line: "May I have a word?" The audience is asked to yell out suggestions to initiate the narrative; they too are part of this collaborative ecosystem. As they activate their bodies and voices, improvisers attune to their partners, and co-create new shared realities to produce a unique show that will never be seen again.

In order to successfully navigate this uncharted territory, actors depend on a set of values and agreements to support one another in this process. Each training school or theater promotes different values and agreements based on the training of the founders and their influences. We are passionate about this craft and its application to individual and organizational growth. Our philosophy is that by prioritizing psychological safety, improv can become an interactive mindfulness practice for any type of group. This supports individuals to joyfully inhabit the present moment, meet uncertainty with enthusiasm, fail good-naturedly, and build deep connections.

Now you may be thinking that improv sounds frightening or that it will scare your patients. Public speaking *sans* script? Being unprepared in front of people? Yet it is the risk and fear of rejection and vulnerability that make it an opportunity for connection, healing, and transformation. When we make ourselves vulnerable and feel supported, it builds our trust and allows us to shift, change, and expand. We are encouraged to make mistakes and suspend judgment of ourselves and others. In improv, we quickly learn that we are returning to the playground and revisiting that childhood freedom and inventiveness that we once knew intimately. Play is powerful. When we commit to the practice of play in our lives, play wins over fear. According to Brown and Vaughan, "(P)lay . . . is about learning to harness a force that has been built into us through millions of years of evolution, a force that allows us to both discover our most essential selves and enlarge our world. We are designed to find fulfillment and creative growth through play" (Brown & Vaughan, 2010 p. 13). Through play, we face our fear with curiosity and enthusiasm.

Improv is for Everyone

All the world's a stage.

—William Shakespeare

You may think that the improviser is born with certain talents, like the ability to think fast and make witty comments. The fact is improvisers are following guidelines to help themselves listen, adapt, and respond in the moment. It is becoming more and more common for non-actors to seek this training as a way of developing the improviser's mindset for its application to daily life.

Based on our work coaching thousands of clients, we know that as we develop the improviser's mindset, our lives off the stage change in positive ways. Individuals and organizations seek out this training for a variety of reasons that range from personal (a desire for improved communication skills, increased optimism, and resilience) to organizational (improved collaboration, increased creativity, innovative thinking, and leadership development). Applying the principles of improv in the academic world and in the business world is becoming more and more prevalent. John Kao from Harvard Business School said, "Improvisation is one of two or three cardinal skills for businesses to learn in the future" (Kao, 2002, pg. 116). Now many top master's of business administration (MBA) schools include classes on improvisation (e.g., Harvard, Stanford, New York University, Massachusetts Institute of Technology, Duke,

University of California, Los Angeles, University of California, Berkeley, and more). Physicians hire us to further develop their empathy skills and increase patient satisfaction. Salespeople see that this practice is beneficial for slowing down, listening, and deeply connecting with clients. Engineering teams hire us to build cross-functional team relationships and foster innovation. This has proven especially effective at Twitter, where Ms. Galvez designed an employee development program that grew from one to six weekly classes over the course of five years. The program is recognized as one of the most popular learning and development offerings at Twitter. Finally, executives turn to improv to help with influencing and crafting culture through these principles.

How Does Improv Support Therapy?

The skills that improv teams use to negotiate on stage while under pressure are the same skills that your clients can use to negotiate any circumstance that requires them to be agile in their own lives. As the therapist, you can leverage these principles to build alliances with colleagues and patients and to confidently approach uncertainty with clinical material. Establishing a common language and forming agreements around these principles helps create deeper connection with others and ourselves. It is common for us to work with clients who have been referred to our improv classes by their therapists. These students often find improv complementary to their therapeutic sessions. Improv provides a creative venue to begin to work through some of life's challenges. It is a safe space to renew our sense of joy, trust, and adventure.

In a classroom, we provide a supportive space to explore creativity and role-playing, and to become more comfortable with uncertainty. As much as we calculate and plan to avoid uncertainty, there will always be something we encounter that we didn't quite anticipate. As much as we try to control things, we simply can't. We like to call improv "training for the unexpected." It is training for those moments when life throws us a curveball and we have to think on our feet and deliver with confidence. The more comfortable we are with the unexpected, the more available we are to be in the moment, and less driven by fear.

We train people by duplicating "on the spot" moments so that this elevated state becomes familiar and does not propel us into fight, flight, or freeze mode. We purposely put ourselves under pressure so that we learn how to not just survive, but to thrive under these conditions. We practice putting ourselves on the spot so that we learn to relax and breathe when challenged. Mimicking the state of being on the spot in the form of play reduces anxiety as we train our bodies to breathe and our minds to focus on the task at hand instead of worrying about future outcomes. Play liberates our fixed states and alters how we see the world. Our exercises push the boundaries of our established patterns and allow us to accept uncertainty and open up to new perspectives.

Whether you or your patient want to tap into creative power, build confidence, connect deeply with others, gain comfort with uncertainty, adapt to change, or become unstuck from a rigid pattern, the improviser's mindset, outlined in this chapter, will provide tools to thrive.

These principles are useful to anyone who wants to increase or improve any of these traits: resilience, buoyancy, courage, confidence, vitality, joy, optimism, presence, openness, flexibility, curiosity, generosity, and empathy. It is also a mindset that is supportive in minimizing or decreasing judgment, anxiety, rumination, and depression.

In this chapter, we will explore the improviser's mindset through the follow-

* Intentional Listening
* Make Your Teammate the Hero
* Power of Presence
* Resilient Response
* Open to Yes
* Voice Your ideas

FIGURE 16.1
ImprovHQ principles courtesy of Betsy Crouch and Zoe Galvez

---

ing ImprovHQ principles:

For each principle, we have included an exercise that you can practice on your own or with others: patients, couples, families, a colleague, or with your own family. Approaching your work with the improviser's mindset will give you a new perspective and new toolkit. Improv exercises are organic and ever-evolving. Use these recommendations as a launching pad to create your own exercises to inspire breakthroughs for yourself and your patients. This type of experiential learning, in a therapeutic environment, is an opportunity to build resilience while experiencing humor and levity. Let's jump in and explore the improviser's mindset. This is an invitation to play and practice these principles to become more resilient, receptive, and ready to face uncertainty with new-found courage.

The ImprovHQ Principles

Principle 1: Intentional Listening

Seek first to understand, then to be understood.

—Stephen R. Covey

IMPROV IS THE ART OF DEEP LISTENING

Our number one goal on stage is to collaborate well. The bottom line is that in order to collaborate well we need to listen well. As improvisers, we must be aware of everything going on around us; we must play actor, director, and writer all at once, while the lights shine on our faces and the audience shouts out suggestions. Listening is challenging when we are under pressure. We must set an intention to hear the words our teammate utters, as well as to receive the information being communicated beyond the words. Intentional listening defines the commitment to be more conscious of our surroundings and our partners at all times. If we walk onstage expecting a certain answer or reaction, we may miss something shared by our fellow players or even the audience. We must hang in suspense as we take in the information rather than formulating a response before the speaker has completed their thought.

Improvisers train to acquire, retain, and reincorporate a large volume of material, including new names in every scene. An improviser needs to develop a keen ability to listen on many levels.

You see . . .	It means . . .
A twinkle in your partner's eye	They have an idea
A subtle hint they are lost	They've forgotten a name
That they are unsure	They need your help
That they're inspired	Drop your idea and add to their offer

We also can differentiate between the actor's emotions (he's nervous tonight) and his character's emotions (he wants to hug me). Our awareness extends to the timing of the show (time to wrap up) as well as the narrative (time for a plot twist). We recognize when the story is taking on a life of its own and all you have to do is surf the narrative wave, letting everything glide into place. Finally, you notice the sound of your own thoughts and quickly decipher whether they are inspirations that propel the story forward or judgments that need to be instantly discarded, as they're not useful in the midst of dynamic collaboration.

Our modern culture requires us to perform this type of juggling act on a daily basis. We are expected to take in the information we've learned and pass it on to others. Yet, in real life, we don't always have the accountability of an audience. As a result, we miss opportunities for deeper connection with others. What ends up happening is a game of "telephone" in which messages are often distorted. We take on more information than we are able to process and we find ourselves overwhelmed by inefficiencies, including having to repeat conversations and meetings.

According to studies, most of us think we are average or above-average communicators (Haney, 1979), yet our listening efficiency is quite low, only 25 percent (Husman, Lahiff, Penrose, 1988). Many people agree that effective listening is important. However, few people feel driven to commit to working on this skill (Spitzberg, 1994). With rare exceptions, most of us have room for improvement. The good news is that you can develop your ability to listen and retain information through practice, whether you want to get on stage or not.

Slowing down to listen can help us better understand verbal messages as well as their underlying meaning. The challenge is that we often stop listening once

FIGURE 16.2
Woman multitasking at desk. (Courtesy of William Koehler)

we think we understand the speaker's point. Have you found yourself quickly coming to a conclusion about someone's diagnosis before hearing their entire story? At this point listening stops, and we begin to formulate our response. There is often more to hear. At the very least, when we slow down and remain curious, the listener has a deeper sense of being heard. Practicing intentional listening is about remaining in that space of curiosity longer than we are accustomed to. With this practice we may discover that there is more to uncover. If we fall into the habit of thinking about how we are going to respond, we often miss key information. If we desire to be better communicators we must stop assuming, and seek to understand, leaving room for the speaker's input. Most people are unaware that we have the capacity for "superhero" listening skills and that with these skills we can positively impact our life and the world around us. This popular performance piece is one of our favorite listening exercises. We use it as a technique to practice listening offstage. Notice that it forces you to slow down.

Exercise: Last Letter, First Letter

Objective: Listen to everything your partner says completely before responding.

Participants: 2–3

Explanation: The last letter of player A's sentence (Andy) is used to start player B's sentence (Betty), and vice versa.

Example:

ANDY: *What a beautiful day it is today.*

[The person responding (Betty) would begin the next sentence with the last letter of Andy's sentence, "y," from the word "today."]

BETTY: *Yes, it is a beautiful day, a great day for sailing.*

[Player A (Andy) would use the last letter of player B's (Betty) sentence, in this case, "g," to start the next sentence.]

ANDY: *Gosh I really believe I can win this regatta!*

BETTY: *Ahoy! The other boats are lining up and ready!*

And so on and so forth.

Tips: Use general content for the conversation like "foods you enjoy," "vacations," or "your favorite restaurant." If you choose to do this listening exercise with clients we do not recommend using clinical material, because it could derail the purpose of the exercise. The purpose of the exercise is to slow down, listen fully, and to connect and have fun!

Daily practice:

This is an exercise you can do in any interaction. Is there someone at home or at work who you would like to connect with at a deeper level? After one or two sentences, drop the spelling component but continue to utilize the pauses for deeper listening. If you find yourself distracted, not fully engaged, or interrupting, bring the spelling component back in.

ERIC'S STORY

A client of ours giggled while sharing with us that he really wanted to become a better listener with his wife, so he used the "last Letter, first letter" technique, for six months, without telling her. He told us that one day she said to him curiously, "Something is different. It seems like you are really hearing what I am saying and listening to me." His tone shifted earnestly, as he shared with us that he was so happy to connect with her on a deeper level and so appreciative for the exercise. It was a moving story and a great example of how you can deepen connections using this technique. This tool simply reminds us to slow down and pause before speaking.

In an improv scene, it is imperative to listen to everything our partner says to create a shared dialogue. If we check out for a moment on stage, because we are wrapped up in our thoughts (or nervousness), then we're no longer attuned to one another and we become stuck. In improv we have to show up with 100 percent of our attention. There isn't any part of us that can be anywhere else. When we do this well, the results are sometimes described by the players and audience as magical. Sometimes the audience does not believe that the story is improvised because it is so well executed. We are capable of achieving this type of flow in our lives. Listening with intention and curiosity helps us hear new possibilities and helps us move out of our stuck places. When we listen with intention, it is an act of generosity. By respecting our teammate's contribution we make them the hero.

Principle 2: Make Your Teammate the Hero

> *Treat a man as he is and he will remain as he is. Treat a man as he can be and should be and he will become as he can and should be.*
>
> —Goethe

IMPROV IS THE ART OF CONNECTION

Inherent to our artform is the promise of uncertainty. Is facing uncertainty scary and uncomfortable? Is it exciting? Uncertainty can feel frightening, especially when we feel we are alone. In improv, we are surrounded by others facing the void with us. We approach the daunting task of facing uncharted territory as an ensemble with a core commitment to look for ways to set one another up for success. The interpersonal connection and commitment to inspire one another on stage, and help each other no matter what, builds a camaraderie and trust which transforms our fear of uncertainty into an enthusiasm for discovery and creation.

To move through our "stuck places," we often need factors in place such as trusting relationships, professional guidance, a safe environment, and clear goals and values. We are all wired for connection. In our style of improv, we create a safe and supportive environment by committing to find ways to inspire and connect with one another. Improv requires us to be generous and serve the team as a whole. We enter into a group rhythm that is bigger than ourselves. As an ensemble, we attune to one another to reach a collective consciousness. It's a form of dynamic collaboration that requires us to constantly take leaps of faith, knowing our partners will be there for us. In the same regard, it is essential that your patient knows that he or she is part of your collaborative team. "Effective therapists are able to form a working alliance with a broad range of clients . . . The working alliance is described as collaborative, purposeful work on the part of the client and the therapist (Wampold, 2011, p.3). It is the working alliance that you form together which provides a basis for treatment. When you think of it in these terms, you are essentially a part of many small teams.

On the stage, one way we practice teamwork is by accepting others and their ideas. Our teammate becomes our lifeline as we maneuver through new territory, traveling into the unknown together with only the rules of improv to keep us afloat. It's critical to look for ways to inspire the collective, draw on each other's resources, and share control. We practice mutual care, honoring our partner's ideas and validating their creative suggestions by using them to build the scene. Improv is an avenue for deeper connection. We look for ways to light each other up onstage knowing that inspiration leads to creativity and better storytelling.

The magic of true teamwork happens as we drop our own agenda to serve the story and serve the show. Even when you see a format like Theatresports, created by Keith Johnstone, where two teams compete, both groups prioritize creating an entertaining show over winning or personal achievement.

This principle, "Make Your Teammate the Hero," encourages a shift from an inward focus, "Am I doing a good job?" to an outward focus whereby players attend to their partners more than themselves. This act of generosity also makes us less self-conscious. The team feels more secure when everyone agrees to look out for each other's well-being. In reflecting on kindness, Seligman (2002) states that kindness "consists in total engagement and in the loss of self-consciousness. Time stops" (p. 9). In class, we often describe this act of benevolence as sending your arrows "out" instead of "in." The interpersonal attentiveness required by improv creates a state whereby the "we" becomes as or more important than the "me," which Dr. Daniel Siegel refers to in his book *Brainstorm* (2013) as "MWe."

In improv, it is essential to create an environment conducive to taking risks and sharing ideas. We strive to create emotional safety so that students can take chances, explore their creativity, and take intelligent risks. It takes time to lay the groundwork for the ensemble to build trust. We use playful exercises such as the ones found in this chapter to build psychological safety. We have found that play, with the intention of creating trust under the guidance of a professional coach, creates emotional safety. Amy Edmondson of Harvard Business School defines psychological safety as a "shared belief that the team is safe for interpersonal risk taking" (2014). Group dynamics affect the tone of the classroom and the success of a show. A lack of psychological safety impedes our ability to collaborate at a peak level.

Our approach to "Make Your Teammate the Hero," is aligned with the Appreciative Inquiry approach, established by Cooperrider and Whitney, which "is the cooperative, coevolutionary search for the best in people, their organizations and communities, and the world around them. It involves systematic discovery of what gives 'life,' to an organization or community when it is most effective and most capable in economic, ecological, and human terms" (Holman, Devane, & Cady, 2009, p. 115) David Cooperrider, who works with the Flourishing Leadership Institute, introduced a simple yet effective way to help organizations and their people learn and grow. This approach rigorously focuses on what is going well by calling upon strengths to provide guidance for change instead of dwelling on problems. By asking questions about the positive experience and applying that knowledge, we are able to celebrate and learn from our success just as we do from failure (see Resilient Response). Using positive reinforcement, we encourage students to voice their ideas and get out of their comfort zone. As instructors, our notes after a scene focus on the strengths of the students. We ask them to apply these techniques to what they may improve. Our approach is to set strong ground rules whereby students do not give each other negative feedback or criticism. Knowing that your idea will be honored and accepted and even transformed into something magical gives us the freedom to express our creativity. This journey of mutual care mimics what Barbara Fredrickson calls positivity resonance. She explains, "Within those moments of interpersonal connection that are characterized by this amplifying symphony—of shared positive emotions, biobehavioral synchrony, and mutual care—life-giving positivity resonates between and among people" (Fredrickson, 2013, p. 17). Bringing your best self to the team is the true spirit of improv. The encouragement, celebration, and positivity can be transformative.

Who is on your team? Certainly your patient is part of the team. Who else is on your team? Are you partnering with a psychiatrist or therapist? Are you working with a coordinator or medical doctor? Are you giving or receiving clinical supervision or training? Are you part of a medical group? Do you have a receptionist? If so, consider all of these connections part of the patient experience and part of your team. If you are in private practice are you working with a consultant or a group of colleagues to support you in your work? Connecting with colleagues can provide a level of comfort, especially when dealing with uncertainty or with difficult cases, or simply to share best practices.

Exercise: Three Things in Common—Building Community
Objective: An exercise you can use to help to deepen the ties in your community is called "Three Things in Common." Whether you are part of a clinical staff at a medical center or you meet with a group of independent practitioners, this exercise is helpful to build trust and find common ground.
Participants: 2–3
Explanation: Pair up with one other person. Time yourself. You have two minutes to find three things in common. Repeat with a different partner. This can also be played in trios. Consider this game for families or couples.
Pro tip: Ask participants to keep topics positive and make eye contact. Dare to dive deeper than obvious commonalities such as "we both live in Chattanooga."

This exercise mimics the purposeful attention we must pay to each other in improv. By creating a safe and supportive environment for our community to connect at a deeper level we provide an atmosphere for transformation.

I took a leave of absence from work and wasn't sure what was next in my life. I suffer from bipolar disorder and the depressive side of my condition was incredibly severe to a point where suicide was practically imminent. During my group therapy, improv was suggested and I was intrigued at the thought of being able to laugh again. I wasn't really sure what improv entailed, but signed up for a class anyways.

Walking into class, my anxiety was off the charts, but within 10 minutes I was "playing" with complete strangers and what happened next was a surprise and a delight. Over the next two hours I found myself "in the moment" forgetting my problems and laughing more than I had in years. Improv reminded me how people in my life want to lift me up and embrace what I have to offer. I think we often forget the joy of the simple things. I remembered what it was like to be "me." These classes spiked creativity that overflowed into other parts of my life as well. I actually started painting again after 18 years and I forgot that I was good at it. I have gone back to work, and still continue improv classes which give me familiar friendly faces that I get to see week after week.

—Gary, student

Improv expands our capacity to accept others and empathize. We inhabit other points of view, relationships, and worlds. We have an opportunity to try on various roles that give us insight into human behavior, helping us appreciate our similarities and differences. Diversity is honored in improv.

Improv also provides us a shame-free space to expand our own sense of self. Exploring different characters through play allows us to step outside of ourselves to embody different behaviors. We explore being larger, smaller, brighter, slower, faster. Embracing a variety of behavioral aspects gives us the flexibility to choose. Our own habits become conscious and visible. We experience that we are freer to change than we may have imagined.

Improv has allowed me to experiment with how I present myself to the world because what I have thought of as "me" is a somewhat arbitrary character that accumulated over the decades. Encountering triggering content in scenework, in a safe ensemble, has allowed me to practice different responses and experience how a different character would respond in a given situation. The result is a newfound confidence, peace, and delight in inhabiting my beautifully imperfect self. I truly believe I have a right to exist and to have a voice of my own, which is an attitude that was unthinkable for me a few short years ago.

—Avery, student

The practice of accepting others leads to an acceptance of self. When we find ourselves open and receptive we are experiencing the Power of Presence.

Daily Practice:

- Set a colleague or collaborator up for success. Ask them: "What can I start doing (or do better) to set you up for success?" Who is someone in your life that you can make the hero?
- Write a thank you note to someone. Take it a step further, call them and read the letter over the phone, or read it in person. Who is someone in your life that has been a hero?

Principle 3: Power of Presence

'What day is it?', asked Winnie the Pooh. 'It's today,' squeaked Piglet. 'My favorite day,' said Pooh.

—A.A. Milne

IMPROV IS THE ART OF INTERACTIVE MINDFULNESS

Improv requires mindfulness. It is an opportunity to bring our solo mindfulness practice into our interactions with others. To describe this experience we began using the phrase "interactive mindfulness practice." In improv our attention is linked with our partners. There is rigorous training that goes on behind the scenes to discipline ourselves and our minds to be focused and present, to listen well, and to adjust in the moment. As we enter into an improv scene, we notice not only our own breath, which tunes us into the emotional life of our character, but our partner's breath and any shift in their expression. We are looking for cues that feed the story and connect our characters. As we bring our attention to these nuanced changes, we align to our partners to create an attuned presence. Every move, every breath, every action is clocked on stage, quieting the saboteur monkey mind. The training exercises we use cultivate a habit of being in the moment, together. When we are truly present in the moment with ourselves and each other, we can fluidly shift from being a leader to being a follower, and back again, adjusting to what the team needs or the story needs. The improviser's mindset teaches us to focus on what is here now, rather than thinking about the past or the future. It is highly motivating to pay attention when there is fear of embarrassment for being lost on stage. We will let our teammates down if we are not following the narrative. On the other side of fear is the realization that we are not alone. The team will create a story from anything that happens, and the audience wants to see us succeed. From that foundation, we are able to experience the true magic of being in the moment together.

"Through spontaneity we are re-formed into ourselves . . . Spontaneity is the moment of personal freedom when we are faced with a reality, and see it, explore it, and act accordingly. In this reality, the bits and pieces of ourselves function as an organic whole. It is the time of discovery, of experiencing, of creative expression." (Spolin, 2000, p. 4) Many people believe that improvising is "making stuff up," and "pulling things out of thin air." From our perspective, the improviser's mindset is about paying attention to what is here now. We play from a place of true spontaneous impulse while paying attention to our surroundings. Perhaps it was your own imagination that kickstarted the scene or an audience member's suggestion. It may be a sound, a thought, or the expression on your colleague's face that inspires your next line. We practice trusting that the scene will unfold organically without the need to worry. We trust that everything we need is here now. We will either see, hear, notice, or feel something that we will name or that will propel an action. If we don't have a "hit," or inspiration, we pause, breathe, and trust that one of our teammates will. Ultimately, it's about creating from what exists in this moment. It is an art form born from deep presence. It's a dive into "now," and as improviser's know firsthand that "now" is ever-changing.

Beginning improvisers sometimes plan instead of listening and reacting. They monologue instead of creating a shared dialogue. Planning what you are going to say, or even worse, creating a plan for what the other person should say or do, will cause you to ignore important information relevant to the scene. You will also be disappointed because your partner may not say or do what you have crafted in your own mind. Your plan has been derailed, which leaves you in a place of panic. It is important to listen to what the other player is saying and to authentically react in real time. This allows you and your partner to organically create the scene together. As a team, you follow the flow of the action that the audience sees, rather than the scenario in your own head. This is the dynamic collaboration that is achieved through both listening and giving up control. This deep connection is created by following the natural progression of the scene. What if something unexpected happens? We make it the character's issue, and part of the story. We embrace the now. Are you embracing the present moment? How can you apply this idea to your own life? How can you apply it to your practice?

What do we do when something unexpected happens in life? How we respond when something unexpected happens reveals how flexible, or how rigid, we are. Often when life throws us a curveball we go into fight, flight, freeze, or even faint mode. Improv teaches us to breathe and relax in these moments, so we can be present and attend to the issue using our whole brain rather than being occupied with survival. As improvisers, we constantly put ourselves on the spot; we enter the stage with nothing: no set, no props, and no preplanned ideas. We ask the audience for a suggestion to begin the story and then jump into the abyss of the unknown. We stare at a blank canvas every show. We write the first words of the book. We rub two sticks together and hope that tonight we will make fire. Sometimes the sparks ignite immediately, and other times it's simply a dim ember which we face. In improv, there is no time to evaluate. We tend to the fire however small or large it may be, with full bravado and acceptance.

Exercise: I am here.
Objective: This exercise is very simple yet extremely powerful because it helps us feel seen, and pulls us into the present moment.
Explanation: This is a group exercise. Stand in a circle. One person at a time enters the middle of the circle when they are inspired to do so. Once they feel fully present with the group they say, "My name is _____, and I am here."

Participants: 4–14
Pro tip: Encourage participants to make eye contact and speak, once they feel truly present.

In our everyday lives, we are often preoccupied by planning, worrying, judging, and running the to-do list through our minds. If we step on stage or into life and just follow what everyone else is doing, without speaking up for our needs, we can experience life as extremely chaotic. On the other hand, if we step on stage with a fixed idea of everything we want to see in the scene, we can become frustrated, angry, and separated from the rest of the ensemble. As improvisers, we enter a state of harmony when we learn to both lead and follow. We trust the dance with our partners, trust the dance with the story, and trust the dance with the moment. Learning to let go of ego, we see clearly when it is necessary to follow instead of lead. We trust that we can start fresh each time, listening for the new song that is now. Practicing detachment from fixed ideas and moments past, we let go of the wonderful scene that had the audience roaring in their seats. We let go of the wave of laughter that lifts our spirits, and erase the masterpiece to begin again and again . . .

Daily practice:

- Set aside time to devote yourself fully to an activity you truly enjoy. Savor that time wholeheartedly.
- Sit someplace different in a room instead of habitually going to the same spot.
- On your daily commute, take a moment to feel the steering wheel in your hands, take a deep breath, and notice something new along your route.
- At your desk, stop working for a moment, take a deep breath. Notice the sounds around you and the temperature in the room. Stretch. Yes, do it!
- Next time you are at dinner with a friend, dare to have a tech-free meal.

This is a practice that can be utilized in daily life. Even when we set intentions for our day, sometimes traffic or some other inconvenience gets in the way. If we surrender to what is happening we are in tune with the universe and give up the struggle to change what we cannot control. In improv, and in life, we can tune into everything in our present surroundings, keep breathing, and open our minds to do our best with what we truly have. As Eckhart Tolle (2004) suggests, "Whatever the present moment contains, accept it as if you had chosen it" (p. 29). By choosing to see everyday as a new dance we can choose to wipe away our old perceptions of ourselves and others, let go of our perceived limitations and play a new song. The magic is in the moment, and we have to be here to experience it!

CLAIRE'S STORY

A young therapist we worked with was given a senior therapist's patient load upon his retirement. She noticed that when the other practitioners in her medical group heard that she would be taking on a certain patient, many responded with, "Good luck, she's tough!" Apparently, the patient had a long history of being difficult. Claire found herself worrying day and night about how this appointment would go. She was dreading taking on a notoriously disagreeable patient. After taking improv, she realized she would not be able to enter the room and have a successful interaction with preconceived notions in mind. By suspending judgment, she was able to have a fresh start with the patient, and noticed that the anticipation of the encounter was much more difficult than the actual event. In fact, she came out with a positive view of the patient and a newfound perception she was able to create from being fully present without interference from the past.

Improv is a tool that helps us cultivate presence, adaptability, and ultimately relinquish control. The level of presence required in improv begins to seep into our existence. Over time, we notice when we are not in the moment and recognize the power that exists when we bring our attention back to now.

Principle 4: Resilient Response

> *Changing the destructive things you say to yourself when you experience the setbacks that life deals all of us is the central skill of optimism.*
> —Martin E. P. Seligman

IMPROV IS THE ART OF BUOYANCY

Fear is a strong force that impedes our ability to take action. When we are stuck it is often fear of failure holding us captive. If we look at failure as the end of the world, or allow it to wrap our identity into its clutches, fear of failure becomes immobilizing. Yet all of us will stumble and fall at some point in our lives. But imagine if Abraham Lincoln had given up on his dream to become president after 8 major political rejections over 25 years? How do we shift from punishing ourselves when we fail to welcoming failure and mistakes as a learning opportunity? How do we transform ourselves from perfectionists to adventurers?

We believe that improvisation is a tool to build resilience. It teaches us to be in relationship with our fear and to show up in spite of it. When you attend improv class, you are inviting your fear or what we call the "monster under the bed" to attend class with you. Whether this monster is your inner critic, your perfectionist, or fear of failure, you have an opportunity to play with that monster, and eventually befriend him.

Improv is an invitation to make mistakes and discover the gifts those mistakes reveal. It is an invitation to allow yourself to be vulnerable, goofy, foolish, and follow the fun into the sublimely ridiculous. It's an opportunity to embrace parts of yourself that you may have suppressed, forgotten, or carefully hidden. You are witnessed and accepted by your peers as you take imperfect action. The former principle, Make Your Teammate the Hero, creates a safe space to approach our fear as a community. There is a level playing field because every student participates in the same exercises. We fail, collectively. It's a community "emotional ropes course" where we learn to face our fears together, building courage as individuals.

As improvisers, we learn that "failure" is natural and that everyone experiences it. We loosen our attachment to perfectionism. When we are in front of an audience, we cannot afford to be stuck in judgment about a mistake. The show must go on! We cannot hide, stop, or go home. Resilient response

FIGURE 16.3
Monster under the bed. (Courtesy of William Koehler)

begins with handling our mistakes with grace. During a show, when a scene fails we have to let it go, stay in the moment, and move into the next scene. We learn that if we dwell on a perceived failure then we are not practicing our Power of Presence. In improv, we learn to laugh at our own mistakes along with the audience. Playing the fool, we discover that we will not die when we make a mistake, and that the audience's attention quickly shifts to how we recover. Failing good-naturedly creates rapport with the audience, as they live vicariously through the improviser's courage to go on. Allowing yourself to be vulnerable can also make you quite likeable on the stage. You become the representative of the audience's own fears, and as you conquer them, they too feel the release. Your job is to surrender judgment first, which quickly gives the audience permission to do the same. It is your courage that often steals the spotlight and your mistake that allows this gift to be revealed.

Mistakes can be miracles. Our relationship to fear of failure maturates as we advance in our improv training. At first we are terrified of making mistakes. Over time, we are more willing to take risks, grow, learn, and discover new things. The repetition and disposability of improv lowers the emotional cost of failure. Improv's temporary worlds change our sense of control over unknown outcomes. The end of the world becomes the end of the scene, and we simply begin anew. Failure becomes familiar, and therefore the dread that may have consumed us dissipates.

Separating our identity from failure helps us to progress. In improv we say, "I failed!" not "I am a failure." In fact, improvisers celebrate mistakes as a way of rewiring themselves to experience risks as opportunities for learning and growth. We learn to channel fear into excitement. Imagine that you are a trapeze artist standing above the crowd ready to take your leap of faith. You find your fingers just missing the fly bar, and the next thing you know you are surrounded by net. Do you cower into the dressing room, or do you get up, put your arms in the air, and celebrate your brave attempt? "Ta-dah!" Matt Smith, a Seattle improviser began applying the circus's traditional bow, "Ta-dah" into his practice as a performer many years ago. This victory stance is a technique that is simple yet transformative, because it changes our physiological response to mistakes. The circus bow has morphed into a variety of bows, dances, and cheers to celebrate the moment of the mistake. We find that the circus bow can be an empowering tool for resilience. In class, we often ask the participants to invent their own way to celebrate failure. Each class has a signature victory call. A popular one is the cheer, "Woo hoo!" When we celebrate failure we recognize our own humanity. It's not an excuse to do shabby work or to enter life halfheartedly. The improviser is asked to step onto the stage boldly.

If we experience something that feels like failure on stage or in a class, the ramifications of that experience certainly can be challenging, emotionally and psychologically. Practicing this counterintuitive response in those moments helps us create new habits that redirect our focus to compassion and learning, instead of criticism. We have been asked, "How do I celebrate failure if I did something that negatively impacted people?" Of course, it is not appropriate to yell "I failed," with arms up in the air, in certain situations in life and at work. Yet, even in our lives when something goes seriously wrong, we can (at some point) accept the mistake and learn from it. We can utter a "woo hoo" inside our minds as an act of self-compassion to counteract the inner critic when it wants to berate us. Practicing resilient response with small mistakes allows us to build this "muscle" and apply it to larger concepts and experiences over time. Celebrating failure involves acceptance, responsibility, compassion, and gratitude for the experience. When we approach challenges in life with the resilient response factor, we are able to move forward and release ourselves from being stuck. We free ourselves from the fear of mistakes and celebrate them as critical to the creative learning process. As we continue to practice resilient response in the improv studio, we notice that same courage and coping strategies begin to show up in our lives. Improvisers adapt quickly, so that mistakes are barely noticeable. We make it look easy because we learn to move faster than our inner critic. We believe that anyone can adopt the self acceptance, compassion, and buoyancy of the improviser.

MICHELLE'S STORY
Michelle had been troubled by her divorce for many years. She initiated the end of the relationship and was holding on to the guilt of hurting her former husband. She described the feeling as a dull undercurrent that colored her ability to start a new relationship. She was driving home from improv class after the resilient response lesson when it suddenly occurred to her . . .

"I was stopped at a red light and said to myself, 'wait a minute, woo hoo! I need to apply my woo hoo! to my failed marriage and forgive myself.'" She realized at that moment that her heart had been stopped at a red light for several years. In the midst of her epiphany, the street light turned green, and she knew she was ready to "drive" ahead. This was the opening that provided her the awareness and courage to seek professional counseling to attend to her own forgiveness.

The resilient response factor is a reminder that we can have compassion for ourselves and others as we venture forth in our day-to-day lives. It is a call to pull yourself up by your bootstraps when life presents challenges, instead of allowing shame to pull us into a vicious downward spiral. How would you like to celebrate failure? How can you, your team or organization practice a way of helping each other through those difficult times? How can you hold more compassion for yourself so that you may be fully available to serve others?

Principle 5: Open to Yes

Those who say yes are rewarded by the adventures they have. Those who say no are rewarded by the safety they attain.

—Keith Johnstone, author, *Impro*

IMPROV IS THE ART OF AFFIRMATION

You may have heard about the improv rule "Yes, and." Tina Fey describes it in her book *Bossypants* (2013), "The rule of agreement reminds you to respect what your partner has created and to at least start from an open-minded place" (p. 84). "Yes, and" is widely accepted as a cornerstone to improvisation. A group of improvisers can create a scene in minutes simply because they've agreed to say yes. "Yes" is the platform for collaboration. "Yes" creates an environment where creativity can thrive because people feel safe to take risks and express themselves. Positive mood enhances creative insight; negativity reduces it (Subramaniam, 2009). We've all heard the phrase "let's agree to disagree." Yet in improv we enter into a space where we "agree to agree." In improv, no idea will be shot down. It is a form of unconditional positive regard. For the improviser this comes in the form of accepting "offers." An "offer" is anything we say or do on stage. It is similar to John Gottman's bids (Gottman & Silver, 1999). Gottman observed in his study that in healthy relationships partners turn toward one another. This is also a must for fellow improvisers.

As improvisers, our job is to acknowledge our partner's offer (or bid) to create a connection and move the story forward. Any idea that is presented on stage will be accepted. Yes is the acknowledgement of the idea. The improviser then takes it a step forward by adding "and." "And" is the building block that adds information, and moves the narrative to new places. We consider "yes, and" a frame of mind. "Open to Yes" is the spirit of availability and openness one can bring into life. It's an opportunity to see new possibilities and solutions. It's true that sometimes in life and at work we have to say no, but is it a kneejerk no? Is it a no out of habit? Or fear? Sometimes we say no too early before we've allowed an idea to have a chance to live and breathe in the room, even if it's just for two minutes. Being "Open to Yes" can help us consider new ways of looking at places where we might be stuck.

When we make room for the power of yes we allow creativity to flow, and we may come up with ideas we didn't realize existed. This is an imperative function of innovation. When we are stuck on a problem, we often play a game called, "Pretend 'no' doesn't exist," until we find a possible solution. We practice playing the "What if" game in the positive light instead of the all too familiar way we often play "What if" when we worry.

Daily practice: Be aware of when and how you use the word "but," and challenge yourself to eliminate it. Try inserting the word "and" instead of "but." Notice how you can deliver the same message.

Open to Yes utilizes the power of optimism. "Optimism is invaluable for the meaningful life. With a firm belief in a positive future you can throw yourself into the service of that which is larger than you are" (Seligman, 2011, p. iv). We ask students to start a scene positively. Narratively speaking, this gives the audience a chance to fall in love with the hero. Some beginning students find this challenging. Fear drives them to play characters who are anxious or inept. You'll see many "first day on the job" scenes so that the actor can play it safe. We ask them to rewind, start again, and play a character who is a confident expert, utilizing their intelligence and joy. With this practice, they begin to manage their fear. As they play confident characters, they too begin to feel that same level of confidence. Playing characters with a positive outlook helps them experience a form of learned optimism. This positivity muscle becomes easier to exercise in daily life.

Open to Yes goes hand in hand with Make Your Teammate the Hero. We celebrate our teammates by accepting their ideas. Interestingly, "yes, and" is being applied to caretakers of Alzheimer's patients. Stobbe and Carter describe their use of this technique to create better connections with Alzheimer's patients in their TED Talk at TEDMED 2015 (Carter & Stobbe). Accepting an Alzheimer's patient's reality provides relief from suffering for the patient and the caregiver. Instead of saying "No, my name isn't Mary," we accept the name given and therefore we accept the memory loss of the patient. Certainly we have seen vast improvements in relationships of all kinds applying this well-known improv rule.

The investment of "yes" goes beyond the words. "Yes, and" can also be encompassed through nonverbal communication such as expression and emotional shifts in the character. When we allow ourselves to let the "offer" really land and allow our character to be emotionally changed, we are "turning toward our partner instead of away" (Gottman & Silver, 1999), with enthusiastic engagement. In Keith Johnstone's book *Impro for Storytellers* (1999, p. 110), he describes it as "over accepting" an offer. It is not the mere words "yes, and" that allow the story to unfold. The characters must be "open to yes" emotionally too, otherwise the narrative can become stuck. Emotional engagement is necessary to set off a chain reaction of emotional truth between characters. We've all heard an apology without the feelings to back it up, and rarely does it lead to reconciliation. Words are sometimes not enough. In improv, at least one of the characters must allow the offer to have impact, otherwise the characters become "stuck" in a cyclical argument on stage.

When two characters enter into a cyclical argument, it isn't interesting to the audience because the plot stops and the characters are not allowing themselves to be altered.

"Yes you did. No, I didn't. Yes, you did. No I didn't." The characters must be vulnerable instead of rigid to allow the action to continue unfolding. If they maintain a state of defensiveness, the scene goes nowhere. The audience wants to see how an action affects the character's emotional state and how it impacts the relationship between the two characters. One of the characters must break the cycle. *"Yes, you're right, I did."* When we respond with "no," the conversation is limited, the ideas are not developed, and the scene spins in a negative direction.

Finding the voice inside you that is a "yes" has been dampened for some of us, but improv helps us practice finding optimism and positivity. The spirit of "yes" can help us become unstuck. Certainly, it is this sense of hope that your patient is looking for in you. "The effective therapist communicates hope and optimism. This communication is relatively easy for motivated clients who are making adequate therapeutic progress. However, those with severe and/or chronic problems typically experience relapses, lack of consistent progress, or other difficulties. The effective therapist acknowledges these issues but continues to communicate hope that the client will achieve realistic goals in the long run" (Wampold, 2011).

"Yes, and," creates an opportunity to advance the story in improv. Being open to yes advances the story of our lives. This expansion of "yes, and" creates motivation, starts conversations, validates contribution, makes room for diverse perspectives, and provides hope. Open to yes is the willingness to approach life with an open attitude and emotional availability. It's the spirit of seeking the positive and allowing yourself to be changed. Being open to yes creates an environment where it's safe to Voice your Ideas.

Daily practice:

Flex your positivity muscle. Next time you sit in a comfortable chair or hold a warm cup of tea, verbalize the positive feeling. Dwell in that positive state rather than allowing it to be a fleeting thought. Increase the amount of time

FIGURE 16.4
Boy playing in cardboard toy car. (Courtesy of William Koehler)

you spend luxuriating in a positive sensory experience. Train your mind to see, appreciate, and truly feel open to yes.

Principle 6: Voice your Ideas

There is a vitality, a life force, an energy, a quickening that is translated through you into action, and because there is only one of you in all of time, this expression is unique. And if you block it, it will never exist through any other medium and it will be lost.
—Martha Graham

IMPROV IS THE ART OF ENGAGEMENT
Our final principle is Voice your Ideas. This principle represents participation and allowing your voice to be heard. It gives you permission to believe in yourself and risk sharing your ideas. On the stage it means following an inspiration and giving a voice to it. In life, it means speaking up and contributing

your perspective. When we are connected to our voice we are connected with our essence. We experience an ease in communication. In any group of people there is potential for a collective creative flow. Just as each individual is unique in their expression, so is every group.

Many ideas flow through an improv exercise or scene. We have countless opportunities to express ourselves. It becomes easier and easier to voice ideas as we're exposed to a constant stream of new scenes, characters, and situations. We teach clients to open up to their ideas, trust their creative voice, and share boldly. It's equally important that we learn to let go of ideas and detach ourselves from the outcome. At first many students treat their ideas as if they are precious. They find it hard to move forward even if the plot moves in another direction. Over time, they recognize that improv is disposable and malleable. They learn to trust that they will have an abundance of fresh ideas and that their creativity is limitless if they trust their own voice and those of the collective.

It is important to honor our similarities and differences and celebrate contributions without judgment. As a group, family, or as a team we can practice honoring all contributions, and behaving in a way that encourages everyone, especially the quieter voices, to contribute. According to Woolley, et al. (2010), equal contribution is critical to uplifting the collective expression, "as long as everyone got a chance to talk, the team did well, but if only one person or a small group spoke all the time, the collective intelligence declined" (Duhigg, p MM20). Think of a time you shared an idea and it was shut down by someone you respected. How willing were you to share future ideas? We all experience disappointments in life and it's normal to resist making ourselves vulnerable. Studying improv exercises with a trusted ensemble creates an opportunity to practice vulnerability in a safe space. We have observed students open up in class, and begin to blossom in their lives.

Some of us have a habit of correcting others or taking responsibility for teaching, even when we're not the authority in the room. New students sometimes correct each other during an exercise. In our sessions, we set ground rules in advance. Students are asked to take care of their own tree while the coach takes care of the forest. Participants learn to take ownership of the energy they bring into the room, leaving their egos at the door. They practice encouraging others without the need to regulate them. This shift from correction to encouragement is essential to develop new habits and unlock our unique voice.

Once trust is established and external factors are addressed, some of us must still examine our negative internal dialogue. In anticipation of being misunderstood or looking foolish, our inner critic often becomes overactive and stifles our creativity. For some of us, that critic is often more demanding than any of the external voices in our lives. Perhaps constant correction and lack of encouragement brought us here.

As a child, we were much less filtered and more authentic. We allowed our voices to be heard, before we were criticized and quieted ourselves to avoid rejection. Practicing improv reminds us to be kind to ourselves. We start tapping into our innate creativity, as we let go of our habit to edit and learn to risk speaking out loud without first thinking it through. We develop the ability to trust our gut and tune into our body's wisdom. We often say the body knows what the next step in the story is before we consciously do. Sometimes our body pulls us out onto the stage! "The only real mistake here is ignoring the inner voice," said Del Close, founder of iO Theater. By trusting our impulses we put a voice to those intuitive "hits" instead of listening to the inner critic. We build our confidence through this journey.

Are you freely expressing your voice or second-guessing yourself? As Brené Brown describes in her book *Daring Greatly* (2012), "Courage starts with showing up, and letting ourselves be seen" (p. 30). Taking the first step is an act of courage that builds as we trust our inner voice. The confidence to trust your expertise, in the moment, even in the face of uncertainty is cultivated by training for the unexpected. That means doing the homework and then letting it go to be fully present to see, hear, and process what is in front of you and inside of you. Some improvisers say, "Don't be prepared." We believe preparation is necessary and plans can help as a guideline. Releasing our tight grip to a plan allows us to serve the moment.

Improv is an ode to process rather than perfectionism. As improvisers, we connect to our voice by doing exercises that help us move faster than our inner critic. The game convergence helps us accomplish quieting our inner critic in a fun way. It expands our capacity to express and accept our ideas and the ideas of others.

Exercise: Convergence
Objective: This exercise is a fun way to practice voicing your ideas. It provides an opportunity to remain connected and resilient when we do not see eye to eye. The challenge and objective of this exercise is for the players to repeat rounds until they say the *same word at the same time*.
Participants: 2
Explanation and Example: To begin, each player thinks of a word, any word. (Don't say your word out loud to your partner). For example Mark thinks "Pumpkin." Beth thinks "Orange."
Round 1: Mark let's Beth know that he is ready by saying "1." Beth let's Mark

know that she is ready by saying "2." In unison, Mark and Beth say together, "one, two, three," and then they both say their word at the same time: Mark says, "Pumpkin," and Beth says, "Orange." We now have two words, "Pumpkin," and "Orange."

Round 2: The players each try to think of a new word that comes to mind when they think of "Pumpkin," and "Orange." A word that associates the two starting words. Either player can begin round 2 by saying "1," to let their partner know they are ready. For example, Beth says, "1." When Mark (player 2) has his word ready he says "2." In unison, Mark and Beth say "one, two, three," then together say their new word at the same time. Mark says, "Jack-o'-lantern," and Beth says, "Halloween."

After each round of this game, the players have reached one of two results. Either:

1. The two players "converged," and said the *same word at the same time.* Or . . .
2. The two players said two different words, and move on to the next round.

If you get two separate words (which is most likely), then again the players try to think of a new word to link the two latest words. Continue, trying to converge by saying the same word at the same time.

Other rules: Do not repeat words from previous rounds. The new words from each round should be based on the most immediate previous round. Words from rounds further back are irrelevant.

Pro tips:

- Keep eye contact.
- Breathe.
- Give your partner an encouraging look and make sure arms are uncrossed.
- Suspend judgment of your word choice or the word choice of your partner.

Some days when you are meeting with clients, the sessions flow . . . convergence! Other days it is challenging, and you don't feel like you are on the same page with clients or colleagues, or both! Convergence is the practice of staying buoyant when we feel stuck. Notice if your inner critic interrupts the flow of this game, even though there are no wrong answers. Once we gain confidence voicing our ideas we become more relaxed and generous in sharing. In an environment where the emphasis is on participation students allow ideas to flow. We use this game to create psychological safety in the classroom.

Daily practice:
When someone holds back their voice or their question, everyone misses the opportunity to learn. Try this exercise to create a safe place to voice ideas. At work, or as a family, have a brainstorming session where each idea is celebrated. Set the timer for five minutes. Agree that the exercise is in divergent thinking. After every person shares an idea, everyone says "that's a great idea," the word "yes," or at least a nod and smile. Decide what works best for your culture. When time is up, explore commonalities among the ideas. Delay the editor. After contributions have been celebrated, discuss what is appropriate based on the realistic restraints that exist: budget, time, resources, etc. By delaying the editor we are free to explore possibilities and encourage innovation.

In improv we learn to honor our own voice and speak with humility and conviction. We begin to see ourselves as courageous, strong, and creative. We worry less as we focus on the joy of playing full out. Together we create an inspiring collective voice!
Conclusion:

Laughter is the shortest distance between two people.

—Victor Borge

Improv is a Catalyst for Change

When we look underneath the laughter and behind the curtain, we see that the art of improvisation holds the power for exceptional collaboration, deep connections, and positive change. Improvisers see each scene as a new canvas, a blank slate, and a new opportunity. Approaching life with the eager curiosity of an improviser helps us create a story we want to be a part of! Improv is an ode to process, and helps us move out of our stuck places by equipping us with tools that help us take action. With practice, we are able to break out of our thoughts, habits, and patterns to forge a new path.

Use the ImprovHQ principles as a framework to adopt the improviser's mindset. Use I-M-P-R-O-V to remind yourself and your community that you hold the power to change, learn, heal, and grow. The improviser's mindset is for the performance called life.

Now go play!

References

Brown, S., & Vaughan, C. (2010). *Play: How it shapes the brain, opens the imagination, and invigorates the soul.* New York: Avery.

Brown, B. (2012). *Daring greatly: How the courage to be vulnerable transforms the way we live, love, parent, and lead.* New York: Penguin.

Carter, M., & Stobbe, K. (2015). Using Improv to improve life with Alzheimer's. *TEDMED.* Retrieved from *www.tedmed.com/talks/show?id=526821*

Edmondson, A. (2014). *Building a psychologically safe workplace* [video file]. Retrieved from *www.youtube.com/watch?v=LhoLuui9gX8*

Fey, T. (2013). *Bossypants.* New York: Reagan Arthur Books/Little, Brown and Company.

Fredrickson, B. L. (2013). *Love 2.0: Finding happiness and health in moments of connection.* New York: Penguin.

Gottman, J., & Silver, N. (1999). *The seven principles for making marriage work: A practical guide from the country's foremost relationship expert.* New York: Three Rivers Press.

Haney, W. V. (1979). *Communication and interpersonal relations.* Homewood, IL: Irwin.

Holman, P., Devane, T., & Cady, S. (2009). *The change handbook: The definitive resource on today's best methods for engaging whole systems.* Vancouver, BC: ReadHowYouWant.

Husman, R. C., Lahiff, J. M., & Penrose, J. M. (1988). *Business communication: Strategies and skills.* Chicago: Dryden Press.

Johnstone, K. (1999). *Impro: Improvisation and the theatre.* New York: Routledge.

Johnstone, K. (1999). *Impro: Improvisation for storytellers.* New York: Routledge.

Kao, J. (2002). The virtues of corporate "disorder." In Pierer, H. V. & Oetinger, B. V. (Eds.). *A passion for ideas: How innovators create the new and shape our world* (pp. 109–123). West Lafayette, IN: Purdue University Press.

Seligman, M. E. (2002). *Authentic happiness: Using the new positive psychology to realize your potential for lasting fulfillment.* New York: Free Press.

Seligman, M. E. (2011). *Learned optimism: How to change your mind and your life.* New York: Vintage Books.

Siegel, D. (2013). *Brainstorm: The power and purpose of the teenage brain.* New York: Penguin Books.

Spitzberg, B. H. (1994). The dark side of (in)competence. In Cupach, W. R. & Spitzberg, B. H. (Eds.). *The dark side of interpersonal communication.* (pp. 25–49) Hillsdale, NJ: Erlbaum.

Spolin, Viola (2000). *Improvisation for the theater: A handbook of teaching and directing techniques.* Evanston, IL: Northwestern University Press.

Tolle, E. (2004). *The power of now: A guide to spiritual enlightenment.* Vancouver, BC: Namaste Publishing.

Subramaniam, K., Kounios, J., Parrish, T., & Jung-Beeman, M. (2009). A brain mechanism for facilitation of insight by positive affect. *Journal of Cognitive Neuroscience, 21*(3), 415–432.

Wampold, B. (2011). Qualities and actions of effective therapists. Retrieved from *www.apa.org/education/ce/effective-therapists.pdf*

Whitney, D., & Cooperrider, D. (2006). Appreciative inquiry: A positive revolution in change. In Holman, P., Devane, T., & Cady, S. (Eds.), *The change handbook.* (pp. 73–88) San Francisco: Berrett-Koehler Publishers.

Woolley, A., Chabris, C. F., Pentland, A., Hashmi, N., & Malone, T. (2010). Evidence for a collective intelligence factor in the performance of human groups. *Science, 330*(6004), 686–688.

17

Cultivating Curiosity, Creativity, Confidence, and Self-Awareness through Mindful Group Therapy for Children and Adolescents

Bonnie Goldstein

GROUP THERAPY HARNESSES the desire to connect, belong, and feel part of a community, as members' reflections about their interactions lead to insight, understanding, and growth. This prepares young people, in particular, to thrive as interdependent adults, working together to foster a climate of kindness, empathy, compassion, and resilience. As part of this therapeutic process, interactions can lead to recollections of earlier painful encounters, as old memories resurface. For example, misattunements and failures of understanding within the group can recreate previous feelings of being misunderstood. The group then provides a wealth of growth opportunities. Transformative moments begin with misreading another group member in the here and now, evoking feelings from past experiences and relationships. By capitalizing on such interchanges, we can lay the foundation for repair and resilience; social-emotional development and growth; and the cultivation of curiosity, creativity, and confidence.

Early in life, the brain develops a set of "social status schema" (Cozolino, 2014, 2015). Experiences within different social groups leave an imprint in our implicit memory—those memories of which we are not consciously aware.

Negative emotions or responses to experiencing fear within the social arena evoke "fight," "freeze," or "flee" responses. Such responses often originally serve to protect the very young child who has not yet developed sufficiently to use higher-level defense mechanisms. Instead, avoidance, disconnection, splitting, and projective identification, or dissociation become automatic responses to pain. Once instilled in the brain, these responses become habitual, and change may be difficult. When defense patterns become entrenched or dysfunctional, change may require new types of interventions to lay the foundation for new neural pathways.

Adolescents may not have had many opportunities to feel accepted and validated by others. This can reinforce mistaken beliefs that they are "awkward" or "different," with something to be ashamed of that they must hide. Although their intention is to avoid trauma by avoiding others, they may wind up cutting themselves off from the beneficial effects of relationships they need to heal and grow (Cozolino, 2015). The question then is, when they are guided to revisit and confront these responses, can change occur?

Research in neuroplasticity shows us that the structure of our brains is continually altering. The potential to change in a positive direction—toward increased calm, compassion, resiliency, and vitality—is foundational to the group therapy experience. As we will see through a case presentation of the interchange between two teenagers, Danielle and Ian, playful interventions within a group environment can foster feelings of safety, as group members allow their hidden selves be seen by the others. "To restore resilience, one must restore *joie de vivre*. As will become clear, there is no better vehicle for that than natural play—the engagement that children themselves devise to pass the living moment" (Trevarthan & Panksepp, in press, p. 29).

Play, Creativity, Vitality, and Safety

Inspired, innovative, and integrative group therapy comes about through co-creating a playful, supportive, safe, nurturing, growth-oriented therapeutic environment. A safe group milieu in which it becomes less shameful to show hidden parts of the self requires finding ways to move past old responses and habitual behavior patterns. Siegel (2013) states, "The playfulness and humor that emerge from the creation of new combinations of things are essential to keep our lives full of vitality" (p. 10). Opportunities arise for group members to address feelings of anger, fear, danger, and other defensive responses. Participants can revisit their evaluation of others, reassess their sense of self in relation to others, and gain reassurance as commonalities between members become evident, collaboratively laying the foundation for shifts in experience.

Observing changes in other members of the group can become an important part of hope for one's self, whether members are engaged in dialogue or participating quietly while actively observing others. The experience of watching one's peers can be helpful for some group members who cannot put into words their own thoughts, feelings, and fears. Yalom, widely recognized as the "father" of group therapy states,

> Therapy groups invariably contain individuals who are at different points along a coping-collapse continuum. Each member thus has considerable contact with others—often individuals with similar problems—who have improved as a result of therapy. I have often heard clients remark at the end of their group therapy how important it was for them to have observed the improvement of others (Yalom & Leszcz, 2005, p. 5).

An overarching goal is to work toward a shifting of group members' consciousness, especially toward increased compassion, or what Barbara Fredrickson (2013) in her book *Love 2.0*, calls "Positivity Resonance," which involves focusing on positivity, while being seen for your authenticity, a resonance receptive to the authentic experience of another. Curiosity fosters this receptivity, and helps to mitigate the emotional reactivity that inevitably arises from time to time through the vibrant interaction of group members.

Through the lens of Sensorimotor Group Psychotherapy for young children, Goldstein and Ogden (2013) describe evoking playful co-curiosity. This includes looking at what comes up in the present moment—in the body, and in the dyadic relationship of child or adolescent and therapist—while integrating somatic understanding. Galvanized by the rich integrative treatment modalities offered by sensorimotor psychotherapy (Ogden, Minton, & Pain 2006; Ogden & Fisher, 2015), these concepts have been applied to the group milieu (Goldstein & Ogden, 2013; Goldstein & Ogden, in press; Ogden & Goldstein, in press), introducing new ways to use the emergent experience, here and now, as experiences transpire in the group.

Transformational experiences arise during which healing can occur collaboratively, as recognition, exploration, and resolution of trauma and developmental issues during the group experience are aided by an essential element of play—inviting curiosity. Sensorimotor psychotherapy for our younger clients, explored by Ogden, Goldstein, and Fisher (2012), prioritizes curiosity about what is emerging in the present moment as collaboratively noting emerging body sensations, along with emotions, thoughts, and feelings. Inviting mindfulness through playful queries, such as "I'm curious," or "I wonder," we offer a collaborative lens that welcomes, in the spirit of play, wondrous and supportive inquisitiveness. This engaged curiosity, foundational in mindfulness practices, fosters a deepening awareness of the present moment experience. We help our clients become mindfully attuned to their experiences, as they emerge in the group experience. Creative and playful modalities help to navigate complicated and contentious relationships, such as will be described in the case example of Danielle and Ian, two teen group members.

The concept of Embedded Relational Mindfulness, proposed by Pat Ogden, and written about extensively in the sensorimotor psychotherapy literature, illustrates the two paths that therapeutic relationships travel. The explicit, conscious path represents what therapist and patient sense they are doing together, supported by theory and technique. In contrast, the implicit journey pertains to what gets enacted beneath the words, beyond technique. Elusive and unconscious, the implicit journey may feel vaguely familiar, leading to outcomes that are not intended or predicted. When treating young clients, Goldstein and Ogden ascertain: "Through the use of directed mindfulness, embedded in relationships, we hope to capitalize on the neuroplasticity of the brain by teaching children to notice the internal somatic indicators that compromise their automatic reactions, and then purposefully direct mindful attention to something they typically do not notice, like deep breathing, thereby creating a new experience" (in press, p. 247).

Ogden and Goldstein (in press) expand on the collaborative nature of interactions, through mindfully witnessing, naming, and supporting what emerges, "bringing attention to these momentary shifts arising during the session and collaboratively deepening into awareness of interactions between client and therapist." Goldstein and Siegel (2012) introduce mindful group psychotherapy as the apex of the emerging group experience: "Mindfulness in the group experience creates a healing ethos that can hold very nearly any member that is a part of it" (p. 220). These ideas build upon concepts of interpersonal neurobiology, in order to elucidate the powerful emerging experience of "feeling felt" through interrelationships.

Similarly, adding neuroscience and somatic components to the traditional group therapy models that emphasize the cognitive-based verbal narrative can shift the emphasis from primarily dialogue and cognitive tasks by also inviting an exploration of present-moment awareness, practicing sensory intelligence, and welcoming experiences of consciousness into the group process. For example, as group members engage with one another in new ways, developing mindful awareness leads to powerful insights, practical skills, and expanded awareness of the body as a source of important insight and information. More significant, the group format offers an authentic experience in which members "feel felt" (Goldstein & Siegel, in press, p. 264).

Goldstein and Ogden (2013) further elucidate the powerful influence of Embedded Relational Mindfulness© to deepen awareness, stating "This kind of mindful awareness offers group members tools for self-reflection, observation, and curiosity about the body's states—the sensations in our chest, our breath (shallow or deep), the rhythm of our breathing, the changes in posture, tilt of the head, angle of the shoulders, muscular tension, and so forth" (p. 135).

Over time, as positive experiences emerge within the framework of group, feelings of safety, comfort, and calm help members to settle into the group. Rick Hanson states that these new positive experiences can start to become "hardwired into our psyche," thereby replacing the bad, and helping to promote positive relationships. Hanson's (2009) book, *Buddha's Brain*, aids mental health professionals to develop effective ways to help patients "light up" the brain circuits that relieve worry and stress, while promoting positive relationships and inner peace.

Hanson suggests that positive experiences that emerge within the group, as illustrated here by the cases of Danielle and Ian, can in turn change the brain for the better. Danielle and Ian's involvement in therapy, and the eventual intersection of their group experience, clarify the power of a group to address interpersonal conflict, bias, and a growing emphasis on difference in our society.

Danielle: Overcoming Isolation, Shame, and Loss

As a young child, Danielle emigrated from the Middle East, fleeing with her mother after a change in government regime resulted in their lives being threatened. Her father remained behind, continuing to reside far from his daughter and wife. Danielle cannot recall the last time she saw her father.

As significant as these losses were, Danielle feels she experienced even greater trauma following September 11, 2001, when both her first and last names were changed. In the ensuing months, her family and others in their community experienced an upsurge of hostility, rage, and racial profiling. Her shame and loss were palpable, and she recalled a moment when she asked her mother "When can I go back to being called Sahair?" Her mother's anxious shout of "never" had not been fully discussed nor its ramifications explored before entering therapy. Consequentially, Danielle never told others how her history had been marked by these traumatic losses. With fearful messages woven throughout the very fabric of her being from a young age, Danielle became afraid of others and hesitant to approach or engage with her peers. Her isolative behaviors had produced a self-fulfilling prophecy—that she would be marginalized and rejected.

Initially, Danielle's diagnosis of depression came through her school counselor, who felt Danielle was not a candidate for school-based social groups due to her feelings of secrecy and shame. At her school counselor's insistence, Danielle began intensive one-on-one therapy with me at the onset of 12th grade. I suggested that group therapy could help her combat her sense of isolation as well as aid in developing awareness of the overarching impact of her traumatic experiences. Danielle agreed to overcome her hesitation and give it a try.

Curbside Therapy: Resourcefully Meeting Clients

On the way to her first group session, despite acquiescing, Danielle felt unable to follow through. She sat outside in her mother's car, unable to come upstairs to the group session. What has been playfully termed "curbside therapy" ensued. Danielle's exasperated mother came upstairs to ask what we should do. I left the group in the skillful hands of my co-leader and went to meet Danielle, sitting on the curb adjacent to their car. Our prior individual therapy session paved the way for the ensuing "curbside therapy," as I acknowledged Danielle's tremendous anxiety and suggested that together we might mitigate her body-based response to these feelings (heart beating painfully; rapid, short, staccato breaths contributing to even more discomfort).

Collaboratively, I led us in an exercise that dropped beneath the context (the situation that presented). I suggested we bring our awareness to our bodies and what was happening at the time (I became acutely aware of my own discomfort about working publicly, beside her car; I somehow felt inadequate in my inability to anticipate this situation, which resulted in my own elevated heart rate, etc.). Together we agreed to become curious about what was arising for each of us as I accompanied her curbside. Dropping beneath the situation at hand, I encouraged her to join me in letting our awareness be filled by the feelings and sensations of the breath, etc., in lieu of discussing the context upon which we met on the curb. Mindfulness inquiries such as "Let's notice our breath," and "Notice, and just becoming aware of what you notice," are prompts that significantly aided in the unfolding awareness of our experience.

Danielle grew calmer and acknowledged that her all-encompassing anxiety about starting group had rendered her unable to mobilize and come to group. Collaboratively, we co-created what Danielle experienced as a new body-based self-calming exercise through awareness of her breath and through her becoming mindful about where her anxiety resided in her body. This awareness led to co-development of resources from within, tools she could employ at future challenging occasions. Our collaboration arose organically, starting with my internal query, "How can I meet each client wherever he or she needs to be?"

To engage our clients wherever they are, following them and evoking curiosity or playful interest in their experience is a key element in building therapeutic relationships with our younger clients. In the same vein, Malcolm Gladwell (2013) describes educators working with unruly kids in a classroom, where he emphasizes, "If the teacher is actually doing something interesting, these kids are quite capable of being engaged. Instead of responding in a 'let me control your behavior' way, the teacher needs to think, 'How can I do something interesting that will prevent you from misbehaving in the first place?'"(p. 206).

The process of becoming client-centered evokes a lens of play by necessity, as play is a hallmark of capturing our younger clients' interest. Sitting curbside with Danielle, she dictated all aspects of our interaction, yet I communicated that I would meet her on her turf, a message she later acknowledged let her know that she mattered. Instead of trying to control her behavior by insisting she come into my office, safety was established by my orienting toward her needs.

Body and Posture as Armor

The following week, Danielle did garner her strength and join the group, albeit with the support that led to our agreement that we first meet pre-group and then enter the group room together, so she would not have to make conversation or face her peers alone. Her fear of being rendered speechless was overarching, as was her habit of not engaging with others. Danielle's body stance implicitly let all members know of her hesitancy. She entered the room with her head down, arms crossed, appearing defiant or avoidant. (She later recognized this posture as self-protective "body armor.") Her initial responses to group members were curt, often one-word answers to their questions. There was no eye contact. Yet Danielle seemed unaware of her self-protective stance.

A few weeks later, the group used a playful exercise during which members were invited to share their experiences of one another. Through group discussion addressing questions ranging from "What was your first impression of group?" to "What was your first impression of one another?" members developed an understanding of how they came across to others, and also began to grow more sensitive toward each another. Danielle accepted feedback suggesting she shift her "body armor" so she appeared less alienating. A large, full-length mirror, stored in the closet yet readily available, was brought out so Danielle could view herself in the stance we were discussing. Others also gazed in the mirror, supported by their peers, encouraged by the leaders, in what became a fun and interactive exercise providing much insight.

From the onset, it was evident that Danielle had difficulties socially, exhibiting behaviors that seemed to contribute to her sense of isolation. Along with her self-protective "body armor," she reportedly remained safely distanced from her peers at school by avoiding school clubs and teams, eating lunch alone in the library, and dodging opportunities to be with other students lest this might precipitate discussion. She felt that her brown skin color contributed to some of her feelings of social isolation, and mentioned that the majority of the students at her Oceanside school were "beach blond, surfer types." She also distanced with her posture and stance. She kept her eye gaze toward the ground, and rarely responded when spoken to, her long black bangs falling over her eyes. Over time, she came to recognize this external message of her inner desire to avoid contact and to hide. Hence, in a social-feedback loop, her avoidant behavior deepened her sense of isolation, and similar behaviors continued, because Danielle didn't yet possess the tools to help mitigate her isolative behavior and avoidant impulses.

Through budding self-understanding, cultivated through her group experience, Danielle started to feel safer, both with people and with her own experiences. This opened a small window toward growing stability and confidence around others. As her burgeoning sense of safety increased, she began venturing into previously uncharted territory socially. For example, Danielle's mother, who modeled similar avoidant behavior, had been reinforcing her isolation (seen as self-protective in this "new country" that she emigrated to almost two decades earlier). Danielle's mother had avoided becoming friends with any of the families who were at Danielle's school and didn't encourage her daughter to invite classmates to their home. Through her group experience Danielle began to consider new possibilities, revisiting issues of self-esteem and trauma, exploring and building upon a new sense of self awareness. Her exchanges with others helped Danielle overcome her hesitancy and begin a new journey, thereby illustrating how "emotional competences and self-regulation strategies develop through our interactions with others, not through cognitive.learning" (Hart, in press, p. 14).

Danielle attained a better sense of the way she carried her body and learned to identify thoughts and feelings that arose. Yet this dyadic resonance went beyond simple mirroring, to serve as the first step of a feedback loop that allowed in true understanding. This understanding was a product of letting her peers join her in learning to co-create safety, listen and hear one-another, and support their fellow members. Moreover, Danielle's intersubjective experience shifted, illustrating how the "group psychotherapy format offers an experiential immersion that fosters awareness and exploration of the ways we know and have a sense of the known within our subjective experience of being alive" (Goldstein & Siegel, in press, p. 260).

"Playing" with Breath

One group exercise focused on bringing members' attention to their body-based experiences (e.g., noticing feelings of curiosity about a new member) or becoming aware of aches in their stomach, legs, and feet (perhaps an urge to mobilize or run). For Danielle, the impulse to bolt could be identified with a tingling in her feet. She noticed her limbs began moving and wiggling and connected it to her instinct to flee the room.

As our group sessions progressed, the members became keener interpreters of their inner body and the mind's signals, and the relational component of our collaborative work together significantly helped all members. This occurred, for example, during a group exercise focused on breath. Danielle was encouraged to sense her breath through guiding phrases, such as "Sense the sound of your breath"; "As you shift your awareness, feel the breath as it comes in and out." Over time, Danielle was encouraged to lead the other members in brief breathwork exercises. Taking a turn leading the group in breathwork further deepened her self-confidence and inspired a growing curiosity about other's experiences.

Learning to be more centered and finding equanimity through these self-calming exercises, which were introduced in a playful manner, Danielle and her fellow group members developed tools to mitigate feelings of shame, anxiety, fear, etc., and were encouraged to practice these nascent skills. Moreover, during a family session, scheduled seasonally with group members and their parents or guardians, Danielle was asked to model the "breathwork" exercises to her mother. She created a series of movements and encouraged her mother to follow (i.e., suggested that her hands resting on her lap, sitting with legs uncrossed, body posture aligned, and spine elongated) offering a powerful learning opportunity. Danielle wasn't just doing the relaxation and confidence-building exercises, she was teaching others to do these exercises, opportunities which deepened her subjective experience and enhanced her own integrative capacity. To practice these exercises prepared Danielle for her conflict-ridden interactions with Ian.

Ian: Playfully Sharing the First Experiences of Group

Ian is a 17-year-old who has long struggled to manage his behavior among his peers. His frequent, ongoing, interpersonal challenges and outbursts led his family to bring him to individual and group therapy so that he could develop self-reflective skills and self-regulation strategies. In the months leading up to the 2016 presidential election, the issues of intolerance, separateness, inclusion, and belonging that were arising nationwide also arose within the therapeutic milieu. Ian seemed to be taken with the heated rhetoric heard during the presidential debates, and reportedly openly taunted his classmates, especially those who might be "different" in some way. He told them he would help "build that wall," arguing "some people don't belong here." Ian cast aspersions without being fully aware of the origin of his hateful feelings or their implications. However, therapy also revealed that Ian had also been teased and called "mutt" by peers because of his olive skin color and mixed ancestry.

Ian's preexisting bias and overarching opinions came to the forefront of the group experience through his interactions with Danielle. Since nursery school, Ian had reportedly been the "identified problem kid," the one who was always stepping on someone's toes, bumping into peers, taking another's toy, or engaging in other problematic behavior. Frequently chastised by his teachers, he had feelings of shame and low self-worth, which were a deep assault on his developing psyche. One goal of group therapy was to ensure that we didn't further evoke shame while exploring these feelings, along with related sense of vulnerability and self-hate. Working collaboratively, the group process fostered Ian's recognition of similar feelings. Group discussion and heightened focus on behaviors that had led to problems in the past were replayed. Ian began to identify his propensity to feel excluded and isolated, "again and again," as he self-reported during our initial sessions. Sensing "there's something wrong with me," he told the group that the reason he was coming to therapy was because he had "problems," which he seemed to feel were insurmountable. Since Ian had come to believe that he was "defective," through the lens of group therapy we explored opportunities to revisit these feelings, while helping him to develop self-compassion, self-acceptance, and the taking and receiving of support.

Ian found that when members offered supportive positive feedback, the way that he held his body changed. His appearance shifted from the confident, cocky bully/rebel, off-putting teen to a more vulnerable, accessible person. This change manifested physically. For example, as he shrugged, Ian's shoulders dropped forward, his eyes turned downcast. At these times he displayed a fleeting, palpable unease and sense of unworthiness. Often he found these feelings intolerable, and would create a minor conflict or use his body provocatively, pushing boundaries or instigating interpersonal conflict to shift the moment or cause a distraction. Ian longed to be seen, recognized, honored, and respected, and these softer feelings were manifested over time in the group. Yet his provocative behavior ensued again with the shadow of the 2016 elections bringing Ian's provocative taunts toward Danielle to the forefront of our group therapy sessions.

Power Pause: Powerful Pauses and Shifting the Pace

Ian's history of creating minor conflicts and his inappropriate behaviors— using his body provocatively, pushing, shoving, and violating boundaries— included an escalation of verbal taunting toward Danielle. The timing of his hostility paralleled the escalation of verbal hostilities in our society (at his school, there was a heightened climate of polarized political feelings). On the one hand, Ian would do things to attract attention, such as bringing pumpkin cupcakes to delight the group at Halloween. On the other hand, he often expressed vociferous opposing feelings and displayed open hostilities toward his groupmates. Three examples come to mind.

On the first session following the end of daylight savings time, because the room was getting dark earlier, members wished for the group to transpire by candlelight. Ian opposed this, saying it was "Ugh . . . so stupid . . . creepy." This upset his fellow members. Later in the session, he expressed feelings toward one of the female group members, calling her "a dumb blonde" for her opinion. The following week, when many in the country were expressing upset about the 2016 election results, he championed the president-elect. He called both male and female members of the group "dumb" and "idiots," and embraced the slogans, "Make America Great Again" and "Build a Wall." He did this while looking at Danielle, and while knowing her insecurity about her background. To address the escalation of feelings in the group, I had to direct their attention to the underlying context and explore the meaning Ian himself ascribed to his comments. Concomitantly, I aimed to illustrate to Ian that he was recreating the type of interpersonal conflict that occurred frequently at school. This required looking at the moment-to-moment experience that was transpiring.

One aspect of group guidelines included an overarching commitment to *Powerful Pauses*. Whenever conflict escalated, group members were encouraged to "down-regulate" by embracing pauses and slowing things down. This worked as follows: I stood up and indicated a stop sign with my hand; I then playfully whispered *"Power-Pause,"* and encouraged group members to be curious about what was emerging as they down-regulated. Members self-examined what thoughts and feelings were coming up and how this manifested in their bodies. In this way, the Power-Pause helped to bring here-and-now experiences into awareness. Were they feeling more nervous, anxious, more awakened or numb as the conflict within group escalated? Some observed with wide-eyed panic (perhaps a flight or freeze response, perhaps reminiscent of other conflicts in interpersonal relationships); others reacted by matching anger, in ever-escalating verbal assault (fight response). By regulating the pace and flow of the group dialogue, I helped group members feel assured of being safely guided through these interactions with support and reinforcement.

> Group therapists help to slow the pace down, modeling patience, curiosity, and mindful attention. For example, when conflict arises in the group, there may be multiple reactions: some group members are on the edge of their chairs ready to fight, some want to get out of the room, and some just freeze or shut down and seem to disappear into the couch. The group therapist encourages each member to access and describe his or her own experience (Goldstein & Ogden, 2013, p. 135).

Addressing Conflict with a Playful Sensorimotor Exercise

One way I helped to pause the conflict-ridden session and shift the pace of the group was to follow an interactive sensorimotor psychotherapy exercise that uses two large therapy balls. A similar proximity-seeking exercise focusing on setting and respecting boundaries exercise with six-year-olds is described in Goldstein and Ogden (in press, p. 241). To address Ian's provocative comments, group members were invited to quietly observe and reflect upon the host of emotions that were emerging while remaining engaged in this learning experience. Meanwhile, Danielle and Ian were offered seats on their own large therapy balls, each placed on opposite sides of the room. They could use gentle bouncing or soothing swaying movements, with feet pushing down on the ground. Gently bouncing on exercise balls releases tension because the ever so slight bouncing and balancing keeps people's feet firmly gripping the floor in order to balance, while the gentle movement is somewhat calming.

Danielle and Ian were asked to select locations where they could gaze at one another, but at a distance they co-created. Once they found their distance (across the room from one another, supportively surrounded by the other group members), their conversation continued as they sat on the ball. Another brief hostile interchange was interwoven with playful giggling as one fell slightly off the ball and had to reestablish balance. Some wobbliness

ensued, as each was encouraged to find a distance between them that felt correct. Danielle moved back until she was out the door, at which point Ian said,
"That's right . . . out . . . no more group for you." Our office doors are glass
sliders, so Danielle's annoyance was visible as she sat on her ball without com-
menting on his incendiary words.

Only after Danielle had moved far outside the group room did Ian indicate
with his hands that she shouldn't keep moving back (note that the glass doors
allowed for each of them to see one another, and the glass "barrier" seemed to
serve the function of offering safety). At that juncture both Danielle and Ian
were instructed to notice what they felt in their bodies. I asked body-oriented
questions to encourage present moment awareness, including "What do you
feel inside your body right now as you face one another?", "What is happening
in your stomach now?" and "Do you feel the anger now that you mentioned
feeling earlier?" Although Ian started to recognize that perhaps he had sent
Danielle too far away, he seemed to have difficulty suggesting she come forward. He was encouraged to notice what happened when he invited her back
into the room with only his eyes and his hand gestures. Peering through the
glass, his hesitancy was palpable. As they cautiously and slowly continued
the exercise, this time coming closer, Ian acquiesced that he had feelings of
anxiety when beckoning her near. Danielle, however, came to a different realization. She said that she had become accustomed to lots of personal space
through years of aloneness, and she was not so quick to move back into the
group room. She noted that she could breathe more easily when there was
plenty of space between her and Ian. She expressed that Ian continued to

FIGURE 17.1
Danielle's journey on the medicine ball. (Courtesy of Bonnie Goldstein)

intermittently remind her of others who had taunted her, and said that she preferred to observe group from outside the glass, looking in.

Little headway was made with respect to their interpersonal conflict until we were able to bring their implicit experience of one another into the room, by dropping beneath the contentious content to the underlying process and feelings. At that point, the pace slowed, to allow for curiosity about what was happening in the present moment. This opened space for members to share their thoughts and feelings, emotions, and cognitions amid the contentious and argumentative banter. As the exercise continued, I instructed Ian to ask Danielle to slowly move toward him while he remained seated on the ball, until he felt that she was just the right distance from his body. In the spirit of curiosity, he was encouraged to use his hands as guides, which he did, initially somewhat reluctantly. After a few moments, the exercise shifted their experience of one another, dispelling the tension over Ian's comments. In time, Ian apologized, not for expressing his beliefs, but for casting aspersions on Danielle. He stated "It's not like I'm kicking you out of the country." Danielle responded, "But you would, and your president-elect will."

In the words of Nelson Mandela, "It never hurts to think too highly of a person, they often act differently because of it." The support and respect Danielle garnered during her experiences in group therapy led to shifts in her sense of self in the world. As a result of the support she received through this playful group experience—particularly after the provocative series of interchanges with Ian—Danielle started to reach out to others at school. Reporting her efforts to her groupmates garnered her even more support. Her subsequent evident growth in confidence and willingness to risk being "seen" were clear manifestations of growth based on her group experience.

In this exercise, through the lens of curiosity and playfulness, the collaborative group experience offered opportunities for connecting and afforded redeeming moments that emerged as members shared with one another, as guided by the support of the group leaders. While the tension in the room continued, some members spoke out against Ian's political beliefs; others offered words of support to Danielle (a unique and gratifying experience for her). In this safe atmosphere, both members could take personal risks, revisit their challenging beliefs, and have an authentic learning experience. Throughout the dyadic exchange, the observing group members were assured that they, too, would have an opportunity to do a similar exercise. They were asked to observe their own feelings, thoughts, and bodily experiences during the exercise Danielle and Ian did together. Group leaders checked in with all the group members, ensuring that interventions were adjusted to meet the needs of the group.

Similar playful exercises are often useful during high-conflict moments in group, allowing for mindful self-awareness to develop in the present moment (during the conflict), with plenty of group opportunities for practice, reinforcement, and the development of new cognizance. Other dyads within the group took turns exploring their own responses to this exercise as Danielle and Ian observed. Reflecting on their experiences and observing groupmate's experiences (similarities and differences) fostered curiosity and often led to uncovering underlying beliefs. Exploring prior experiences, perhaps ones that might have felt shameful in the past, within the safety of the group milieu, helps to forge bonds of connections with others. We sense their thoughts and feelings as we deepen into relationship.

In a follow-up session, Danielle played for group members the song "For Good" from the musical *Wicked*. She focused on the lines "Because I knew you, I have been changed for the better . . . I have been changed for good." Danielle's affinity for *Wicked* was touching, as the musical parallels her own journey, exploring issues of diversity occurring in a complicated lifelong friendship.

A Playful Introduction to Window of Tolerance

Thus far, I have discussed playful and creative ways to work interactively with young clients in a group setting that are effective in promoting confidence and self-awareness. In conjunction with these techniques, I use colorful materials that facilitate these clients' abilities to recognize and regulate affect. This is critical, especially in group settings, because intense feelings are often challenging for young people and can cause them to avoid or withdraw from a group, as we saw with Danielle.

Siegel's *window of tolerance* offers a conceptual framework that is useful when emotions, thoughts, and feelings emerge within the group. Siegel (2012) states:

> Each of us has a 'window of tolerance' in which various intensities of emotional arousal can be processed without disrupting the functioning of the system. For some people, high degrees of intensity feel comfortable, and allow them to think behave, and feel with balance and effectiveness. For others, certain emotions (such as anger or sadness), or all emotions, may be quite disruptive to functioning if they are active in even mild degrees (p. 283).

Along the same lines, Goldstein and Siegel state, "A client's window of tolerance for experiencing interactions that could be interpreted as isolating or rejecting would be widened, so that he or she could maintain equilibrium even in the face of such unsupportive experiences" (in press). Although working with the window of tolerance can be of value for all ages, I find it particularly useful with young clients in a group setting who otherwise might not be sufficiently open to the experience.

Ogden and colleagues (Ogden, Minton, & Pain, 2006; Ogden & Fisher, 2015) did pioneering work to extend the concept of the window of tolerance through the lens of sensorimotor psychotherapy. This window of tolerance model has been constructed to be accessible to children and adolescents (Ogden, Goldstein, & Fisher, 2012; Goldstein & Ogden, in press). Self-awareness skills include recognizing and understanding the oscillations of emotions as they rise and fall (identifying thoughts, feelings, and body cues, as they fluctuate in their emergent experience); and fostering curiosity and collaborative experimentation through the group milieu (i.e., understanding their shifting arousal levels, developing a heightened sense of awareness and of wonder). Often these processes are unrecognized, with clients remaining unaware, until small bits of learning, bite-size moments, allow for new learning within the therapeutic milieu.

For young clients, Ogden, Goldstein, and Fisher (2012) describe an exercise integrating the window of tolerance using a magnetic board and

> (e)xplaining to children in age-appropriate language and metaphor what the higher and lower arousal levels mean. Choosing from a set of brightly colored, appealing magnets, children are invited to place their magnets on the window of tolerance at the appropriate place to represent their own arousal. As arousal fluctuates throughout the session in response to different stimuli, the magnet can be moved accordingly, and children can be asked to show and describe how the level of arousal is reflected in their body (p. 235).

Worksheets (see Figures 16.2 and 16.3) have been designed for therapists and clients using this exercise to work at the edges of the regulatory boundaries of the window of tolerance. With the help of these worksheets, clients can better understand their autonomic arousal patterns. These include signs of high or hyperarousal, low or hypoarousal, and regulated arousal within the window of tolerance. The worksheets are also useful for helping clients identify triggers and signs of dysregulated arousal. The design of these playful worksheets invites curiosity while further illustrating the concepts of high and low arousal. In addition to the aforementioned worksheets, a character-free worksheet presenting evocative colors (hot red indicating high arousal, ocean blue representing optimal arousal, dull gray representing hypoarousal), help

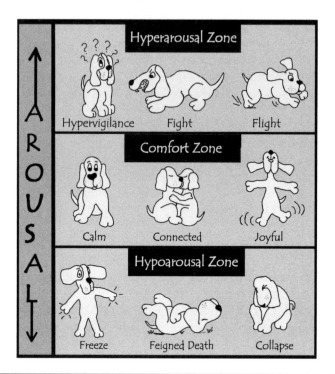

FIGURE 17.2

Window of tolerance chart. (Courtesy of Bonnie Goldstein; artwork by Terry Marks-Tarlow)

cultivate young clients' abilities to identify their arousal and to promote new feelings as they emerge. At the same time, clients in a group can collaboratively identify feelings and learn to tolerate whatever emerges (i.e., tolerating upset, frustration, anger), in service of expanding their window of tolerance (slowly expanding their ability to tolerate adverse feelings).

As part of their dyadic exercise, Danielle and Ian were each invited to select one of the three window of tolerance worksheets with the aim of identifying, understanding, modulating, regulating, and titrating their respective feelings of upset. This exercise helped them to slow their rapid, moment-to-moment, verbal and nonverbal interactions and shift their physical arousal. I observed this shift reflected in their bodies, for example in Danielle's collapsed posture and in Ian's raised chin and puffed out chest. Shifting their interaction fostered greater understanding, and they become increasingly effective at hear-

peedy's brain goes 100 mph

Max sometimes has a hard time understand everything his teacher says.

Ricky cannot help getting into trouble in the playground.

Windows of Tolerance
Optimal Arousal Zone

Robby likes school but Sometimes it's hard for him to get up for school.

Jacob wants to get good grades but his teacher says he needs to remember to bring in his homework assignments.

John sometimes loses focus in class and starts daydreaming.

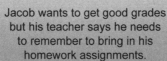

FIGURE 17.3

Window of tolerance chart designed for young children. (Courtesy of Bonnie Goldstein)

ing one another. Danielle expressed some surprise about how effective this exercise was because she did not generally have positive expectations about her interactions with others. Slowing things down helped Ian self-regulate and "think before he spoke," thereby combatting his propensity toward impulsively speaking out. Focusing on the window of tolerance with the aid of the worksheets stimulated a robust group discussion about the messages shared nonverbally, as well as the conflict-ridden exchange between Ian and Danielle. The participants learned to be open and receptive within the moment-to-moment experiential context of the group experience.

Conclusion

Working with children and adolescents in the group milieu creates new possibilities for interactions, self-understanding, and confident engagement with others. This is all the more important now that politics and prejudice—a lethal combination—have found their way into the lives of young people, mirroring the escalation of larger societal conflicts. Cohesive therapy groups can thrive when members are kept emotionally safe within the group despite the inevitable interpersonal conflict. The group can model acceptance by not ostracizing anyone or by not allowing a member to be exiled or "killed off." By prioritizing playful communication and movement exercises, group members can explore emerging internal conflicts, become more mindful of their moment-to-moment experience, and delve beneath the verbal content of presenting problems. All of this can lead to qualitative and quantitative healing and growth, as new neural pathways are created. Healing occurs when we understand how prejudices are mirrored in the body and how they prevent us from both feeling accepted and accepting others.

We have the opportunity to help young clients early in life, before their behaviors become deeply ingrained into the fabric of self and patterns of behavior. These familiar patterns inevitably emerge in the group milieu. Group therapy helps members to view things anew, as emergent experiences arise naturally through the interpersonal interchange, resulting in shifts in sense of self and other. For example, one group member told another, "I found compassion in your eyes. I felt that I didn't have to hide myself from you." Another group member said, "The relationship I feel with other group members and the group as a whole calms me down, even on days when there is not group."

Learning to acknowledge differences and developing tolerance for these differences are our overarching goals. For many young clients, such as Ian and Danielle, who struggle every day in a world that magnifies isolation and insecurity, intolerance and prejudice, group therapy provides an opportunity to grow understanding, build a sense of safety, and celebrate diversity and self-acceptance. It provides a framework for healing that can make all the difference. In the words of Anne Frank (1949), "How wonderful that nobody need wait a single minute before starting to change the world."

References

Brewer, J., Davis, J., & Goldstein, J. (2013). Why is it so hard to pay attention, or is it? Mindfulness, the factors of awakening and reward-based learning. *Mindfulness*, 4(1), 75–80.

Cozolino, L. (2010). *The neuroscience of psychotherapy: Healing the social brain* (Second Edition). New York: W. W. Norton & Company.

Cozolino, L. (2014). *The neuroscience of human relationships: Attachment and the developing social brain* (Second Edition). New York: W. W. Norton & Company.

Cozolino, L. (2015). *Why therapy works: Using your mind to change your brain*. New York: W. W. Norton & Company.

Frank, A. (1949). *Anne Frank's tales from the secret annex*. New York: Penguin, Random House.

Fredrickson, B. (2013). *Love 2.0: Finding happiness and health in moments of connection*. New York: Plume.

Gladwell, M. (2013). *David and Goliath: Underdogs, misfits, and the art of battling giants*. New York: Back Bay Books.

Goldstein, B., & Ogden, P. (2013). Sensorimotor psychotherapy as a foundation of group therapy with younger clients. In Gantt, S. P. & Badenoch, B. (Eds.). *The interpersonal neurobiology of group psychotherapy and group process* (pp. 123–145). London, UK: Karnac Books.

Goldstein, B. & Ogden, P. (In Press). Playing with possibilities: Sensorimotor psychotherapy with younger clients in individual, family, and group psychotherapy. In Hart, S. (Ed.). *Inclusion, play and empathy: Neuroaffective development in children's groups*. London, UK: Kingsley Publishers.

Goldstein, B. & Siegel, D. J. (In Press). Feeling felt: Co-creating an emergent experience of connection, safety, and awareness in psychotherapy. In M. J. Solomon & D. J. Siegel, *How people change: Relationships and neuroplasticity in psychotherapy*. New York: W. W. Norton & Company.

Hart, S. (In Press). Empathy and compassion are acquired skills, In Hart, S. (Ed.). *Inclusion, play and empathy: Neuroaffective development in children's groups*. London, UK: Kingsley Publishers.

Hanson, R. (2009). *Buddha's brain: The practical neuroscience of happiness, love and wisdom*, Oakland, CA: New Harbinger.

Mark-Goldstein, B. & Siegel, D. J. (2013). The mindful group: Using mind–body–brain interactions in group therapy to foster resilience and integration. In Siegel, D. J. & Solomon, M. (Eds.). *Healing moments in psychotherapy* (pp. 217–242). New York: W. W. Norton & Company.

Ogden, P., Minton, K., & Pain, C. (2006). *Trauma and the body: A sensorimotor approach to psychotherapy*. New York: W. W. Norton & Company.

Odgen, P. & Goldstein, B. (In Press). Embedded relational mindfulness (ERM) in child and adolescent treatment: A sensorimotor psychotherapy perspective. In Buckwalter, K. &

Reed, D. (Eds.). *Attachment theory in action: Building connections between children and parents*. New York: Rowman & Littlefield.

Ogden, P., Goldstein, B., & Fisher, J. (2012). Brain-to-brain, body-to-body: A sensorimotor psychotherapy approach for the treatment of children and adolescents. In Longo, R., Prescott, D., Bergman, J., & Creeden, K. (Eds.), *Current perspectives & applications in neurobiology: Working with young persons who are victims and perpetrators of sexual abuse* (pp. 229–255). London, UK: Karnac Books.

Ogden, P. & Fisher, J. (2015) *Sensorimotor psychotherapy: Interventions for trauma and attachment*. New York: W. W. Norton & Company.

Ogden, P. & Goldstein. B. (In Press). Embedded relational mindfulness (ERM). In *Child and adolescent treatment: A sensorimotor psychotherapy perspective* (pp. 233–255). New York: Rowman & Littlefield.

Siegel, D. J. (1999, 2012). *The developing mind, Second Edition*. New York: The Guilford Press.

Siegel, D. J. (2013). *Brainstorm: the power and purpose of the teenage brain*. New York: Penguin Group.

Trevarthan, C. & Panksepp, J. (In Press). In tune with feeling: Musical play with emotions of creativity, inspiring neuroaffective development and self-confidence for learning in company. In Hart, S. (Ed.) *Inclusion, play and empathy: Neuroaffective development in children's groups*. London, UK: Kingsley Publishers.

Yalom, I. & Leszcz, M. (2005). *The theory and practice of group psychotherapy, Fifth Edition*. New York: Basic Books.

18

The Power of Optimism

Steve Gross

BY WAY OF introduction, my name is Steven Gross and I am a clinical social worker whose mission is to help nurture the healthy social, emotional, and psychological development of children whose lives have been deeply impacted by acute and/or chronic trauma. I am also a Playmaker whose mission is to build *O'playsis* and spread the power of *Optimism* to wounded children in a way that helps them access their true, inherent *Superpowers*. Believe it or not, both of these sentences say the exact same thing—just in a different language and from a slightly different perspective. Allow me to explain.

I work with a team out of Boston called Life is Good. Most people know Life is Good as a T-shirt company but few know that Life is Good is an integrated for-profit and not-for-profit company whose sole mission is to spread the power of optimism. The for-profit side of the company accomplishes this in part by creating original artwork and pairing it with simple words of wisdom to create a line of lifestyle products that help consumers build community and "spread good vibes." The not-for-profit side of the company—also known as The Life is Good Kids Foundation—accomplishes this by partnering with leading childcare organizations to improve the quality of care delivered to our nation's most vulnerable children. More specifically, The Life is Good Kids Foundation delivers training as well as personal and professional development resources to men and woman who dedicate their careers to building healing, life-changing relationships with children. These frontline heroes—we call them Playmakers—are committed to "growing the good" in the lives of children.

Playmakers

The origin of the word Playmaker comes from the world of sports. In sports, a playmaker is a player who steps up when the game is on the line and does something that makes a positive, game-changing difference. We use the world Playmaker within the human-service field to describe a care provider who steps up at an important time in a person's life and makes a positive, life-changing difference. Playmakers for children are present in many different fields. Some are teachers. Some are social workers. Some are child life specialists. Some are psychotherapists. Some are coaches, mentor, afterschool providers, or summer camp counselors. The one thing that Playmakers have in common is that all of them—regardless of their field— are in the life-changing relationship business.

Being a Playmaker requires an important balance of professional skills and personal disposition. Professional skills pertain to the occupational skills and qualifications that a person acquires through formal training and experience. For example, social workers, teachers, psychologists, child life specialists all need to complete a rigorous course of study both inside and outside of the classroom before they are able to enter the field as a professional. As a result, they possess skills and knowledge that people outside of their profession do

FIGURE 18.1

Courtesy of Aimee Corrigan

not. It is difficult to imagine a person being an effective psychotherapist, social worker, or teacher without proper education and training.

Personal disposition, on the other hand, pertains to the inherent and nurtured qualities that make up a person's character. For example, is a person positive? Open-minded? Loving? Compassionate? Grateful? Authentic? Fun? Creative? Just as it is difficult to imagine a psychotherapist being effective without formal training, it is perhaps more difficult to imagine a psychotherapist—especially one who works with our most vulnerable children—being effective without possessing many of these important human qualities. After all, outstanding human services require outstanding humans.

Optimism

In addition to being in the life-changing relationship business, Playmakers are also in the spreading the power of optimism business. Optimism is commonly defined as hopefulness and/or confidence about the future. However, my team and I define it simply as "choosing to see and focus on the good." More specifically, choosing to see and focus on the good in one's self, the good in others, and the good in the world around you.

Contrary to popular opinion, optimism and realism are not mutually exclusive. Optimism is not about denying the existence of hardships, pain, injustice, fear, and/or despair. Instead, it is about not allowing the "darkness" of life to eclipse one's ability to see the light that exists within it all. When I think about optimism in this way, I find it difficult to think of a more important human characteristic or a stronger indicator of psychological wellbeing. As

FIGURE 18.2
Optimism involves seeing the glass as half full

psychotherapists—and as Playmakers—helping to nurture a sense of optimism in the people we serve must be one of our highest priorities.

Toxic Stress

The seeds of optimism—especially in young children—can be extremely sensitive to environmental stressors. Having an optimistic approach toward life may be a good plan, but as former heavyweight boxing champion Mike Tyson reminds us, "Everyone has a plan 'til they get punched in the mouth." Tragically, for many children in America, life sure can throw some pretty mean punches. Some are of the knockout variety, and come out of nowhere with devastating force (acute trauma), while others come in the form of a steady stream of pounding jabs (chronic trauma) that over time wear a person down and break their spirit. According to a study funded by the Centers for Disease Control, exposure to adverse childhood experiences is one of the greatest health threats facing our nation's children. The Adverse Childhood Experiences (ACE) study showed that toxic stress—resulting from overwhelming environmental threats, such as abuse, neglect and household dysfunction, can disrupt healthy brain development and lead to severe social, emotional, and cognitive impairments (Felitti, et al., 1998). These impairments make it extremely difficult for survivors of trauma to see and focus on the good in themselves, the good in others, and the good in the world around them. To seek relief, many adopt a host of maladaptive coping strategies, such as substance use, promiscuous sexual behavior, and eating disorders, that may be effective in temporarily interrupting their suffering, but that over time erode overall health and can eventually lead to disease, disability, and in some cases, early death (Felitti, et al., 1998).

For children—and other young mammals—one of the most tragic consequences of toxic stress is that it stops them from playing. Neuroscientific research with rat pups provides us with some fascinating insights regarding the effects of play on neurodevelopment and the destructive impact that toxic stress has on play behavior. Diamond and her team created three different kinds of living environments for rat pups (Diamond, Krech, & Rosenzweig, 1964). The first environment—which they called the "impoverished environment"—consisted of an empty cage with only food and water. The second environment—which they called the "standard environment"—replicated typical experimental conditions at the time, a small cage with three rats, food, and water. The third environment—which they called the "enriched environment"—was more like a rat playground. It was decked out with exercise wheels to run on, tunnels to crawl through, and most importantly, a whole bunch of other rats. They then studied and compared the brains of the rats that living in the three different environments.

You can probably guess what Diamond's lab discovered. The rats that lived in the enriched environments had significantly more cortical development (including dendrite growth, increased nerve cell size, etc.) than their buddies living on the other side of the tracks. And the rats living in the impoverished environment had significantly less cortical development than the rats in the standard environment (Diamond, et al., 1964). As a result, the enriched group had more evolved cognitive functioning (they could learn to navigate mazes, while the unenriched rats could not) as well as social functioning (they could differentiate between the friendly and aggressive gestures of other rats, while the unenriched rats could not). In other words, Diamond's research confirmed what everyone who has ever worked with children already knows—that when young mammals are raised in an environment where they are free to engage, connect, and explore, their brains develop better. (Maybe this is why my wife and I currently spend more money per year sending our children to preschool then we spent on college tuition for ourselves. But I digress . . .)

What Jaak Panksepp discovered next was even more interesting. He observed high levels of play behavior in a group of rat pups living in an enriched environment. In fact, the play behavior of these rats looked quite similar to the play behavior of other young mammal (including human children), highlighted by exuberant running, chasing, and tussling. Then, seemingly out of nowhere, he and his team observed a sudden, dramatic drop in play behavior. Baffled by this, Panksepp and his team looked for explanations, and quickly found one. One of the lab technicians who happened to have a cat came to work with some cat hair on her clothing and inadvertently introduced it into the enriched environment. The presence of the cat hair triggered an acute stress response in the rats (i.e., When the cat's not away, the rats won't play). Panksepp and his team thoroughly cleaned the cage to rid it of any trace of cat hair, but sadly, the play behavior of the rats never resumed to anywhere close to their pre-cat hair levels (Panksepp, 1998).

So what do exercise wheels, rats, and cat hair have to do with play and psychotherapy? The first thing we can take from this experiment is that play supports the healthy social, emotional, and cognitive development of young mammals. The second thing we can take from this experiment is that environment matters. It matters a lot. If an environment is not conducive to mammals engaging, connecting, and exploring, then play behavior—and subsequently brain development—is compromised. The third thing we can take from this experiment is that a sense of safety is essential in order for young mammals to play, and that overwhelming fear or trauma is arch enemy number one to play.

FIGURE 18.3

Courtesy of Aimee Corrigan

But I have some good news for you. You ready for it? We're not rats! Although human children react in similar ways to rat pups when faced with life-threatening stressors, their human caregivers have far greater capacity to respond to them in ways that promote healing and that enable them to play again. More specifically, these Playmakers have the capacity to build enriched environments, detect and remove "cat hair," and to help kids regain the strength to play again.

Play

Most people think that play—like work—is primarily characterized by activity type. For example tag, hide-and-seek, soccer, and swinging on swings are usually considered play activities, while mowing the lawn, doing the dishes, painting the fence, and cleaning the house are usually considered work activities. Categorizing play this way is far too limiting, as it fails to capture the true essence of play. My team and I define play as freely and joyfully engaging with, connecting with, and exploring the surrounding world. In other words, play is not about what you do. Play is the spirit in which you do everything that you do.

FIGURE 18.4

Courtesy of Steve Gross

A game of soccer may be more like work than play for some players, while painting a fence may be more like play than work for some workers (just ask Tom Sawyer). For example, if a couple of painters are enjoying each other's company, are engaged in the task at hand, feel a sense of joy in painting, and feel pride in their ability to do the job well, then I would say that those painters were *playing* not *working*.

Let me give you an entirely different example. Several years ago, my sister invited me to watch my nephew play soccer. After watching the game, she asked me how I thought he played. I told her that from my perspective, he didn't *play* soccer. He *did* soccer. She looked at me like I had three heads (a look I have seen many times throughout my life) and asked me what I meant. I told her that in order for Josh to be *playing* soccer he (1) had to feel some sense of *joyfulness* while playing; he (2) had to feel some sense of *social connection* toward his teammates; he (3) had to feel some level of *active engagement* in the game; and he (4) had to feel some sense of *internal control* or competency in his abilities as a player. During the game that I watched, Josh didn't appear to feel any of these feelings. Instead, I observed him insecurely—almost sadly— lumbering around the field, disconnected from his teammates and disengaged from the action. Now in case you're wondering, that particular game was an isolated experience for Josh. As the season rolled on, Josh really started getting into soccer. He made a bunch of friends, developed confidence in his abilities, and began having a lot of fun *playing*. He now plays for the United States Olympic team. It's a true story—all except for the last sentence.

The Four Domains of Play

Joyfulness, social connection, active engagement, and internal control are what my team and I refer to as the four domains of play. We believe that in order for an activity to be considered play, the person participating in the activity needs to experience all four of these key ingredients.

Joyfulness

The simplest definition of joyfulness that I've come across is *enduring positivity*. Joyfulness is a deep, felt sense of appreciation and contentment regardless of circumstances. Joyfulness can be experienced as a fleeting, emotional state— like when we celebrate the birth of a child—but it can also be practiced and nurtured into becoming a stable trait that becomes part of a person's overall character. Joy is not the absence of sadness. Instead, it exists along the same emotional continuum. Like the swinging of a pendulum, it is difficult to imagine reaching the highest heights of joy without also experiencing the lowest depths of despair. One can't exist without the other.

When people are joyful, they attend to the present moment and celebrate all that is good in it. Sometimes, joyfulness is expressed with exuberance, through smiles and laughter. At other times, joy is expressed more internally and is difficult to observe. Whether or not it is expressed through quiet contentment or exuberance, joy is a celebration of the positive aspects of any moment, whether it is dancing to a favorite song, listening to the wind through the trees, or spending time with a good friend. In the absence of joy, there can be no play.

Social Connection

Documentary filmmaker Ric Burns once said that the "the quality of a person's life is in direct proportion to the quality of their relationships." I couldn't agree more. Being connected to others is our most important and powerful human drive. Human beings are unable to survive without connection to others. We are herd animals. Feeling a sense of belonging is crucial to our overall well-being. Starting with parents and caregivers, infants immediately seek connection and develop strong bonds, in order to feel loved and protected. It is through these most basic connections that children develop the confidence to more independently explore the world around them. Just knowing that they have a safe base to return to, children can be socially connected even while playing alone.

Our drive to play with others is deeply rooted in our desire to belong and to be considered a valued part of a community. Allow me to share a powerful example of this with you. Not long after the 2010 earthquake that devastated Haiti, I was in Port-au-Prince working with a local non-governmental organization (NGO) that was providing emergency medical services to a particularly hard-hit village there. One of the members of the medical team—who also happened to be a colleague of mine, and knew of my experience working with children—asked if I'd be willing to run a small playgroup for some kids whose parents were receiving treatment. I told him that since I was "flying solo" and did not have the staff support to properly supervise a large group of children, I was reluctant to say yes. He told me that this village was particularly hard hit by the earthquake and that, as a result, he assured me that were only a handful of kids, maybe 10 or so, who were healthy enough to play. The others were too sick, too tired, too hungry, and/or too scared to participate. So I grabbed a small play parachute from my supply kit, headed over to the makeshift medical clinic, and began playing some games with this small group of children. It didn't take long for the children's cautious exploration to morph into loud, exuberant, joyful play.

FIGURE 18.4

The glorious sound of laughter and playful giddiness filled the space, and soon echoed throughout the village. Curious kids eventually started peeking their heads out from inside their makeshift shelters, and slowly, one by one, ventured over to see what was going on. Most of them couldn't resist joining in on the fun. Before long we had to abandon the play parachute because it was way too small to accommodate the huge group of children who were eager to play. Driven by their desire for connection, children who moments before were not well enough to play, had somehow almost miraculously mustered the strength to do so—further evidence that a child's drive to play is primal, in that it serves as their leading vehicle for relationship building. In the absence of social connection a child can never fully engage in play.

Active Engagement

Active engagement is basically a person's capacity to "be here now." With regard to play, active engagement is a person's ability to be enthusiastically immersed in activity. At the risk of sounding "too Eastern" (whatever the heck that means), everything takes place in the present moment. Nothing ever happens in the past or in the future. Although most of us spend a great deal of our lives reminiscing about the past and anticipating the future, the acts of reminiscing and anticipating can only be done in the present moment.

Renowned psychologist Mihály Csíkczentmihályi (1997) describes "flow" as a deep, effortless involvement in an activity in which the person loses sense of self and time. When we are actively engaged, we are fully present in the moment, not preoccupied with the past or the future, but focused on the activity at hand. When children are actively engaged they explore with passion and gusto, are curious and inquisitive, and are primed for exploration and creation.

This reminds me of another story. I once took a very difficult yoga class. Actually, calling this class "difficult" is an understatement. The room was 103 degrees, the class was 80 minutes long, the instruction was fast paced, and the difficulty of the poses far exceeded my ability to even attempt them. As I struggled not to pass out and vomit, I kept looking at the clock on the wall, hoping desperately for the speedy passage of time. The instructor noticed my looking at the clock, and said to me (in a very yoga-like tone), "Be here now. Because if you're not here, you're nowhere." All of a sudden it hit me that I would rather be nowhere than in that yoga class. So I left.

After reflecting on this experience for some time I took something very powerful from it. I took that when the present moment is overwhelming, we disengage from it. And when we disengage from the present moment, we cease to play.

Internal Control

Internal control is about a person's sense of safety, worth, and competence. As we learned from Jaak Panksepp's (1998) research, young rats stop playing the moment threat is introduced into their environment. Even once the threat is removed, the rats do not return to their pre-threat levels of play. All young mammals, including children, cannot fully engage in play if their basic safety needs are not met. Only once their basic safety needs are met, can children develop a sense of confidence, freedom and belief in their ability meet life's challenges with success. One of my favorite internal control stories is of a three-year-old girl who is drawing a picture in her preschool art class. The teacher asks the little girl what she's drawing, and the little girl says, "I'm drawing a picture of God." The teacher says, "But sweetie, nobody knows what God looks like." To which the little girl boldly replies, "They will when I'm done."

All people, especially children, need to feel that they are special and powerful. In describing a young child's need to feel special, one of my social work professors at Boston College taught me that every toddler should be made to believe that they "shit gold." That everything about them, including the "fruits" of their bodily functions, are pure and original works of art that deserve to be celebrated. Children cannot play if they are unable to experience some sense of internal control.

When we look at the four domains of play and compare them with some common responses to toxic stress and trauma, we begin to see that in many ways play is the opposite experience of trauma. While play brings about feelings of joy, trauma brings about feelings of hopelessness and despair. While play serves to unite us, trauma serves to isolate us. While play motivates us to actively engage in the moment, trauma motivates us to fight and flee from it. And while play allows us to control our environment, trauma occurs when our environment controls us. Therefore it is essential that psychotherapists and other interventionist working with survivors of trauma prioritize the creation of safe, loving, joyful, and engaging environments for the children in their care. If trauma and play are indeed at the opposite ends of the continuum of human experience, then play has the potential to serve as an antidote and powerful corrective experience to trauma when integrated into treatment.

O'playsis

We define the word *oasis* as a pleasant place that serves as a refuge from what is difficult. We define the word *play* as freely and joyfully engaging, connecting, and exploring the surrounding world. We melded these two words together (because nobody told us that we couldn't), to create the word O'playsis. We define O'playsis as a refuge where one can freely and joyfully engage, connect, and explore. In a perfect world, every educational, medical, or enrichment program that serves children—especially those who have been wounded by life's cruelest and most unfair challenges—would be an O'playsis. Come to think of it, an O'playsis is the optimal environment for just about anybody to do just about anything. Even bottom-line driven, for-profit businesses across the country have discovered that joyful, engaged, connected, and empowered employees are far more productive than their unhappy, disengaged, isolated, and anxious counterparts (duh). This has driven many businesses to allocate resources to optimizing their work environments and improving their corporate cultures.

At the Life is Good Kids Foundation we created a scale called the Organizational Optimism Profile that is used to help human service organizations measure levels of joyfulness, social connection, internal control, and active engagement throughout the workplace. By asking employees a series of 22 questions, such as, "I feel like I am part of a team," "I feel that my ideas and opinions are heard and acted on" and "I get to do things that I enjoy doing, while at work," organizational leaders can begin to quantify the abstract concept of O'playsis within their work environments and create strategies to strengthen it.

Superpowers

Just about every superhero story follows a similar archetype. They generally take place in a kingdom, village or metropolis where life for the most part is pretty darn good. That is, until a destructive force moves in and threatens to destroy it. The people, too weak and helpless to defeat the bad guys on their own, call on a superhero to fight their battle. The superhero invariably possesses superpowers. These superpowers usually come in the form of super-human physical prowess (i.e. the ability to fly, breath under water, leap tall buildings in a single bound, look through walls, beat people up, travel faster than the speed of light, etc.) that enable them to defeat the villain, restore goodness, and ultimately save the day.

The truth of the matter is that most of the problems that plague society today are not ones that can be solved by use of superhuman physical strength. Solving society's most challenging problems will require us to figure out "technologies" that will enable us to increase our social, emotional, and cognitive superpowers. Can you imagine how the world might be different if we were able to increase our global capacity to love by as little as even 10 percent? How many armed conflicts would be averted? How might violent crime be reduced? How many lives would be saved? How much suffering would be averted? What if we were able to do the same with our global capacity for creativity, compassion, courage, or gratitude?

At Life is Good we define "superpowers" as the traits that bring out the best in humanity. Our 10 favorites are love, compassion, authenticity, courage, fun, creativity, gratitude, humor, simplicity, and openness. We believe that children possess all of these superpowers in their truest, most pure form. When I ask childcare professionals what superpower they admire most in children, they often tell me . . .

- I admire how kid's imaginations work and how creative they are.
- I admire how real and authentic kids are; what you see is what you get.
- I admire that kids are able to have fun doing even the simplest little things.
- I admire how enthusiastic kids are and how open they are to trying new things.
- I admire how loving kids are and how willing they are to forgive.
- I admire how funny kids are and how much they love to laugh.

FIGURE 18.6

Courtesy of Aimee Corrigan

Picasso is quoted as saying that, "All children are born artists. The trick is remaining an artist as we grow old." I think that the same holds true for many of our superpowers. If we're not careful, the wear and tear of everyday life and the stress that comes along with it can erode our ability to engage life with a sense of childlike wonder, openness, fun, creativity, and love. And as our capacity to play diminishes, so does our vitality. George Bernard Shaw once said, "We don't stop playing because we grow old, we grow old because we stop playing." I wish I had said that.

One of my favorite kid superheroes stories also comes from Haiti. It happened while my team and I were observing a preschool in Port-au-Prince. Having not met many foreigners, the children were all extremely excited by our visit. I inconspicuously (or so I thought) gave one of the little girls a friendly smile and a fist bump. Her friend witnessed our interaction and decided that she too wanted a fist bump. This quickly escalated into all of the kids wanting fist bumps. Suddenly an overzealous group of around 40 preschoolers began crowding around us to get theirs. As anyone who knows preschoolers might guess, pushing and shoving ensued, until the teacher decided that it was time to put an end to the commotion. In an unmistakably firm voice she told the children to "sit their bodies in their chairs immediately." The children did exactly as they were told. One little boy who was next in line for his fist bump sat is his seat looking slightly defeated. A few seconds later however he perked up. With a huge smile on his face and a sense of purpose in his eyes, he put both hands on each side of his chair and bounced both himself and the chair across the room to claim his fist bump. Talk about putting your superpowers to good use! This little boy possessed the *love* to pursuit new friendships, the *creativity* to play by his teacher's rules while still getting what he wanted, and the *courage* to put his brilliant plan into action. Let this be a lesson to all of us in not letting anything get in the way of us making meaningful social connections!

Personal Playmaker Practice

You can't spread what you don't have. Or as legendary jazz saxophone player Charlie Parker once said, "If you don't live it, it won't come out of your horn." If you want to help children discover a sense of joy in their lives, you need to have joy in yours. If you want to help inspire children, then you need to be inspired. If you want to help children feel safe and powerful, than you need to feel safe and powerful. These things tend to be *caught by* children not to *taught to* them.

In 1989, I started a program called Project Joy. Project Joy worked with early childhood educators to help them support the healthy social and emotional development of their children through play. It quickly became evident to me that many of the teachers who were struggling to effectively nurture their children's social and emotional development were not struggling because they lacked knowledge, but because they themselves were socially and emotionally depleted. Again, you can't spread what you do not have.

With this in mind, we believe that is essential that Playmakers apply these same Playmaker principles to their own lives, both inside and outside of work. It is a lifelong practice for every person to cultivate their most optimistic disposition. However, for those of us who have chosen to be in the life-changing relationship/spreading the power of optimism business, this practice must be one of our top priorities.

One simple way that we work to accomplish this is by encouraging our Playmakers to create Personal Playmaker Practice plans. These plans ask Playmakers to apply the four domains of play and O'playsis into their own lives by having them answer these four questions.

1. What are you going to do to bring more joy into your life?
2. What are you going to do to keep yourself strong and balanced?
3. Who are you going to "play with"?
4. What are you going to do to nurture you sense of inspiration and creativity?

We ask our Playmakers to share their Personal Playmaker Practice plans with a few trusted colleagues in an effort to help them feel more accountable to adhering to them. We also ask our Playmakers to revisit their plans consistently and modify them as needed. Things change. We change. Personal Playmaker Practice plans change. The bottom line is this: if we're going to be successful in building O'playsis for others, we need to be successful in building O'playsis for ourselves.

The Optimism Tree

The best way to sum up this chapter is with a visual. I invite you to imagine a tree rooted in rich soil that is bursting with ripe fruit. The soil of this tree represents O'playsis, the roots represent optimism, and the fruits represent our superpowers. The seeds of optimism are inherent in all human beings. We couldn't exist without them. However, for the seeds of optimism to take root and grow, they must be planted in soil that is rich in the nutrients of joyfulness, social connection, active engagement, and internal control. Con-

FIGURE 18.7

The optimism tree

versely, optimism cannot take root in soil that is rich in despair, loneliness, fear, and disengagement. As the seeds of optimism take root and extract nutrients from the soil (O'playsis), the tree yields fruit (superpowers). The fruits of the tree nourish all who consume them. The fruits that fall to the ground will eventually become part of the very same soil in which new seeds will root and grow.

It's a pretty beautiful picture, isn't it? However, we know that trees, especially young ones, are susceptible to environmental factors. Just as drought, insects, and natural disasters can destroy healthy trees, environmental factors—both natural and manmade—can destroy healthy children. As Playmakers it is our responsibility to create and maintain the right soil for growth, while also replanting the trees that have been uprooted by the destructive storms of life.

References

Csíkszentmihályi, M. (1997). *Finding flow. The psychology of engagement with everyday life.* New York: Basic Books.

Diamond, M. C., Krech, D., & Rosenzweig, M. R. (1964). The effects of an enriched environment on the rat cerebral cortex. *Journal of Comparative Neurology, 123*(1), 111–119.

Felitti, V. J., Anda, R. F., Nordenberg, D., Williamson, D. F., Spitz, A. M., Edwards, V., Koss, M. P., & Marks, J. S. (1998). Relationship of childhood abuse and household dysfunction to many of the leading causes of death in adults. The Adverse Childhood Experiences (ACE) study. *American Journal of Preventive Medicine, 14*(4), 245–258.

Panksepp, J. (1998). *Affective neuroscience: The foundations of human and animal emotions.* New York: Oxford University Press.

Index

In this index, *f* denotes figure and *t* denotes table.

AAI. *See* Adult Attachment Interview (AAI)
abuse. *See* childhood abuse
ACE (adverse childhood experience scale), 182
active engagement, 368
The Act of Creation (Koestler), 299
actors, 174–75, 182
   See also performance artists
addiction. *See* drug abuse, ADHD and
ADHD, 249–50, 252, 253, 254–61, 263
adolescents. *See* ADHD; mindful group therapy
Adult Attachment Interview (AAI), 173–74,
   175, 182
Adverse Childhood Experiences (ACE)
   study, 362
adverse childhood experience scale (ACE), 182
affective neuroscience, 243–46
   See also emotional regulation
affirmation, art of, 329–32, 332*f*
Ainsworth, M., 68
Alighieri, D., 17
Allen, W., 292
Ambady, N., 96
amygdala, 71–72
anger. *See* rage and anger
animals, 26–27, 169
   See also bears; deer-flavored morality tale;
     dogs; goats; rats; tiger cubs
anoetic and autonoetic memories, 245
anterior cingulate, 73
Anticevic, A., 43
anxiety, 157, 171
Aposhyan, S., 85, 102
Appreciative Inquiry approach, 319
approach behavior. *See* grasping; pulling;
   reaching

armor, body and posture as, 344–46, 347–48
Arnold, K., 77
arousal. *See* emotional regulation; window of
   tolerance
artification hypothesis, 80–84, 83*f*
artists, 167, 168–69, 171–72, 174, 177
   See also Kandinsky, W.; Marks-Tarlow, T.;
     performance artists
The Art of Loving (Fromm), 69
attachment, 69–71, 174
   See also maternal love
attachment states. *See* Adult Attachment Interview (AAI); secure attachment
attachment theory, 65, 172–73, 277
attention. *See* focused attention (FA)
attention deficit hyperactivity disorders.
   See ADHD
attunement, 139, 194–95, 200, 227–30
   See also clinical intuition; empathic
     attunement
audience, 289–90
audiences, nature of, 291–92
auditory imagination, 213
awareness. *See* choiceless awareness; consciousness; Intentional Listening; mindfulness
   and meditation

babies. *See* infants
Bainbridge-Cohen, B., 97
Baird, B., 46
Bandura, A., 32–33
Barrett, J., 72
Barsalou, L., 49, 50
Bartels, A., 75, 77
bears, 23*f*, 26

Beaty, R., 45
Beebe, B., 72, 146
Bekoff, M., 27
Bem, D., 152
Benedek, M., 45
Benny, J., 292
Be Your Self (Marks-Tarlow), 151f
Biederman, J., 257
Bion, W., 205
Bizahaloni, V., 113
Black Elk, 123
body and posture as armor, 344–46, 347–48
body play, 34
 See also physical play
Borge, V., 289
Bos, M., 47
Bossypants (Fey), 329
Boston Change Process Study Group, 146, 192
Boucard, C., 49
Bowlby, J., 68, 101, 146, 219, 223, 223f, 224
the brain, creative socialization of, 247–54,
 248f, 251f, 253f
brain activity, music improvisation and, 202–3,
 203f, 204
brain development, 243–45, 246, 363
brain lateralization, 149, 149f
 See also left hemisphere; right hemisphere
brain structures. *See* hand model of the brain;
 specific structures
breath awareness meditation, 49–50, 343, 346
Brewer, J., 50, 54
broaden-and-build theory, 126
Bromberg, P., 150
Brown, B., 334
Brown, S., 28f, 74, 266, 311
Buddha's Brain (Hanson), 342
Burns, R., 366

Calvino, I., 211
Campbell, D., 19
Cannon, B., 96
caregiving play, 34, 34f
CARE system, 247, 252, 266
Carter, M., 330
central executive network (CEN), 43, 44f, 45,
 49, 50
Chandrasekhar, S., 18
Chavez-Eakle, R., 77
Child Care and the Growth of Love (Bowlby), 68
childhood abuse, 176, 180
children. *See* ADHD; mindful group therapy
choiceless awareness, 50, 51
Chong, S., 81
Christoff, K., 45

circles, 117–18, 123
 See also medicine wheels
Civilization and Its Discontents (Freud), 64, 290
client-centered processes, 343–44
 See also therapeutic alliance
clinical intuition, 145, 146, 148, 151–52
Close, D., 334
clowns, 111
cognitive control, 45, 51, 54
Cohen, S., 302
comedy and comedians, 289–90, 291, 292–95,
 297–98
 See also humor, as pain substitute
Commoner, B., 19
communication, 73, 75, 77, 81, 198–99
 See also Intentional Listening; nonverbal
 communication
concentration meditation, 50, 51
confidence. *See* self-efficacy
Connally, J., 23
connection, 317–21
 See also social connectedness
consciousness, 17–18, 19, 43, 48
control. *See* cognitive control; internal
 control
Cooperrider, D., 319
co-regulation, 233–34, 235f
couples therapy, nesting dolls and, 271–85
Cozolino, L., 133f
Creative Confidence (Kelley & Kelley), 33
creativity
 about, 169–70
 attachment and, 173, 174
 brain structures and, 45, 46, 47, 51, 65,
 77, 84
 capacity for joy and, 299
 educated imagination and, 17
 as idiosyncrasy, 161–62
 latent inhibition and, 204
 movement and, 96
 mutual love and, 77–78
 playfulness and, 18
 small versus capital "C," 19–20
 See also flow; ImprovHQ principles; improvisation; novelty
Creswell, J., 50
Crohn's disease, 302–3
crowd psychology, 289
 See also audiences, nature of
Cruts, B., 84
Csíkszentmihályi, M., 177, 368
cultural perspectives of play, 110–27
"Culture of Me," 274, 280
curbside therapy, 343–44

curiosity. *See* mindful group therapy; mindfulness and meditation
cymatics, 197, 197*f*

Damasio, A., 41, 115
dance and dancers
    dance of psychotherapy, 147, 147*f*
    "Exploring Connections," 175*f*
    "Exuberant Dedication," 183*f*
    "Flamenco Passion," 178*f*
    "Interdependence," 181*f*
    "Lost and Found and Lost Again," 176*f*
    Navajo culture, 111
    "Quiet Beauty," 179*f*
    "Silent Guardian," 172*f*
    "Tapping Joy," 169*f*
    See also performance artists
Daring Greatly (Brown), 334
Darwin, C., 66
Davanloo, H., 303
Davidson, R., 46
Davis, M., 134
daydream effect, 35–36
Decety, J., 157
deer-flavored morality tale, 13–15
default mode network (DMN), 40–47, 44*f*, 49, 50–51, 56–57
DeForest, I., 86
de Manzano, O., 179
depression
    antidotes for, 251, 254, 266
    fantasy proneness and, 171
    as imagination deficit, 156–57
    paradoxical injunction and, 303–4
Diamond, M., 362–63
directors, as psychotherapists, 287–89
Diski, J., 306
Dissayanake, E., 66, 70, 73, 74, 75, 81, 82, 153
diversity, 144–45
    See also cultural perspectives of play
Djiksterhuis, A., 47
DMN. *See* default mode network (DMN)
dogs, 30*f*, 34*f*, 158
Doll, A., 49
dolls. *See* nesting dolls
dorsal vagal system, 98, 99
drama, 290–91
drug abuse, ADHD and, 256–59
drug therapy. *See* medications
drum lessons, 132–33

Eberle, S., 36
Edmondson, A., 319
educated imagination, 170, 177

efficiency versus love, 16–17
Ehrenswieg, A., 209
Eliot, T., 213
Embedded Relational Mindfulness©, 341, 342
emotional regulation
    love, attachment, and, 69–71, 73–74
    Power-Pauses, 348–49
    in rats, 245
    through play, 79–80, 81–82
emotions. *See* affective neuroscience; facial expressions
empathic attunement, 199–201, 202, 204
empathy, 157
engagement, 219*f*, 332–36, 368
entrainment, 196–97
    See also rhythmic synchronization
Erskine, R., 194
eudemonia versus hedonia, 17
eureka moments, 47
evolution, socialization and, 280–81
excited love, 68, 68*f*, 69, 71, 72, 78
exploratory play, 34
The Expression of Emotions in Man and Animals (Darwin), 66
exuberance at play, 76*f*
Eyre, R., 296

FA. *See* focused attention (FA)
face-to-face play, 121, 126
facial expressions
    distress, 228*f*
    emotional regulation and, 70, 77, 81
    exuberance, 76*f*, 183*f*
    joy, 80*f*, 255*f*
    love, 67*f*, 68*f*
    in play, 82
    right hemisphere and, 73
    sadness, 222*f*
Fagen, B., 26
failure, celebration of, 327–28
fantasy play, 158, 159*f*
fantasy proneness, 170, 171, 175, 176, 180
Farb, N., 51
farce. *See* tragedy-farce continuum
Ferenczi, S., 64, 85
Fey, T., 329
Feydeau, G., 296
Fisher, J., 340, 353
flow
    about, 17, 32, 368
    creativity and, 177–79, 180
    implicit relational knowing and, 146–47, 147*f*
    See also consciousness; creativity; daydream effect; empathic attunement; novelty

focused attention (FA), 48–49, 53, 54
food play, 76*f*
Frank, A., 357
Frank, R., 100, 104
Fredrickson, B., 126–27, 340
Freeman, W., 156
free play, 158, 250, 261, 262
Free play (Marks-Tarlow), 159*f*
Freud, A., 92
Freud, S., 64, 66, 85, 200, 290
Fromm, E., 68–69, 85
frontal lobes, 265–66
    See also prefrontal cortex
Frye, Northrup, 170

Gable, S., 47
Galvez, Z., 312
games and sports, 35, 365–66
genetics, 242–43, 245, 259
The German Ideology (Marx & Engels), 16
gestures, 96, 120
Gilbert, D., 46, 56
Gladwell, M., 344
Glee! (Marks-Tarlow), 160*f*
goats, 248*f*
Golding, K., 232
Goldstein, B., 340, 341, 342, 349, 352, 353
Goodall, J., 26
Gordon, A., 45
Gottman, J., 329
grasping, 103–5, 104*f*
    See also reaching
group behavior, 289
    See also audiences, nature of
group therapy. *See* mindful group therapy

habits. *See* movement habits; rituals
Haiti earthquake survivors, 367–68, 367*f*, 372
hand knowledge, 119–20
hand model of the brain, 118–19
Hanson, R., 342
Hasenkamp, W., 49, 50
hedonia versus eudemonia, 17
Heifetz, J., 141, 142*f*
Here I Am (Jernberg, Hurst, Lyman), 223
The Hidden Order of Art (Ehrenswieg), 209
Hirsch, I., 86
Hölzel, B., 49
homogeneity, 144–45
Hopper, E., 47
Hughes, D., 232
humor, as intervention, 160–61, 303–5, 304*f*
humor, as pain substitute, 299, 300–301, 300*f*, 301*f*, 307

See also comedy and comedians

idiosyncrasies, 152, 161–62, 162*f*
image thinking, 115–16
imagination, 156–57, 170, 177, 199–200, 213
    See also creativity; metaphorical thinking;
    trauma and traumatized imagination
implicit relational knowing, 145–48, 147*f*, 152
Impro for Storytellers (Johnstone), 330
ImprovHQ principles, 313*f*, 314–36, 315*f*, 326*f*, 332*f*
improvisation
    about, 201–4, 203*f*, 309–12
    artwork, 209*f*
    brain activity and music, 56–57, 84, 202–3, 203*f*, 204
    as support to psychotherapy, 312–14
Improvisation (Kandinsky), 209*f*
improvisational play, 201–2
    See also free play
impulse control development, 265–66
impulse control issues, 254, 255, 259, 266
    See also ADHD
In a Silent Way, 135
Infancy in Uganda (Ainsworth), 68
infants, 70, 72–73
    See also mother-infant relationships
inhibition. *See* latent inhibition
Insel, T., 251
Integration and Self Healing (Krystal), 87
intelligence, social connectedness and, 135–36
Intentional Listening, 314–17, 315*f*
internal control, 369
interpersonal neurobiology, 148, 194–95
interpretation, 210
intrinsic motivation, 32–33, 177
intuition, 86
    See also clinical intuition

Jack, A., 50
Jay, T., 289
Jaynes, J., 84
Jensen, H., 84
Jernberg, A., 219, 222, 224, 225
Johnson, N., 96
Johnstone, K., 318, 330
Jones, D., 43, 45
Josipovic, Z., 53
joy, expressions of, 80*f*, 255*f*
joyfulness, 266, 366
Jung, C., 117

Kabat-Zinn,, 52
Kandinsky, W., 205, 206*f*, 209*f*, 212*f*

Kane, J., 84
Kao, J., 311
Kaufmann, S., 45
Kelley, D., 33
Kelley, T., 33
Kessel, P., 86
Killingsworth, M., 46, 56
Kilpatrick, L., 52
Klein, G., 15
Kluckholm, C., 144, 145
Koestler, A., 299
Kolb, B., 243
Korean culture, 115–16, 116f, 117
Krystal, H., 87
Kurtz, R., 100

LaBarre, F., 100
Lakoff, G., 96
language, thought and, 120
latent inhibition, 204
laugh, baby's first, 112
laughter, 289, 290, 291, 292, 297f
   See also comedy and comedians; humor topics
Layers of experience, each enfolded in the last (Marks-Tarlow), 276f
The Leaven of Love (DeForest), 86
left hemisphere
   arousal and, 70
   functions of, 64, 65, 149
   storytelling and, 118
   Western culture and, 122
Lego® Serious Play®, 119–20
letting go. See yielding
Levinson D., 46
Li, W., 41
Liberty in Hand (Marks-Tarlow), 162f
Lieberman, M., 275
Life is Good Kids Foundation, 359, 370, 371–72
Limb, C., 202, 204
Lindell, A., 85
listening. See Intentional Listening; therapeutic ear, fine-tuning of
Liu, C., 41
loneliness, 280, 285
love, 65, 66–71, 67f, 68f, 84–87
   See also mutual love; quiet love
Love 2.0 (Fredricksen), 340
Love and War in Intimate Relationships (Solomon & Tatkin), 271, 282
love versus efficiency, 16–17
loving-kindness meditation, 50, 51
Lowenfeld, M., 115
ludus, 18

Lynn, J., 299
Lynn, R., 298
Lyons-Ruth, K., 192

MacLean, P., 71
Mai, X., 41
Make Your Teammate the Hero, 317–21
   See also social connectedness; socialization
mammalian brain systems, 29–30
Mandela, N., 351
Marks-Tarlow, T.
   about, 79, 82, 85, 86, 201
   Be Your Self, 151f
   Free play, 159f
   Glee! 160f
   Layers of experience, each enfolded in the last, 276f
   Liberty in Hand, 162f
   The music of psychotherapy, 208f
   Safe surprises, 150f
   The Vertebrates, 149f
   We never outgrow the earliest germs of self, 278f
   The Wild Woman, 154f
Marschak Interaction Method (MIM), 227, 228, 231
Martindale, C., 77
Marx, G., 295
Marx, K., 16
The Master and His Emissary (McGilchrist), 117
maternal love, 66, 67–69, 67f, 68f, 71
   See also mutual love
matryoshka dolls. See nesting dolls
Mayseless, N., 84
McGilchrist, I., 65, 114, 117–18, 120, 122, 126
McLaughlin, J., 134–35, 134f
McNeil, D., 120
medial prefrontal cortex (mPFC), 41–42, 50, 51, 53
medications, 180
   See also psychostimulants
medicine men, 121
medicine wheels, 122, 123f, 126
meditation. See mindfulness and meditation
Medowar, P., 15
"Me" generation, 274, 280
Memorial Foundation for Lost Children, 263
memories. See anoetic and autonoetic memories
memory reconsolidation, 248, 249
mental health promotion, 250, 251–53
metaphorical thinking, 119, 120, 155–56, 194, 207
   See also nonverbal thinking; Wild Woman
Mihov, K., 84
MIM. See Marschak Interaction Method (MIM)
mindful group therapy, 338–57

mindfulness and meditation, 48–54, 52t, 55
See also Embedded Relational Mindfulness©;
empathic attunement; presence, power of
mind-wandering, 45–47, 56, 58–59
Mitchell, R., 206
Mnemosyne, 167, 168, 169
Modell, A., 156
Mortimer, J., 296
mother-infant relationships, 70, 72–74, 75,
77, 81
See also maternal love
motivation. See intrinsic motivation
mourning. See unresolved mourning
movement, 94, 95–97
See also specific movements
movement habits
about, 92–93, 94
in psychotherapy, 99, 101, 103, 105, 106,
107, 108
mPFC. See medial prefrontal cortex (mPFC)
Mrazek, M., 47
Murray, H., 144, 145
musical dimensions of psychotherapy, 191–215
music and musicians
about, 195–98, 197f, 214–15
brain activity and improvisation, 202–3,
203f, 204
communal celebration of, 168f
creation of safe spaces through, 132–35
oxytocin and, 82–83
psychotherapy for, 182
See also Cozolino, L.; Heifetz, J.; McLaughlin, J.; performance artists
The music of psychotherapy (Marks-Tarlow), 208f
mutual love, 70, 71–75, 77
See also maternal love

National Geographic Society, 26–27
National Institute for Play, 27
national play initiative, 252, 253, 256
Native Americans, 123, 126
See also Navajo culture
nature versus nurture, 243, 245–46
Navajo culture, 110–14, 114f, 117, 118–19, 120,
121, 122
NDM. See non-directed meditation (NDM)
neocortex versus subcortical regions, 243–
45, 246
nesting dolls, 271–85, 272f, 273f, 284f
neural integration, play and, 57–58
neuroscience. See affective neuroscience; brain
activity; music improvisation and
non-directed meditation (NDM), 49, 56
non-dual awareness (NDA), 49, 54

nonverbal communication, 204–8, 208f
See also facial expressions; gestures; movement habits
nonverbal thinking, 115–16
Nordgren, L., 47
Noriuchi, M., 73
novelty, 34–35, 65, 149–50
See also creativity
nurture. See nature versus nurture

OATS network (Others And The Self), 41
object play, 33
Ogden, P., 340, 341, 342, 349, 353
Ogden, T., 200, 211
open monitoring (OM), 49, 50, 53, 54
Open to Yes, 329–32, 332f
Opezzo, M., 96
O'playsis, 369–70
See also optimism tree
optimism, 361–62, 361f
optimism tree, 373–74, 374f
orbitofrontal cortex, 73, 74
Organizational Optimism Profile, 370
Orpheus, 211
oxytocin, 82–83

Pagnoni, G., 51
paideia, 18
PANIC system, 252, 253, 266
Panksepp, J., 29, 122, 157–58, 226, 243,
363, 369
paradoxical injunction, 303
parasympathetic system, 124, 126
parent education, 234, 236, 236f, 237–39, 263
Parker, C., 372
PCC. See posterior cingulate cortex (PCC)
perceptual decoupling, 45
performance artists, 171–72, 177, 179–82
See also actors; dance and dancers; music and
musicians
Perls, F., 280
Personal Playmaker Practice plans, 373
physical play, 249, 252
See also rough-and-tumble play
Picasso, P., 372
Plato, 167, 261
Platt, C., 84
play
about, 27, 29, 364–66, 364f, 365f
ADHD and pro-social effects of, 259–61
biases against, 37
cultural perspectives of, 110–27
daydream effect of, 35–36
discord and harmony in, 31–32

DMN and, 43, 45–47
domains of, 366–69, 367*f*
Finland's policy on, 250
functions of, 21, 22*f*, 35, 39–40, 158, 232
importance of, 249, 250–51
intrinsic motivation of, 32–33
as novelty pursuit, 34–35
psychotherapy as, 307–8
science of, 29–31
stages of, 36–37
trauma versus, 369
See also ImprovHQ principles; improvisation;
    specific types
PLAY affective system
    about, 122–23, 157–58
    prosocial maturation and, 249–50, 251–52,
        253, 264, 266
play deprivation, 24–25, 26, 30, 266, 362–63
playfulness
    creativity and, 18
    emotionally interactive, 220*f*
    functions of, 32, 254
    Navajo culture and, 111, 112
    psychostimulants and, 250, 256
    See also couples therapy, nesting dolls and
Play: How it Shapes the Brain (Brown), 30
Playmakers, 360–61, 373
play model of healing and growth, 157–61,
    159*f*, 160*f*
play paradox, 31
play personalities, 33–34
plays. *See* comedy and comedians
play sanctuaries, 264
play therapists, 121, 155
polyvagal definition of play, 121, 124
Porges, S., 57, 121, 124, 225, 226
positivity resonance, 319, 340
posterior cingulate cortex (PCC), 41, 45, 49,
    50–51, 54
post-traumatic stress disorder (PTSD), 168,
    169, 171–72
    See also trauma and traumatized imagination;
        unresolved mourning
posture. *See* body and posture as armor
Power-Pauses, 348–49
precuneus, 41, 45
prefrontal cortex, 84
    See also medial prefrontal cortex (mPFC)
preschoolers, 262, 265, 369, 372
presence, power of, 321–25
    See also mindfulness and meditation
Prestera, H., 100
preventive medicine, 38
primary intersubjectivity, 75–80, 76*f*, 78*f*, 79*f*, 80*f*

projective testing, 137, 141
Project Joy, 372–73
prosody, 198–99
Proust, M., 214
psychoeducation, 56
    See also parent education
psychological safety, 319
psychostimulants, 249–50, 252, 256–59
psychotherapists
    body as instrument of, 207–8, 208*f*
    directors as, 287–89
    empathic attunement of, 199–201, 202, 204
    honoring self-expression of, 150–51, 151*f*
    imagination and empathy of, 157
    interpersonal neurobiology and, 194–95
    as musical, 193
    role for play and, 37–38
    therapeutic ear, fine-tuning of, 204–7, 206*f*
    translation and, 211–13
    unconscious scanning of, 209–10
    See also play therapists
psychotherapist training challenges, 129–31,
    137–42, 142*f*, 304–5
psychotherapy
    about, 58
    art of, 153–56, 154*f*
    client-centered process of, 343–44
    creativity in, 85
    goals of, 15–16, 96, 155–56
    homogeneity versus diversity versus unique-
        ness in, 144–45
    humor in, 160–61
    implicit relational knowing and, 145–
        48, 147*f*
    improvisation as support to, 312–14
    love in, 84–87
    movement habits in, 99, 101, 103, 105,
        106, 107
    musical dimensions of, 191–215
    for performing artists, 179–82
    play in, 85, 307–8
    play model of healing and growth, 157–61,
        159*f*, 160*f*
    rupture and repair in, 158–59
    therapeutic alliance in, 192–94, 213–
        14, 318
    See also couples therapy, nesting dolls and;
        humor, as intervention; mindful group
        therapy; Theraplay® model
PTSD. *See* post-traumatic stress disorder
    (PTSD)
pulling, 105–7, 106*f*
    See also yielding
pushing, 99–101, 100*f*, 102–3

quiet love, 67–68, 67f, 69, 71, 78, 81

rage and anger, 293, 295, 300–301, 302–5
Raichle, M., 40
Ratey, J., 94
rats
    ADHD studies with, 258, 259
    play and gene expression in, 250
    social play and decorticated, 244–
        45, 244f
    toxic stress and, 362–63, 369
reaching, 101–3, 102f
reciprocal eye gaze, 221f
Reik, T., 77
relationships. See attachment theory; couples
        therapy, nesting dolls and; mother-infant
        relationships
relaxing. See yielding
resilience, 124, 125f, 126, 156
Resilient Responses, 325–29, 326f
resonance, 194, 195
    See also positivity resonance
rhythmic synchronization, 197–98, 197f
right hemisphere
    attachment and, 70, 77–78
    circles and, 117–18
    functions of, 64, 65, 83, 149, 149f, 206–7
    love and, 71
    prosody and, 199
    sand tray modality and, 116
    storytelling and, 118
    See also nonverbal communication
risk-taking, joy of, 80f
rituals, 74, 81, 82
    See also movement habits
Rivers, J., 291, 295
Robertson, J. and J., 223
Rodman, B., 301
Rogers, C., 2
Rogers, W., 289
Rorschach testing, 137
rough-and-tumble play, 35, 244, 244f, 259,
        263, 264
    See also physical play
rupture and repair, 158–59, 227–30, 228f

Sacks, O., 83
sacred clowns, 111
safe spaces, creation of, 132–35
    See also O'playsis; play sanctuaries; psycho-
        logical safety
safe surprises, 150
Safe surprises (Marks-Tarlow), 150f
salience network (SN), 42–43, 44f, 49

Salk, J., 135–36, 136f
sand tray modality, 113–17, 114f, 116f
Schooler, J., 45, 46, 47
Schore, A., 65, 67, 70, 73, 83, 84, 114, 161,
        195, 239
Schore, J., 83, 239
Schwartz, D., 96
secure attachment, 174
    See also maternal love
SEEKING system, 249–50, 251–52, 253,
        258, 264
Segment Bleu (Kandinsky), 206f
self-centeredness. See "Culture of Me"
self-efficacy, 33
self-expression, of psychotherapists, 150–
        51, 151f
Seligman, M., 318
sensorimotor group psychotherapy, 340,
        349–50, 350f
    See also Embedded Relational Mindfulness©
separation anxiety. See PANIC system
Shamay-Tsoory, S., 84
shame, 137, 159, 170, 171, 181
Shaw, D., 86
Shaw, G., 372
Shewmon, D., 244
shopping, learning how to, 79f
Short-Term Dynamic Psychotherapy
        (STDP), 303
Siegel, D., 115, 118, 124, 194, 318, 339,
        341, 352
Silvia, P., 45
simulation theory, 42
Skynner, R., 303–4
sleep and play, 30, 31, 266
Slepian, M., 96
Smallwood, J., 45, 46
Smith, M., 327
Smith, R., 45
SN. See salience network (SN)
social connectedness, 135–36, 366–68
social engagement system, 57, 121, 124,
        126, 225
    See also default mode network (DMN); win-
        dow of tolerance
socialization
    the brain and creativity and, 247–54, 248f,
        251f, 253f
    DMN and, 41
    evolution and, 280–81
social learning theory, 32–33
    See also intrinsic motivation
social play, 34, 262
social status schema, 338–39

Sood, A., 43, 45
Sorg, C., 49
Sperry, R., 94
STDP (Short-Term Dynamic Psychotherapy), 303
Stern, D., 72, 146, 155
Stobbe, K., 330
Stoppard, T., 291
storytelling, 116, 118
stress. *See* toxic stress
Strick, M., 47
Sunderlans, M., 254
supernatural belief systems, 176–77
superpowers, 371
Swart, I., 83
sympathetic system, 121, 124, 126
synchrony, 194, 195
    See also rhythmic synchronization

TAT. *See* Thematic Apperception Test (TAT)
Tatkin, S., 271
Taylor, V., 51
teenagers. *See* adolescents
Tees, C., 243
temporoparietal junction (TPJ), 41, 45
Thaut, M., 197
theater, 291–92
Thematic Apperception Test (TAT), 141
themes and variations, 210–11
theory of mind capacity, 181
therapeutic alliance, 192–94, 213–14, 318
therapeutic ear, fine-tuning of, 204–7, 206f,
    210–11
Theraplay (Jernberg), 219
Theraplay, 3rd ed. (Booth & Jernberg), 224
Theraplay® model, 218–39
There He Goes (Jernberg, Hurst, Lyman), 223
tiger cubs, 265f
Todd, M., 95
Tolle, E., 324
toxic stress, 362–64
TPJ. *See* temporoparietal junction (TPJ)
tragedy-farce continuum, 294f, 296–97, 298
translation, 211–13
trauma, play versus, 369
trauma and traumatized imagination, 170–72,
    175, 176, 180
traumatic situations, development in, 275f
    See also toxic stress
Trevarthen, C., 72

Tronick, E., 72, 202
Tyson, M., 362

the unconscious
    attunement through, 200
    interpretation of, 210, 211
    nesting dolls and, 278–79, 281f, 282f
unconscious scanning, 209–10
uniqueness, 144–45
    See also idiosyncrasies
To the Unknown Voice (Kandinsky), 212f
unresolved mourning, 174–77

value laden adaptive map deficiency, 266
van der Kolk, B., 161, 171
Vaughn, C., 311
The Vertebrates (Marks-Tarlow), 149f
Voice your Ideas, 332–36

walking, 96
Wampold, B., 193
Wan, X., 84
Weber, M., 16
We never outgrow the earliest germs of self (Marks-
    Tarlow), 278f
Western culture, 117–18, 121–22, 123, 126
Whitman, C., 23–25
Whitney, D., 319
Wilde, O., 150
Wild Woman, 153–55, 154f
The Wild Woman (Marks-Tarlow), 154f
Williams, R., 293, 295
Wilson, F., 119
window of tolerance
    about, 93–94, 93f, 98
    mindful group therapy and, 352–54, 354f,
    355f, 356
Winnicott, D., 40, 64, 67, 69, 71, 85, 96, 201–2,
    205, 223, 224, 307
Wohlschlager, A., 49
Woolley, A., 333

Xu, J., 53

Yalom, I., 340
"Yes, and," 329–32, 332f
yielding, 97–99, 97f
Youngman, H., 294

Zeki, S., 75, 77